Weimar Communism as Mass Movement

1918–1933

Weimar Communism as Mass Movement
1918-1933

Edited by Ralf Hoffrogge and Norman LaPorte

Part of the Studies in Twentieth Century Communism Series

Series Editors: Norman LaPorte, Kevin Morgan and Matthew Worley

Lawrence and Wishart
London 2017

Lawrence and Wishart Limited
Central Books Building
Freshwater Road
Chadwell Heath
RM8 1RX

© Lawrence & Wishart 2017
Individual articles © author

The authors have asserted their rights under the Copyright, Design and Patents Act, 1998 to be identified as the authors of this work.

All rights reserved. Apart from fair dealing for the purpose of private study, research, criticism or review, no part of this publication may be reproduced, stored in a retrieval system, or transmitted, in any form or by any means, electronic, electrical, chemical, mechanical, optical, photocopying, recording or otherwise, without the prior permission of the copyright owner.

ISBN 9781910448984

British Library Cataloguing in Publication Data.
A catalogue record for this book is available from the British Library

Typesetting: e-type
Cover design: Andrew Corbett
Cover image: Bundesarchiv photo by Georg Pahl, 1 May 1930

Contents

Acknowledgement	vii
Acronyms and abbreviations	viii
Timeline	xi
Note on organisation	xix
Note on 'seizure of power'	xxi
Ralf Hoffrogge and Norman LaPorte, Weimar Communism as Mass Movement: An Introduction	1

(I) Revolutionary Origins

1. Gerhard Engel, The International Communists of Germany, 1916-1919   25

2. Ottokar Luban, The Role of the Spartacist Group after 9 November 1918 and the Formation of the KPD   45

(II) The KPD between Revolution and *Realpolitik*

3. Florian Wilde, Building a Mass Party: Ernst Meyer and the United Front Policy, 1921-1922   66

4. Ralf Hoffrogge, Class against Class: the 'Ultra-left' Berlin Opposition, 1921-1923   87

5. Mario Kessler, Resisting Moscow? Ruth Fischer and the KPD, 1923-1926   109

6. Norman LaPorte, The Rise of Ernst Thälmann and the Hamburg Left, 1921-1923   129

7. Marcel Bois, Opposing Hitler and Stalin: Left Wing Communists after Expulsion from the KPD   150

(III) Communism and the Trade Unions

8. Constance Margain, The German Section of the International of Sailors and Harbour Workers — 170

9. Stefan Heinz, The 'Red Unions' and their Resistance to National Socialism: The Unity Union of the Berlin Metal Workers, 1930-1935 — 187

(IV) Reaching Beyond the Party?

10. Sebastian Zehetmair, The KPD and Farmers: Approaches to a Neglected Research Problem — 205

11. Ben Fowkes, Communism and the Avant-Garde in Weimar Germany — 220

12. Fredrik Petersson, Willi Münzenberg: A Propagandist Reaching Beyond the Party and Class — 240

(V) Stalin, the 'Third Period' and the German Catastrophe

13. Bernhard H. Bayerlein, The Entangled Catastrophe: Hitler's 1933 'Seizure of Power' and the Power Triangle – New Evidence on the Historic Failure of the KPD, the Comintern, and the Soviet Union — 260

Notes on Contributors — 281

Index — 285

Acknowledgement

This translation was made possible thanks to a Nina Fishman Translation Award from the Barry Amiel and Norman Melburn Trust. The objectives of the Trust are to advance public education, learning and knowledge in all aspects of the philosophy of Marxism, the history of socialism, and the working-class movement. Nina Fishman was a long-term Trustee. She was also an important political thinker, activist and historian. The award commemorates her legacy by enabling the publication of significant works on topics that would have interested her. For further information please see http://www.ninafishman.org/

Acronyms and abbreviations

ADGB	General Confederation of German Trade Unions (*Allgemeiner Deutscher Gewerkschaftsbund*)
ARBKD	Association of German Revolutionary Visual Artists (*Assoziation revolutionärer bildender Künstler*)
BBZ	*Bremer Bürgerzeitung*
BPRS	League of Proletarian Revolutionary Writers (*Bund proletarisch-revolutionärer Schriftsteller*)
BVP	Bavarian People's Party (*Bayerische Volkspartei*)
Comintern	Communist International
DEV	German Railway Workers' Union (*Deutscher Eisenbahner-Verband*)
DAF	German Labour Front (*Deutsche Arbeitsfront*)
DMV	Metal Workers' Union (*Deutscher Metallarbeiterverband*)
DNVP	German National People's Party (*Deutschnationale Volkspartei*)
DVFP	Freedom Party (*Deutschvölkische Freiheitspartei*)
ECCI	Executive Committee of the Comintern
EVMB	Unity Union of Berlin Metalworkers (*Einheitsverband der Metallarbeiter Berlins*)
EVSHBD	Unity Union of Seamen, Harbour Workers and Bargemen (*Einheitsverband der Seeleute, Hafenarbeiter und Binnenschiffer Deutschlands*)
FAUD	Free Workers' Union of Germany (*Freie Arbeiter-Union Deutschlands*)
GDR	German Democratic Republic
IKD	International Communists of Germany (*Internationale Kommunisten Deutschlands*)
IAFC	International Anti-Fascist Committee
IAH	International Workers' Relief (*Internationale Arbeiterhilfe*)
ISH	International Union of Seamen and Harbour Workers (*Einheitsverband der Seeleute, Hafenarbeiter und Binnenschiffer Deutschlands*)

ACRONYMS AND ABBREVIATIONS

ISPD	International Socialist Party of Germany (*Internationale Sozialistische Partei Deutschlands*)
IFTU	International Federation of Trade Unions
ITF	International Transport Workers' Federation
KAG	Communist Working Group (*Kommunistische Arbeitsgemeinschaft*)
KAPD	Communist Workers' Party of Germany (*Kommunistische Arbeiter-Partei Deutschlands*)
KPD	Communist Party of Germany (*Kommunistische Partei Deutschlands*)
KPO	Communist Party of Germany (Opposition)
LACO	League Against Colonial Oppression
LAI	League Against Imperialism and for National Independence
LSI	Labour and Socialist International
Profintern	see RILU
RDEBA	National Union of German Railway Employees (*Reichsgewerkschaft deutscher Eisenbahnbeamter und Angestellter*)
RAPP	Russian Association of Proletarian Writers
RFB	League of Red Front Fighters (*Rote Frontkämpferbund*)
RILU	Red International of Labour Unions, also known as Profintern
RGO	Revolutionary Trade Union Opposition (*Revolutionäre Gewerkschafts-Opposition*)
RKP	Communist Party of Russia (*Russische Kommunistische Partei*)
RSS	Revolutionary Shop Stewards (*Revolutionare Obleute*)
SAG	Social Democratic Working Group (*Sozialdemokratische Arbeitsgemeinschaft*)
SAPD	Socialist Workers' Party of Germany (*Sozialistische Arbeiter-Partei Deutschlands*)
SPD	Social Democratic Party (*Sozialdemokratische Partei Deutschlands*)
SDVB	Social Democratic Organisation of Bremen (*Sozialdemokratischer Verein Bremen*)
USPD	Independent Social Democratic Party (*Unabhängige Sozialdemokratische Partei Deutschlands*)
VAPP	All-Russian Association of Proletarian Writers

VKPD   United Communist Party (*Vereinigte Kommunistische Partei Deutschlands*) (denomination of KPD shortly used in 1920-1921 after its merger with the left wing of the USPD)

Timeline

1914

4 August: German SPD supports war bonds in the Reichstag

2 December: Karl Liebknecht is the first Reichstag deputy to oppose war bonds.

1915

5-8 September: Zimmerwald Conference brought together anti-war Socialists; beginning of Zimmerwald left around Lenin.

1916

28 June: Mass strike in Berlin against the arrest of Karl Liebknecht.

4 July: Bremen shipyard workers' strike begins.

1917

6-8 April: USPD formed by anti-war social democrats from both left and right wings of the party.

16-23 April: Anti-war mass strikes in Berlin and Leipzig.

1918

January: Mass strikes in several German cities, workers' councils emerge as strike leaderships.

3 November: Sailors' revolt at Kiel.

4-9 November: Spread of workers' and soldiers' councils throughout Germany.

9 November: Abdication of Wilhelm II; Social Democrat Friedrich Ebert becomes Chancellor of the republic.

10 November: Formation the Council of People's Representatives between MSPD and USPD.

11 November: Armistice signed.

16-20 December: First nationwide Congress of Workers' and Soldiers' Councils in Berlin.

29 December: USPD leaves Council of People's Representatives.

31 December (to 1 January 1919): Founding convention of the KPD.

1919

5-11 January: So-called 'Spartacist Rising' in Berlin.

15 January: Murders of Karl Liebknecht and Rosa Luxemburg.

19 January: Elections to National Assembly, boycotted by KPD.

6 February: Opening of National Assembly in Weimar due to continued unrest in Berlin.

11 February: National Assembly elects Friedrich Ebert as Reich President.

13 February: formation of Weimar Coalition of SPD, Democratic Party and Catholic Centre Party under Philip Scheidemann.

February-May: Strikes and civil unrest throughout much of the country.

2-6 March: Founding Congress of Communist International (Comintern).

7 April-2 May: Munich Soviet Republic (*Räterepublik*).

28 June: Versailles Treaty signed by German delegation (comes into force 10 January 1920).

October: Second KPD Congress; Heidelberg Split removing syndicalist-inspired members.

1920

25-26 February: Third KPD Congress.

13-17 March: Kapp-Lüttwitz Putsch and general strike.

March-April: Fighting between Red Army of the Ruhr against the Free Corps and Reichswehr.

27 March: Müller (SPD) cabinet of parties of Weimar Coalition (SPD, DDP and Catholic Centre).

14-15 April: Fourth KPD Congress.

6 June: Reichstag elections, Weimar Coalition defeated; formation of the minority coalition under Konstantin Fehrenbach of the Catholic Centre Party; SPD leaves government but 'tolerates' it (i.e. confidence and supply).

19 July-7 August: Second Congress of Communist International.

12-19 October: Halle Congress of USPD; split of the party on the question of affiliation with Communist International, a majority agrees to merge with KPD.

1-3 November, 3 December: Fifth KPD Congress.

4-7 December: Sixth (Unification) KPD Congress; left-wing of USPD merges with KPD.

1921

8 March: Allied troops occupy Duisburg, Ruhrort and Düsseldorf in stand-off over Versailles Treaty.

20 March: KPD's March action, and uprising largely limited to central Germany, begins.

22 June-12 July: Third Congress of Comintern; announces United Front policy; intensified factional tensions in KPD.

10 May: New coalition government under Chancellor Wirth and Foreign Minister Walter Rathenau; dominance of issues surrounding peace treaty.

3 July: Foundation of the Red International of Labour Unions (Profintern).

22-26 August: Seventh KPD Congress.

26 August: Murder of former finance minister Matthias Erzberger by völkisch nationalists.

1922

1-7 February: Railway workers' strike.

16 April: Treaty of Rapallo between Germany and Soviet Russia.

18 July: Reichstag passes Law for the Protection of the Republic, directed against right-wing terrorism, later used mostly against the political left.

24 September: Rump USPD merges with SPD.

5 November-5 December: Fourth Congress of the Comintern.

14 November: Wirth government resigns; minority conservative cabinet under Wilhelm Cuno, a shipping magnate who was nominally non-party but close to the German People's Party (DVP).

23 November: National Works Council Congress.

1923

28 January-1 February: Eighth KPD Congress.

10 January: Germany defaults on reparations.

10-13 January: German defaults on reparations payments under Versailles Treaty; French and Belgian armies occupy the Ruhr; Cuno government calls for 'passive resistance' (i.e. strikes).

August-September: Various secret meetings in Moscow to determine policy surrounding 'German October'; plans fails to materialise nationally.

12 August: Fall of Cuno government; formation of Grand Coalition of SPD, Centre Party, Democratic Party (DDP) and German People's Party (DVP) under Chancellor Gustav Stresemann.

26 September: Passive resistance in Ruhr called off.

27 September: State of Emergency throughout Germany declared by President Ebert.

21 October: Congress of Works Councils, Chemnitz

23 October: Hamburg rising begins.

29 October: Military suppression of legally-constituted coalition governments of SPD and KPD in Saxon and Thuringian Diets.

2 November: SPD ministers resign from Grand Coalition.

8-9 November: Hitler Putsch in Munich; President Ebert passes executive power to General von Seeckt (State of Emergency lasting until 13 March 1924).

23 November: Fall of Stresemann government (he becomes Foreign Minister); formation of minority government under Chancellor Wilhelm Marx (Catholic Centre Party).

23 November (to 29 February 1924): KPD banned.

1924

21 January: Lenin dies.

7-10 April: Ninth KPD Congress.

16 April: German government accepts Dawes Plan as means fulfilling Versailles Treaty.

4 May: Reichstag election; gains by KPD and 'anti-system' parties of nationalist right.

17 June-8 July: Fifth Congress of the Comintern; Bolshevisation announced for all member parties.

15 July: Formation of KPD's paramilitary association, the League of Red Front-Fighters (RFB).

7 December: Second Reichstag election; losses by KPD and radical right.

1925

15 January: Hans Luther forms first 'bourgeois bloc' (*Bürgerblock*) cabinet, including monarchist German National People's Party (DNVP).

27 February: Re-foundation of the Nazi Party.

28 February: Death of President Ebert.

26 April: Field Marshall Paul von Hindenburg elected president, with Ernst Thälmann standing as KPD candidate.

12-17 July: Tenth KPD Congress.

31 October-1 November: First Party Conference; deposes Ruth Fischer and the 'ultra-left' confirms new leadership under party chairman Ernst Thälmann. United Front becomes official party line.

1926

19 January: Second Luther Cabinet; conservative minority government now without DNVP.

24 April: German-Soviet treaty of friendship and neutrality (the Berlin Treaty).

12 May: Luther government falls; Wilhelm Marx (Catholic Centre Party) forms minority government.

20 June: Plebiscite to expropriate former German princely houses; initiated by KPD and narrowly loses.

17 December: Fall of Marx cabinet.

1927

29 January: Marx heads another bourgeois bloc government, including DNVP.

10 February: Foundation of League against Imperialism in Brussels.

10-14 February: Congress against Colonialism and Imperialism.

2-7 March: Eleventh KPD Congress.

16 July: Labour Exchanges and Unemployment Insurance Law.

1928

20 May: Reichstag elections; rise in KPD and especially SPD vote.

17 July-1 September: Sixth Comintern Congress; ends United Front and begins Class against Class policy.

28 June: Chancellor Hermann Müller (SPD) forms Great Coalition Cabinet.

October-December 1928: Ruhr iron and steel lock-out.

3-4 November: Second Reich Conference of KPD.

1929

9-10 March: Anti-Fascist Congress

1 May: So-called 'Bloody May' street fighting in Berlin with thirty-three dead after SPD-led Prussian government bans outdoor parades.

3 May: The KPD's paramilitary League of Red Front Fighters is banned.

8-15 June: Twelfth KPD Congress.

7 June: Young Plan to settle reparations issue.

9 July: DVNP, the Stahlhelm veterans paramilitary association and the Nazi Party begin to campaign against the Young Plan; origins of ultra-nationalist Harzburg Front.

3 October: Death of Stresemann.

24 October: 'Black Thursday' on New York Stock Exchange; begins world economic crisis.

21 December: Stalin's fiftieth birthday; cult of personality begins.

22 December: Referendum to reject Young Plan gets only 13.8 per cent of vote.

1930

27 March: Hermann Müller (SPD) cabinet resigns.

30 March: Heinrich Brüning (Catholic Centre Party) appointed Chancellor; first presidential government and begins period of deflationary emergency decrees and mass unemployment.

14 September: Reichstag elections; gains by KPD but especially the Nazi Party.

3 October: Formation of the League of Struggle against Fascism (*Kampfbund gegen den Faschismus*) as partial replacement organisation for the League of Red Front-Fighters.

1931

11-14 February: Sailors' and harbour workers' strikes.

13 July: Banking crisis, German bank collapses.

9 October: Second Brüning Cabinet.

16 December: Formation of Iron Front of SPD, trade unions and the pro-republic Reichsbanner paramilitary association.

1932

10 April: Hindenburg re-elected Reich President, with Thälmann standing for KPD.

24 April: SPD-led Weimar Coalition in Prussia loses majority.

30 May: Brüning Cabinet resigns.

1 June: Franz von Papen forms government of 'national concentration'.

20 July: Prussian government ousted by Papen.

31 July: Reichstag elections; Nazis become largest party.

27-29 August: World Congress against War held in Amsterdam.

15-18 October: Third Reich Conference of KPD.

6 November: Reichstag elections; Nazi vote falls while KPD vote continues to rise.

17 November: Fall of Papen government.

3 December: Kurt von Schleicher forms presidential regime.

1933

28 January: Schleicher resigns

30 January: Hitler appointed Chancellor.

27 February: Reichstag fire.

5 March: Reichstag election, but no longer free and fair. KPD and SPD

are banned from campaigning, but nevertheless receive 12.3 and 18.3 per cent of the vote.

23 March: Enabling Act; political opposition proscribed. KPD banned.

1935

Over the course of the year 1935 the now illegal structures of the KPD are destroyed by the Nazi regime.

25 July-21 August: Seventh Comintern Congress; People's Front policy announced.

Note on Party Organisation

At the KPD's founding congress, the assembled delegates endorsed a federal organisational structure; the aim was to allow flexibility of action and propaganda, at a time when the party had largely to operate under conditions of illegality. By the party's second congress in October 1919, federalism had begun to be subordinated to greater centralism. There remained considerable local autonomy in the press, in the election of officials by the membership and in campaigning, as long as these were within the agreed framework set down by the central leadership. Issues of party organisation were a prominent reason for the party split that took place at this point, which ended the more syndicalist-type organisations.

From the unification of the KPD and the left-wing of the USPD in December 1920, until 1925, the party's evolving organisational statutes tightened centralism and with it party discipline, using the Leninist nomenclature 'democratic centralism' as set out in the Communist International's '21 Conditions'.

Importantly, this note on organisation clarifies not only the complexity of party structures, but also issues of translation, where German terms offer no direct equivalents in English. Initially, the most important organisational unit of the KPD as a mass-based party was the *Zentrale*, which was an inner leadership grouping similar to the Bolsheviks' central committee. However, at least formally, greater power lay in the hands of the *Zentralausschuss* (or central commission), which comprised a clear majority of delegates from the party's district organisations (*Bezirke*). This, in principle, meant that the *Zentrale* could be outvoted. In practice, however, the Executive Committee of the Communist International and its emissaries, who attended KPD meetings in Berlin, held considerable influence. But, in these early years, the *Zentralausschuss* had the authority to rule in cases of differences of opinion, and was charged with running day-to-day party activity on the lines set down by the then annual party congresses.

The organisational statute adopted at the Seventh Congress (1921) stated that lower party organisations must 'unconditionally implement' decisions of higher party authorities, but it was not until the

Bolshevisation Statute, adopted at the Tenth Congress (1925), that this was given organisational power. The *Zentrale* was reconstituted as the *Zentralkomitee* (central committee) on the Bolshevik model and the *Zentralausschuss* which had represented the regions – and the party's many locally based factions – was abolished.

In turn, as the membership of the *Zentralkomitee* expanded, its actual power contracted. The political and organisational hub transferred to the narrower *Politbüro* (political bureau) and *Orgburo* (organisational bureau). The latter of these was dissolved in 1926 and its remit was transferred to the actual leadership, the *Sekretariat of the Politbüro*, which comprised three members. After 1925, there were only two further party congresses during the Weimar Republic – 1927 and 1929. The party conference, which replaced the *Zentralausschuss* in 1925, met only three times before the fall of the republic.

Centralisation of the national leadership found its equivalent at district level. The membership, and their delegates to district congresses, were initially able to elect the leadership and party officials, but this was subsequently superseded by their appointment from above. At national, district and sub-district (*Unterbezirke*) levels, the leaderships were expected to set up divisions to run campaigning, from agitation and propaganda, to work in trade unions and sports organisations, to work among women and youth, to film production and distribution.

Despite repeated organisational drives, the KPD – a party increasingly comprised of unemployed and unskilled workers – resisted moves to make factory cells the main building block of party organisation; the lowest party unit continued to be the street cell. These incremental organisational changes, which enabled the sidelining of the membership's democratic input from below, are evidence of the aspiration – even if this did not become the reality – to construct a 'monolithic' party driven by the leadership and its apparatus of full-time officials. Such changes were the foundation of what is referred to as the 'Stalinisation' of the KPD.

Sources

Hermann Weber, *Wandlung des deutschen Kommunismus. Die Stalinisierung der KPD in der Weimarer Republik*, Frankfurt: Europäische Verlagsanstalt, 1969, pp251ff.
Ben Fowkes, *Communism in Germany under the Weimar Republic*, London: Macmillan, 1994, pp.183ff.

Note on 'seizure of power'

Historians use quotation marks to qualify the term 'seizure of power' when referring to Hitler's accession, to convey that it was more a transfer of power, from the old political elites around President Hindenburg, to the Nazi Party during 1933 and 1934. This was in addition to the use of violence by the Nazis, whether political opponents or other targeted groups.

Weimar Communism as Mass Movement: An Introduction

Ralf Hoffrogge and Norman LaPorte

IN THE YEARS immediately following the October Revolution of 1917, revolutionary workers and also intellectuals across the globe were inspired to believe that Marx's 'spectre of communism' was not only haunting Europe but had taken on material substance. This situation had grown out of the impact of 'total war', which began in 1914 and ended the 'long nineteenth century'. In Europe, the Romanov, Habsburg and Wilhelmine empires fell and, in Britain, Ireland went from anti-colonial uprising in 1916 to civil war. There were mass-based strike movements, including those with political aims, and workers and soldiers organised councils which sat uneasily alongside national parliaments. Above all in the colonised East, the 'revolutionary wave' also witnessed anti-imperial revolts which aimed to bring about national self-determination.[1] Even if this proved to be a 'red mirage', at the time it was understood by the Bolsheviks and their supporters internationally as the first rays of a new socialist dawn spreading across the globe from Petrograd, as war and revolution pulled down the old, nineteenth-century order and began to define a new epoch.[2]

These events inspired the Bolsheviks to found the Communist International (Comintern) in 1919 as a 'world party' to overthrow global capitalism.[3] However, Bolshevik victory in the Russian civil war allowed the initial consolidation of the Soviet state at the same time as the 'revolutionary wave' began to ebb across Western Europe. Almost from the outset, the ensuing tensions this generated between the 'centre' and 'periphery' of the world communist movement meant that the communist parties were increasingly defined by their orientation towards the 'actually existing' model and defence of the Soviet state, even if idealism remained part of a communist identity.[4]

Yet, as the essays below detail, this did not mean that the world communist movement was 'monolithic', even if this became the stated aim of many leading Communists. To understand the 'cracks in the monolith' of inter-war communism, it is especially important to understand the inner life not only of the Russian Communist Party (RCP), but also of the Comintern's 'national sections'.[5] In this respect, the German Communist Party (*Kommunistische Partei Deutschlands*, KPD) has a special importance for the global history of communism, as it was the largest party outside of the Soviet Union. Its size and the country's relative proximity to Soviet Russia ensured that communism's opponents – from Social Democrats to the old political and economic elites – 'defined their political identities, established their political agendas, and secured their political powers largely in opposition to German and international communism'.[6]

When communism collapsed between 1989 and 1991, the force that had shaped so much of the twentieth century became history. At the same time, research beyond the earlier cold-war confines of Kremlinology – a type of informed guesswork – was facilitated by the opening of the archives. This produced a 'boom' in communism studies, even if research into the KPD remained a relatively 'small boom' compared to interest in the German Democratic Republic (GDR).[7] However, too little of this new research on the KPD has been available to those who do not read German. This edited volume is a first step towards remedying this, making this field of research available in English for the first time, as well as making a distinct contribution to the field of study in its own right. To allow readers to gain a sense of the KPD's political development, we have presented the chapters (broadly) chronologically while focussing on some main themes. First, we address the party's revolutionary origins between 1918 and 1920; then the influences – domestic and Soviet – shaping its consolidation and role as a mass party; this is followed by the vexed relationship between communism and the trade unions; the penultimate section looks at attempts to win support beyond communism's core constituency among the industrial working class; and the final section examines the implications of the so-called 'Third Period' surrounding the Nazi Party's 'seizure of power' (for a further explanation of this term, see p.xii) in January 1933 and Moscow's intransigent role in this.

The long formation of the KPD, August 1914-December 1920

Against the backdrop of the Cold War, the split in the labour movement between social democracy and communism appeared to be an inevitable process, particularly in divided Germany. While West German authors focused on communism's anti-democratic tendencies from the outset, in East Germany, the establishment of the KPD was regarded as one of the most important outcomes of the German Revolution.[8] According to Marxist-Leninist historians, the founding of the KPD followed a world-historical process that began in Russia with the split between the Mensheviks and the Bolsheviks in 1903.[9] Even dissident Marxists clung to this narrative for a long time, as in the case of Pierre Broué's standard work *The German Revolution*. In the foreword to the book's reissue in 2005, Eric D. Weitz noted that, 'For Broué, the Bolshevik Revolution remained the correct model of revolutionary practice and V.I. Lenin the key strategist and thinker'.[10] Yet the founding generation of the KPD did not view Lenin or the Bolsheviks as its ultimate model. Rosa Luxemburg criticised Lenin's vision for the party until the bitter end.[11] In particular, she regarded the split in German social democracy as undesirable, even after the shock of 1914. For a long time, Luxemburg and her Spartacus Group remained hopeful that there would be a party conference ending the Social Democratic Party's (*Sozialdemokratische Partei Deutschlands*, SPD) support for the Kaiser's war. In Germany, the start of the war was followed by months of shock and disorganisation. When anti-war members of the SPD founded the Independent Social Democratic Party (*Unabhängige Sozialdemokratische Partei Deutschlands*, USPD) in 1917, they adopted the SPD's Erfurt Programme of 1891. Their objective was not communism as a new beginning but rather a return to their social-democratic roots. Accordingly, this meant that the new party not only included the left wing of the SPD around Luxemburg and Karl Liebknecht, but also their old adversaries Eduard Bernstein, the father of revisionism, and Karl Kautsky, who represented the 'Marxist centre'.[12]

The establishment of German communism, thus, did not follow the Bolsheviks' example from the outset, but was characterised by being an extended process from 1914 to 1920. The KPD did not grow out of an orderly split along the familiar lines of intra-party conflict, as Schorske's early influential study asserted.[13] Instead, it was an open-ended process, which was shaped by political contradictions and alliances of convenience.

Admittedly, since the late 1950s, West German historiography developed a nuanced view of the German Revolution of 1918/19 and of the council movement; the view conceded that the councils represented an independent social movement and were not a merely an imitation of the Russian soviets.[14] Yet, all too often, the KPD was dismissed as a 'totalitarian' party from the outset, despite its close connections to the council movement. A change came only after Herman Weber's 'Stalinisation thesis', which made clear that in order to understand the KPD, account must be made of the its revolutionary and democratic origins. Weber traced these radical roots back into the pre-war SPD, whose traditions were carried into the anti-war USPD, not least by the German Marxism of the Spartacus Group until the foundation of the KPD on the last day of 1918.[15]

In influential studies by Hartfrid Krause and David Morgan, the USPD is defined as having a centre-left socialist tendency, standing between the KPD and the SPD,[16] which came to an end in 1922 when its right wing reunited with the SPD. More importantly in the consolidation of communism as a mass movement, the USPD's left wing split off in October 1920 and merged with the KPD the following December. The split was over the Communist International's (Comintern) 'Twenty-One Conditions' of entry which, in essence, reconstituted German communism as a Leninist 'party of a new type', adhering to the principles of 'democratic centralism'. Yet, even if the KPD's 'second foundation' officially proclaimed the values of 'centralism', as we will discuss below in relation to the processes of Bolshevisation and Stalinisation, there remained a diversity of competing tendencies and political orientations under its organisational umbrella well into the 1920s.

The first chapter in this volume emphasises the KPD's democratic inheritance. Ottokar Luban traces the development of the Spartacus Group from its roots in the pre-war SPD. He emphasises its character as an informal network that arose from a circle of intellectual friends and that expanded its influence through the newspapers *Internationale* and *Spartacus Letters*. But there was no initial attempt to establish a party. Instead, its members intended to use these newspapers and flyers to change the SPD's orientation from within. Again, after joining the USPD in 1917, the Spartacists operated in similar manner.

Had it not been for the November Revolution of 1918, they might never have hoped that an independent revolutionary party could assume leadership of the labour movement. That hope was always controversial and, as Luban shows, it was ultimately ill-founded. At its founding congress on 30 December 1918, the KPD was unable to integrate leading actors, such as the Revolutionary Shop Stewards (*Revolutionäre Obleute*, RSS), for example, who, as a trade-union network, had organised the mass strikes of 1916-1918 and shaped the council movement.[17] The Shop Stewards opted to remain within the USPD, although they soon shared a traumatic experience with the new KPD: the January Uprising of 1919 in Berlin. This ended in a disastrous defeat and the death of KPD leaders Luxemburg and Liebknecht. As Luban explains, the 'premature' founding of the party was based on the assumption that the SPD government had entirely lost the support of the working class. The National Assembly elections on 19 January 1919 proved the opposite: the SPD received 37 per cent of the vote while the KPD boycotted the election.

The decision to boycott the elections essentially grew out of the influence of a second group that had participated in the founding of the KPD, the International Communists of Germany (*Internationale Kommunisten Deutschlands*, IKD). Based in Bremen and north-western Germany, the IKD had its origins in a group of anti-war Socialists around Anton Pannekoek, Karl Radek and Johann Knief. Gerhard Engel explains the origins of this as yet little-researched group that was one of the founding organisations of German communism.[18] It had called for the formation of a new party to the left of the SPD as early as 1916, significantly earlier than the Spartacus Group. The 'Bremen Left Radicals', as they were known on account of their regional stronghold, were only able to implement that goal with the onset of the German Revolution. Shortly thereafter, they merged with the Spartacists at the founding congress of the KPD.

As the IKD rejected parliamentarianism and the existing trade unions, most of its supporters were expelled from the KPD at the party's Heidelberg Congress in October 1919. These Left Radicals alternated between putschism and support for council democracy, making them the embodiment of the revolutionary turmoil that gave rise to German communism. But the historiographical focus on the Comintern and the Leninist tradition has meant that this link between Left Radicals, syndicalism, and communism has been given little scholarly attention.[19] That shortcoming is offset here by providing equal consideration for both of the KPD's founding groups.

Between Revolution and Realpolitik: the development of the KPD during the Weimar Republik c. 1921-1933

The merger with the left wing of the USPD consolidated the new 'United KPD' (VKPD), as it was briefly known, as the largest communist party outside of Soviet Russia. The party now organised some 400,000 members and, like the new party leadership, they represented in their majority former Social Democrats who had been radicalised by war and the post-war revolutionary crises.[20] Above all in the early years of the Weimar Republic – before the impact of structural unemployment from the mid 1920s – Communists were also a significant, if minority and localised, presence in the trade-union movement.[21] There was also a diversity of 'mass organisations', the largest of which was the League of Red Front Fighters (*Rote Frontkämpferbund*, RFB) which, in the middle years of the Republic, organised some 100,000 activists who furnished the party with a conspicuous and, for the party's opponents, intimidating presence on the streets of major cities.[22] Beyond this the party also had a core electorate of some 2 million during the mid 1920s, which, during the final crises of the Great Depression, surged to 6 million or 16.9 per cent of the popular vote – only a few percentage points behind the SPD – in the Reichstag elections of November 1932.[23]

The KPD began the early 1920s as a 'broad church', which continued to house a plurality of workers' radicalisms in a country characterised by strong regional and local traditions. The tensions that this generated informed the KPD's tactical relationship with the SPD and the Republic, as well as its relationship of deepening dependence on the Comintern. The early intersection of Soviet foreign policy and the pursuit of the German revolution were personified by Karl Radek. Not only was Radek the Comintern's emissary to the KPD, he also played a key role in the negotiations surrounding the Rapallo Treaty (1922), which established diplomatic relations between Berlin and Moscow. At this time, Radek was received by none less than the German Chancellor. Yet he also headed the Comintern's commission, which was charged with launching the aborted uprising known as 'German October' in 1923.[24]

However, the dynamics in the central and local party organisations also continued to influence how policy was implemented. Despite what amounted to a diverse spectrum of overlapping and diverging political positions, it is possible to distil two main orientations.[25] Firstly, one wing of the party accepted the need for the 'united front' policy. This involved a form of Leninist *realpolitik* in the trade unions and municipal parliaments, including voting with the Social Democrats, in order to win concessions at the local level. At the same time, the policy aimed to generate mass mobilisations – such as strikes and other campaigns concerning workers' standard of living – which would 'unmask' the leaders of the SPD and the trade unions as unable to fight for workers' interests, thus winning these workers over to the communist project.[26] Florian Wilde's chapter uses a number of examples of the 'united front' under the leadership of Ernst Meyer in 1921/22 and the policy's reprise in the mid 1920s. Using this tactic, the KPD was able to rebuild its strength and influence after the membership loss precipitated by the so-called 'March Action' (1921), which was the new mass party's first uprising attempt in its central German strongholds. Communists played a leading role in a strike of railway workers in 1922 and participated in the wave of workers' protests after the Foreign Minister, Walter Rathenau, was murdered by far-right nationalists who had aimed to destabilise the Weimar Republic. Wilde also shows how, in 1925/26, the KPD led the referendum campaign to expropriate the former Kaiser and old monarchies of the Second Reich, which had fallen from power in 1918 but had retained their material assets.[27] As the former German Communist and later political historian, Ossip Flechtheim, put it: this Leninist *realpolitik* had the potential to enable the party to become the successor to the pre-war SPD as a party of radical opposition to the new republic.[28]

Some KPD leaders were able to grasp that the early 1920s marked a moment in which most workers wanted to defend the Republic – however flawed – against their traditional enemies on the far right. The KPD's (ultra-)radical wing, however, had stronger support among the membership, especially in northern and western Germany. For this reason, making even the tactical concessions demanded by the 'united front' always met with significant resistance at both local and leadership level. For the 'Left Opposition', which crystallised in early 1921 and rose to take the leadership in 1924, the immediate memory of how the SPD had suppressed workers' radicalism during the revolution – including the murders of Rosa Luxemburg and Karl Liebknecht – informed their hostility towards all compromise.[29] This is the theme which runs through the following chapters. Ralf Hoffrogge's chapter details the origins and rise of the Berlin-based 'Left Opposition', which was often labelled the 'ultra-left' by its adversaries. Hoffrogge's archival research offers two correctives to earlier research on these leftists who held a Leninist world view while rejecting the Comintern's 'united front' policy in the early 1920s. Firstly, the group did not only include intellectuals – such as Ruth Fischer, Werner Scholem, Arthur Rosenberg and Karl Korsch – as previous research thought. Rather, its ranks were also filled by workers, including many militant trade unionists, who had pursued the German Revolution from the factories in 1918/19. Secondly, Hoffrogge stresses that the KPD in 1923 was not prepared to inflame anti-Semitism for tactical reasons. The author concedes that Ruth Fischer – who was herself from a Jewish background, like Werner Scholem – used ill-chosen words to attack both German and 'Jewish capitalism' at a meeting of far-right nationalist students. But, using previously inaccessible archival sources, he details how the Berlin Left remained opposed to Radek's so-called 'Schlageter Line' of 'neutralising' fascism by winning over its rank-and-file supporters.

In his biographical contribution, Mario Kessler begins by outlining Ruth Fischer's rise in the communist movement to become, firstly, a leader of the Berlin Left, before becoming the first woman – at only twenty-nine years of age – to head a mass party in Germany.[30] The author also details Fischer's central role in the KPD during 1923 – including the Comintern's preparations for a 'German October' – and how this catapulted her into the national leadership in early 1924. Fischer and the KPD's Left took power in a groundswell of support within the party for their policies of outright rejection of Social Democracy and the 'bourgeois Republic'. But, in a drive to reshape German communism as a revolutionary vanguard party modelled on the seemingly successful Soviet model, Kessler details Fischer's role in the 'Bolshevisation' of the KPD. The policy, which was adopted by the Fifth World Congress of the Communist International in July 1924, imposed strict organisational centralisation and the elimination of dissenting voices in waves of purges of so-called 'Rightists'. As Kessler concludes, 'Bolshevisation meant the destruction of internal party democracy; Stalinisation – the process that followed – meant slavish subordination of the party to the short-term needs of Stalin's policy'. Fischer Bolshevised the KPD, only to be ousted herself in the ensuing process of Stalinisation. She, as well as Scholem, lost their positions in 1925 and were expelled from the KPD in November 1926. The new head of German Communism was Ernst Thälmann, whose appointment followed a direct and highly public intervention by the Comintern in September 1925.

Thälmann, a former transport worker in the Hamburg docks, is the subject of Norman LaPorte's chapter. LaPorte argues that Thälmann's early ultra-radicalism was rooted in local industrial and political experiences and, with significant support among party workers, he felt emboldened to oppose the 'united front' despite his resolute 'loyalty' to Moscow. The Hamburg Left, which he headed, entered into an alliance with the Berlin Left – which now began to be organised nationally as a faction – over the course of 1922. This enabled his rise with Ruth Fischer into the KPD's national leadership in April 1923 and his prominent role as a national leader thereafter. During the Comintern's preparations for the 'German October', he was an outspoken opponent of the 'united front' policy which aimed at winning over the left wing of Social Democracy for revolution and warned of overestimating any common cause. The so-called 'Hamburg Rising', the party's last attempted insurrection, was a failure, an isolated putsch without active support even among workers in the Hamburg docks. But the long-underestimated Thälmann was able to use his credentials as a 'genuine proletarian' with proven credentials as someone prepared to fight against the odds, in order to become party leader and Germany's best known Communist.[31]

Biographical approaches to the history of the KPD have helped shed new light on the party's Stalinisation, and to qualify earlier research. For example, the literature has tended to present Heinrich Brandler and Ernst Meyer, even at the end of the 1920s, as the heirs of Rosa Luxemburg and the 'democratic communism' of the early years of the Weimar Republic.[32] These advocates of the 'united front' policy did indeed defend internal party democracy against Stalinism, but so too did their adversaries, the 'ultra left', who Meyer and Brandler helped 'purge' from the party in 1926. While the sectarian Left protested against Stalinism from the very beginning, the 'moderate' wing continued to work within an increasingly Stalinised party for two more years. This paradox is addressed by recent biographical studies of leading 'ultra-left' leaders; the main findings of this research are presented in the chapters by Hoffrogge and Kessler in this volume.[33] In fact, the central issue was tactics: how to promote revolution in Germany, when the moment returned. Not only did party leaders and members change factional alignments at one time or another, but Stalin and the Comintern never actually subscribed to these currents in more than a tactical and momentary manner. Importantly, democracy, as defined by later historians, was at no time a defining category for the 'ultra-left' or the proponents of the 'united front'. Both political orientations defended internal party democracy at certain points, but it was never an end in itself. Stalin made use of this in order to bring about changes in the party line, which enabled him to purge 'leftists' and 'rightists' one after another if they did not subordinate their views to the new 'official' policy. The mere notion of a 'left' and 'right' in the revolutionary communist movement – and the use of terms such as 'ultra-leftism' – originate in Stalinist polemics. In these struggles, both wings of the KPD were willing to align themselves with Stalin. Scholem, Fischer, and the Left did so in 1924, in order to oust Brandler; then, Brandler and Meyer used their positions in the leadership to purge the 'ultra-left' between 1926 and 1928. Thälmann represented the culmination of the party subordination to Moscow, as a leftist who became Stalin's willing executor.

This section of the book concludes with Marcel Bois's chapter, which outlines the fate of Left Communism from the mid 1920s until the collapse of the Weimar Republic in 1933. Based on his extensive archival research,[34] Bois details how, despite their common anti-Stalinism, these groupings were unable to unite. Instead, differences continually surfaced over such issues as: the extent to which criticism should only be voiced inside the party; whether Soviet communism could be reformed; or whether opposition required forming a new party. A minority, notably the 'Intransigent Left', around Karl Korsch and Iwan Katz, openly accused the Soviet Union of 'imperialism'.[35] But few felt comfortable with open statements about the degeneration of the October Revolution, let alone with contemplating life outside the 'official' communist movement. The largest grouping was the 'Wedding Opposition' – a nationwide umbrella grouping of leftists who were predominantly industrial workers. It was able to campaign within the party until 1928 precisely because of its relative moderation.

But the Stalinists – not least Thälmann – knew how to hammer on divisions between and within these groupings and appealed to their 'party discipline'. Only after the most resolute of these Communists had been expelled from the party did they form a common platform. But the *Leninbund*, which was founded by Ruth Fischer and Hugo Urbahns in 1928, was almost immediately confronted by the Stalinists' renewed 'left turn'.[36] The group fragmented and Fischer and Maslow applied, unsuccessfully, to be readmitted to the KPD. At the same time, the tactic allowed for the purge of the last remaining non-Stalinist groupings, the 'Right' around Brandler and Meyer. During the Great Depression and the impending Nazi 'seizure of power', some of these left-wing Communist abandoned their long-standing dogma and cooperated with the SPD and other left-wing splinter groups on the streets in 'united front' actions. Their inspiration had come from the now exiled Leon Trotsky, whose extensive writing advocated these policies internationally.

Communist Trade Unionism

In the KPD's approach to the trade unions in this period, it is instructive to take the long view. From the foundation of the KPD onwards, its relationship with the trade unions was defined in countless factional struggles. During the German Revolution, the KPD had been undecided about whether it should work within the existing framework of the General Confederation of German Trade Unions (*Allgemeiner Deutscher Gewerkschaftsbund*, ADGB), or whether this would be futile because of SPD hegemony. When the Moscow-based Red International of Labour Unions (RILU or, more commonly, Profintern)[37] was founded in 1921, two forms of trade unionism were affiliated to the KPD. There was the Union of Manual and Intellectual Workers, a syndicalist union that had converted to communism and was independent of the ADGB;[38] and, at the same time, communists also formed factions within the unions of ADGB with the objective of winning them over. But the 'March Action' in 1921 and the 'abortive uprising' of October 1923 undermined communists' efforts to gain ground. In 1924, official party policy was that all party members had to work within their respective unions and, in 1925, the Union of Manual and Intellectual Workers was dissolved. Finally, five years after its foundation, the KPD undertook a systematic approach towards trade unionism that was guided by the politics of the 'united front'. This, however, was ended only three years later by the Comintern's 'ultra-left turn' in the course of 1927-28, and party policy focussed on exacerbating tensions between the ADGB affiliated union leadership and their rank-and-file member. The policy of promoting the Revolutionary Trade Union Opposition (*Revolutionäre Gewerkschafts-Opposition*, RGO) led to expulsions and finally to the formation of separate 'red unions'.

Two of those 'red unions' are presented in detail in this volume. Stefan Heinz addresses the Unity Union of Berlin Metalworkers (*Einheitsverband der Metallarbeiter Berlins*, EVMB) and Constance Margain deals with the International Union of Seamen and Harbour Workers (*Einheitsverband der Seeleute, Hafenerbeiter und Binnenschiffer Deutschlands*, ISH). In his chapter, Heinz challenges the notion that trade union policy merely followed top-down party lines issued from Berlin and Moscow. Instead, he highlights the dynamics of radicalisation from below that took place during the Great Depression. Although the 'red unions' ultimately failed in the sense that they did not mobilise the masses, their appeal to a significant minority reflected genuine dissatisfaction within the ADGB-affiliated German Metal Workers' Union (*Deutscher Metallarbeiterverband*, DMV). The DMV followed the ADGB's policy of avoiding strikes, in the belief that it lacked the strength to do so at a time of mass unemployment. The 'Unity Union' opposed this policy and was able to organise some 10,000 workers in Berlin, half of whom were unemployed. It was, therefore, one the largest of the 'red unions', although its support failed to transfer to the national level. Yet, when the KPD began to move away from the policy of founding independent 'red' unions, the Berlin membership resisted and asserted a certain autonomy vis-à-vis the party leadership. Indeed, the demands for equal pay, gender equality and political struggle attracted many women, who comprised some 30-40 per cent of members – a figure far in excess of the DMV's support among women. After 1933, the 'Unity Unions' autonomy helped facilitate the setting up of networks of resistance to the Nazis which functioned into the mid 1930s, a finding which is also highlighted in recent biographical research.[39]

Political radicalisation during the Great Depression is also a *leitmotiv* of Constance Margain's chapter.[40] Founded in Hamburg in October 1930, the ISH was a product of the policy pursued by the Moscow-based

Profintern; in Germany, its national section was known as the Unity Union of Sailors, Harbour Workers and Bargemen (*Einheitsverband der Seeleute, Hafenerbeiter und Binnenschiffer Deutschlands*, EVSHBD). As was the case with the Berlin metal workers, this 'Unity Union' aspired to organise all workers under the banner of communism. But both of these 'red' unions fell short of this ambition – even if this organisation also numbered some 10,000 members. Its minority status prevented the successes of strikes in German ports. But there were other successes, notably in strikes against German owned ships harboured in Soviet waters, which endorsed political demands against Chancellor Brüning's austerity policies. The strikes had the support of the ISH's 'Interclubs', which provided meeting points for sailors and, initially at least, also the Soviet authorities. Nevertheless, the action collapsed after ten days. The reasons for this were a lack of support among sailors, who feared unemployment, but also the contradictory agendas of different Soviet authorities. While the Profintern supported the strike, the Commissariat of Foreign Affairs did not want to jeopardise German-Soviet relations. Ironically, Soviet Russia failed to support precisely the sort of transnational strike that had originally defined the foundation of the Comintern and Profintern. This entanglement of different Soviet interests is also brought out in Bernhard Bayerlein's chapter below.

Reaching Beyond the Party? The Countryside, Middle Class Intellectuals and Avant-Garde Artists

As we have seen, the KPD was a resolutely proletarian party in terms of its ideology and sociology and it had its strongholds in the centres of heavy industry. The opposing side of this was that the KPD had minimal electoral support in small-town and rural Germany, where a majority of the population continued to live. Only 2.2 per cent of the party members were agricultural workers, which amounted to 0.06 per cent of this important section of the population.[41] It was a phenomenon specific to Weimar Germany. In France, Italy, Eastern Europe and the Balkans, there was significantly more, if varied, support for communism in the countryside.[42] In general terms, the period from 1914 until 1933 was characterised by vast social change and economic upheaval which drove a process of political radicalisation and party-political realignment.[43] The origins of this rural protest can be located in the wartime economy, which requisitioned foodstuffs for the front and fixed prices for urban consumers. These hostilities toward the 'urban revolution' were intensified during the early years of the Republic by the belief that 'socialist' governments privileged urban consumers and, from the mid-1920s, the early onset of the world agricultural depression turned the countryside vehemently against the so-called Weimar 'system', even before the Great Depression. By the end of the 1920s, the rural areas – notably in the north and east – denounced the alleged 'Sovietisation of Germany'. No amount of propaganda about how harmoniously the traditional and the modern could happily cohabit in Soviet Russian villages had any prospect of success.[44] The beneficiary was the ultra-nationalist, anti-Bolshevik Nazi movement, which witnessed its earliest breakthrough in the countryside and took the leadership of rural professional associations before absorbing the votes of small town and rural Germany in a process peaking in July 1932.

Yet, as Sebastian Zehetmair details below, the KPD – to some extent influenced by the October Revolution – was the first political party to have an agricultural programme (1920) and an organisational division in the leadership devoted to rural campaigning. In reality, however, the content of the KPD's programme – like that of the SPD's – had little appeal beyond to agricultural labourers, as it advocated the socialisation of the rural economy and continued to regard small rural producers as a 'dying class', as anticipated by Marx.[45] In the early 1930s, Bruno von Salomon, a prominent leader of the north German rural protest movement, did join the KPD and voiced support for the KPD's 'Peasants' Aid Programme' (1931).[46] But this was an exception in a countryside which was turning 'brown' not 'red'. Explaining this is the most original part of Zehetmair's essay, which sheds new light on the urban-rural fault line running through Weimar politics and society. He argues that, while the KPD was firmly located within the workers' milieu spanning the trade unions and other organisations common to all (employed) workers, the party had no organisational points of contacts allowing it to transmit their message in the countryside.

Where the KPD and the Comintern did have much more success in reaching a wider audience and organising support for the 'New Russia' was among intellectuals and artists. In reaching this audience, the communist movement's main asset was the 'visionary propagandist', Willi Münzenberg – as Fredrik Petersson terms him in his contribution below. Münzenberg had been a member of the pre-war socialist youth, whose activism had led to a period of exile in Switzerland where he had become close to Lenin and other Russian exiles. It was recognition of his organisational and journalistic abilities as well as his insights into how to project a communist message to a non-communist audience, which catapulted him into the role of the Comintern's *de facto* minister for propaganda with access to a wealth of financial resources.[47] In 1921, Münzenberg was charged with organising the international campaign for famine relief in the West for Soviet Russia and out of this he built the Berlin-based 'International Workers' Relief' (*Internationale Arbeiterhilfe*, IAH).[48] The IAH was at the epicentre of what became known as the 'Münzenberg *Konzern*', which distributed pro-Soviet propaganda worldwide using a vast array of mass media. Above all, Münzenberg's innovation was based around the realisation that visual propaganda was more likely to create a penumbra of supporters and sympathisers beyond the party than dogmatic pamphlets. It was this that led to his lasting collaboration with the photomontage artist John Heartfield, not least in the images used to convey pro-Soviet sentiments in the *Illustrierte-Arbeiterzeitung*.[49]

To use Walter Laqueur's phrase, Münzenberg was also 'a cultural impresario of genius', who used the contemporary resonance of issues such as anti-imperialism and support for peace in an increasingly anxious post-war Europe as a means of winning the support of prominent intellectuals, most of whom were not Communists.[50] Among the prominent international figures participating in Münzenberg's congresses and committees and signing their manifestos were: the Indian nationalist, Nehru; the Harvard-educated American civil liberties activist, Roger Baldwin; the French Communist and anti-war writer, Henri Barbusse; and the renowned German scientist and pacifist activist, Albert Einstein, who had supported Münzenberg's activities since 1921.[51]

In detailing the anti-imperialist and peace congresses held in Brussels, Berlin, and Amsterdam between 1927 and 1932, Petersson shows how Münzenberg was in constant contact with the Comintern, which ultimately determined policy while leaving sufficient latitude for the great impresario to reach a mass audience. Interestingly, while the KPD was tied to the Stalinist 'Class against Class' policy after 1928, Münzenberg was able to distance himself from the party in order to maintain prominent public roles for 'bourgeois' intellectuals in a manner more like the 'united front' of the mid 1920s and, arguably, anticipating the 'Popular Front' of the 1930s, which depended on the creation of broad cross-class support in defence of the Soviet Union. Anti-communism after the fact is one reason why, until recently, historians paid little attention to Münzenberg's break with Stalinism, let alone trying to explain it as an important theme in interwar political history, as Petersson does in this volume.[52]

In his chapter, Ben Fowkes addresses how avant-garde artists and intellectuals, like so many German Communists, had been deeply influenced by the trauma of the war. Now, above all, during Weimar's 'golden twenties', their creative protest could be expressed. Even if the extent of cultural liberalisation after 1918 has been qualified by recent studies, it is hard to dispute that Germany imposed less censorship than perhaps any other European state. In Berlin many of the leading figures in modern art rose to become the new cultural elite. They enjoyed official patronage and had access to the cultural infrastructure of museums, art galleries, theatres and the opera, as well as being home to the radical journalism of *Die Weltbühne*.[53] For a moment at least, to use Peter Gay's term, the avant-garde 'outsider' had become an 'insider'.[54]

Importantly, however, as Benjamin Ziemann has recently argued, it would be a mistake to see the metropolis as representative of wider German developments, as much of the literature on Weimar's artistic and intellectual achievements tends to do. Its reception in the countryside and small town provinces was largely hostile. Ziemann, instead, invites us to see 'Weimar as Weimar', the small Thuringian town with a nineteenth-century cultural heritage, which expelled the architects of the Bauhaus movement in 1925.[55]

Ben Fowkes' chapter contributes the first study that explains this estrangement, by detailing the KPD's cultural policy during the Weimar Republic. The reader is introduced to five stages in the party's relationship to left-wing, non-communist artistic and intellectual innovation. After the brief period in which the nascent party welcomed the avant-garde's rejection of the old order, by 1920 the KPD adopted a policy hostile to it as a 'distraction' from political revolution. This was relaxed during the Republic's middle years and was welcomed by many fellow-travelling left-wing intellectuals and artists, but cooperation turned to outright condemnation of 'bourgeois culture' when the Comintern introduced the policy of 'Class against Class' in 1928. Then, again in line with Soviet cultural policy, from 1932 the policy was incrementally abandoned as 'socialist realism' became official policy instead. With the introduction of the 'Popular Front' in the mid-1930s, all thought of forming a new, independently organised 'proletarian culture' evaporated. Had the KPD been able to moderate the Comintern's sectarianism in the early 1930s, there was considerable potential for a broad front drawing in 'public intellectuals' against the rise of Nazis, as the role of Münzenberg shows – but the party's Stalinisation prevented this.

'Class against Class', c.1929-33

As the essays in this volume illustrate, historians of the KPD during the final fateful years of the Weimar Republic continue to differ in the emphasis they place on the importance of exogenous and endogenous factors shaping the policies of communist policy.[56] Yet, a synthesis of both is best suited to explaining the formation of policy in Moscow and how it could be carried out in Germany, if in some localities more than others.[57] Increasingly pushed out of the factories from the mid-1920s onwards, the KPD during the Great Depression became a vehicle for articulating the protest of the unemployed and underemployed workers on the streets.[58] The treatment of the KPD's constituency by the SPD at regional level – above all in Prussia, which was by far the largest federal state – is also at the centre of these accounts. As Marcel Bois details in this volume, the SPD's Police President in Berlin, Karl Zörgiebel, was a communist hate figure. This was reinforced by his use of force to break up the party's May Day celebrations in 1929 and, following these events, the SPD's Minister of the Interior in Prussia, Carl Severing, banned the League of Red Front Fighters shortly after relaxing the ban on Hitler addressing mass rallies.

The classic social history perspective remains that of Eve Rosenhaft, who argued that, when combined with the SPD administration's cuts to pay and welfare benefits, it seemed to ordinary Communists that there really was a 'united front' extending from the SPD to the Nazis.[59] The responses of Communists in Berlin to the austerity politics of the Great Depression, however, were far from universal, as more recent local studies detail.[60] Furthermore, the KPD's support for progressive issues – for example, the campaign for legal abortion in 1931 – remind us of the diversity of expressions of German communism, even after its Stalinisation.[61]

Importantly, however, the availability of new documentation in Moscow and Berlin makes clear that, if we are discussing the formation of policy in Moscow and its rigid, top-down imposition on the KPD leadership, it is impossible to deny the primacy of Soviet interests of state. Bernhard H. Bayerlein has been at the cutting edge of this new wave of archival research and his contribution to this volume draws on the three-volume documentary collection *Deutschland, Russland, Komintern*.[62] He argues that Stalin and his inner circle failed to anticipate the Nazi 'seizure of power' and, thereafter, prioritised maintaining good bilateral relations. As German Communists were being murdered, imprisoned, and sent to the camps in early 1933, Soviet diplomats assured their German counterparts that the fate of the KPD was an internal German matter. In 1933 and 1934, the Comintern held to its existing policy of treating Social Democrats as the 'main enemy', despite some convoluted statements about a 'communist united front'. The Comintern leader, Dimitri Manuilsky, even asserted that the Nazis' wave of terror against its political opponents would shatter any remaining 'democratic illusions' and ease the path to revolution. The head of the Profintern, Solomon Lozovsky, even welcomed the destruction of the SPD-led trade unions. At the centre of Bayerlein's chapter, however, is the argument that all these seemingly revolutionary utterances were a mere charade behind which stood the actual desire to strike a deal with Hitler.

The centrality of Stalin's role since the mid-1920s in formulating Comintern policy is now generally accepted, as is his disregard for the tensions generated in the KPD leadership because of these policies.[63] There has also been much speculation about what Stalin actually wanted in Germany, including favouring a military dictatorship to sweep aside the Republic and with it the risk of 'western orientation' in foreign policy, as championed by the SPD.[64] On the basis of archival evidence, Bayerlein's essay confirms that Stalin's priority was 'socialism in one country' and defence of the Soviet 'fatherland'. Soviet industrialisation under the Five Year Plans – including modernisation of the military – was paramount and the German revolution and revolutionaries were, when necessary, to be left to their fate.

Looking Ahead: Research Agendas

The authors in this volume bring into English translation new research which would otherwise be unavailable beyond a German readership. While they reflect a diversity of interpretations of the origins, development and role of the KPD as a mass party in the political system of Weimar Germany, taken collectively they shed light on the diversity and complexity of the party beyond the Soviet 'monolith' and other seeming certainties of the Cold War period. They also identify areas that are under-researched. In terms of the KPD's origins, the focus had rightly been on the Spartacists, but had wrongly neglected the importance of the 'Left Radicals' as an important and enduring influence shaping German communism. The attraction of the 'myth' of the Russian Revolution has long been known to have greater appeal to fellow-travelling intellectuals and artists than the communist parties. But the authors in this volume have elucidated how the KPD reflected the urban-rural split in Weimar Germany. In short, despite developing a peasant programme from the outset, the party could not reach a significant section of society, which inhabited a separate milieu. By contrast, the party leadership's focus on narrowly political aims limited the possibilities open to it among the urban-based artistic avant-garde. If we now know more about the importance of Willi Münzenberg in mobilising the middle classes beyond the party, we still know all too little about the KPD and its (mis)understandings of rural and small-town Germany. This is part of a wider under-researched theme locating German communism within the domestic political system: the importance of local and regional influences shaping the parties and tendencies within these parties. Finally, as polyglot researchers inform us about the relationship between Moscow and Berlin, we still know much less about the dynamics beyond the 'centre' and 'periphery' – the relations between communist parties, which also sheds light on difference as well as similarity.[65]

Notes

1. Jean-François Fayet, '1919', in S. A. Smith (ed.), *The Oxford Handbook of Communism*, Oxford: Oxford University Press, 2014, pp109-24.
2. Michael Buckmiller, 'Bilanz eines russisch-deutschen Forschungsproject', in Michael Buckmiller/Klaus Meschkat (eds), *Biographisches Handbuch*

zur *Geschichte der Kommunistischen Internationale*, Akademie Verlag: Berlin, 2007, pp19-20; David J. Mitchell, *1919. Red Mirage*, London: Jonathan Cape, 1970.
3. Kevin McDermott and Jeremy Agnew, *The Comintern. A History of International Communism from Lenin to Stalin*, Basingstoke: Macmillan, 1996, pxix.
4. For a documentary collection and introduction to this topic, Wladislaw Hedeler and Alexander Vatlin (eds), *Die Weltpartei aus Moskau. Der Grundungskongress der Kommunistischen Internationale 1919*, Berlin: Akademie Verlag, 2008.
5. On this issue, see Norman LaPorte, 'Introduction: Local communisms within a global movement', in *Twentieth Century Communism*, 5, 2011, pp5-21.
6. Eric Weitz, *Creating German Communism, 1890-1990*, Princeton: Princeton University Press, 1997, p4.
7. Marcel Bois and Florian Wilde, 'Ein kleiner Boom: Entwicklungen und Tendenzen der KPD-Forschung seit 1989/90', in *Jahrbuch für Historische Kommunismusforschung* (2010), pp309-322.
8. For an in-depth reconstruction of German historiography of the 1918 Revolution, see Wolfgang Niess, *Die Revolution von 1918/19 in der deutschen Geschichtsschreibung. Deutungen von der Weimarer Republik bis ins 21. Jahrhundert*, Berlin: De Gruyter, 2013.
9. On the limitations of a 'Leninist' narrative for interpreting the formation of German communism, see Klaus Kinner, *Der Deutsche Kommunismus. Selbstverständnis und Realität*, Berlin: Dietz, 1999, pp9-21. Attempts in the GDR to challenge the 'Leninist' narrative of this period were suppressed in 1958, see Mario Keßler, *Die Novemberrevolution und ihre Räte. Die DDR-Debatten des Jahres 1958 und die internationale Forschung*, Berlin: HellePanke, 2008.
10. Eric D. Weitz, 'Foreword', in Pierre Broué, *The German Revolution, 1917-1923*, Chicago: Haymarket Books, 2006, ppxi-xii.
11. The ninetieth anniversary of the German Revolution spurred debate on this issue. See Ottokar Luban, *Rosa Luxemburgs Demokratiekonzept. Ihre Kritik an Lenin und ihr politisches Wirken 1913-1919*. Leipzig: GNN, 2008; Ulla Plener, *Rosa Luxemburg und Lenin. Gemeinsamkeiten und Kontroversen*, Berlin: Nora, 2009.
12. On the pre-war SPD see Dieter Groh, *Negative Integration und revolutionärer Attentismus. Die deutsche Sozialdemokratie am Vorabend des Ersten Weltkrieges*, Frankfurt: Propyläen, 1972; Paul Blackledge, 'Karl Kautsky and Marxist Historiography' in *Science and Society*, 70, 3, 2006, pp337-359.
13. Carl E. Schorske, *German Social Democracy, 1905-1917. The Development of the Great Schism*, Cambridge: Harvard University Press, 1955.
14. Eberhard Kolb, *Die Arbeiterräte in der deutschen Innenpolitik. 1918-1919*, Düsseldorf: Droste, 1962; Peter von Oertzen, *Betriebsräte in*

der *Novemberrevolution*, Düsseldorf: Droste, 1963; Dirk Müller, *Gewerkschaftliche Versammlungsdemokratie und Arbeiterdelegierte von 1918. Ein Beitrag zur Geschichte des Lokalismus, des Syndikalismus und der entstehende Rätebewegung*. Berlin: Colloquium, 1985.

15. Hermann Weber, *Die Wandlung des Deutschen Kommunismus*, Frankfurt: EVA, 1969; *idem*, 'The Stalinization of the KPD: Old and New Views', in Norman LaPorte, Kevin Morgan and Matthew Worley (eds), *Bolshevism, Stalinism and the Comintern*, Basingstoke: Palgrave Macmillan, 2008, pp22-44.
16. David W. Morgan, *The Socialist Left and the German Revolution. A History of the German Independent Social Democratic Party, 1917-1922*, Ithaca: Cornell University Press, 1975; Hartfrid Krause, *USPD. Zur Geschichte der Unabhängigen Sozialdemokratischen Partei Deutschlands*, Frankfurt am Main: EVA, 1975.
17. Ralf Hoffrogge, *Working-Class Politics in the German Revolution. Richard Müller, the Revolutionary Shop Stewards and the Origins of the Council Movement*, Leiden: Brill, 2014.
18. See two recently published biographical accounts on IKD members: *Paul Frölich: Im radikalen Lager. Politische Autobiographie 1890-1921* (edited by Reiner Tosstorf), Berlin: Basisdruck, 2013; Gerhard Engel, *Johann Knief – ein unvollendetes Leben*, Berlin: Dietz, 2011.
19. A remarkable exception is the study by Hans Manfred Bock, *Syndikalismus und Linkskommunismus von 1918 bis 1923. Ein Beitrag zur Sozial – und Ideengeschichte der frühen Weimarer Republik*, Meisenheim: Anton Hain, 1969.
20. In 1928, some 61 per cent of KPD members had previously been members of the SPD or USPD, see Klaus-Michael Mallmann, 'Milieu, Radikalismus and locale Gesellschaft: Zur Sozialgeschichte der Weimerer Republik', in *Geschichte und Gesellschaft*, 21, 1, 1995, pp11-12.
21. Freya Eisner also emphasises the lack of pragmatism in communist policy in the unions as the reason for the decline of the party's influence. See *idem, Das Verhältnis der KPD zu den Gewerkschaften in der Weimarer Republik*, Cologne: Europäische Verlagsanstalt, 1977.
22. For the RFB's presence on the streets see, for example, Marie-Luise Ehls, *Protest und Propaganda: Demonstrationen in Berlin zur Zeit der Weimarer Republik*, Berlin: De Gruyter, 1997, pp113-28
23. 'Einleitung', in Herman Weber and Andreas Herbst (eds), *Deutsche Kommunisten. Biographisches Handbuch 1918 bis 1945*, Berlin: Dietz, 2008, pp13-15.
24. For a review of recent literature on this topic, see Norman LaPorte, 'Something Old, Something New, Something Borrowed and Something Blue', in *Moving the Social*, 55, 2016, pp113-40.
25. For an account of these political orientations from a prosopographical perspective, see Weber and Herbst, *Deutsche Kommunisten*, pp19-21.

26. See John Riddell (ed. and translator), *Toward the United Front: Proceedings of the Fourth Congress of the Communist International, 1922*, Leiden: Brill, 2012.
27. For a summary of this campaign, see Heinrich August Winkler, *Der Schein der Normalität. Arbeiter und Arbeiterbewegung in der Weimarer Republik*, Bonn: Dietz, 1987, pp270ff.
28. For a summary of Flechtheim's argument in English, see *idem*, 'The Role of the Communist Party', in Lawrence Wilson (trans.), *The Road to Dictatorship. Germany 1918-1933*, London: Oswald Wolff, 1964, pp93-110.
29. On the importance of Communist perceptions – or misperceptions – of the Republic, see Klaus Kinner, *Kommunismus und Linkssozialismus*, pp33-34.
30. Mario Kessler, *Ruth Fischer. Ein Leben mit und gegen Kommunisten (1895-1961)*, Cologne: Böhlau, 2013.
31. For a review of recent literature, see Norman LaPorte, 'Man and Myth: Ernst Thälmann', in *International Newsletter of Communist Studies*, 20/21, 27-28, 2014-2015, pp58-72.
32. See, for example, Jens Becker, *Heinrich Brandler. Eine politische Biographie*, Hamburg: SVA, 2001; Florian Wilde, 'Ernst Meyer (1887-1930) – vergessene Führungsfigur des deutschen Kommunismus. Eine politische Biographie', PhD Thesis, University of Hamburg, 2012.
33. Mario Keßler, *Arthur Rosenberg. Ein Historiker im Zeitalter der Katastrophen (1889-1943)*, Cologne: Böhlau, 2003; *idem, Ruth Fischer (1895-1961). Ein Leben mit und gegen Kommunisten*, Cologne: Böhlau, 2013; Ralf Hoffrogge, *A Jewish Communist in Weimar Germany. The Life of Werner Scholem (1895-1940)*, Leiden: Brill, 2017.
34. Marcel Bois, *Kommunisten gegen Hitler und Stalin. Die linke Opposition der KPD in der Weimarer Republik. Eine Gesamtdarstellung*, Essen: Klartext, 2014.
35. For a valuable discussion of the literature and key documents, see Ben Fowkes, *The German Left and the Weimar Republic. A Selection of Documents*, Leiden: Brill, 2014, pp334-60.
36. Rüdiger Zimmermann, *Der Leninbund. Linke Kommunisten in der Weimarer Republik*, Düsseldorf: Droste, 1978.
37. Rainer Tosstorff, *The Red International of Labour Unions (RILU) 1920-1937*, Leiden: Brill, 2016.
38. Jochen Weichold: *Die Union der Hand – und Kopfarbeiter Deutschlands (Räteorganisation)*, in *Jahrbuch für Forschungen zur Geschichte der Arbeiterbewegung*, 1, 2005, pp99-106.
39. Siegfried Mielke and Stefan Heinz, *Emigrierte Metallgewerkschafter im Kampf gegen das NS-Regime*, Berlin: Metropol, 2014.
40. Constance Margain, 'L'Internationale des gens de la mer (1930-1937): activités, parcours militants et résistance au nazisme d'un syndicat communiste de marins et dockers', PhD Thesis, Université du Havre 2, 2014.

41. Ben Fowkes, *Communism in Germany under the Weimar Republic*, Basingstoke: Macmillan, 1984, p173.
42. See, for example, Laird Boswell, 'The French Rural Communist Electorate', in *Journal of Interdisciplinary History*, 23, 4, 1993, pp719-49; George D. Jackson, *Comintern and Peasant in Eastern Europe*, New York: Columbia University Press, 1966.
43. For a valuable survey of more recent research which emphasises the early alienation of the countryside from the Republic, see Matthew Stibbe, *Germany 1914-1933. Politics, Society and Culture*, London: Routledge, 2010, pp117-23.
44. See, for example, the propaganda image reprinted in Weitz, *German Communism*, p239.
45. Ben Fowkes, *The German Left*, pp279-80.
46. James Ward, '"Smash the Fascists": German Communist Efforts to Counter the Nazis, 1930-1931, in *Central European History*, 14, 1, 1981, p53.
47. For a biographical sketch, see Herbst and Weber, *Deutsche Kommunisten*, pp521-24; see also Robert Service, *Comrades. Communism: A World History*, Basingstoke: Macmillan, 2007, pp109-10.
48. Kaspar Brasken, *The International Workers' Relief, Communism, and Transnational Solidarity. Willi Münzenberg in Weimar Germany*, Basingstoke: Macmillan, 2015, esp. pp29ff.
49. Cristina Cuevas-Wolf, 'Montage as Weapon', in *New German Critique*, 36, 2, 2009, p189; on the use of film, see, for example, Vance Kepley, 'The Workers' International Relief and the Cinema of the Left, 1921-1935', in *Cinema Journal*, 23, 1, 1983, pp7-23.
50. Walter Laqueur, *Weimar. A Cultural History 1918-1933*, London: Wiedenfeld and Nicolson, 1974, pp43, 51-52.
51. John Willett, *New Sobriety. Art and Politics in the Weimar Period 1917-32*, Hampshire: Thames and Hudson, 1978, p71.
52. See, for example, Sean McMeekin, *The Red Millionaire: A Political Biography of Willy Münzenberg, Moscow's Secret Propaganda Tsar in the West, 1917-1940*, Yale: Yale University Press, 2004; Stephen Koch, *Double Lives: Stalin, Willi Münzenberg and the Seduction of the Intellectuals*, London: HarperCollins, 1995.
53. Alexandra Richie, *Faust's Metropolis. A History of Berlin*, London: HarperCollins, 1998, pp331, 341.
54. This was the title of Gay's book, but also informed his main argument, see *idem, Weimar Culture. The Outsider as Insider*, New York: Harper Row, 1968.
55. Benjamin Ziemann, 'Weimar was Weimar: Politics, Culture and the Emplotment of the German Republic', in *German History*, 28, 4, 2010, pp542-571.
56. See, for example, Sigrid Koch-Baumgarten, 'Eine Wende in der Geschichtsschreibung der KPD?', in *Internationale Wissenschaftliche*

Korrespondenz zur Geschichte der Arbeiterbewegung, 46, 1, 1998, pp82-89.
57. On the various milieux in which the KPD operated, see Klaus-Michael Mallmann, *Kommunisten in der Weimarer Republik. Sozialgeschichte einer revolutionären Bewegung*, Darmstadt: Wissenschaftliche Buchgesellschaft, 1996, pp365-80.
58. Weitz, *German Communism*, pp160ff.
59. Eve Rosenhaft, *Beating the Fascists? The German Communists and Political Violence, 1929-1933*, Cambridge: CUP, 1983, esp. 7ff, 18ff, 26, 211; see also Andreas Wirsching, *Von Weltkrieg zum Bürgerkrieg? Politischer Extremismus in Deutschland und Frankreich 1918-1933/39*, Munich: Oldenburg, 1999, esp. pp22, 325, 360, 410, 610. For a review of the wider literature, see Norman LaPorte, 'Local Communisms within a global movement', in *Twentieth Century Communism*, 5.
60. For developments in Saxony, see Norman LaPorte, *The German Communist Party in Saxony*, Oxford: Peter Lang, 2003.
61. See Fowkes, *The German Left*, pp241ff.
62. Bernhard H. Bayerlein *et al* (eds), *Deutschland, Russland, Komintern. Neue Perspektiven auf die Geschichte der KPD und deutsch-russischen Beziehungen (1918-1943)*, Berlin: De Gruyter, 2014.
63. Kevin McDermott, 'Recent Literature on the Comintern: Problems of Interpretation', in Narinsky and Rojahn (eds), *Centre and Periphery. The History of the Comintern in the Light of New Documents*, Amsterdam: Institute of Social History, 1996, pp25-32; Bert Hoppe, *In Stalins Gefolgschaft. Moskau und die KPD, 1928-1933*, Munich: Oldenburg, 2007.
64. For a discussion of this literature, see Heinrich August Winkler, *Der Weg in die Katastrophe. Arbeiter und Arbeiterbewegung in der Weimarer Republik*, Bonn: Dietz, 1987, pp734ff.
65. This was the aim of LaPorte, Morgan and Worley (eds), *Bolshevism, Stalinism and the Comintern*.

The International Communists of Germany, 1916-1919

Gerhard Engel

THE COMMUNIST PARTY of Germany grew out of two previously existing organisations: the internationally recognised Spartacus Group and the smaller, less well known International Communists of Germany (IKD).[1] But it was the IKD that initially called for the establishment of a party to the left of the Social Democrats, which is why it is examined first in the chronological sequence of the essays in this book.

The IKD came into existence under the particular conditions of the labour movement in Bremen and north-western Germany. Early in the twentieth century, Bremen was rapidly developing into an industrialised urban centre dominated by shipyard labour. Thousands of qualified metalworkers arrived, along with many unskilled workers, proletarianised peasants, and an urban petty bourgeoisie. Between 1888 and 1907, the number of industrial labourers in Bremen grew six-fold to 33,000.[2] The rapidly growing population suffered from a shortage of housing and high rents while business owners and shareholders, who were making enormous profits, forced their employees to do extra work without increasing their wages amid rising costs. What labour rights did exist in the sense of social services, industrial safety, and freedom of association were disregarded. An undemocratic system for electing Bremen's local parliament, known as the *Bürgerschaft*, limited the capacity of the unions and the SPD to take political action.[3] The intensifying social and political conflict led to increasingly bitter fighting, in which business owners would respond to strikes – for social demands by individual groups of workers – by locking out their entire staff.

In the conflict between Marxism and revisionism at the turn of the century, radical Socialists took majority control of the Social-

Democratic Organisation of Bremen (SDVB), as the local iteration of the SPD called itself. They set the organisation's direction through their daily newspaper the *Bremer Bürgerzeitung* (BBZ), which opposed reformism, supported using the political mass strike as a new weapon, and called on the unions to adopt revolutionary politics in the fight for workers' economic and social demands.[4] The SDVB's political influence extended far beyond the workforce; it organised powerful actions in support of democratic suffrage in Bremen and supported the democratic school reform movement. Among its most fervent supporters were Social Democratic teachers, including Johann Knief, who would become the spokesman for the 'Bremen Left Radicals'. This was the title claimed by Social Democrats who not only disassociated themselves from the 'opportunism' of the SPD's right wing but were also increasingly at odds with the party's 'Marxist Centre' around Karl Kautsky, which had a penchant for radical language but in practice was willing to compromise with right-wing Socialists in the name of party unity. The three tendencies that typified the pre-war SPD therefore established themselves in Bremen: the reformist right wing, the party centre, and the left wing, which insisted on revolutionary action against imperialism and militarism. These tendencies each came to different conclusions with respect to the question of how socialist goals were to be reached in a world altered by 'monopoly capitalism' and 'imperialism'.

The radical left did not initially disassociate itself from the broader left wing of the SPD. The circumstances in Bremen, however, were particular. The party's reformists and the union bureaucrats quickly became the minority, which meant that the most important battles over the party's orientation were fought between the so-called party centre and the radical left.

Two international socialists, theoreticians and writers played a preeminent role in establishing the Bremen Social Democrats' radical left group. Dutchman Anton Pannekoek, a resolute defender of the mass strike, was assigned to work in Bremen as an 'academic instructor' by the education committee of the union cartel and the SDVB in 1910. In his socialist theory courses and articles in the *BBZ*, he opposed Kautsky's 'strategy of exhaustion' to wear out the opponent, yet opposed to any attempt to seek a 'final battle'.[5] Pannekoek described Kautsky's strategy as a 'theory of passively waiting'. During a 'period of imperialism in decline', he said, it is the workers' job to eliminate the ruling classes through extra-parliamentary action. He believed that parliamentary struggle was just 'one means to an end'. Arsenal building and belligerent policy were imperialism's essential characteristics. War, as the 'worst of all evils', would have to be prevented through mass action. Pannekoek was counting on a wave of spontaneous resistance if the threat of war became acute.[6]

Karl Radek, a leading member of the Party of Social Democracy of the Kingdom of Poland and Lithuania, had come to Germany in 1908 and earned a reputation as a brilliant writer on the Marxist left. He also worked for the *BBZ* and found political allies among the radical left in Bremen, where he moved to in 1912. Like Pannekoek, Radek would maintain close ties with Bremen's radicals even during the war.

In 1912, Radek published his most important theoretical work, *Imperialism and the German Working Class*,[7] in Bremen, where the radical left adopted his analysis. That analysis offered a theoretical foundation for their view that imperialism was heading toward a world war, which is why the capitalist social order that supported it had to be overcome through mass actions, and replaced by a socialist order. From then on, partisanship in support of Pannekoek and Radek's outlook was the inescapable criterion by which the radical left in Bremen would measure the politics of the SPD's right wing, as well as the party centre's unwillingness to act.[8]

When the SPD leadership threatened Radek with expulsion in the wake of disputes within the Polish party, Bremen's radical left resolutely defended his membership and the possibility of his continued work with the German Social Democrats. This happened, for example, during the mass strike debates, when the radicals again demonstrated their willingness to stand up as a minority against the party majority. What became known as the 'Radek Affair' intensified solidarity among left-wing radicals in Bremen. *BBZ* editor-in-chief and Reichstag deputy, Alfred Henke, who had once been a radical leftist trailblazer himself, was inconsistent in his defence of Radek; this led to the first rifts between him and his representative at the *BBZ*, Johann Knief, who was a passionate campaigner for Radek.[9] As noted above, Knief, a teacher who had emerged from the left opposition in the Bremen school-reform movement, would become the radicals' spokesman.

Far more so than even during the 'Radek Affair', Knief's radical outlook became evident in the mass strike debate of 1913.[10] He supported using the political mass strike not only as a defensive measure or threatening gesture but also as an offensive weapon. Mass actions, he explained, sometimes occur in the context of offensive and sometimes of defensive actions ranging from peaceful mass demonstrations and demonstrations of strikers to 'long-term mass strikes that might lead to popular uprisings'. In his view, the party could not plan such developments but would have to explain the mass strike and organise the action. Each individual mass action would be 'an episode in our struggle for power'. Partial goals would have to be pursued with an eye toward the intended final goal: a socialist society.

The debate about the mass strike escalated in conjunction with the shipyard workers' strike of 1913,[11] which the workers initiated against union leaders' wishes. Open conflict erupted between the union's members and its officials, leading to acrimonious debates about both authorisation for spontaneous action and the relationship between leaders and those they led. Anger and resentment over union bureaucrats' strikebreaking policies was seminal for both Bremen's left and the shipyard workers. For years it would define their attitude toward reformist unions and the 'radicals' within the SDVB who, like Alfred Henke, had voted to break the strike.

As was the case throughout the left wing of the SPD, it had become clear to the Bremen radicals long before August 1914 that the looming war would be nothing other than an imperialist war on all sides. They adhered all the more definitively to the Second International's anti-war resolutions based on that insight. Moreover, they were convinced that social democracy would defend peace to the end and, if they should fail, would respond to the outbreak of war with powerful actions. This idea was reinforced by the nationwide worker protests against the threat of war that lasted right up until the war actually started. The bewilderment was therefore all the more pronounced in Bremen when the SPD Reichstag faction approved the imperial government's demand for war bonds on 4 August 1914 and the party executive and union leadership called for the fatherland to be defended while announcing a 'civil peace' (*Burgfrieden*) between the labour movement and the state for the duration of the war.[12] Johann Knief and his supporters regarded 4 August as a logical outcome of the way that pre-war social democracy had developed. On the day that he was shipped to the Western Front, Knief, who had been conscripted immediately upon the outbreak of war, wrote that:

It is not the labour movement that has suffered a defeat but its leaders. They have ensured that Social Democracy has ceased to exist. [...] The masses will have to carve their own path; their leaders are finished. Until now the masses have not been taken into account. But they will make their demands. Long live the future!¹³

Although these dramatically stated and emotionally loaded lines are unprogrammatic, and the expectations they expressed were bitterly disappointed in the months that followed, they nonetheless show the direction in which radical left thought would move over the course of the war. What they clearly reveal is the anticipation of a split within social democracy and a belief that the working masses would be able to rise to take control of their own actions, against the will of their leaders.

Notably, the radical left worked for a revolutionary peace movement within the SPD. They declared their solidarity with the nascent 'international' group around Rosa Luxemburg and Karl Liebknecht, with whom they were in constant contact. They also welcomed Liebknecht's public 'No' vote against war bonds on 2 December 1914 and protested against the half-hearted attitude of those Reichstag deputies who, after opposing war bonds within their faction, abandoned Liebknecht in parliament. These included Bremen's own Alfred Henke. The split between the radical left and the 'centrists', already apparent before the war, grew significantly deeper.

At the end of 1914, Knief, who was convalescing after a mental breakdown at the front, took stock of the labour movement's course up to that point, in a blistering critique of the Social Democrats.¹⁴ He questioned their nature as a workers' party in pursuit of a socialist society and began searching for an alternative configuration for the socialist movement, which he claimed had emerged independent of and in opposition to the Social Democrats, and above all against the party and union bureaucracies.

In August 1915, his search for like-minded people led to initial contacts with the radical left in Hamburg. Although the Hamburg radicals around Heinrich Laufenberg and Fritz Wolffheim had a great many theoretical and tactical weaknesses, which the Bremen emissaries Knief and Paul Frölich – who from 1916 jointly edited the weekly newspaper, *Arbeiterpolitik* – felt the need to expose,¹⁵ the left radical movements in the two cities grew steadily closer.¹⁶

The conflicts within the SDVB came to a head in 1915. Beginning that January, a discussion group that included leaders of the radical left, the so-called party centre around Henke, and supporters of official SPD policy, debated the problems of the party's orientation during the war. The pro-war minority left the group the following May, having been completely isolated. The discussion thereafter was dominated by the radical left and the group began evolving into an 'organisational core' of the party opposition. It was primarily supported by the Bremen shipyard workers, where an illegal network of radical shop stewards emerged. In the discussion group, radical left soldiers in the Bremen Infantry Regiment, who were then engaged in trench warfare on the Western Front, called for anti-war actions. The soldiers expressed their mistrust of the SPD and suggested that, where possible, the left should work to create its own organisation even while the war continued.[17]

Conflict with the moderate Henke grew when Knief returned to Bremen in October 1915 and set the tone for the debates that followed. In the debates about nation and internationalism, Knief called for a reawakening of workers' internationalist class consciousness as a precondition for mass action.[18] It was necessary, he believed, to analyse the war based on Marxist principles:

> It is not that the war emerged from humanity's 'faults and follies', nor the question of whether it is 'rational' or not – whether it meets certain 'goals' that, from a scientific standpoint, can impress us. The only question is which social forces led to its emergence and what new social forces it will unleash.[19]

Knief's views prevailed within the group; Henke's influence reached a new low when he again refused to join Karl Liebknecht and Otto Rühle in voting against war bonds in the Reichstag. He justified his position by saying that a no vote could cause the party to be expelled from parliament and the *BBZ* to be banned.

At that point Henke and his small handful of supporters also left the group, which consequently became a radical leftist cell. It ceased to be only a place for discussion and was from then on the driver for anti-war action in Bremen. In December 1915, Knief called for a break with the obsession with legality. Because the party centrists considered mass action necessary yet unfeasible under wartime conditions, responsibility fell on the radical left to mobilise the masses for anti-war action.[20]

Knief's group succeeded in winning this position in the Bremen SPD. Even when Henke became one of the eighteen party centrist representatives who began voting against war bonds in December 1915, the deep rift between him and the radical left remained as pronounced as ever. He believed that the German government should initiate a peace without annexations as soon as its national borders and independence could be assured and when Germany was in a favourable position with respect to the war. Knief's group, however, categorically rejected the 'national defence' argument and fought for extra-parliamentary mobilisations for peace with socialist goals.

Long after the radical left broke with the politicians supporting the 'civil peace', another schism began to develop because of the half measures of the centrist party opposition. The *BBZ*, which presented the perspective of its editors Johann Knief and Paul Frölich, who had taken over in late 1915/early 1916, declared that:

> Unity has made the party great. That is certain. But only unity based on class struggle. Any other unity is just a sham, a formula obscuring decay. We have been concerned with unity built on class struggle from the outset and we will not give up this ideal for a moment. Our struggle is directed only toward this unity.[21]

These words also encapsulated the position that Johann Knief took up on behalf of Bremen's radical left at the national conference of left-wing party opposition leaders on 2 January 1916. Like all the participants, the delegation from Bremen agreed with Rosa Luxemburg's 'Principles of International Social Democracy'. But they joined with the representatives of Hamburg's radical left and a few other members of the Spartacus Group in criticising the 'Principles' for not articulating a sufficiently decisive break with the right wing of the party and not being disassociated systematically from the 'Centre' group. They also bemoaned the lack of more concrete tasks for everyday actions by the left-wing party opposition. From that moment, the radical left began drifting away from the Spartacus Group. The Bremen group and like-minded people in other places regarded themselves as independent. They accepted the authority of the Spartacus Group around Karl Liebknecht, Rosa Luxemburg, and Franz Mehring in the struggle against the war and its proponents, which they saw as the core of opposition to official Social Democracy. But they insisted on their independence and autonomy in developing their own tactics. In January 1916, SDVB officials loyal to the party executive set up their own press organ to counter the party opposition.²² This marked the beginning of the organisational split within the SPD in Bremen. Until May 1916, the majority of party members who supported the radical left managed to exclude numerous 'war socialists' from party positions and offices. Their majority in the local party organisation, out of all proportion to their position in the national party, initially reinforced the view on the radical left that its supporters' drive toward a renewed socialist workers' party would succeed by ousting opportunists of every stripe. The *BBZ* proclaimed that:

> It is a matter of fact that party unity must no longer be preserved. A split will and must come. [...] The organisation of the Social Democratic Party today already comprises opposing parties and that bond has not yet been broken simply because the internal struggle has not yet been won. And that struggle is for the hearts and minds of the party membership and their instruments of power: the organisational apparatus and their press.²³

For the radical leftists (who at this time were also known as the International Socialists of Germany), a battle for hearts and minds always meant the sharpest dissociation not only from the right wing of the party but also from the 'party centre'. Unlike the Spartacus Group, this corresponded to their declared affiliation with the Zimmerwald Left, the European opposition that had formed under Lenin's leadership at the Zimmerwald Conference in September 1915.²⁴ Bremen's radical left primarily maintained close contact with the Bolshevik leaders in their Swiss exile through Karl Radek. They participated in the second Zimmerwald Conference in April 1916 in Kienthal, Switzerland, through their representative Paul Frölich.²⁵

When food riots erupted in Bremen in May and June 1916, they grew into a wave of protest against Karl Liebknecht's arrest and conviction, which had taken place after his anti-war protest at Potsdamer Platz in Berlin on 1 May 1916. Supported by the radical shop stewards of Bremen's Weser shipyard, approximately 4000 shipyard workers engaged in one of the first major strike actions of the war early that July – a very significant number given the size of the workforce. (In Berlin, 50,000 metalworkers had in fact gone on strike on 28 June under the leadership of the Revolutionary Shop Stewards.) They made social demands and declared their solidarity with Liebknecht. These developments encouraged the radicals' belief in their anti-war strategy of mass actions, which evolved out of the mainstream of the Social Democratic anti-war opposition.

After that, the split between the group around Alfred Henke and the radical majority became more apparent in Bremen. In March 1916, Henke, along with seventeen other Social Democratic Reichstag representatives, rejected the government's war budget, after which they were all expelled from the party's parliamentary faction. The group formed their own faction under the rubric of the Social Democratic Working Group (*Sozialdemokratische Arbeitsgemeinschaft*, SAG). Because they restricted their anti-war efforts to parliamentary action and continued to press for party unity, the radicals' criticism of Henke and his colleagues only grew. Henke responded by openly distancing himself from the International Socialists of Germany and the Spartacist Group, which he branded a 'sectarian formation'.[26] In Bremen, the cleft between the radicals and the moderate party opposition was now just as deep as between both groups and the party executive. Johann Knief wrote that, 'This makes the three-way division among the Social Democrats clear. It must continue'.[27]

For the radicals, this largely meant losing access to the *BBZ*, where Knief had published his articles, but which was dominated by Henke. Yet despite a great deal of difficulty, they soon took another step toward independence: the first edition of *Arbeiterpolitik. Wochenschrift für wissenschaftlichen Sozialismus* (Workers' Politics. A Weekly Journal for Scientific Socialism), which was edited by Knief, was published on 24 June 1916.[28] From then on, the radicals were able to openly disseminate their views – if admittedly under conditions of censorship – and to unite like-minded people. In the months that followed, they gained subscribers and readers among workers, soldiers, and sailors, above all in north-western Germany but also in the Ruhr region, Dresden, Berlin, Munich, and other left-wing centres.[29]

One of the main topics of discussion in 1916 was a complete break with the party that had voted in parliament in support of the war effort on 4 August. The radical left considered it necessary to wage class struggle against this party just the same as against the imperialist bourgeoisie. *Arbeiterpolitik* appealed to the Spartacus Group to join this discussion. That call shows Knief's supporters to be among the earliest forerunners of the German Communist Party (KPD). Karl Radek sent most of the main articles on the subject from Switzerland to Bremen, where Knief and Wilhelm Eildermann printed them as their own positions. Their arguments regarding imperialism and opportunism matched the analysis Lenin had formulated in his writings. They included harsh criticism of the SAG, which the radicals saw as an internal party opposition, and which only confirmed the left's irreconcilable antagonism towards official Social Democracy. As a result of all the debates around 'opportunism', *Arbeiterpolitik* in August 1916 contemplated 'the possibility and necessity of establishing an independent organisation for proletarian socialism, the formation of a socialist party that represents the politics of the radical left for the first time'.[30] They hoped that members of the SPD would take up their revolutionary anti-war perspective – and they succeeded in Bremen, where they had a solid majority. On 1 December 1916, the SDVB cut off its membership dues to the party executive. In turn, the party executive immediately expelled the entire Bremen organisation from the SPD. The local right-wing socialist minority established a new organisation in Bremen and assumed leadership of the *BBZ*. With that, the organisational split between the official SPD and the local party opposition was complete.

In January 1917, the SPD executive also expelled the SAG and its supporters, who promptly announced the establishment of their own anti-war opposition party. With this, the radicals declared that, 'despite everything we are up against, now is the time to start our own party'.[31] Knief published a resolution 'for mutual understanding among the radical left'. At its centre were three theses:

> 1. The split among the Social Democrats due to the 4 August policy is irreversible; 2. Acknowledging this split means recognising the need to consolidate the 'oppositional organisations and groups in a new, proletarian party'; 3. If agreement among them is achieved with respect to questions pertaining to the condition of the working class in the era of imperialism, then there should be a conference to establish the new International Socialist Party of Germany. The Spartacus group should assume leadership.[32]

But the Spartacists did not take on the overall leadership. In April 1917, when the Independent Social Democratic Party of Germany

(*Unabhängige Sozialdemokratische Partei Deutschlands*, USPD) was founded, its members included not only the SAG, which in essence was a parliamentary faction within the Reichstag, but also thousands of workers who saw in it both the promise of a return to pre-war revolutionary social democracy and a vehicle for waging a revolutionary struggle against the war. To ensure its capacity to directly influence the development of the USPD's base, the Spartacus Group aligned itself with the party with the proviso that its own independence would be preserved. The radical left vehemently criticised this, pointing out 'the Bolsheviks' independent emergence' in the revolution that had already begun in Russia.[33] International circumstances at that moment demanded that a radical party be established in Germany, they argued. Leftists' membership of what they understood to be a moderate party would be political suicide, an outright betrayal. For that reason, the radicals in Bremen and Hamburg never joined the USPD and opposed those on the left who did.[34]

Arbeiterpolitik responded to the establishment of the USPD and the Spartacus Group's participation with a certain degree of confusion. Calls for the formation of a separate radical party were at times pushed to the background. And while it appealed to the left to drive a revolutionary wedge into the unions, it also published articles advocating their abolition altogether. The radical left in Hamburg published a resolution rejecting a labour movement in which the party and unions were divided, and called for a unified organisation. *Arbeiterpolitik* then lost both Knief and Frölich and with them the direction that they had set out. Knief went underground in April 1917, and was arrested in January 1918; he remained in 'protective custody' until the Revolution the following November. Frölich was conscripted into the military again. He would later state that '*Arbeiterpolitik* during the later stages of the war cannot be regarded as an expression of the radical left movement'.[35]

It was only in late July 1917 that steps toward establishing a radical party resumed – but this time without the Spartacus Group.[36] A call stated that groups had been established in several places and had informed *Arbeiterpolitik* of their endorsement of a new party. This meant that the conditions had been met for creating an International Socialist Party of Germany (*Internationale Sozialistische Partei Deutschlands*, ISPD). A working committee took up the task and called on the radical left to submit proposals for the party programme and statutes. They made it clear, however, that the new party could not be a top-down organisation dominated by the leadership. Thirteen delegates from local radical left groups met conspiratorially in Berlin on 26 August 1917 to establish the party, but the police broke up the gathering and seized the drafts of the founding documents. Those papers defined the new party they strived for as giving new leadership to the labour movement in place of the old SPD, which had forfeited its leadership position through its war policy and destruction of intra-party democracy. The new party likewise distanced itself from what they saw as the USPD's half-hearted opposition. The ISPD, the delegates claimed, would be based on the principle of proletarian internationalism; it would consider itself 'a member of the nascent Third International' and part of the Zimmerwald Left. The party's organisational identity would borrow from anarcho-syndicalism in that it defined itself as a 'unity organisation', combining party and union.

After the failed attempt to establish the party in August 1917, Knief raised the issue again the following December.[37] He had concluded that it was necessary as it followed the Bolsheviks' role in the successful October Revolution which had been enthusiastically applauded among the radical left. As he had prior to the establishment of the USPD, Knief called on the Spartacus Group to break away from the USPD and create a separate radical party. He was the first person to raise the issue of establishing a *de facto* communist party in Germany in the wake of the Russian Revolution.

When revolution came to Germany in November 1918, radical leftists believed that it would have to be pushed beyond the formation of a republic with bourgeois-democratic laws to produce a socialist upheaval in German society. Their goal was a 'dictatorship of the proletariat' led by revolutionary workers' and soldiers' councils, free of right-wing socialists and supported by reliable armed workers.

By 10 November 1918, Bremen's radical left was already discussing constituting itself as the International Communists of Germany (*Internationale Kommunisten Deutschlands*, IKD), Bremen Branch, and creating a daily newspaper. On 16 November, the Dresden radicals published a newspaper called *Der Kommunist*. This self-identification of radical leftists as communists and of their groups as the International Communists of Germany was a reference to Marx and Engels' Communist Manifesto, and indicated a position among the revolutionaries on the far left wing. The foremost newspaper with that tendency was another daily, called *Der Kommunist*, this one published in Bremen – with the first issue on 27 November – and edited by Knief. The radical left demanded that the Revolution should be the moment to achieve what had previously eluded them: the establishment of a new revolutionary party. It was nonetheless clear to them that they would be unable to act without what was now termed the Spartacus League. However because the Spartacists were still betting on the possibility of winning over the majority of the revolutionary oriented USPD members, the radical left decided to lead the movement itself, form local organisations made upwards of their supporters, and put pressure on the Spartacus League through their organisational links. To attentive observers, it became apparent within the first few weeks that the German Revolution had stalled and that the right-wing socialists had allied themselves with the old powers. For its part, the radical left viewed this as evidence of the need for a new revolutionary party that would lead the masses in a proletarian revolution.

The IKD grew quickly in Bremen. They had a core of about fifty people and a base of 500 to 1000 supporters, mostly shipyard workers who had been expelled from the SPD.[38] Local IKD groups sprang up in north-western Germany (including Bremen, Bremerhaven, Vegesack, Hamburg, Wilhelmshaven, Rüstringen and Hanover) as well as in Saxony, Berlin, the Rhine-Ruhr region, Württemberg, and Bavaria.[39]

Delegates from some ten local IKD groups met in Berlin from 15-18 December 1918 for their first national conference.[40] In a misunderstanding of the balance of political power during the Revolution, the 'founding declaration' drafted by the Dresden branch of the IKD identified the party's goal as the immediate 'establishment of communism'. The path to that goal was to be, in the short-term, a dictatorship of the proletariat over the bourgeoisie, with the support of armed communist workers. IKD members in the workers' councils were called on to isolate and oust SPD supporters. This meant that they were making demands over the heads of the majority of workers, who were still behind the SPD during the Revolution, thereby effectively isolating themselves, instead of collaborating with the workers in pursuit of comprehensible interim goals. The idea, championed above all by Knief, that the path to a socialist revolution had to be paved by a longer period of mass actions, was brushed aside despite the fact that the revolution had proven Knief correct in that regard.[41] So the cornerstone of the IKD's constitution as a party intent on bringing together 'all communists [...] be they previously Spartacists, radical leftists, or otherwise identified',[42] was an unrealistic, sectarian platform. They envisaged a federated organisational structure based on intraparty democracy; for the IKD, the Bolsheviks were an example of a party leading a revolution, but not a model for party organisation. The IKD's dissociation from the old Social Democrats included rejecting a centralised party structure. It also viewed the Spartacus League as a 'leading organisation' with suspicion, believing that what was needed instead was:

> [E]quality, independence, will, and the strength of each individual's own action. [...] Mass movements cannot be leaderless, but nor can they be driven by their leaders. [...] The masses are racing and pushing forward and in their midst are their leaders, scarcely visible, cheering, stirring, and guiding![43]

Unity of action, they argued, could only be guaranteed by the movement's 'unity of mind' if the individual groups were completely independent.[44] So while the IKD considered a representative democracy expedient where the state was concerned, it insisted on direct democracy within the party that was to lead it.[45]

The first national IKD conference left one question unanswered: should Communists participate in the National Assembly elections on 19 January 1919? The delegates called on the rank and file to quickly inform the organisation of their views. Opinions were divided. Many of them considered council power and acknowledgement of a bourgeois parliamentary legislature to be fundamentally irreconcilable, while others, such as Knief, pleaded for a radical left-wing parliamentary faction as a mouthpiece for revolutionary ideas for as long as the majority of the workers, faced with the power of counterrevolution, were unprepared for a socialist revolution.[46]

The IKD delegates met again in Berlin on 24 December 1918 for their second national conference. Against Knief's opposition, they decided to boycott the elections. At the same time, however, they also rescinded their decision not to unite their organisation with the Spartacus League. Karl Radek, now a guest from Soviet Russia at the national council congress in Berlin, had convinced Knief to give up his aversion to joining with the Spartacists on the previous night. His change of opinion was also helped by developments in the Spartacus League itself. Internal support for withdrawal from the USPD was growing due to party leaders' refusal to convene a national conference, where the Spartacists had hoped to win the majority over to their views.[47] A resolution adopted at the national IKD conference stated that this development had overridden the theoretical and tactical contradictions between the Spartacus League and the radical leftists and reduced them to 'different ways of articulating the same ideas'. Their differences on organisational issues would resolve themselves over the course of the revolution. The delegates to the national conference declared their 'absolute consent to uniting the IKD with the Spartacus League' and proposed to the Spartacists that a 'founding conference for the Communist Party of Germany (Spartacus League) (KPD-S)' be called.[48]

The national conference that would become the KPD's founding party convention began on 30 December 1918. Knief, the intellectual leader of the IKD, welcomed the creation of the party enthusiastically. He saw only one problem area that was contentious, albeit manageable: the relationship between the independence of the rank and file and the central leadership of the movement, wherein he advocated a bottom-up organisational structure and decision-making process.[49] Because the IKD bound its representatives to the majority decisions of the grassroots, Knief, as an opponent of the electoral boycott, could not be a delegate to the founding convention. Moreover, he fell seriously ill shortly before the year's end and died on 6 April 1919.

Twenty-nine delegates from fourteen local IKD groups participated in the founding KPD conference.[50] Karl Becker of Dresden read out the IKD declaration that stated its desire to merge with the Spartacus League and formally dissolved its own institutions. A second IKD declaration emphasised the need to merge but also pointed out the contradictions that had prevented such an action to date:

> While this work was illegal, it was unavoidable that preparation for revolution would start from various centres. And due to the disparities in the political and economic character of the distinct fields of work, theoretical and tactical differences were bound to arise. The IKD organisations grew and developed from below; the illegal

organisation of the Spartacus League was led from above. The IKD proclaimed its categorical support for breaking away from both the old Social Democratic Party as well as the USPD; the Spartacus League took on the task of undermining the old parties from the inside out. That caused a series of contradictions at the conferences of what would become the Third International [...] These contradictions have now vanished. Both tendencies have been welded together through the fire of revolution. [...] In a joint Communist Party, we will apply all of our powers to uncompromising completion of the proletarian revolution and work for a clear, principled party policy.[51]

With that declaration, the IKD now emphasised its desire for unity while simultaneously pointing to its own pioneering role in the process of creating the new party. The declaration also affirmed the IKD's directly democratic conception of a revolutionary party, its pursuit of a Third International led by the Zimmerwald Left (which is to say by Lenin), and a party politics that would continue the revolutionary process toward a socialist revolution through a dictatorship of the proletariat. The IKD delegates voted against Communists' participation in the National Assembly elections. They also proposed the creation of a 'unity organisation' and the departure of Communists from reformist unions. The IKD therefore made no small contribution to the plurality of viewpoints at the establishment of the KPD.

When the factional struggles that convulsed the KPD during the first decade of its existence were over, the International Communists of Germany, though an organisational co-founder of the KPD, found itself marginalised. Only a minority of its members were relatively at ease with the party's changing leadership and political orientation, which increasingly reflected the Comintern's Bolshevisation and ultimately its Stalinisation. The IKD's position on the trade union issue and parliamentarism were revised no later than during the KPD's Heidelberg Conference in October 1919 under party chairman Paul Levi. Former IKD supporters with an anarcho-syndicalist outlook then sought a political home in the schismatic Communist Workers' Party of Germany (*Kommunistische Arbeiter-Partei Deutschlands*, KAPD) that had been formed in April 1920 by KPD-members expelled at Heidelberg or the Free Workers' Union of Germany (*Freie Arbeiter-Union Deutschlands*, FAUD). Other former IKD-members, who had stayed with the KPD during the 1920s, criticised the Bolshevised KPD in 1928-1929, and made up a significant proportion of the founders of the break-away Communist Party of Germany (Opposition) at around the same time. Others, including Paul Frölich, the one-time close colleague of Knief, would join the Socialist Workers' Party of Germany (*Sozialistische Arbeiter-Partei Deutschlands*, SAPD) in 1931.[52] Although it had an important role in establishing the KPD, it is thus clear that the short-lived IKD would have less influence on its subsequent history than would the various communist and left-socialist tendencies that rejected or criticised it from within the German labour movement before 1933.

Translated by Joe Keady

Notes

1. This essay is partly based on the author's book *Johann Knief – ein unvollendetes Leben*, Berlin: Karl Dietz Verlag, 2011.
2. Peter Kuckuk, 'Industrialisierung, Sozialstruktur und Arbeiterschaft in Bremen', in Hartmut Müller (ed.), *Bremer Arbeiterbewegung 1918-1945. Trotz alledem. Katalogbuch*, Berlin: Elefanten Press, 1983, pp10-14; Herbert Schwarzwälder, *Geschichte der Freien Hansestadt Bremen*, vol. 2, Bremen: Christians, 1995, pp469-479.
3. Schwarzwälder, *op. cit.*, pp511-514.
4. Karl-Ernst Moring, *Die Sozialdemokratische Partei in Bremen 1890-1914*, Hanover: Verlag für Literatur und Zeitgeschehen, 1968, p102; Schwarzwälder, *Geschichte der Freien Hansestadt*, pp526-554.
5. Karl Kautsky, *Was Nun?* in *Die Neue Zeit*, 28, 2, 1910.
6. Hans Manfred Bock, 'Anton Pannekoek in der Vorkriegssozialdemokratie', in *Arbeiterbewegung. Theorie und Geschichte. Jahrbuch*, Band 3, Frankfurt am Main: Fischer, 1975, pp103-167.
7. Karl Radek, *In den Reihen der deutschen Revolution 1909-1921*, Munich: Wolff, 1921, pp48-155.
8. The conceptual foundations of the Radical Left in Bremen between 1910 and 1914 is explored in detail in Hansgeorg Conert, *Reformismus und Linksradikalismus in der bremischen Sozialdemokratie vor 1914. Die Herausbildung der 'Bremer Linken' zwischen 1904 und 1914*, Bremen: Universität Bremen, 1985, pp243-383.
9. Gerhard Engel, *Johann Knief - ein unvollendetes Leben*, Berlin: Dietz, 2011, pp128-138, 143-151.
10. Johann Knief, 'Die neue Massenstreikdiskussion', in *BBZ*, 26, 27, and 28 June 1913.

11. Helmut Kral, *Streik auf den Helgen*, Berlin: Tribüne Verlag, 1964, pp225-227; Dirk Hemje-Oltmanns, *Materielle Bedingungen der Entwicklung des Verhältnisses von Sozialreform und Revolution in Deutschland (1890-1929) unter besonderer Berücksichtigung der Bremer Werftarbeiterbewegung*, München: Minerva, 1983, pp104-109.
12. Paul Frölich, *Im radikalen Lager. Politische Autobiographie 1890-1921*, Berlin: BasisDruck, 2013, pp102-106.
13. 'Letter from Johann Knief to Rudolf Franz', 23 August 1914, in Bundesarchiv (BArch), N 2078/2, Bl. 4-5.
14. 'Letter from Knief to Franz', 31 December 1914, in BArch, N 2078/2, Bl. 36-38.
15. 'Letter from Knief to Franz', 15 August 1915, *op. cit.*, Bl. 91; Volker Ullrich, *Die Hamburger Arbeiterbewegung vom Vorabend des Ersten Weltkrieges bis zur Revolution 1918/19*, Band 1, Hamburg: Lüdke, 1976, pp218-220.
16. Ullrich, *op. cit.*, pp312-313, 334.
17. Wilhelm Eildermann, *Jugend im ersten Weltkrieg. Briefe, Tagebücher, Erinnerungen*, Berlin: Dietz Verlag, 1972, pp246-248; Gerhard Engel, *Rote in Feldgrau. Kriegs- und Feldpostbriefe junger linkssozialistischer Soldaten des Ersten Weltkrieges*, Berlin: trafo Wissenschaftsverlag, 2008, pp61, 71, 96-97, 101, 107.
18. Eildermann, *op. cit.*, pp273-274; *Lichtstrahlen*, 3, 6, 1915/1916, pp137-140.
19. *Lichtstrahlen*, 3, 6, 1915/1916, p140.
20. Stiftung Archiv der Parteien und Massenorganisationen der DDR im Bundesarchiv (SAPMO), Sg Y 30/0188, Bl. 391.
21. 'Eine zeitgemäße Mahnung', in *BBZ*, 20 December 1915.
22. Erhard Lucas, *Die Sozialdemokratie in Bremen während des Ersten Weltkrieges*, Bremen: Carl Schünemann Verlag, 1969, pp43-44.
23. *BBZ*, 15 May 1916.
24. Horst Lademacher (ed.), *Die Zimmerwalder Bewegung. Protokolle und Korrespondenz*, Band 2, The Hague-Paris: Mouton, 1967, pp327, 298-299, 325, 327-328.
25. Frölich, *Im radikalen Lager*, pp119-124.
26. *BBZ*, 17 June 1916.
27. 'Letter from Knief to Franz', 30 June 1916, in BArch, N 2078/2, Bl. 105.
28. Frölich, *Im radikalen Lager*, pp125-127; Gerhard Engel, 'Einleitung', in *Arbeiterpolitik. Unveränderter Neudruck*, Leipzig: Zentralantiquariat der DDR, 1975, ppiii-xvii.
29. Peter Kuckuk, 'Bremer Linksradikale bzw. Kommunisten von der Militärrevolte im November 1918 bis zum Kapp-Putsch im März 1920', PhD Thesis, University of Hamburg, 1970, p68.
30. 'Einheit oder Spaltung der Partei?', in *Arbeiterpolitik* 1, 10, 1916, p76; Gerhard Engel, 'Johann Knief – Biographisches zu seinem Platz in der Geschichte der deutschen Linken', in *Jahrbuch für Forschungen zur Geschichte der Arbeiterbewegung*, 4, 3, 2005, p125.

31. 'Die Spaltung der Partei und das Zentrum', in *Arbeiterpolitik*, 2, 6, 1917, p44.
32. 'Die Verständigung der Linksradikalen', in *Arbeiterpolitik* 2, 8, 1917, pp57-59.
33. 'Das Kompromiß von Gotha', in *Arbeiterpolitik*, 2, 15, 1917, pp113-115.
34. 'Die Konferenz der Arbeitsgemeinschaft', in *Arbeiterpolitik*, 2, 13, 1917, p97.
35. P. Frölich, *Im radikalen Lager*, p126.
36. 'An die linksradikalen Ortsgruppen und Genossen!', in *Arbeiterpolitik*, 2, 30, 1917, p225; Ullrich, *Hamburger Arbeiterbewegung*, pp412-416; Engel, *Johann Knief*, pp318-320.
37. P[eter] Unruh (Johann Knief), 'Eine dringende Notwendigkeit', in *Arbeiterpolitik*, 2, 50, 1917, pp374-375.
38. Peter Kuckuk, *Bremen in der Deutschen Revolution 1918/1919. Revolution, Räterepublik, Restauration*, Bremen: Steintor, 1986, p32.
39. Kuckuk, *Bremer Linksradikale*, p68.
40. *Der Kommunist* (Bremen), 21 December 1918.
41. Johann Knief, 'Internationale Kommunisten und Unabhängige', in *Arbeiterpolitik*, 3, 48, 1918, pp289-292.
42. *Dokumente und Materialien zur Geschichte der deutschen Arbeiterbewegung* [henceforth: *DuM*], Reihe II, Band 2, Berlin: Dietz Verlag, 1957, p610.
43. 'Partei und Bewegung', in *Arbeiterpolitik* 2, 11, 1917, pp83-84; 'Partei und Führer', in *Arbeiterpolitik*, 2, 37, 1917, pp284-286.
44. *Der Kommunist* (Bremen), 6 December 1918.
45. Gerhard Engel, 'Demokratie in Theorie und Praxis der Bremer Linksradikalen', in Rainer Holze and Siegfried Prokop (eds.), *Basisdemokratie und Arbeiterbewegung*, Berlin: Karl Dietz Verlag, 2012, pp98-106.
46. Johann Knief, 'Die Konsequenzen', in *Der Kommunist* (Bremen), 24 December 1918.
47. Jakow S. Drabkin, *Die Novemberrevolution 1918 in Deutschland*, Berlin: Deutscher Verlag der Wissenschaften, 1968, pp444-447.
48. *DuM*, Reihe II, Band 2, p653.
49. Johann Knief, 'Spartakus und wir', in *Der Kommunist* (Bremen), 1 January 1919.
50. Hermann Weber (ed.), *Die Gründung der KPD. Protokolle und Materialien des Gründungsparteitages der KPD 1918/1919*, Berlin: Dietz Verlag, 1993, p318.
51. Weber, *Die Gründung*, p171.
52. These developments are explained in Theodor Bergmann, '*Gegen den Strom'. Die Geschichte der KPD-(Opposition)*, 2nd Edition, Hamburg: VSA Verlag, 2001; Hanno Drechsler, *Die Sozialistische Arbeiterpartei Deutschlands (SAPD). Ein Beitrag zur Geschichte der deutschen Arbeiterbewegung am Ende der Weimarer Republik*, Meisenheim am Glan:

Hain, 1965; Reiner Tosttorff, 'Paul Frölichs unvollendete Erinnerungen', in Paul Frölich, *Im radikalen Lager*, pp341-343.

The Role of the Spartacist Group after 9 November 1918 and the Formation of the KPD

Ottokar Luban

The Background

CONTRARY TO THE resolutions passed by the Socialist International, the Social Democratic Party of Germany deputies in the Reichstag on 4 August 1914 voted unanimously in favour of war credits.[1] The most intense criticism of that decision came from a group of left-wing Social Democrats who came together under the rubric of the Spartacus Group (later the Spartacus League). Their numbers grew and the Spartacists became the voice of the socialist anti-war movement, although under the state of siege they could not work other than as a loose clandestine network. It was only with the freedom of the press and freedom to organise that followed the November 1918 revolution, as well as the release of leaders and sympathisers from prison, that the stage was set for a new party to be established: the Communist Party of Germany made its first appearance at a national conference at the turn of 1918/19.

This chapter will look at the founding of the party and the events leading up to it from August 1914 until the failed upheaval in January 1919, which ended with the murders of Rosa Luxemburg and Karl Liebknecht. It will emphasise the continuities between social democracy and early communism and address the fragility of that beginning phase, which was not only threatened by external repression but was also persistently contested from within. Certain leading figures within the Spartacus group, such as Clara Zetkin and Leo Jogiches, doubted the value of establishing a new party until the very last, preferring to remain in the partially revolutionary Independent Social Democratic Party of Germany (USPD).

The Shock of 4 August

While the left wing of the SPD was mired in a passive state of shock in August 1914, the circle of radicals around Rosa Luxemburg in Berlin attempted an internal protest against the change of course without any initial success. Nonetheless, that group, which included Franz Mehring, Clara Zetkin, Ernst Meyer, Julian Marchlewski (a.k.a. Karski), Wilhelm Pieck, Hugo Eberlein, Leo Jogiches, Käte and Hermann Duncker, and, from late August 1914, Reichstag member Karl Liebknecht, campaigned – following the anti-war resolution of the Socialist International – for a consistent anti-war policy and for democracy through mass actions up to and including revolutionary uprising. They promoted their ideas verbally at party events and among small groups of radical comrades and they widely distributed illegal pamphlets. These were initially directed at SPD members, but their focus increasingly shifted toward the workforce as a whole as the war progressed. The Luxemburg circle adopted the name International Group (*Gruppe Internationale*) after the newspaper *Die Internationale*, published in April 1915. The group operated autonomously within the SPD and, after the party split, within the USPD. The name Spartacus Group, derived from the illegal newspaper *Spartacus*, gained currency starting in 1916. Given that the group was only an informal network, it had neither an executive committee nor any formal membership. Anyone committed to the views espoused in *Spartacus* and involved in the dissemination of its content could be considered a 'member'.

The Spartacus Group during the Last Two Years of the War

The International Group was badly weakened by the arrests of two of its leaders, Rosa Luxemburg and Karl Liebknecht. Luxemburg was in prison from February 1915 until February 1916 and then in 'protective custody' from July 1916 until 8 November 1918. A great deal of her writing for pamphlets and *Spartacus* articles was smuggled out, but her oratory talents were missed at assemblies and demonstrations. Worst of all, she was unable to contribute to the revolutionary left-wing socialist uprising in Berlin on 9-10 November 1918 because she only reached Berlin on the evening of 10 November, following her release from prison in Breslau (Wrocław).

Starting with his rejection of war credits on 2 December 1914,

Liebknecht's consistent anti-militarist politics made him a symbol of the peace movement. After he was arrested at a demonstration on 1 May 1916 and sentenced to four years and one month in prison, the harsh conditions of his imprisonment left him isolated and deprived him of any political impact.

It is primarily thanks to the efforts of Rosa Luxemburg's long-time comrade Leo Jogiches – a journalist born in Vilna in 1867 who had been active before the war among the exiled Russian social democrats in Switzerland and Berlin – that the Spartacus Group was able to effectively influence mass actions among German workers between 1916 and early 1918. His great experience in conspiratorial political work helped him to build a clandestine network of backers within the Berlin SPD and, later, the USPD, with connections to supporters nationwide. In Berlin, he focused on the Teltow-Beeskow-Charlottenburg electoral organisation, which was the only party organisation outside Hanau in which the Spartacus Group had a majority. Under the guise of being a building cooperative, Spartacus supporters met in various neighbourhoods to discuss their illegal work. Jogiches had a large number of pamphlets printed, shipped, and distributed. The Spartacus Group's main strongholds were in Stuttgart, Hanau, Chemnitz, Braunschweig, and Duisburg. Oppositional members of the socialist youth organisation made up a separate network.[2] There were also radical left-wing organisations in Bremen and Hamburg. However, from mid-1916 onward they demanded the founding of a radical party that would unify party and trade union, which was rejected by the Spartacus leadership.

The pamphlets made their way to a wide array of locations. Other people, including Ernst Meyer, worked to assist Jogiches; most of these were long-term SPD or USPD members or functionaries.[3] Spartacus supporters also received internal memoranda on certain occasions. They met with Jogiches and other main organisers for discussions at events like the national SPD conference in Berlin in September 1916 or the founding USPD conference in Gotha in April 1917. However, after this, there were no further national gatherings of the Spartacus Group until 13 October 1918 in Berlin, due to difficulties paying for travel expenses and the significant risk of arrest.[4]

Because of the Spartacus Group's loose organisational structure, they did not organise the mass political strikes of June 1916, April 1917 and January 1918. These were instead organised by a network of oppositional union leaders who would be known after the German Revolution of 1918 as the Revolutionary Shop Stewards (*Revolutionare Obleute*, RSS).[5] Jogiches organised a network distributing pamphlets, which aimed to radicalise the shop stewards and the union rank and file. For example, during the revolutionary mass strike in late January 1918, in which approximately three quarters of a million people participated in Berlin and other cities, eight Spartacus pamphlets were produced, each with a print run of 25,000-100,000.[6] Jogiches began preparing for another mass action in March 1918 after the January strike of that year, but he and his group of supporters were arrested in late March. The authorities uncovered and destroyed almost the entire Spartacus network in the process.[7]

Mathilde Jacob, a friend of and intermediary for the imprisoned Rosa Luxemburg, as well as one of Jogiches' associates, worked painstakingly to win over new recruits for the Spartacus Group. It was only in May 1918 that the thirty-four year-old blacksmith and Labour Secretary Karl Schulz, who had just deserted the military, was able to rebuild the Spartacus Group and restart pamphlet distribution. However, he was arrested on 15 August 1918, together with his closest aides Susanne Leonhard and Erich Anspach. The newly re-established network was again destroyed, after the authorities found a list of Spartacus Group members' names and addresses on Leonhard; the group did not revive until the November Revolution.[8] Following their arrests, the RSS, with whom Jogiches had worked closely, cut off contact with Spartacus Group members due to fear of infiltration by informers.[9]

After his amnesty on 23 October 1918, Karl Liebknecht had only modest success in reviving the Spartacus networks, although he personally worked intensively to prepare for the November 1918 uprising in Berlin. By that point, the RSS, together with the Spartacus Group and various leftist USPD leaders, such as Ernst Däumig and Georg Ledebour, had formed a committee they were already calling a 'workers' council' to prepare for a mass action. What they had in mind, however, was not another strike, but an armed uprising. It should be emphasised, however, that neither the USPD nor the Spartacus Group had voting authority in that committee; instead, they served only in an advisory capacity. The shop stewards alone set the date of the uprising for 11 November. However, they revised that decision in favour of 9 November, in response to changing circumstances and, to some extent, pressure from Liebknecht, who participated in the discussions as the Spartacus Group representative.¹⁰ The uprising was successful and the *Kaiserreich* came to an end.

The Role of the Spartacus Group after 9 November 1918

On the day of the uprising,[11] Liebknecht joined members of the revolutionary committee at the front of marches, addressed assemblies, and proclaimed the existence of a Socialist Republic from the window of the *Stadtschloss* in the heart of Berlin. A short while before that, however, SPD politician Philipp Scheidemann had already declared a German Republic from a balcony of the Reichstag building. At noon, with the imperial government ceding to the pressure by the victorious revolutionary masses, the title of Chancellor was transferred from Max von Baden to the SPD leader Friedrich Ebert, who announced the formation of a new government comprised of SPD and USPD representatives.

When Liebknecht arrived at the Reichstag in the early evening for negotiations with the other insurgents, he was urged by soldiers to affiliate with the SPD-USPD unity government that the SPD had proclaimed. After resisting for a long time, he finally accepted a government office, provided that it would only last for three days until an armistice could be established. But, after Jogiches had informed him of his strong disagreement, and the USPD had abandoned the left-wing positions that were the conditions of his participation, he rescinded the agreement.[12]

The political decision to form a SPD-USPD government on 9 November was made largely without the participation of the people who had organised the successful uprising. This is because almost all the members of the Spartacus Group, the left wing of the USPD and the RSS who were involved in in the revolution were marching with the workers through the streets of Berlin, giving speeches, and helping to occupy government buildings.

The rank and file only came back into the picture thanks to the efforts of RSS leader Emil Barth, after the negotiations in the Reichstag building between the SPD and the USPD on the formation of a new government were almost finished. At an assembly in the Reichstag building on the evening of 9 November, at which soldiers were present, Barth got a resolution passed that would allow Berlin's factories and garrisons to elect workers' and soldiers' councils on the morning of 10 November, which would then elect a revolutionary socialist government that afternoon.[13] However, this plenary assembly of Berlin's workers' and soldiers' councils proved to be a disaster for the revolutionary left. The SPD won a majority among the soldiers and, using its party newspaper, *Vorwärts*, and the preliminary discussion, skilfully exploited the soldiers' and workers' need for unity.[14] Before and during the assembly, the Spartacus Group had distributed a pamphlet with the slogan 'No votes for the government socialists', but this was pilloried by a soldier over the course of the meeting 'with vigorous applause'.[15]

A letter to August Thalheimer (written, in all likelihood, by Jogiches), dated 11 November 1918 and obviously influenced by this tremendous defeat for the left, offers a remarkably prosaic assessment of the balance of political power: 'The Revolution [...] is, above all, a soldiers' mutiny. It was executed *by* soldiers who were dissatisfied with their lot *as* soldiers. [...] Certainly the masses contributed to the Revolution, but for the moment its social core remains completely shrouded in darkness.' Jogiches realistically assumed that 'Many or most of the working people still support the majority Social Democrats'. That majority, however, was 'not only slowing down the Revolution but directly counter-revolutionary'. The task of the Spartacus Group was therefore 'to expose the counter-revolutionary nature of the majority socialists before the masses by initiating a wave of agitation against them. We must then expose the social core of the events that have taken place and thereby turn this from a soldiers' revolt into a true proletarian revolution'.[16]

Founding the Party Prematurely in December 1918

It might have been possible for the Spartacus Group to lawfully propagate its political goals at its own assemblies and through its own newspaper in order to build an organisation. But the links between the leadership and its supporters had largely been destroyed during the war due to the large numbers of arrests and conscriptions. When the leaders first met with Rosa Luxemburg on 11 November, following her arrival in Berlin the evening after her release from 'protective custody' in Breslau, the group adopted the name Spartacus League to clarify its claim to a larger federation even as it remained within the USPD. Where its illegal work during the wartime state of siege had largely been limited to agitational pamphleteering, various tasks were now delegated to fourteen different people. Not only did they plan on publishing a daily newspaper but also a weekly theoretical journal called *Die Internationale* as well as newspapers directed at soldiers, women, and young people. Between 11 and 17 November, however, they had no publication at all. The editorial offices of the bourgeois publishing company Scherl Verlag had been occupied during the Revolution on 9 November and used to publish the *Rote Fahne* on 9 and 10 November 1918, in lieu of the *Berliner Lokalanzeiger*. But the occupiers were unable to hold the premises, and Luxemburg and the rest of the Spartacus leadership spent more than a week looking for a publisher with a printing press for their own newspaper, before the *Rote Fahne* finally resumed publication on 18 November 1918. Yet even then, a shortage of paper and staff restricted editions to four pages. Luxemburg was so burdened as editor-in-chief that she was hardly able to appear at the Spartacus League's public assemblies, costing the organisation its most dynamic orator.[17] All of these circumstances combined to delay the Spartacus Group's composition as a cohesive organisation.

By contrast, although the opponents of a socialist revolution had no functional mass organisations at their disposal, they were nonetheless able to monopolise state power, as Liebknecht made clear in a sober analysis dated 21 November 1918: 'the "socialist" government has maintained or even reinstated the entire administrative apparatus and the old military machinery – institutions which are nearly impossible to control for the workers' and soldiers' councils; the enormous economic power of the ruling classes has not been touched, and some of their social powers will continue for a long time'. Liebknecht emphatically called for the Revolution to move forward, writing that: 'The working masses must defend what they have gained and proceed to conquer the remaining positions of power in order to bring the ruling classes to their knees and to make proletarian rule come true in flesh and blood'.[18] The question at that point was whether Liebknecht and the other leaders of the Spartacus League would be able to use this realistic assessment to draw level-headed conclusions for future political action.

For Rosa Luxemburg, this was not the case. As in early 1916, she drastically overestimated the revolutionary mood among the workers. In a letter to Clara Zetkin dated 29 November 1918, she wrote that

USPD members, including 'Däumig, Eichhorn and others, argued for taking a stand entirely on the same grounds as ours, and the same was true for Ledebour, Zietz, Kurt Rosenfeld – and the masses!'[19] In her revolutionary impatience and wishful thinking, Luxemburg had evidently entered into an inauspicious alliance.

Based on that erroneous assessment, she believed that the time had come to assume leadership of the left wing of the labour movement. On 14 December 1918, she published the manifesto 'What Does the Spartacus League Want?' in the *Rote Fahne* and on 15 December she proposed that the USPD withdraw from the government at the party's general assembly in Berlin. She called for party members to reject a national assembly, take power immediately through the workers' and soldiers' councils, and convoke a national party congress immediately. But her resolution received only 29 per cent of the delegates' votes versus 71 per cent for a proposal by Rudolf Hilferding. This proposal supported allowing the USPD representatives to remain in the joint revolutionary government with the majority Social Democrats, participating in the national assembly elections, and holding a USPD congress only after those elections. That outlook was not limited to USPD delegates; the working population of Berlin shared it as well. When the Berlin workers' council delegates to the national council congress were elected on 14 December, the SPD, with eleven delegates, won significantly more support than the USPD with seven delegates. The SPD's majority in the soldiers' councils was even larger. It is therefore incomprehensible that Rosa Luxemburg still believed that there would be a left-wing majority at the National Congress of Councils, which opened on 16 December in Berlin, and she was disappointed when the delegates voted for a national assembly, cursing them afterwards as 'Ebert's Mamluks'.

That mid-December, Luxemburg and the other Spartacus leaders could no longer ignore the actual views of the proletarian masses delegated from Berlin and across Germany. Over the weeks that followed, they doggedly campaigned for their views within the USPD (some of whose members already leaned toward supporting the Spartacus League) in an attempt to win a majority or be able to take a significant number of party members with them to form a new, left-wing socialist party in the event of a split. At the same time, quickly forming a new party carried the risk of isolation, which is why Luxemburg had opposed dividing the party during the war.

There was also no shortage of urgent pleas from left-wing USPD officials to hold off on founding a separate left-wing socialist party. In a conversation on 20 or 21 December 1918, Wilhelm Koenen, chairman of the USPD's large Halle-Merseburg branch, emphatically pointed out to Luxemburg that Spartacus sympathisers within his chapter needed more time to build a majority in favour of forming a new, radical party. But Luxemburg insisted on doing so quickly.[20] In a letter dated 17 November 1918, Clara Zetkin also argued with Luxemburg against establishing a party too soon, writing that, 'Given our well-known lack of leaders and resources, it would make it considerably more difficult for us to reach the masses [...] I think we should stay in the USP[D] for now as its relentless critics'.[21] Zetkin, who was unable to travel to Berlin for health reasons, was evidently not immediately informed of the resolution to form a new party, which was subsequently passed at the national Spartacus conference on 30-31 December 1918. Jacob Walcher, a delegate from Stuttgart who participated in the founding KPD conference, would later recall her 'irritation at the choice of an inauspicious moment' for it.[22] In an as yet undiscovered letter to Luxemburg in early January 1919, Zetkin evidently vigorously criticised the decision, as we can deduce from Luxemburg's reply dated 11 January 1919.[23]

The Founding Congress of the KPD

The source materials do not provide an unambiguous explanation as to when exactly the preliminary decision to establish the KPD was made. The *Rote Fahne* mentions a 'national Spartacus League conference' on 23 December and again in a lead article dated 29 December. A decision to form the party is supposed to have been passed on the evening of 29 December when the Spartacus leadership met for a discussion with several delegates. That is when the name Communist Party was chosen over Luxemburg's preferred Socialist Party.[24] There was talk at the conference itself of a national conference and a founding party convention but it was only at its conclusion that Liebknecht declared it the official founding party conference.[25]

While Luxemburg's 'What Does the Spartacus League Want?' advanced a vision of socialism with an unambiguously grassroots-democratic and socialist orientation, it was counteracted at the founding party conference by the prevailing anarcho-syndicalist and putschist currents among the delegates. That ultra-left outlook led the party to reject participation in the forthcoming national assembly elections despite the fact that the entire Spartacus leadership, with Luxemburg and Liebknecht at the helm, had supported participation. The risk of a resolution hostile to the existing unions and their replacement by a single unity organisation that merged party and union was only averted by handing the matter over to a programme committee, where Luxemburg's proposed basic programme could also be discussed and augmented.[26] The radical current among the Spartacus League's delegates was widespread and it was supplemented by the twenty-nine delegates from the International Communists of Germany (*Internationale Kommunisten Deutschlands*, IKD), which had constituted itself as a party in late November 1918 and had strongholds in Bremen, Hamburg, and Dresden.[27] It had merged with the Spartacus League at the conference, where they combined to form a radical majority. On the other hand, the union-based RSS ultimately did not participate in the conference despite hours of negotiations with Liebknecht.[28] As a result, the new party lacked a mass base among the workers of Berlin. Karl Radek, who participated in the congress as an emissary of the Bolshevik government and whose speech was greeted with thunderous applause, came to a drastically negative conclusion, writing that: 'The party conference was a glaring demonstration of the party's youth and inexperience. Its connections with the masses were extremely weak [...] I did not believe that I was looking at an actual party'.[29]

By breaking away from the USPD in late December 1918, Luxemburg and the other Spartacus League leaders also broke with the conviction that doing so would isolate them from the proletarian masses, as they had believed in 1916-17. As the discussion, speeches, and resolutions at the founding congress show, the leaders had particularly surrendered themselves to the pressures of a radical spectrum whose illusory expectations were far removed from what most workers had in mind. If the Spartacus League had remained in the USPD, that party would likely have pledged its unambiguous commitment to the council system at its subsequent party conference in early March 1919, and thereafter advocated a revolutionary politics with an emphasis on mass action. A revolutionary socialist mass party in Germany might therefore have been possible by March 1919.

What Effect Did the Bolsheviks Have on the Formation of the KPD?

Given that the Bolsheviks' representative, Karl Radek, had been in Berlin since 19 December 1918, the question has arisen of whether or not he and Adolph A. Joffe, the Soviet ambassador in Berlin between late April and 4 November 1918, had pushed for the establishment of a separate party.[30] The archival sources cannot confirm that they did. Neither the correspondence between Spartacus leaders Hermann and Käte Duncker between May and October 1918,[31] nor the letters sent to Moscow by Joffe and other Bolshevik emissaries in Berlin during the same period, discuss the notion of forming a party. On the contrary, Joffe's reports on the USPD and the Spartacus Group repeatedly state that the USPD was too passive and the Spartacus Group too weak to be able to actively push for a revolution.[32] After the Russian embassy was expelled from Germany on 4 November 1918, contact with a Bolshevik representative was only re-established with Radek's arrival on 19 December 1918. However, given Radek's long-standing animosity toward Luxemburg and Jogiches, it was impossible for him to influence the leaders of the Spartacus Group. He only succeeded with his old friends among the left-wing radicals in Bremen (particularly Johann Knief, who opposed merging with the Spartacus League), where the IKD were preparing to form a joint party.[33] The decision to establish the KPD some time near the end of the national council congress on 20 December 1918 was therefore taken quite autonomously by the Spartacus League's leaders.

It is well known that Luxemburg and Lenin had considerable political differences.[34] They clashed repeatedly, as in 1904 and 1911, over Luxemburg's conception of a grass-roots democratic mass proletarian movement.[35] In an incomplete draft of a manuscript Luxemburg wrote on the Russian Revolution, she rejected the terror that the Bolshevik government directed at its political enemies. Most other leaders of the Spartacus Group shared that opinion, as Angelica Balabanoff wrote after speaking with them, in a letter to Lenin dated 19 October 1918.[36]

The leaders of the KPD also opposed Lenin's plans to establish a Communist International, on the grounds that such an undertaking could only be successful if there were a mass base for socialist parties in Europe.[37] But despite all their differences, Rosa Luxemburg and her political colleagues worked closely with the Bolsheviks. In mid-December 1918, cultural historian Eduard Fuchs, a long-standing confidant of the Spartacus League's leaders, was sent on an arduous journey to Moscow with a letter from Rosa Luxemburg and verbal messages about the situation in Germany.[38] Leo Jogiches, who assumed leadership of the KPD after Luxemburg was murdered, maintained that contact, with his early February 1919 letter informing Lenin of the situation in the German labour movement and, in the wake of Fuchs' return from Russia with money for the KPD, asking for additional financial support.[39] Nonetheless, the KPD leadership did not satisfy Lenin's wish for their approval of the Communist International. On the contrary, they decided to send fellow party organiser Hugo Eberlein to Moscow with an explicit mandate to vote against its establishment.[40] Thus we can say that the leaders of the KPD preserved their autonomy from the outset.

The KPD in the Berlin January Upheaval of 1919

Luxemburg's article 'The First Party Congress', first published in the *Rote Fahne* on 3 January 1919,[41] gives no indication that she expected revolution to come soon or to run its course quickly. She did not anticipate a revolutionary turning point in the near future but rather a longer maturation process.[42]

Late at night on Saturday 4 January 1919, the RSS, KPD leaders Liebknecht and Pieck, and the Berlin branch of the USPD issued a call for a demonstration in protest against the dismissal of Berlin Police Superintendent Emil Eichhorn, a USPD member, by the SPD government. The USPD had left the government in late December and the office of police superintendent was its only remaining position of official power. Despite the short notice, several hundred thousand people participated in the demonstration in central Berlin on 5 January. The organisers, who were caught off guard by the enormous turnout, had not called for any concrete objective other than protest against the Ebert-Scheidemann government, but participants nonetheless spontaneously occupied several newspaper offices that evening, including the Social Democrats' *Vorwärts*.

Despite the enormous scale of the demonstration that Sunday, the coverage in the Monday edition of the *Rote Fahne* on 6 January was relatively reserved. There was nothing to suggest that Luxemburg or the rest of the KPD leadership planned a decisive power struggle against the Social Democrat government in the days that followed.

Nor is there any hint of this in Luxemburg's patently realistic reply to Karl Radek on 6 January 1919, in response to his question regarding the goal of the mass action. Radek, quoting her, wrote that, 'The strike was a protest strike. We wanted to see how far Ebert would go and how the workers in the countryside would respond to the events in Berlin. Then we would see.'[43]

In contrast to Luxemburg's cautious outlook, Liebknecht and Pieck let themselves get carried away by the euphoric mood among the RSS on the evening of 5 January. With only six votes against, an overwhelming majority passed a resolution calling for a general strike on 6 January for the purpose of toppling the SPD government. However, the extremely short announcement did not include any direct call to remove the government. At Pieck's request, a Revolutionary Committee made up of thirty-three members was formed, including co-chairmen Ledebour, Liebknecht, and Shop Steward Paul Scholze. The demonstration already had the appearance of a popular uprising, due to its hundreds of thousands of participants and, without any preparation, the left-wing socialists of Berlin suddenly attempted to turn it into a new insurrection. Richard Müller, who had organised the mass strikes during the war, warned against exceeding the scope of the protest due to the lack of organisational structure and planning. He and five other shop stewards did not participate, depriving the Revolutionary Committee of skilled organisers.

With nearly half a million participants, the mass demonstration on Monday 6 January was even larger than on Sunday. The Revolutionary Committee sent armed troops to occupy government buildings, legitimising their authority with a document written by Pieck declaring that the SPD government was no longer in control and that the Revolutionary Committee had taken power; at the bottom of this document were the names of Karl Liebknecht, Georg Ledebour and Paul Scholze. The public and the other KPD leaders would only learn of the existence of the declaration when a facsimile was published in *Vorwärts* on 14 January. While the Revolutionary Committee were more than satisfied with the response to their call for a general strike on 6 January, they were deeply disappointed by the troops stationed in Berlin, which either remained neutral or were loyal to the SPD government.

Liebknecht and Pieck, the two members of the KPD leadership who were also part of the Revolutionary Committee, had spent their time since Saturday 4 January in a nearly uninterrupted string of meetings and speeches at demonstrations, without any opportunity to coordinate with the other KPD leaders. It was only on the evening of Monday 6 January that Jogiches and Paul Levi were able to make contact with Liebknecht and Pieck.

Impressed by the success of the general strike on 6 January, Luxemburg now also saw a possibility to take power. In her lead article in the *Rote Fahne* on 7 January (therefore written on the evening of 6 January) titled 'What Are the Leaders Doing?' she proclaimed the goal of 'occupying all positions of power,' a clear reference to the fall of the government.[44] The first meeting of the KPD leadership with Liebknecht and Pieck was held that Tuesday noon. 'Comrades Luxemburg and Jogiches urged a more definitive leadership of the struggle and clear slogans.'[45] Historians have previously been unaware of the discussion on 7 January between the Spartacists – and their representatives on the Revolutionary Committee Liebknecht and Pieck – and the push by Jogiches and Luxemburg for the Committee to take more forceful action. This KPD leaders' meeting was evidently suppressed in subsequent writings on the German Revolution produced by both the KPD and the Socialist Unity Party of Germany (SED) as a way of constructing the myth that party leaders – particularly Rosa Luxemburg – rejected the idea of overthrowing the government. Luxemburg's lead article 'Neglected Duty', dated 8 January (but written the day before), shows that by 7 January she had indeed concluded that the time to fight for control had come. She repeatedly mentions that 'the Ebert-Scheidemann government must be removed' if the revolution is to be continued and socialism implemented. However, she does clearly oppose an outright coup, writing: 'Removing the Ebert-Scheidemann government does not mean storming the Reich Chancellery and chasing off or arresting a few people. Above all it means seizing all actual positions of power and *keeping* and *using* them.'[46] Here, Luxemburg focuses on institutions that would facilitate the distribution of revolutionary propaganda with intensive involvement by prominent USPD leaders Ledebour and Däumig.

The coup d'état proclamation that Pieck wrote and Liebknecht signed was attacked both by Rosa Luxemburg immediately after the failed insurrection attempt and by historians later on. That criticism is, in my view, unjustified. On 7 January, it appeared as though most of the workers in Berlin were insisting that the Ebert-Scheidemann government be replaced. The planned takeover by the RSS and the attempt to occupy government buildings therefore did not amount to a putsch by a small revolutionary group; instead, they were the product of a mass movement made up of the majority of the workers of Berlin (albeit only on that particular Monday and Tuesday). Those steps and the coup declaration were what gave them revolutionary legitimacy in Berlin – just as the overthrow on 9-10 November 1918 had. The scale of the majority in favour of replacing the SPD government among the rank and file is apparent in two resolutions passed by the plenary assembly of the Greater Berlin local workers' councils on 10 January, which almost unanimously called for the resignation of the government – including support from most of the SPD delegates.[47]

The argument that a Ledebour-Liebknecht government with the RSS would have been limited to the capital and a few industrial centres is true, but this is only apparent in hindsight. In November 1918, information about the workers' willingness to engage in a revolutionary uprising nationwide had appeared extremely unfavourable at the moment when the spark was lit, making it possible that a similar movement could have arisen in January 1919 as well. The action in January 1919 only became a putsch as of Wednesday 8 January, when the majority of Berlin's workers no longer supported the Revolutionary Committee taking power.

The KPD leaders held a meeting that Wednesday evening, after the factory workers' willingness to strike had begun to wane and the first small skirmishes between government troops and revolutionaries had started. Given the flagging appetite for conflict among the working people of Berlin and the majority SPD government's discernible preparations to put down the revolution by force, Jogiches forcefully called for Liebknecht and Pieck to resign from the Revolutionary Committee. A majority passed the proposal over dissenting votes from Pieck and Liebknecht, and Liebknecht announced that he would not comply with the resolution, thereby initiating a split among the KPD leaders. Jogiches went so far as to propose that the group publicly distance itself from Liebknecht in the *Rote Fahne*. That proposal was rendered meaningless, however, when the RSS held a meeting late that evening and adopted both a pamphlet written by Hugo Haase and Liebknecht's call for a general strike. Luxemburg and most of the Spartacus leaders regarded this renewed willingness on the part of the RSS and the

USPD leadership to engage in conflict as a sign that the mass movement might be reviving, but it was not enough to move the workers to continue fighting. On the contrary, a mass movement with an entirely different objective developed in the factories of Berlin on 9 January. Workers called for unity on socialist principles between the 'ordinary' members of the SPD, USPD and KPD to end the bloodletting without recourse to their leaders. The unity movement consisted of over 200,000 workers in Berlin and it spread to other industrial centres across Germany. Workplace assemblies elected worker delegations, usually on a parity basis (i.e. each of the three socialist parties had the same number of delegates), and these were sent to the SPD central council, the USPD, the RSS and Liebknecht to demand the resignation of the government and of all socialist party leaders in order to stop the fighting in Berlin. The parity-based workers' committees were to take over management at all levels. Furthermore, the workers called for unification of the three socialist parties, and new workers' council elections. The USPD fully supported this spontaneous mass movement, but the leaders of both the SPD and the KPD rejected its objective.[48] Luxemburg saw the USPD as its intellectual author and she sharply criticised them for it. The fact that the Social Democrats had also rejected all the unity movement's demands was not sufficient to convince Luxemburg to reconsider her position.[49] For her, it was reminiscent of the unity slogans of 9-10 November 1918, when the SPD, which had previously worked against the revolution, was able to win a majority against the revolutionary forces by employing the same rhetoric of unity. But had the KPD supported the new unity movement, it might have made it possible to preserve the masses' revolutionary energy and strengthen the party.

The unity movement thus failed to achieve its objective and, contrary to the hopes of the revolutionary left, the mass movement did not regain momentum on 9-10 January. With Liebknecht's consent, the KPD leadership decided on the 10 January 'to abandon joint actions with the shop stewards and only to participate in their meetings in order to exchange information'.[50]

Rosa Luxemburg published an article in the *Rote Fahne* on 12 January under the headline 'And Still the Revolution Will Win!', in which she commented on the seizure of the *Vorwärts* building by government troops and the SPD government's military victory. Although she no longer regarded the fall of the government as imminent, she nonetheless saw it as almost inevitable in the near future, writing that Ebert and Scheidemann could 'enjoy only a final, brief reprieve' for their 'glorious rule' which was built 'on dead bodies' and required 'the grace of the bourgeoisie'. A letter Luxemburg wrote to Clara Zetkin on 11 January shows that this was not merely optimistic agitation but in fact corresponded to Luxemburg's illusory expectations. Despite the unambiguous defeat, she remained hopeful, writing, 'if the course of events continues as it has so far, it will prove to be highly questionable whether things will even reach the point of elections and a National Assembly'.[51] Just how badly her assessment deviated from the popular mood would become apparent eight days later during the National Assembly elections. At the start of the January uprising, it appeared as though a great majority of Berlin's working people would side with the revolutionary left. But on 19 January, the SPD won 36.4 per cent of the votes in Berlin – a significant gain against the USPD, which only took 27.6 per cent of the vote.[52] In keeping with the decision made at its founding congress, the KPD had boycotted the elections.

When analysing and assessing the *Rote Fahne* and the policies of the KPD leadership during the fighting in January 1919, we must keep in mind the fact that the situation changed repeatedly from hour to hour. Rosa Luxemburg and the other editors and other leaders were under enormous stress, the printing press and the editorial offices of the *Rote Fahne* were being attacked by government troops, and articles had to be written in safe houses.[53]

After changing houses several times, Luxemburg and Karl Liebknecht went into hiding in the home of some comrades in Berlin's Wilmersdorf district, where they were arrested on 15 January 1919 and murdered by *Freikorps* troops. The murders weakened the prospects for democracy not only within the KPD but also in the Communist International as a whole. As the story of its establishment shows, the first generation of leaders was not only independent in terms of the strategies they pursued, but also in their concept of democracy. Rosa Luxemburg in particular typified that autonomy. If she had not been murdered, with her concept of a humane basic democratic socialism, she surely would have influenced the political left efficiently and might have prevented or at least significantly hampered Stalinism's triumph in the Comintern.

Translated by Joe Keady

Notes

1. After the foundation of the USPD, the SPD was often referred to as the *Mehrheits*-SPD, or Majority SPD. To avoid confusion we have left the party's name as SPD throughout.
2. Mathilde Jacob, *Rosa Luxemburg. An Intimate Portrait*, London: Lawrence and Wishart, 2000, pp69, 74-84; Ottokar Luban, 'Ermittlungen der Strafverfolgungsbehörden gegen Mathilde Jacob und Leo Jogiches (1915-1918). Ergänzungen zu ihren politischen Biographien', in *Internationale wissenschaftliche Korrespondenz zur Geschichte der deutschen Arbeiterbewegung (IWK)*, 31, 3, 1995, pp307-331; idem, 'Die Auswirkungen der Jenaer Jugendkonferenz 1916 und die Beziehungen der Zentrale der revolutionären Arbeiterjugend zur Führung der Spartakusgruppe', in *Archiv für Sozialgeschichte* (AfS), XI, 1971, pp185-223 http://library.fes.de/jportal/receive/jportal_jpvolume_00010019;jsessionid=4423 9AA6FFEF6B9B5A72D5884EB736CB?XSL.view.objectmetadata.SESSION=true&XSL.toc.pos.SESSION=1; Ernst Meyer (ed.), *Spartakus im Kriege. Die illegalen Flugblätter des Spartakusbundes im Krieg*, Berlin, 1927.http://resolver.staatsbibliothek-berlin.de/SBB0000994F00000000 - _blank
3. Ottokar Luban, 'Führung und Basis des Rosa-Luxemburg-Kreises (Spartakusgruppe), 1915-1918. Biographien und soziale Zusammensetzung', in idem, *Rosa Luxemburgs Demokratiekonzept. Ihre Kritik an Lenin und ihr politisches Wirken 1913-1919*, Leipzig: Rosa Luxemburg Stiftung, 2008, pp172-195.
4. Ottokar Luban, 'Neue Forschungsergebnisse über die Spartakuskonferenz im Oktober 1918', in Ulla Plener (ed.), *Die Novemberrevolution 1918/19 in Deutschland. Für bürgerliche und sozialistische Demokratie*, Berlin: De Gruyter, 2009, pp68-78.
5. See Ralf Hoffrogge, *Working Class Politics in the German Revolution. Richard Müller, the Revolutionary Shop Stewards and the Origins of the Council Movement*, Brill: Leiden, 2014, pp35-60.
6. Ottokar Luban, 'Julius Gerson und Eduard Fuchs, die Spendensammler für die Flugschriftenagitation der Spartakusgruppe – Verbindungen zwischen Linkssozialisten und bürgerlichen Pazifisten', in idem (ed.), *Rosa Luxemburgs Demokratiekonzept*, pp286-305; idem, 'Spartakusgruppe, revolutionäre Obleute und die politischen Massenstreiks in Deutschland während des Ersten Weltkrieges', in *ibid.*, pp127-171.
7. For the proceedings against Jogiches, see 'Die Ermittlungsakten zu Jogiches und Genossen', in Bundesarchiv Berlin (henceforth: BArch), R 3003, C 83/18.
8. See, BArch, R 3003, J 638/18, No. 1, Bl.1, 6 and a Berlin political police report from September 1918, in Landesarchiv Berlin, A Pr. Br. Rep. 030, No. 15842, Bl.131.

9. Jean-Claude Montant, 'La propagande extérieure de la France pendant la Première Guerre Mondiale. Exemple de quelques neutres européennes', PhD Thesis, Université Paris I Panthéon-Sorbonne, 1988, p1489.
10. For more on the relationship between the shop stewards and the Spartacus Group, see Luban, 'Spartakusgruppe, revolutionäre Obleute und die politischen Massenstreiks in Deutschland während des Ersten Weltkrieges', pp164-171.
11. For details on this and what follows, see, for example, Pierre Broué, *The German Revolution, 1917-1923*, Chicago: Haymarket, 2006, pp157-207; David W. Morgan, *The Socialist Left and the German Revolution. A History of the German Independent Social Democratic Party, 1917-1922*, London: Ithaca, 1975, pp118-211; Eberhard Kolb, *Die Arbeiterräte in der deutschen Innenpolitik 1918-1919*, Frankfurt/M: Ullstein, 1978, pp114-214.
12. Jacob Walcher to the author, 8 July 1969.
13. Kolb, *Arbeiterräte*, p116.
14. Stenographic notes by journalist Richard Bernstein, in Gerhard Engel, Bärbel Holtz, Ingo Materna (eds), *Groß-Berliner Arbeiter- und Soldatenräte in der Revolution 1918/19. Dokumente der Vollversammlungen und des Vollzugsrates. Vom Ausbruch der Revolution bis zum 1. Reichsrätekongreß*, Berlin: Akademie, 1993, pp17ff.
15. *Ibid.*, pp15-24.
16. SgY 17, No. 1, Bl.85, 86, in BArch Berlin. There is nothing in the letter about the proposed state form.
17. Heinz Wohlgemuth, *Die Entstehung der KPD. Ein Überblick*, Berlin: Dietz, 1978, pp242ff.
18. For Liebknecht's article, see Gabriel Kuhn (ed.), *All Power to the Councils! A Documentary History of the German Revolution of 1918 -1919*, Oakland: PM Press, 2012, pp.93ff; for the online version, see: http://libcom.org/files/Allpower%20to%20the%20councils.pdf.
19. Georg Laschitza, Peter Adler, Annalies Hudis (eds), *The Letters of Rosa Luxemburg*, trans. George Shriver, London/New York: Verso, 2011, p482.
20. BArch Berlin, NY 4072, No. 138, Bl.81 f.
21. 'Letter from Clara Zetkin to Rosa Luxemburg', 17 November 1918, in Marga Voigt (ed.), *Clara Zetkin. Die Kriegsbriefe (1914-1918)*, Berlin: Karl Dietz, 2016, p440.
22. 'Letter from Jacob Walchers to Karl Bittel', 9 March 1966, in BArch Berlin, NY 4127, No. 68, Bl.269.
23. Laschitza *et al.* (eds), *Letters of Rosa Luxemburg*, pp491ff.
24. Hermann Weber, 'Einleitung', in idem (ed.), *Die Gründung der KPD. Protokoll*, Berlin: Dietz, 1993, pp38ff.
25. *Ibid.*, p290.
26. Ibid, pp154, 164f.
27. Paul Frölich, *Im radikalen Lager. Polititische Autobiographie, 1890-1921*,

ed. Reiner Tosstorff, Berlin: BasisDruck, 2013; Gerhard Engel, *Johann Knief. Ein unvollendetes Leben*, Berlin: Dietz, 2011, pp368ff, 397-406.
28. Weber, *Gründung der KPD*, pp270-280 (Liebknecht).
29. Karl Radek, 'November – Eine kleine Seite aus meinen Erinnerungen', in Otto-Ernst Schüddekopf, *Karl Radek in Berlin. Ein Kapitel deutsch-russischer Beziehungen im Jahre 1919*, in *AfS* II, 1962, pp119-159, 136. Also available online: http://library.fes.de/jportal/servlets/MCRFileNodeServlet/jportal_derivate_00020003/afs-1962-087.pdf.
30. See Ottokar Luban, 'Russische Bolschewiki und deutsche Linkssozialisten am Vorabend der deutschen Novemberrevolution. Beziehungen und Einflussnahme', in *Jahrbuch für historische Kommunismusforschung (2009)*, pp283-298; *ibid.*, 'Rosa Luxemburg's Critique of Lenin's Ultra Centralistic Party Concept and of the Bolshevik Revolution,' *Critique. Journal of Socialist Theory*, 40, 3, 2012, pp357-365.
31. Heinz Deutschland (ed.), *Käte und Hermann Duncker. Ein Tagebuch in Briefen (1894-1953)*, Berlin: Karl Dietz, 2016, with complete correspondence, documents, and images on a USB-card, here: pp. 1914/2331-1918/3047.
32. Luban, 'Russische Bolschewiki', pp283-298.
33. Jean-François Fayet, *Karl Radek (1885-1939). Biographie politique*, Berne: Peter Lang, 2004, pp262-270; Ottokar Luban, 'Karl Radek im Januaraufstand 1919 in Berlin. Drei Dokumente', *IWK*, 36, 3, 2000, esp. p392; Engel, *Johann Knief*, 407ff; Frölich, *Im radikalen Lager*, 166ff.
34. Nonetheless, some scholars have attempted to downplay or even deny these differences right up to the present day, see Ulla Plener, *Rosa Luxemburg und Lenin. Gemeinsamkeiten und Kontroversen*, Berlin: Nora, 2009.
35. Peter Hudis and Kevin B. Anderson, *The Rosa Luxemburg Reader*, New York: Monthly Review Press, 2004, pp.248-65, 266-80.
36. Rossijskij Gosudarstwennyj archiv sozial'no-polititscheskoi Istori (Russian State Archive of Socio-Political History, RGASPI), Moscow, f.5, op.3, d.80, 2.
37. *Ibid.*, f. 495, op. 124, d. 539, 42 (Henryk Walecki's handwritten report in German).
38. 'Letter from Rosa Luxemburg to Lenin', 20 December 1918, in Laschitza *et al.* (eds), *Letters of Rosa Luxemburg*, p486.
39. 'Letter: Leo Jogiches to Lenin', 4 February 1919, in Hermann Weber, Jakov Drabkin and Bernhard H. Bayerlein (eds), *Deutschland, Russland, Komintern. II. Dokumente (1918-1943)*, Volume 1 [1918-1933], Berlin: De Gruyter, 2015, pp77-80.
40. Hugo Eberlein, 'Spartakus und die Dritte Internationale,' *Internationale Pressekorrespondenz*, Vienna, 4, 1924, No. 28, 29, p306.
41. Rosa Luxemburg-Stiftung (ed.), Rosa Luxemburg, *Gesammelte Werke*, Volume 4 [August 1914 to January 1919], Berlin: Rosa-Luxemburg-Stiftung, 2000 [henceforth: Luxemburg, *GW* 4], p514.

42. See Ottokar Luban, 'Rosa at a Loss Rosa. The KPD Leadership and the Berlin Uprising of January 1919. Legend and Reality', *Revolutionary History*, 8, 4, 2004, pp19-45.
43. Radek, 'November', p137.
44. Luxemburg, *Gesammelte Werke*, 4, pp516-518.
45. Wilhelm Pieck, 'Zur Parteigeschichte der KPD', in BArch Berlin, NY 4036/384, Bl.122. The manuscript contains important information that is not included in the versions that were printed subsequently.
46. Luxemburg, *Gesammelte Werke*, 4, pp519-522.
47. Gerhard Engel, Bärbel Holtz, Gaby Huch, Ingo Materna (eds.), *Groß-Berliner Arbeiter- und Soldatenräte in der Revolution 1918/19. Dokumente der Vollversammlungen und des Vollzugsrates. Vom I. Reichsrätekongreß bis zum Generalstreikbeschluß am 3. März 1919*, Berlin: Akademie, 1997, pp183f, pp200f.
48. Pieck, 'Manuscript', Bl.125f; Kolb, *Arbeiterräte*, pp235-237; Morgan, *Socialist Left*, p217.
49. 'Das Versagen der Führer', in Luxemburg, *Gesammelte Werke*, 4, pp523-526.
50. Pieck, 'Manuscript', Bl. 128f.
51. Laschitza *et al.* (eds), *Letters of Rosa Luxemburg*, p491.
52. Susanne Miller, *Die Bürde der Macht. Die deutsche Sozialdemokratie 1918-1920*, Düsseldorf: Droste, 1978, p452.
53. Jacob, *Rosa Luxemburg*, pp94f, 97-100.

Building a Mass Party: Ernst Meyer and the United Front Policy, 1921-22

Florian Wilde

Ernst Meyer (1887-1930): A Forgotten Leader of German Communism

DESPITE BEING 'ONE of the most notable leaders of the German communist movement', Ernst Meyer remains relatively unknown. In English, the only widely available text relating to him is the autobiography of his wife, Rosa Meyer-Leviné.[1] Yet Meyer was an important figure in the left wing of the German labour movement from the time he joined the Social Democratic Party in 1908, until his death over twenty years later. A friend and collaborator of Rosa Luxemburg, during the war he was also one of the founding and leading members of the Spartacus League, which is discussed in the chapter by Ottokar Luban above. He was a delegate to the international anti-war socialist conferences at Zimmerwald (1915) and Kienthal (1916). Elected to the Communist Party of Germany's *Zentrale* at its founding conference at the turn of 1918/19,[2] Meyer maintained leadership roles almost continuously in the years to come. He also represented the party at the second and fourth World Congresses of the Communist International (1920 and 1922).

Following the arrest of KPD chairman Heinrich Brandler in April 1921,[3] Meyer assumed acting leadership of the organisation and was elected head of the *Polbüro* (Political Bureau) at the August 1921 Party Congress in Jena.[4] During that period it was Meyer's 'united front' policy – an attempt to organise coordinated mass actions involving the KPD, the SPD, and the trade unions – that was primarily responsible for the KPD's consolidation as a mass party. This essay will focus on Ernst Meyer's role in the development of the 'united front' policy during this period as a contemporary form of 'revolutionary realpolitik'.

From the 'Theory of the Offensive' to the United Front

In the summer of 1921, Meyer became one of the main protagonists in a form of revolutionary *realpolitik*. Prior to that, however, he had intermittently supported a very different outlook: the theory of the 'revolutionary offensive'. The latter policy arose out of an interpretation of the persistence of post-war revolutionary conditions. Alongside Paul Frölich, Hugo Eberlein, August Thalheimer, and Heinrich Brandler, Meyer became a voice for a widespread mood of revolutionary impatience after the merger with the left-wing of the Independent Socialist Party made the KPD a mass party. The policy's failure notably turned all of these men into Communist pragmatists, a tendency later vilified by their intraparty adversaries as 'right wing'.

In March 1920, intensifying regional disputes in central Germany appeared to provide the United Communist Party leadership with an opportunity to take the offensive and trigger a new wave of revolutionary upheaval. The party tried to use these events to catalyse a nationwide uprising in what would be remembered as the disastrous 'March Action'. Hundreds of Communists were killed, approximately 6000 were arrested, and 4000 were convicted. The latter included party chairman Heinrich Brandler, whose position would be taken over (provisionally at first) by Ernst Meyer. Party membership plummeted due to an ensuing membership exodus. The number of members immediately after unification is disputed, with estimates ranging from 350,000 to 448,500, but by August 1921 there were only 180,443.[5] Due to its putschism, the party was now completely isolated within the labour movement.

As a consequence of the 'March Action's' catastrophic outcome and the dissipation of what was termed the 'post-war revolutionary wave', the Comintern ushered in the 'united front' policy at its Third World Congress in the summer of 1921, with the slogan 'To the Masses'. The 'united front' concept aimed to allow communist parties to preserve their revolutionary identity during non-revolutionary periods while remaining open to the politics of wider alliances, which aimed to win the masses over to communism.

But the resolutions that were passed at the World Congress were relatively vague. It was up to the various parties to experiment with putting the new line into practice.[6] This included the KPD, which was now officially led by Ernst Meyer after the party congress in Jena from

22-26 August 1921. Meyer had initially been reluctant to give up the earlier policy, but now became an enduring and energetic advocate of the new line, particularly in light of the KPD's positive practical experience with it under his leadership.

The 'United Front' and Taxation

In late 1921, members of the Reichstag attempted to increase taxes on sales as a way of funding the burden of debt which had been produced by reparations payments under the Treaty of Versailles. The KPD opposed this, demanding instead higher taxes on wealth and the seizures of assets instead – and it employed the 'united front' strategy in pursuit of those demands.

In the party's main paper, Ernst Meyer wrote that the guiding principle behind the Communists' tax policy was, 'to prevent the living standards of the broad masses from deteriorating' and 'to shift the entire tax burden onto the propertied classes'. For that reason, the KPD's parliamentary deputies would 'resist all taxes that worsen the living standards of the proletariat'. Unlike the purely parliamentary approach of the other parties, however, the KPD would try to 'pressure the government and the bourgeoisie to prevent [sales] taxes by all extra-parliamentary means'. If the Communists were unable to stop the new taxes, they would intensify the struggle for higher wages, Meyer said. The KPD's principal task was to 'harness all proletarian forces for this extra-parliamentary struggle'. To that end, the party would be prepared to support the proposals of other workers' parties 'if these proposals provide a basis for initiating struggles and thus accelerating the establishment of a "united front" of the entire proletariat against the capitalists'.[7] For Meyer, the struggle for 'partial goals' was therefore linked to the Communists' 'final goals', a point he emphasised at the party conference in November when he said that, 'We are fighting taxes in order to shift the balance of power'.[8]

The KPD's demand for the seizures of assets entailed the state's expropriation of a portion of stocks, bonds, landholdings, factories, and mines. Party members believed that this was how Germany's debts should be paid off, and how higher wages and an active social policy could be financed. This, they hoped, would make it possible for all workers to participate in common defensive actions, especially as the trade unions and the SPD were on record as backing similar proposals. The KPD proposed to both the trade union and the SPD executive committees that they establish a coordinated working-class mobilisation to implement the asset seizures and to defend the eight-hour workday and the right to strike.

The *Zentrale* issued a national newsletter explaining that the asset seizures were 'a spark to ignite revolutionary struggles with limited goals and to broaden those struggles from a fight over taxes into general confrontations with the bourgeoisie'.[9] This explanation was necessary because the asset seizure campaign was far from uncontroversial even within the KPD: the party's left wing derided it as 'reformist' and sharply criticised the leadership.

In an article for International Press Correspondence (*Inprekorr*), the newspaper of the Communist International, Meyer countered that the call for asset seizures was admittedly not 'inherently communist', but:

> attempting to implement it means intensifying the class struggle against all capitalist parties, who will oppose these demands with all their power [...] Attempting to implement this also means rejecting any coalition with the bourgeoisie and, moreover, it presages replacing bourgeois parliamentary government with a purely socialist one.[10]

Thus the goal of the 'united front' policy was to make demands that were in the interest of the entire working class, shared by other workers' organisations, and necessitated an intensified confrontation with capital. The demands were to be achieved primarily through extra-parliamentary action, beyond the scope of parliament-oriented, social-democratic politics.

The Railway Workers' Strike

The 'united front' policy was put to the test as during the great railway strike from 1-7 February 1922.[11] Public employees, including railway workers, were particularly hard hit by the government's financial policies because the state was unwilling to increase its employees' wages to keep up with inflation. The German government under Chancellor Joseph Wirth refused to yield to the railway workers' wage demands;

instead, it attempted to dismiss 20,000 employees and to extend the working hours of those remaining in employment. The German Railway Workers' Union (*Deutsche Eisenbahner-Verband*, DEV) was unwilling to put pressure on the SPD, which was supporting the Wirth government in the Reichstag, but the National Union of German Railway Employees (*Reichsgewerkschaft deutscher Eisenbahnbeamter und Angestellter*, RDEBA), which organised 270,000 traditionally more conservative workers among white-collar staff, decided to strike on 1 February 1922. It was 'Germany's first significant civil servants' strike' as these workers were on the state's payroll.[12] The response of the Social Democratic President, Friedrich Ebert, was immediately to ban both the strike and all agitation in support of it. The government threatened disciplinary action and had members of the strike leadership arrested.

The KPD backed the strikers' demands without reservation from the outset, calling on the leaders of the DEV, and the General Confederation of Trade Unions (*Allgemeiner Deutscher Gewerkschaftsbund*, ADGB) and the SPD and USPD to discuss measures in support of the strikers and, above all, to act in defence of the workers' right to strike.[13] They refused, however, and the SPD leadership went so far as to position itself firmly against the strike. Similarly, on 3 February the leaders of the ADGB called on the strikers to 'go back to work immediately' because 'working people in particular are suffering the consequences' and the strike was 'having a genuinely catastrophic effect on Germany's foreign policy'.[14] By contrast, on 5 February 1922, the KPD's *Zentrale* issued a call 'to all working people', which called for 'solidarity with those in struggle! [...] A defeat for the workers in this strike would be [...] a defeat for socialism, a failure for the unions, and a victory for Stinnes. The powerful united front of all workers and public employees must prevail against this attack!'[15]

At the local level at least, the KPD's 'united front' efforts had a measure of success. Party members in other cities issued solidarity statements, and workers organised in the SPD-dominated ADGB participated in the strike. In Rhineland-Westphalia, the KPD and USPD issued a joint call to support the strikers.[16]

But ultimately the Communists were the only ones who offered significant support for the railway strike, which ended inconclusively on 8 February. Where the strike's immediate goals were concerned, the KPD refrained from making its own demands, as Meyer pointed out in the Prussian *Landtag* (state parliament): 'They will not be able to find a single statement showing that we wanted to do anything with this movement other than actively support the striking workers'.[17] Nonetheless the KPD made known its secondary objectives, such as making the railways economically viable through a 'state takeover of the coal and iron ore plants under the leadership of their workers' and promoting the idea that the right to strike must be defended 'with an extremely aggressive fight against the government, [including] the overthrow of the government, and the establishment of a workers' government'.[18] The KPD tried to inform the railway workers that their struggle was inevitably political in nature because 'a conflict between a government and its civil servants [...] is never a purely economic struggle but also a struggle for political power',[19] and emphasised the need to call a general strike to support the railway workers. Nonetheless, the KPD never made its support for the strike conditional on the strikers' adoption of its demands, nor did it try to impose its demands on the strikers. Instead, it showed 'great restraint' in order to 'avoid confusing' the railway workers, as Meyer would later say.[20]

According to its leaders, the strike involved 800,000 railway workers by the time it ended, making it 'the largest transport strike in German history'.[21] The Wirth government itself described it as a 'revolt in the civil service'.[22] Despite the fact that the strikers were ultimately defeated, the action was a success for the KPD. It had shown that the 'reformist' unions would not defend their own members' interests, including the right to strike.[23] As Reisberg noted, 'the KPD came out of the strike [...] with new authority'.[24] That is why, at a meeting the day after the strike ended, its leadership felt that, 'We have reason to be very pleased with our party's conduct during the entire strike action'.[25] In his report on the political situation at the Zentrale meeting on 15 February, Meyer summarised the situation by stating that, 'Our partial isolation from the workers has been eliminated. Our influence among government employees and their faith in us have grown tremendously due to the strike action'.[26]

Meyer again presented a very positive assessment of the KPD's role in the railway strike in his report at the May meeting of the *Zentralausschuss*, claiming that government employees had grown more sympathetic toward the party and that, 'the tactic we pursued during the strike not only proved its effectiveness but also established the potential to build on newly formed relationships in future actions taken up by government employees'.[27] At the Fourth World Congress of the Comintern in autumn 1922, even its leftist chairman, Grigory Zinoviev, praised the KPD's policy during the railway strike as a 'textbook example of the proper application of the united front tactic'.[28]

The political lesson Meyer derived from the railway strike was that KPD propaganda had to pursue 'the demand for a workers' government'.[29] The reason he gave for this was that 'the striking workers [had] abandoned their struggle because they were afraid to continue a fight for governing power without the USPD or the SPD'. During any future railways workers' strike, he continued, 'the demand for a workers' government should not come at the end but at the beginning. A workers' government is the only way to achieve employees' economic demands'.[30]

United Front against the Right: The Campaign after the Rathenau Assassination

The assassination of German Foreign Minister, Walther Rathenau, by a far-right fanatic on 24 June 1922 gave the KPD a significant opportunity to apply the 'united front' tactic to a major political issue.[31] Rathenau's murder was one of many murders of left-wing and Jewish politicians during the early years of the Weimar Republic, which had claimed the lives of 354 often little known individuals by 1922; most of the perpetrators went unpunished.[32] At this time, the radical right had propagated the slogan, 'Take out Walther Rathenau, he's a goddamned Jewish sow'.[33]

The Rathenau assassination unleashed a wave of anger and outrage in the republican camp and among working people. In a Reichstag speech on 25 June, even Chancellor Wirth exclaimed, 'The enemy [...] is on the right!'[34] The killing provoked spontaneous protest demonstrations and strikes. The first mass demonstrations took place on 25 June and were repeated in the days that followed. According to Wolfgang Abendroth, those demonstrations were, at the time, 'probably the largest ever in German history' because they had been called not only by workers' organisations but in some places also by bourgeois democrats.[35] When the unions called for a nationwide half-day general strike on 27 June, the Communists retracted their call for a general strike on 26 June and supported the unions. The general strike was accompanied by enormous demonstrations with up to 800,000 people in Berlin, 200,000 in Leipzig, and up to 80,000 in Kiel.

Meyer wrote that the Rathenau assassination created 'for the first time an opportunity to test this [united front] tactic nationwide on a large scale'.[36] A few hours after the assassination was announced, the KPD took the initiative and called for a conference to be convened immediately with the SPD and USPD to discuss defensive measures against right-wing terrorism. The Communists' basis for negotiation included taking drastic steps against the far right, including purging the bureaucracy of monarchists and reactionaries, an amnesty for imprisoned workers, arming the workforce, establishing proletarian supervisory committees, and calling for a general strike.[37] That meant that the Communists were pursuing the very politics that the SPD had at least verbally advocated in the wake of the Kapp Putsch – a coup attempt by the far-right in Berlin in 1920 – and had expressed in the 'Bielefeld Agreement', to which the KPD now explicitly referred.[38] The SPD initially rejected the Communists' 'united front' offer but, under pressure from its own rank and file to finally take decisive action against the far right, it was ultimately forced to negotiate with the Communists. The SPD nonetheless made it clear from the outset that it was unwilling to meet most of the Communists' demands and insisted that the negotiations be kept secret.

The workers' organisations reached an initial accord on 26 June based on proposals from trade union representatives demanding that the fight against the far right be intensified. Ernst Meyer was among the KPD's representatives at the negotiations and the subsequent meetings with leading workers' organisations. They agreed that, 'for as long as a common struggle must be waged against reactionary elements, in-fighting among the parties must cease'.[39] At the national level, the most important accord was known as the 'Berlin Agreement' of 27 June between the ADGB, the General Free Federation of Employees (*Allgemeiner freier Angestelltenbund*, AfA-Bund), the SPD, the USPD, and the KPD. Ernst Meyer and Wilhelm Koenen signed on behalf of the Communist Party. These organisations jointly called for a law to protect the Republic that would include, among other things, 'an immediate ban on and strict punishment of any monarchist or anti-republican agitation [...] a ban on and immediate dissolution of all monarchist and anti-republican affiliations, [and] a ban on monarchist colours and banners' as well as streamlined procedures for arresting violators of these provisions, the creation of a national criminal police organisation, and an amnesty for incarcerated workers.[40] The Communists signed the 'Agreement' despite the fact that, on the one hand, many of their demands – such as their call for another general strike, arming the workers, and establishing proletarian supervisory committees – were not adopted, and, on the other hand, that a law protecting the Republic could, in the hands of a reactionary judiciary, rapidly be turned against the KPD itself. The KPD's central organ, *Die Rote Fahne*, posed the question: what guarantees are there that these resolutions will be put into effect, answering: 'Today there is none' – only 'extra-parliamentary action by the workers' could guarantee it.[41]

Yet, in the wake of the Rathenau assassination, an unprecedented number of meetings were held among various workers' organisations, not only at the national level but at the regional and local levels as well.[42] On 4 July, there were more work stoppages and mass demonstrations across Germany in response to a call by the signatories to the 'Berlin Agreement'.[43] Some 700,000 people participated in the demonstrations in Berlin, approximately 100,000 in each of Dresden, Frankfurt, Wuppertal, and Munich, 60,000 in Düsseldorf, 50,000 in Königsberg, and 40,000 in Kiel. These demonstrations were more militant than those of the previous week. For example, monarchist emblems were destroyed (the 'Berlin Agreement' had called for their removal) and there were violent confrontations with the police, leaving several people dead.

Meyer's letters to his wife during those days are enthusiastic: 'Tonight [there is] a print run of 80,000, tomorrow morning 120,000. Hurrah!! We are in a magnificent situation – both agreements and Tuesday's demonstrations together but also open criticism of the SPD and USP. The unions have a lot of respect for us'.[44] And in a letter that was probably written on 8 July 1922, he wrote: 'Zwickau is in the workers' hands. Spontaneous outbreaks everywhere. Good situation for our party. SPD's attempts to isolate us rejected. Negotiations with all organisations tomorrow despite our extremely harsh open criticism!'[45]

But tensions among the organisations that had signed the 'Berlin Agreement' had been growing significantly in the run-up to 4 July. While the KPD was oriented toward intensifying extra-parliamentary actions, another general strike, new elections, and the installation of a 'workers' government' to implement the decisions in the 'Berlin Agreement', the leaders of the SPD, the USPD and the unions were trying to push the movement back toward a parliamentary course, which would be easier for them to control, and above all to pass a 'law for the Protection of the Republic'.[46] To achieve this parliamentary aim, the SPD repeatedly appealed to right-wing parties – including the monarchist German National People's Party (*Deutschnationale Volkspartei*, DNVP) – to support the law instead of calling on its own rank and file to implement the 'Berlin Agreement'.[47] For this reason, in the Prussian *Landtag*, Meyer accused the SPD of, 'not thinking of steps that the workers can take to put pressure on [the state] parliaments themselves. Instead, from the outset they only think of the balance of parliamentary power'. That, he stated, 'is the fundamental difference between social-democratic and communist tactics and politics'.[48] The SPD parliamentary faction in the Prussian *Landtag* voted against a bill to amnesty proletarian prisoners and, with trade union leaders, looked for a way to end the 'united front' with the KPD. They repeatedly made demands that would hardly be reasonable for the Communists to accept in the hope that the KPD would be forced to break off their unity of action.

The split between the participants in the 'Berlin Agreement' finally came on 8 July. The KPD was notified that, due to its militant activities, it had forfeited the right to remain part of this week-old accord. On 18 July, the Reichstag passed the 'Law for the Protection of the Republic' over the dissenting votes of the KPD (and the parties of the far right).

Meyer's Understanding of the United Front Policy, 1921-1922

Meyer's interpretation of the united front policy during 1921 and 1922 was not static, but rather developed in response to the KPD's practical experiences. While many Communists, including Meyer himself, initially saw the united front policy as a temporary tactic and primarily regarded it as a means to expose 'reformist' leaders, it nonetheless gradually became an overarching KPD strategy. Meyer moved incrementally away from a more 'tactical' understanding of the 'united front' policy and increasingly came to regard it as *the* appropriate method for winning over Social Democrats during non-revolutionary periods. At the Fourth World Congress of the Comintern in November 1922, Meyer said that the 'united front' policy 'must not be regarded as an episode, but rather as a period of Communist tactics'.[49]

A consistent core element of Meyer's interpretation of the 'united front' was his approach to what were known as 'partial' or 'transitional' demands. This grew out of the KPD's experience during the March Action. He had learned how quickly a fight which had begun with 'maximalist' demands could lead to isolation. Thereafter he would no longer regard the inherent radicalism of a demand as a deciding factor, but rather the radicalising potential in the establishment of (inherently reformist) 'partial' or 'transitional' demands whose implementation was only conceivable in the form of broad mass struggles against the bourgeoisie and the government. From his perspective, the immanent, radicalising dynamic of such struggles would ultimately transcend the framework of 'reformist' parliamentary politics – a point that is essential to Meyer's understanding of the 'united front' policy. This was the basis of Meyer's emphasis on the importance of 'partial' or 'transitional' demands as starting points for workers' collective struggles. He would express this outlook again and again, such as when he stated his willingness to support demands that, from the KPD's perspective, would lead to insufficient tangible gains, 'provided that they cause conflict to erupt and thereby accelerate the formation of the united front of the entire proletariat against the capitalists',[50] or when, on the occasion of the 'Berlin Agreement' after the Rathenau assassination, he said, 'a few demands more or less will not determine the strength of the movement today. It is much more important for the most modest demands to be carried out through the workers' own action'.[51]

For Meyer, pragmatically achievable 'partial' demands did not contradict the ultimate communist objective; on the contrary, that objective could only be attained by fighting for 'partial' demands because, as Meyer wrote in an article in *Inprekorr*, that struggle: 'truly fought out, must immediately turn [...] into struggles to achieve the final goal'. Meyer was concerned primarily with the dynamic arising from the struggle for such demands and less with the implementation of those demands as such:

> Making such demands does not mean that they will all actually be achieved in their stated form. They need only be rallying points for

struggle by the broad masses. The struggle for one of these demands can reel in the entire front of the class struggle and lead to the establishment of a council dictatorship.[52]

For Meyer, therefore, the 'united front' policy in no way meant surrendering the goal of revolution and should not be misconstrued as synonymous with 'reformist' politics. For Meyer, the united front policy was the practical side of the problem of 'with which means and under what slogans the communists of all countries could most quickly and most successfully achieve the goal of realising communism'.[53] Accordingly, Meyer no longer regarded the KPD's 'partial' demands as 'reformist'. For him, even 'reformist' demands could be implemented most rapidly through the 'revolutionary' means of extraparliamentary struggle. Indeed, he wrote that, 'Work for reform is only successful when it is done in a revolutionary spirit and when it leads directly to revolutionary struggle'.[54]

Meyer's stance on the question of the Communists' relationship to the Weimar Republic (a controversial topic within the KPD) is worth noting. For him, the need for Communists to defend the Republic absolutely against all right-wing attacks was as far beyond dispute as the communist goal of overcoming it and replacing it with a dictatorship of the proletariat based on workers' councils. Like 'partial' demands, he primarily regarded negotiating with the leaders of other workers' organisations as a means to involve the entire working class in joint extra-parliamentary conflict. That is why, at the May 1922 meeting of the *Zentralausschuss*, he said:

> The united front tactic [...] means that, beyond detouring into loose discussions with the central committees of the other workers' organisations, we want to gain an opportunity to meet with workers and members of those other parties. We are well aware that those discussions must not be an end unto themselves – for us, they are only a means [to an end]. But rejecting them would mean failing to carry out the united front tactic altogether.[55]

Elsewhere Meyer expressed the opinion that negotiations with leaders of other organisations had no objective other than 'inducing workers' collective action'.[56] If the other organisations rejected the KPD's offer of high-level negotiations, the Communists would then be able to claim that they were unwilling to fight for their supporters' interests. But, if they accepted the offer, the KPD hoped joint actions would show that the Communists were the ones fighting most forcefully on the workers' behalf. Meyer, however, believed that the call for united action must never be directed toward the leaders alone but always at the entire organisation made up of the leadership and the rank and file – and if there were negotiations, they would have to be conducted openly and thus in a way that was accountable to the working class.[57]

In Meyer's view, the greatest danger in applying the 'united front' policy was the risk that the Communists might not be sufficiently able to maintain their 'independent face'. In other words, negotiations with these leaders would force the KPD to refrain from 'adequately harsh and thorough criticism' of other organisations both in joint actions and particularly during high-level negotiations.[58] In brief: he saw 'opportunism' as the biggest threat. That is why Meyer regarded 'the deepening of all members' theoretical knowledge, organisational consolidation of the party, and strict discipline' as the 'unavoidable preconditions for successful application of this tactic'.[59]

An Assessment of the United Front Policy 1921-22

Given that neither the Third World Congress of the Comintern nor the KPD's Jena Party Congress issued concrete instructions for implementing the new 'united front' policy, the KPD had to establish its form as it was put into practice. Meyer's influence in that process was significant. In 1921 and 1922, KPD policy essentially coincided with Meyer's understanding of the tactic, even when the left wing of the party opposed it. All told, Meyer's approach to 'partial' demands appears to have been a core element of the KPD's 'united front' tactic, particularly after the Jena Congress.

The KPD's experience through an array of united front initiatives varied. For example, while its use in economic debates (particularly in the railway strike) was unambiguously positive, in the political matter of the Rathenau campaign, it raised a series of problems for the party. These were partly the result of the party's lack of experience with high-stakes negotiations, but also derived from the pressure put on the leadership by the KPD's left wing, as detailed by Ralf Hoffrogge and Mario Kessler elsewhere in this volume. It was not easy to find a reasonable way forward between, on the one hand, the risk of 'opportunism' and the attendant loss of the party's 'independent face', and, on the other hand, sectarianism and the isolation from the wider workers' movement that this caused. Nonetheless, there were strong signs of the tactic's success; an unprecedented number of joint meetings between workers' movement organisations took place;[60] 'Control Committees' were created, which brought together Social Democrats and Communists in opposition to rising food prices and, by July 1923, numbered 800; the 'Proletarian Hundreds', which had their origins during the Rathenau campaign, emerged as a proletarian paramilitary defence organisation;[61] and there was overall growth in the membership and influence of the KPD.

The same can be said of the 'National Works Council Congress' (*Reichsbetriebsrätekongress*), which the KPD had initially called on the ADGB to convene in the summer of 1922. In the event, this was organised by a communist Works Council Assembly after SPD-led trade union leaders rejected the proposal. Some 802 delegates gathered in Berlin on 23 November 1922, and the meeting was clearly dominated by Communists.[62] Yet, if the participants did not include many non-Communist Works Councils, it did reveal the extent of Communist influence in the workplace among more generally.

The KPD's significant role in the mobilisation of workers' organisations following the murder of Foreign Minister Walter Rathenau by right-wing extremists, as discussed above, also showed how the 'united front' tactic had enabled the KPD to end its isolation within the workers' movement, which had been greatly exacerbated by the 'March Action'.

For all of these reasons, Meyer could enthusiastically defend the KPD's use of the 'united front' policy at the Fourth World Congress of the Communist International at the end of 1922. He opposed the notion that the 'united front' could be applied to economics but not to politics, stating that: 'Our experience shows that such a distinction is absolutely impossible in the present situation'.[63]

Consolidation of the KPD under Meyer

When Ernst Meyer assumed the leadership of the KPD, the impact of the 'March Action' – the abortive putsch with an epicentre in the party's central German strongholds – had produced something approaching self destruction.[64] But Meyer and the 'united front' tactic restored the party's fortunes. Its membership had risen from a low point of 180,443 in 1921 to 224,689 a year later.[65] A report on the development of the party's membership, given at the Eighth Congress in Leipzig in January 1923, was even able to state that the rise in numbers, 'in no way reflects the greater influence that the KPD has achieved through its efforts among the working masses in the course of the period under review'.[66] Meyer's report to the Congress stressed that, had party organisations got over their fear of ideological dilution, even more new members would have been registered. His solution was to open up the party, while intensifying the education and training of these new recruits to communism.[67]

The KPD's application of the 'united front' tactic under Meyer resulted in a demonstrable increase in Communists' influence in the unions. Through its support for the railway strike, the party's influence in the Railway Workers' Union increased significantly. In 1922, the Communists took control of the DEV in Berlin and Leipzig, and one in five delegates at the union's conference that year were party members. They also took the leadership of the Building Workers' Union in Berlin and Düsseldorf as well as the Metalworkers' Union in Stuttgart. Every eighth delegate at the ADGB congress in June 1922 was a Communist, and the same figure applied to the Congress of Municipal Workers. At the Congress of the Transport Workers' Union, KPD members made up 10 per cent of the delegates.[68] In January 1923, the KPD Congress could boast of having 997 fractions in trade union branches and a majority in sixty local ADGB committees.[69] The 'united front' policy, as Meyer emphasised, had evidently satisfied expectations with respect to increasing Communist influence within labour organisations, and the factories more generally.[70]

The KPD also recorded successes at the ballot box in 1922, where it 'almost uniformly received a sizeable increase in votes'.[71] In the *Landtag* elections in Saxony in November, it received 267,700 votes as compared with 117,359 the year before.[72] At the start of 1923, Communists represented the sole governing party in more than eighty municipalities and were the strongest party in 170 others; in many hundreds more they acted with the SPD to form an overall majority. Over 6000 Communists were in local councils and municipal administrations.[73]

Not only did Meyer's leadership see the party's consolidation – both in terms of rising membership and greater influence within the wider workers' movement – but he also worked effectively to integrate the various factions with differing tactical orientations. Unlike in 1919 or, very much more so, in the mid 1920s – as Marcel Bois details below – there were no major splits weakening the KPD. Meyer achieved this by ensuring open discussion, which he regarded as an 'absolute necessity', including free debate in the pages of the party's newspapers and journals.[74]

If the KPD's difficulties had made it the Comintern's problem child in 1921, the following year Zinoviev stated that, 'I think we can say, quite rightly and without exaggeration, that our sister party in Germany is one of the most stable and well organised at the Fourth World Congress [...] as well as [being] the most politically clear-sighted'.[75] He then avowed: 'Nobody will deny that our German sister party has intensified its influence quite substantially'. Indeed, it had 'made tremendous strides. Unless all the evidence is deceiving, the path of the proletarian revolution leads from Russia through Germany'.[76]

This is also the view of the KPD's historians, who point to Meyer's role in using the 'united front' to reconsolidate the KPD as a mass-based movement after the fiasco of the 'March Action'.[77] In doing so, he also made it a force that would once again be in a position to seriously consider taking power in October 1923.

Between Isolation and a Return to Party Leadership: Meyer after 1922

Heinrich Brandler's return to Germany in August 1922 prompted a gradual decline in Meyer's power and status, in a shift supported by the Comintern. Meyer was not re-elected to the *Zentrale* at the January 1923 Party Congress, but would assume a leading role in circles opposing the ascendancy of the party's left wing around Ruth Fischer, Arkadij Maslow, and Werner Scholem in early 1924.

In 1926, Meyer returned to the leadership as a key member of the so-called 'Centre Group' and, together with Ernst Thälmann, was the 'actual leader of the party' in the mid 1920s; he again had a 'substantial impact upon its [the KPD's] fortunes'.[78] Some of the KPD's most successful 'united front' projects came about during that period, including the campaign to expropriate the old Imperial aristocratic elites of the Kaiserreich that had kept large portions of their feudal property. The 'expropriation campaign' was initiated by the KPD and its appeal brought united action across all worker organisations. The campaign for a referendum convinced 14.5 million people to vote to expropriate Germany's former 'Princely Houses' – a level of support higher than the combined total the workers' parties had achieved at any national election.[79] Yet, in 1929, Meyer was again removed from leadership and politically marginalised after the KPD's 'ultra-left turn' in 1928. However, by that point, he had already been gravely ill for some time. Ernst Meyer died on 2 February 1930 and was buried alongside other prominent socialists in Friedrichsfelde Cemetery in Berlin.

Translated by Joe Keady

Notes

1. Rosa-Leviné-Meyer, *Inside German Communism. Memoirs of Party Life in the Weimar Republic*, London: Pluto, 1977. The present author's main publications include his doctoral thesis which has been published as, *Ernst Meyer - ein vergessener Parteiführer*, Berlin: Dietz, 2015. See also idem, '"Freedom of Discussion inside the Party is Absolutely Necessary": KPD Chairperson Ernst Meyer 1921/22', in *Historical Materialism*, 22, 2014, pp104-28.
2. Until 1925, the KPD leadership was organised as a twelve-member *Zentrale* (party headquarters). Above the *Zentrale* stood the *Zentralausschuss*, a body of delegates from the party's regional committees that convened quarterly. As these terms have no direct English equivalents, the German terms will be retained in this article.
3. For biographical details of other KPD members mentioned in this article, see Hermann Weber and Andreas Herbst, *Deutsche Kommunisten. Biographisches Handbuch 1918 bis 1945*, Berlin: Dietz Verlag, 2nd edition 2008.
4. The KPD *Zentrale* was formally composed of 'equal members'. Meyer, along with Wilhelm Pieck, received the most votes at the Jena Party Congress and was elected chairperson of the Polbüro at the *Zentrale*'s first session. During that period, his influence on KPD policy was decisive, see Weber and Herbst, *Deutsche Kommunisten*, p43.
5. For a discussion of the debates surrounding the 'March Action' and these figures, see Wilde, *Ernst Meyer*, p226. The most extensive coverage of the 'March Action' is in, Sigrid Koch-Baumgarten, *Aufstand der Avantgarde. Die Märzaktion der KPD 1921*, Frankfurt: Campus, 1986.
6. See John Riddell (ed. and translator), *To the Masses: Proceedings of the Third Congress of the Communist International*, Leiden: Brill, 2015.

7. Meyer, Ernst: 'Steuerfragen', *Die Rote Fahne*, 19 August 1921.
8. 'Die Tagung des ZA der KPD', *Die Rote Fahne*, 20 November 1921.
9. 'Politisches Rundschreiben der Zentrale vom 28.10.21', in Institut für Marxismus-Leninismus (ed.), *Dokumente und Materialien zur Geschichte der deutschen Arbeiterbewegung* [henceforth: *DuM*], Band 7/1 (February 1919 to December 1921), Berlin [Ost], 1966, p600.
10. Ernst Meyer, 'Zur Regierungsbildung in Deutschland', in *Inprekorr*, 1, 15, 27 October 1921, p122.
11. For more on the railway strike, see Arnold Reisberg, *An den Quellen der Einheitsfrontpolitik. Der Kampf der KPD um die Aktionseinheit in Deutschland 1921-1922*, Berlin [Ost]: Dietz, 1971, pp365-379 – in his section 'Quellen' Reisberg presents otherwise unpublished sources that are used as reference in the following; see also Werner Angress, *Die Kampfzeit der KPD 1921-1923*, Düsseldorf: Droste Verlag, 1963, pp264f.
12. Anette Neumann, 'Grundzüge der Gewerkschaftspolitik der KPD von Aug. 1921 bis Dez. 1922', *Jahrbuch für Geschichte*, 38, 1989, p224.
13. See 'Schreiben der Zentrale der KPD an die Vorstände von ADGB, SPD und USPD', in *DuM*, Band 7/2 (January 1922 to December 1923), Berlin [Ost], 1966, pp28ff.
14. 'Gemeinsamer Aufruf des ADGB und anderer Arbeitnehmervertretungen, "An die Beamten, Arbeiter u[nd] Angestelltend" vom 3.2.22' in *DuM*, Bd.7/2, p30f.
15. 'Aufruf der Zentrale der KPD: "An die gesamte werktätige Bevölkerung"' in *DuM* Bd.7/2, p33. Hugo Stinnes, an industrialist and politician, was often used by the KPD to symbolise the entire capitalist class.
16. See Lore Heer-Kleinert, *Die Gewerkschaftspolitik der KPD in der Weimarer Republik*, Frankfurt: Klartext, 1983, p174.
17. Sitzungsberichte des Preußischen Landtags, 1. Wahlperiode, 5. Band, 85. bis 107 (16 December 1921 to 25 February 1922), Berlin 1922, p101; *ibid.*, Sitzung 18 February 1922, Sp.7107.
18. Cited in Reisberg, *Quellen*, p378.
19. 'Politisches Rundschreiben der Zentrale der KPD', 11 February 1922, in *DuM* Vol.7/2, p34.
20. Ernst Meyer, 'Politischer Bericht der Zentrale und die internationale Einheitsfront, gehalten auf der Sitzung des Zentralausschusses der KPD am 14 und 15 Mai 1922', in Stiftung Archiv der Parteien und Massenorganisationen der DDR im Bundesarchiv (SAPMO), RY I 2/1/9, Bl.25.
21. Reisberg, *Quellen*, p374.
22. *Ibid.*, p375.
23. Chris Harman, *The Lost Revolution: Germany 1918 to 1923*, London: Bookmarks, 1982, p294.
24. Reisberg, *Quellen*, p379.

25. 'Protokoll der Sitzung der KPD-Zentrale vom 8.2.22', in SAPMO, RY 1/I 2/2/14, Bl.77f.
26. 'Protokoll der Zentrale-Sitzung vom 15.2.22', in SAPMO, RY 1/I 2/2/14, Bl.84. See also Ernst Meyer, 'Politik und Eisenbahnerstreik', *Inprekorr* 2, 16/17, 11 February 1922, p125.
27. Ernst Meyer, 'Politischer Bericht der Zentrale und die internationale Einheitsfront, gehalten auf der Sitzung des Zentralausschusses der KPD am 14 und 15 Mai 1922', in SAPMO, RY I 2/1/9, Bl.26. The *Zentralausschuss* was a body composed of regional delegates designed to supervise the decisions of the *Zentrale*.
28. 'Protokoll des Vierten Kongresses der Kommunistischen Internationale'. Petrograd-Moscow from 5 November until 5 December 1922, Hamburg, 1923 [henceforth: Protokoll IV. Weltkongress], p35. See also John Riddell, 'The Comintern in 1922. The Periphery Pushes Back', in *Historical Materialism*, 22, 3/4, 2014, pp52-103.
29. 'Protokoll der Sitzung der KPD-Zentrale dated 15.2.22', in SAPMO, RY 1/I 2/2/14, Bl.84.
30. Meyer, 'Politik und Eisenbahnerstreik', p125.
31. For the Rathenau assassination and ensuing movement, see Heinrich August Winkler, Von der *Revolution zur Stabilisierung. Arbeiter und Arbeiterbewegung in der Weimarer Republik*, Bonn: JHW Dietz, pp427ff; Angress, *Kampfzeit*, pp275ff. For published documents concerning the KPD's politics following the Rathenau assassination, see in particular Reisberg, *Quellen*, pp485-535.
32. Angress, *Kampfzeit*, p275; Susanne Miller and Heinrich Potthoff, *Kleine Geschichte der SPD. Darstellung und Dokumentation 1848-1990*, Bonn: JHW Dietz, p100.
33. Cited in Reisberg, *Quellen*, p494.
34. Cited in Winkler, *Revolution zur Stabilisierung*, p427.
35. Wolfgang Abendroth, *Einführung in die Geschichte der Arbeiterbewegung*, Berlin: Distel, 1996, p209. According to Reisberg, 250,000 people participated in the demonstration in Berlin on 25 June, see Reisberg, *Quellen*, p501.
36. Ernst Meyer, 'Zur Praxis der Einheitsfronttaktik', in *Die Internationale*, 5, 3, 1 August 1922, p54.
37. 'Forderungen der Zentrale der KPD vom 24.6.22 an die Leitungen von SPD und USPD als Verhandlungsgrundlage für die Organisierung gemeinsamer Protestaktionen nach dem Rathenaumord', in *DuM* Bd.7/2, pp100ff.
38. The 'Bielefelder Abkommen', in *DuM* Vol. 7/1, pp231ff. For more on the Bielefeld Agreement, see Winkler, *Revolution zur Stabilisierung*, pp328ff.
39. Cited in Heer-Kleinert, *Gewerkschaftspolitik*, p181.
40. For the 'Berliner Abkommen', see *DuM*, Band 7/2, pp103-105.
41. Cited in Reisberg, *Quellen*, p509.

42. See Harman, *Revolution*, p295.
43. See 'Aufruf an das republikanische Volk', in *DuM* Bd.7/2, p106f. Meyer und Koenen again signed this call on behalf of the KPD.
44. 'Letter from Ernst Meyer to Rosa Meyer-Leviné', 30 June 1922, in Rosa Meyer-Leviné, *Inside German Communism* pp46ff.
45. Cited in *ibid*.
46. Heer-Kleinert, *Gewerkschaftspolitik*, p182.
47. See Reisberg, *Quellen*, pp510ff.
48. *Sitzungsberichte des Preußischen Landtags am 7.7.22*, Sp.11782.
49. *Protokoll IV. Weltkongress*, p73.
50. Meyer, 'Steuerfragen'.
51. Ernst Meyer, 'Der Kessel ist zum Platzen voll', *Inprekorr*, 2, No.135, 18 July 1922, p858; see also 'Protokoll der Tagung des Zentralausschusses der KPD vom 23.7.22', in SAPMO, RY 1/I 2/1/14, Bl.16.
52. Meyer, 'Der Kessel'.
53. 'Protokoll der Tagung des Zentralausschusses der KPD vom 14-15.5.22', in SAPMO, RY 1/I 2/1/13, Bl.167.
54. Ernst Meyer, 'Die Aufgaben des 4.Weltkongresses', *Inprekorr*, 2, 196, p1316.
55. 'Protokoll der Tagung des Zentralausschusses der KPD vom 14-15.5.22', in SAPMO, RY 1/I 2/1/13, Bl.167.
56. *Protokoll IV. Weltkongress*, p74.
57. *Bericht über die Verhandlungen des 3. [8.] Parteitages der Kommunistischen Partei Deutschlands (Sektion der Kommunistischen Internationale), abgehalten in Leipzig vom 28. Januar bis 1. Februar 1923*, Berlin, 1923, pp210f. [Henceforth: *Bericht 8. Parteitag.*]
58. *Bericht 8. Parteitag*, p212.
59. Ernst Meyer, 'Die deutsche Partei während der Rathenau-Kampagne', in *Die Kommunistische Internationale*, 4, 22, 13 September 1922, p29.
60. Harman, *Revolution*, p295.
61. Ossip K. Flechtheim, *Die KPD in der Weimarer Republik*, Hamburg: Julius Verlag, 1986, p170; Reisberg, *Quellen*, p522.
62. Otto Wenzel, *1923 – Die gescheiterte Deutsche Oktoberrevolution*, Berlin: Lit-Verlag, 2003, pp35ff.
63. Protokoll IV. Weltkongress, p74.
64. Angress, *Aufstand*, p315.
65. *Bericht 8. Parteitag*, p63.
66. *Ibid.*, p63.
67. *Ibid.*, pp63, 214ff.
68. Harman, *Revolution*, pp297ff.
69. *Bericht 8. Parteitag*, pp75ff.
70. The KPD was also able to win votes in various Works Council elections and had a majority of the members in the Works Councils at several large companies. At Siemens, for example, the KPD was able to increase its

share of the votes from 25 per cent in 1921 to 40 per cent in 1922. For details, see Neumann, *Grundzüge*, p233.
71. *Bericht 8. Parteitag*, p39.
72. *Ibid.*, p43.
73. *Ibid.*, p100.
74. For an extended discussion of these issues, see Florian Wilde, '"Freedom of Discussion"' Inside the Party is Absolutely Necessary" pp104-28.
75. *Protokoll IV. Weltkongress*, p34.
76. *Ibid.*, p36f.
77. See, for example, Hermann Weber's assessment in *idem*, *Die Wandlung des deutschen Kommunismus: Die Stalinisierung der KPD in der Weimarer Republik*, Frankfurt: E.V.A., 1969, p42; *idem*, 'Vorwort', in, Bernhard H Bayerlein *et al.* (eds), *Deutscher Oktober 1923. Ein Revolutionsplan und sein Scheitern*, Berlin: Aufbau, 2003, pp19-34; Flechtheim, *Die KPD*, p167; Angress, *Kampfzeit*, p286.
78. Hermann Weber and Andreas Herbst, *Deutsche Kommunisten. Biographisches Handbuch* 1918 bis 1945, Berlin: Dietz, 2004, p503.
79. Wilde, 'Ernst Meyer', pp443-447.

Class against Class: the 'Ultra-left' Berlin Opposition, 1921-1923

Ralf Hoffrogge

A NEW LEFT OPPOSITION emerged within the KPD around 1921. Unlike the left-wing communism of 1919 and 1920, which was identified with Anton Pannekoek and Hermann Gorter, this new opposition had neither links to nor similarities with syndicalism. On the contrary, its protagonists embraced Lenin's '21 Conditions' and the concept of democratic centralism. But, like the earlier dissenting currents, it was centred in Berlin and Hamburg and was extremely critical of attempts to forge a 'united front' with the SPD. Their leftism, or, as it was called by later opponents, 'ultra-leftism', was based on the belief that world revolution was underway and would be ruined by ill-advised compromises. The ultra left were represented by figures like Ruth Fischer, Arkadij Maslow, and Werner Scholem, who assumed the party leadership in 1924. But they soon lost power as their tactics failed, resulting in the party's political isolation. Eventually the 'ultra-leftists' were expelled from the party because of their resistance to Stalin's subordination of the KPD to the Communist International. In 1928, events took a surprising turn: Stalin adopted a policy formerly advocated by the ultra-left. The Soviet leader declared that a 'Third Period' of capitalist crisis had begun, calling for a struggle of 'class against class'. But the now expelled Berlin ultra-leftists had to watch from the outside.

Unlike Stalin's ill-fated ultra-leftism after 1928, the development of this earlier ultra-left tendency has been given scant attention. This essay will outline its emergence through the lens of the Berlin KPD focusing particularly on the role of Werner Scholem (1895-1940).[1] Special attention is paid to how its early opposition to the 'united front' policy took a strongly antinationalist stance. While the 'Third Period' policy is often associated with nationalism, it is noteworthy that the Berlin Left of 1923 spoke out against the KPD leadership's 'national revolutionary' tactics in the summer of 1923. This stance has remained eclipsed by the controversy surrounding Ruth Fischer's use of anti-Semitic language in the summer of 1923, as Mario Kessler's chapter discusses. Yet, importantly, other members of the KPD Left opposed the so-called 'national revolutionary' politics of this time.

Workers and Intellectuals in the Berlin KPD

In 1921, the Berlin KPD was led by Ruth Fischer and Arkadi Maslow. Both came from well-to-do Jewish families, having broken with their middle-class backgrounds and now part of the party's educated, intellectual wing.[2] Two other figures of the Berlin Left had a similar background: the journalist and member of the Prussian Landtag, Werner Scholem, and his close friend, the historian Arthur Rosenberg, both of them from middle-class Jewish families.[3]

The intellectual makeup of the Berlin district leadership is striking. In conflicts, they were branded a clique of academic scatterbrains whose actions were disconnected from the 'proletarian masses'. Clara Zetkin once said that:

> The opposition did not recruit supporters from the party masses so much as from the ranks of certain underwhelming, semi-educated bureaucrats. That is why they had a relatively easy time making their presence felt [...] Their only support among the wider masses within the party lay where the rank and file were effectively politically untrained and recruited emotionally on 'revolutionary' terms. Party comrades such as these imposed Maslow's cynical brashness, Ruth Fischer's resounding rhetoric, and Scholem's scatter-brained impudence.[4]

This notion that the intellectuals were outsiders and demagogues has also been passed on in the historiography. Werner T. Angress wrote that:

> On average they were ten years younger than the party leaders in the *Zentrale* and almost all of them came from the bourgeoisie. [...] In contrast to the class consciousness of their older comrades, who came of age in the school of militant social struggle with strikes,

lockouts, and often imprisonment, they lacked political experience, class pride, and maturity.⁵

Maslow, Fischer, and Rosenberg may fit this image, but the stereotype starts to break down with Werner Scholem. He had spent ten months in a military prison in 1917 for participating in an anti-war demonstration. Contrary to the prevailing image, many Communists from working-class backgrounds were active in the Berlin district leadership. Among them were the mechanic Anton Grylewicz, who was the head of the KPD in Berlin in 1920-21; toolmaker Hans Pfeiffer; and locksmith Ottomar Geschke – the latter two both came from the Spartacus Group. Another working-class functionary was Paul Schlecht, who also made a living as a toolmaker.⁶ And finally, this list would be incomplete without Max Hesse, whose father had been a co-founder of the German Metalworkers Union. Hesse was the same age as Scholem and they both joined the SPD's youth organisation in 1912. It is striking that Hesse, Schlect, Pfeiffer, Geschke and Grylewicz were all members of the Revolutionary Shop Stewards (*Revolutionäre Obleute*, RSS) during the First World War.⁷ This socialist anti-war movement only accepted veteran union members into its conspiratorial ranks.⁸ Such a cluster of so many old shop stewards indicates that there was a well-organised network within the KPD's Berlin district leadership,⁹ which is to say that the 'Berlin Opposition' had a symbiotic structure. It was not made up exclusively of intellectuals, but had just as many radical workers and trade unionists.¹⁰ While the intellectuals may have been the opposition's front line, evidence of tension between them and union veterans is scarce.¹¹ Oskar Wischeropp, a lathe operator and member of the district leadership, was explicitly opposed to anti-intellectualism, stating that: 'As far as acting against the intellectuals is concerned, I have to say that I'm against [...] For me, a man only has a part to play if he represents the interests of the party, whether he's a worker or an intellectual.'¹²

Maslow, Scholem, and Ruth Fischer's Jewish backgrounds did not appear to be an issue within the Berlin KPD. In this regard, the Berlin KPD of 1921 appeared to be similar to the pre-war SPD. For example, in 1915, Werner Scholem had noted that: 'None of that is very noticeable in Berlin because anti-Semitism generally amounts to nothing there. It is something you only notice when you leave [Berlin].'¹³ Among the Left Opposition outside Berlin Jews also worked with non-Jews and intellectuals with workers on equal terms. Merchant's son Iwan Katz, for example, operated as an advocate of the left in Hanover. Another opposition stronghold was the northern German KPD district of Wasserkante, led by primary school teacher Hugo Urbahns and Ernst Thälmann, who had started his working life as a transporter worker.[14] The Left Opposition was far from merely an intellectual circle that would have remained an 'isolated clique' without the 'proletarian backup' of men like Thälmann.[15] The Berlin example shows just how distinctly it fell within the tradition of local working-class radicalism.

The Left Opposition in 1921

But what did this 'Left Opposition' really amount to? According to Ruth Fischer's writings from 1948, there was a prevailing scepticism towards Soviet politics from the outset.[16] Fischer wrote this as part of a later critique of Stalinism, whose origins she traced back to the early Leninist phase of the Comintern. The fact is, however, that the opposition movement that developed during the course of 1921 was grounded in Leninism. Neither Scholem nor Fischer spoke of any 'degeneration' in Soviet Russia in 1921. The opposition had accepted Soviet-style centralism, fought for the Comintern's '21 Conditions', and clearly distanced itself from the syndicalist Communist Workers' Party, which it polemically derided as 'anarchistic'. Werner Scholem repeatedly railed against the 'KAPist, anti-Bolshevist, and anti-centralist tendencies' within the movement.[17] His choice of words shows that the incipient opposition had nothing in common with the syndicalist tendencies that arose during the founding phase of the KPD.

To date, the most valuable source of information on the development of the Left Opposition is an article by Scholem from 1924.[18] In spring 1921, a gathering of lower- and middle-ranking KPD officials in Berlin 'energetically rejected' the tactics of party chairman Paul Levi. This specifically referred to the united-front policy he had invoked in early 1921 (before the 'March Action' fiasco) with an 'Open Letter', which Levi hoped would win over workers from the SPD. As would happen again later, the left wing of the party at this point opposed any attempt to draw the masses to the KPD by reform-oriented demands concerning bread and butter issues. Scholem suspected Levi of having 'political views that, as a liquidationist tendency, must be resisted in a proletarian way'.[19] The new opposition regarded anything to do with the 'Open Letter', the 'united front', union policy, or other actions in alliance with the SPD as a 'right-wing threat' that was tantamount to 'liquidationism' – which is to say pushing for the dissolution of the KPD. Their stance was therefore essentially a negative one. Levi's expulsion from the KPD after the 'March Action' of 1921 and the merger of his dissenting Communist Working Group (*Kommunistische Arbeitsgemeinschaft*, KAG) with the SPD in 1922 thus seemed to amount to strong evidence of the danger of 'liquidationism'. The Berlin Left criticised the sympathetic treatment of former KAG members who, unlike Levi, did not leave the KPD but stayed in the party. They felt that while others were spared any criticism, they themselves were the object of the leadership's discrimination: 'proposals and suggestions were often rejected simply because they came from opposition comrades'.[20] Party headquarters, they believed, 'systematically portrayed the opposition as a gang of "brawlers", "intellectual jokers" and the like'.[21]

While the Berlin Left considered itself the guardian of communist principles against an onslaught of reformism, the leadership regarded them as a horde of intellectual troublemakers with no programme. Zetkin claimed that, 'in the interest of party purity and independence, [they] would ultimately render all politics impossible until there was nothing left but the propaganda of a small, pure sect'.[22]

However, as Zetkin noted, the Left's tendency toward isolation had roots in the political situation that had developed since 1918. Prior to 1914, coalition building was rarely an issue for the SPD. Then, it was the only workers' party and was politically isolated within an autocratic system. Under Weimar democracy, however, there were two workers' parties and voting determined the composition of the government. Therefore, if the Communists were able to use united-front tactics to pull the SPD to the left, the question of a coalition government would emerge and the KPD would become dependent on their Social Democratic adversaries. In such a constellation, the parliamentary logic of elections threatened to displace the idea of a revolutionary uprising.

It therefore seems reasonable that a strong current within the KPD would demand that the party rely on its own revolutionary power instead of trying to lure trade unions and Social Democrats to the left. For the KPD's Left, the greatest threat to world revolution was not radical isolationism, but being mired in opportunism – a phenomenon most of its members had seen in the SPD before 1914 and during the war. Both former soldiers like Werner Scholem and radical trade-union activists had criticised the SPD as 'opportunistic'. To them, left-wing radicalism was conceivable not despite but because of their many years of experience in the social-democratic labour movement.²³

In the context of such experiences, Ruth Fischer deplored the way the united-front policy was handled by the leadership as early as the Jena Party Conference in August 1921 and called for a 'more dynamic course'.²⁴ But during that early stage, the Left primarily called for official policy to be modified. In response, the *Zentrale* drafted a radical transitional programme that would establish state involvement in large businesses through the compulsory establishment of trusts, of which the state would then nationalise half the shares.²⁵ The Left criticised the programme as unrealistic and misleading. Scholem believed that a 'bourgeois government' neither could nor would ever implement it. For that reason, it was absolutely necessary to add a demand for a 'workers' government'.²⁶ This was still friendly criticism, as the Left was essentially in favour of the united-front tactic. For example, in April 1922, Werner Scholem praised the KPD and SPD's joint appearance at mass demonstrations as a 'starting point for building an international "united front" of the worldwide proletariat'.²⁷

Scholem was receptive to this as the KPD dominated the demonstrations, which had a bottom-up approach – the 'united front from below'. But top-level negotiations imposed on the KPD by moderates were soundly rejected. Scholem was therefore critical of the campaign after the assassination of Foreign Minister Walter Rathenau by *völkisch* nationalists in June 1922: 'The KPD is letting itself be bound by an agreement with the SPD and the union bureaucracy while hiding its "communist face" from the masses'.²⁸ Should the KPD campaign to save liberal democracy? Scholem opposed this and he observed that it was leading to an escalation of the party feud:

> The left organisations' strong criticism of the *Zentrale*'s approach after the Rathenau action [...] created that ominous anti-opposition mood in the *Zentrale*, which has seriously poisoned conditions within the party since then. That was when the plan emerged to forcefully remove the Berlin-Brandenburg district leadership to get rid of the 'roisterers and brawlers'.²⁹

In fact, already on 11 April 1922, a Politburo resolution had stated that the Berlin organisation had to present all its resolutions to the *Zentrale* for approval.[30] On 1 August 1922, the Politburo told the KPD that, 'There is agreement that the current leadership in Greater Berlin is using its organisational influence to agitate against the overall party line and particularly against the *Zentrale*'.[31] Party officials at the national level took it upon themselves to name Heinrich Brandler 'upper district secretary' for the Berlin-Brandenburg, charging him with 'the task of systematically bringing the full force of the *Z[entrale]* to bear [in order] to influence the Greater Berlin organisation'.[32] The effort to disempower the Opposition could not be stated more clearly. But the plan failed and the Left kept control of the Berlin district. Indeed, the intra-party conflict escalated, and became an open split by the following summer.

However, what was decisive in interpreting the 'face of communism' was not the party's grass roots alone, but also the Comintern in Moscow. Shortly before the start of the Fourth World Congress of the Comintern in November 1922, the Berlin Communists therefore held a mass meeting with 3000 delegates. There the KPD chairman Ernst Meyer's 'transitional programme' was denounced and Ruth Fischer was elected as a delegate to attend the congress in Moscow.[33] This meant that, on the international stage, the KPD no longer spoke with a unified voice. As had happened after the March Action in 1921, the Comintern was called on to adjudicate German affairs – a basic model that would be applied to disputes in the years to come.

But the Comintern was also weakened in 1922. The hope of world revolution had not come to fruition and the Soviet government had to make concessions to small-scale capitalism in their own country with the New Economic Policy (NEP). Although the Berlin KPD's revolutionary orientation did not resonate during this period of retreat, the Opposition was nonetheless able to hold its ground in Moscow. Along with Ernst Meyer, dissidents Ruth Fischer and Hugo Urbahns were summoned to a clandestine meeting in a salon in the Kremlin. Here, leading Bolsheviks Leon Trotsky, Karl Radek, and Grigory Zinoviev tried to mediate in the German conflict while Lenin, who was also present, at first only listened silently before ultimately rejecting Meyer's ideas for a 'German NEP' as a transitional programme.[34] Admittedly, a public resolution endorsed Meyer's 'united front' policies, but the secret meeting, attended by such prominent participants, meant the upgrading of the Opposition tendency from a local phenomenon in Berlin and Hamburg to one of international standing.

Consequently, the Opposition was invigorated and the conflict within the KPD persisted. This was apparent at the KPD's Leipzig Party Conference from 28 January to 1 February 1923. In Scholem's words, the conference had 'two sharply divided factions'.[35] In light of increased worker militancy due to the Ruhr crisis, programmatic proposals from the Opposition and the *Zentrale* were now on opposing sides for the first time. In the Ruhr region, the French army had initiated a large-scale operation to occupy major mines and had started confiscating coal as compensation for non-payment of reparations by the German government. The result was the paradox of a strike endorsed by mine owners and the government. It was accompanied by a large nationalist mobilisation, which encouraged fascist militias to commit acts of sabotage. In the midst of this mess, the KPD had to take a stand. Werner Angress summarised the conflict at the Leipzig Party Conference as follows:

> While the Left emphasised action, organising, initiative, and arming the workers, the majority proposals focused on defence against 'fascistic' aggression and the need to confront the Social Democrats with a policy of attrition. Their vision involved taking power gradually and improving the workers' position on the political stage through constant struggle.[36]

After a crucial vote, the majority sided with the *Zentrale* and its united-front policy. Werner Scholem sharply criticised this, writing that:

> The majority proposals in Leipzig were a clear articulation of the new communist revisionism, which abolishes the dictatorship of the proletariat as an immediate goal and regards bourgeois democracy as the 'framework' within which the Communist Party, through the workers' government that it will create through parliamentary means, will conduct its struggle.[37]

Although both factions talked about a 'united front' and a 'workers' government', they meant entirely different things.

One faction anticipated parliamentary alliances with the SPD and attempted to put that tactic into practice. In the spring of 1923, the KPD facilitated an SPD minority government in Saxony and there were similar developments in Thuringia.[38] But the Opposition wanted revolution from below. They wanted to radicalise both the legal works councils and the Control Committees, which were unofficial bodies that had assumed the power to fix food prices in some regions when prices skyrocketed due to hyperinflation. By Scholem's definition, a 'workers' government' was not a parliamentary coalition but 'the demolition of the structure of bourgeois democracy and the onset of civil war'.[39] For the Opposition, a 'united front' was only possible 'from below' and never by means of alliance with the SPD leadership. The party congress in Leipzig ended with an open split between the two factions when a list of candidates for the *Zentrale* did not include a single oppositional candidate. With that, the Opposition took the unprecedented step of boycotting the vote.

Before the party conference, the Berlin Opposition assumed that Ruth Fischer would be given a seat in the new leadership. But this was not so. One result of the Leipzig election boycott was that subsequently four members of the Opposition were elected to the new *Zentrale* under Heinrich Brandler. They were not the Opposition's leaders, however, but officials handpicked by the *Zentrale* to allow the leadership to overcome the organised challenge to its policies. An emergency meeting of the Berlin leadership immediately after the party conference erupted in heated debate. Scholem in particular criticised 'our delegation's poor conduct'. The dissenters, he believed, had stabbed the Left in the back 'just when the Opposition wanted to show the International that it was politically cohesive'.[40] Nonetheless, he told Brandler, who was also present, that: 'If you lead the struggle against the bourgeoisie and the SPD clearly and decisively, you will find every last man in the Berlin Opposition behind you'.[41]

Ruth Fischer also emphasised her accommodating intentions, stating: 'I have always believed that, when the comrades see that we are not just crazy students [...] but also honourable workers, the *Zentrale* will come to its senses and stop rejecting the offer of our hand'.[42] In Leipzig, Brandler himself had launched harsh diatribes against the intellectuals for bringing nothing but confusion into the movement.[43] While in right-wing parties such anti-intellectualism almost inevitably came with anti-Semitism, it is noteworthy that this was not the case in the KPD's ongoing feuds. Rosenberg was derided because of his university position and lack of working-class credentials, Fischer mentions being called a 'crazy student'. But archival sources give no evidence of discrimination because of their Jewish family backgrounds.

In spite of all this, in the new *Zentrale* there was a surprising degree of cooperation between different groups. However, sections of the Left being co-opted onto the leadership did not resolve the conflict. As Werner Scholem subsequently explained: 'The conference had not forged the party into a unified whole but tore it in half. One side was dominated by the central apparatus and the other by the large district organisations. The most ferocious conflicts were soon to occur.'[44]

Ruhrkampf 1923

This intra-Party conflict was triggered by the 1923 *Ruhrkampf* (Ruhr conflict), in which both the German government and German businessmen encouraged workers to strike against the French occupation of the region.[45] Werner Scholem was critical of the KPD's response to the crisis, writing that:

> Again and again the Opposition has vainly pointed out the fact that decisions on the coming revolutionary movement have to be made in the industrial regions and especially the Ruhr. In its failure to take a clear stand against the German bourgeoisie, the party is not taking the right approach to the Ruhrkampf.[46]

In fact, the KPD congress in February 1923 had refused offensive action. In the following months when the *Ruhrkampf* unfolded to become a huge nationalist mobilisation, the party even tried to capitalise on the German government's campaign with an 'anti-imperialist' interpretation of the crisis, portraying Germany as a victim of French imperialism. This meant that the *Zentrale* did not distance itself from the prevailing nationalism, while the Opposition explicitly demanded that the German bourgeoisie be confronted, and not just the French.[47] As a form of protest, Scholem and Fischer travelled to the occupied Ruhr several times in March 1923 and participated as delegates in the KPD Rhineland-Westphalia North district conference in Essen. There they helped pass a resolution calling for workers' control of production.[48] The *Zentrale* strongly disapproved and Scholem was accused of having called for the immediate occupations of factories at a meeting in Dortmund.[49] The KPD Reich leadership regarded this as a breach of discipline and a deliberate attempt to 'annul' the party's tactic.[50] At a meeting, Scholem defended himself against the charges, saying that: 'All this outrage can only be understood if you know what is happening here, namely that some of the comrades have broken away from us'.[51] Scholem now openly stated that he regarded the KPD leadership as a political adversary. Brandler intervened personally and called on the Opposition to 'get [Scholem and Fischer] on the right track,' claiming that it was the only way any understanding could be reached. Otherwise, 'Nothing can save us but organisational means, which is to say expulsion from the party'.[52] This was the first time that Scholem was threatened with expulsion from the KPD. He was not intimidated, however, and instead engaged the *Zentrale* directly, protesting that the leadership would have him 'decapitated' for merely expressing his opinion.[53] Scholem claimed the right to free expression and internal party democracy while Brandler insisted that the opposition had to back legitimate majority decisions. This raised the dilemma of 'democratic centralism': how much latitude could an oppositional movement have and when did criticism amount to a breach of party discipline?

In light of these threats, Scholem rejected Brandler's offer of rapprochement, arguing that the offer was only made out of fear: 'Because the party's Rhineland-Westphalia North district conference has made you afraid that we will have a majority behind us if we work within the party until the next congress'.[54] The meeting was adjourned and the following day Brandler summarised the situation by stating: 'I'll tell you quite openly that no rapprochement is possible on this basis, [there will be] a power struggle and war within the party'.[55]

The pressure from Scholem and Fischer for a social-revolutionary policy in the spring of 1923 caused the conflict between the Opposition and the *Zentrale* to develop into an open power struggle. It was only in further negotiations which included representatives from Hamburg and the Rhineland that a seeming compromise could be reached.[56] But the conflict soon resumed. Scholem proposed that a revolutionary policy in the Ruhr would start with a strike for higher wages as an alternative to the government's officially-sanctioned policy of resistance. He also proposed anti-fascist campaigns as a means of clearly distinguishing the KPD's actions from those of the far right, who had launched a nationalist campaign, including acts of sabotage.⁵⁷ In March 1923, Arkadi Maslow had also warned that the radicalisation produced by the crisis would not benefit the KPD but the right, stating:

> Now we have a competitor, namely Hitler and his National Socialist propaganda. He does not appeal to democratic illusions, but to democratic disillusions. He is against parliament because the masses are disillusioned by parliament. Hitler talks about a strong government and we couldn't lure a dog from a furnace with our modified type of fulfilment policy.⁵⁸

The term 'fulfilment policy' describes the German government's approach. It complied with France's demands to the letter in order to show that the German Reich did not have the financial resources to pay such high reparations. Maslow criticised both the transitional programme drafted by the Zentrale and the theories that had arisen within the KPD of an 'objectively revolutionary' bourgeoisie fighting against the imperialist Treaty of Versailles. He opposed the refrain 'Beat Poincaré on the Ruhr and Cuno on the Spree', which suggested that the working class could fight against the French Prime Minister's imperialism in the Ruhr region without subordinating their cause to German Chancellor Cuno, who resided in Berlin on the banks of the river Spree. With this slogan, the KPD justified its de-facto support for the government as an anti-imperialist struggle in the Ruhr, which Maslow found particularly misguided. In that regard he was in agreement with the Berlin Left. In January 1923, two oppositional Communists from Berlin were fired from the editorial staff at *Die Rote Fahne* for having unilaterally altered this phrase.⁵⁹ While Maslow seemed to admire the far right for its radicalism, like Scholem and Fischer, he strongly repudiated the nationalism of the Ruhr struggle.

Nonetheless, in the summer of 1923, Ruth Fischer supported the *Zentrale* in an attempt to neutralise nationalist agitation using what became known as the 'Schlageter approach'. The occasion was the execution of Leo Schlageter by French troops on 26 May 1923. Schlageter, a member of the Nazi Party, had been part of a sabotage group that had rendered railway tracks impassable in order to prevent coal being transported to France. The *völkisch* right soon established a martyr's cult around him, and the KPD wanted to benefit from it as well. In his infamous 'Schlageter speech', Karl Radek raised the topic at a meeting of the enlarged Executive Committee of the Comintern (ECCI) on 20 June 1923.⁶⁰ He described Schlageter as a 'courageous soldier of the counter-revolution' who deserved 'to be faithfully honoured as an honest man by us [as] soldiers of the revolution'. Radek particularly wanted to honour Schlageter's devotion – but not his goals. He called Schlageter a 'wanderer into the void' whose sacrifice had been for nothing. Only under the banner of communism, Radek continued, could the people who supported fascism today become 'wanderers into a better future for all mankind'.

The speech was therefore not a call for cooperation between Communists and Fascists. Notably, Radek described fascism as a hammer that would smash the proletariat 'in the interest of big business', and he stressed that the KPD would fight anyone who remained in the fascist camp 'with all available means'. As Harald Jentsch has detailed, Radek's 'Schlageter approach' should be regarded as a tactical manoeuvre.⁶¹ It was intended to hamstring the fascist movement in the intensifying social struggles given that, apart from the army and the police, the armed right-wing organisations would constitute the decisive obstacle to a revolution. Even more important was the desired political impact on the petty bourgeoisie and the middle classes, whose radicalisation during the hyper-inflationary crisis had primarily benefitted the fascists. The KPD hoped to win over this radicalism to the internationalist left. Despite its tactical nature, Radek's speech also had to be a serious appeal to the masses of people under the influence of fascist ideas, which meant appropriating nationalist rhetoric. The KPD published Radek's text in *Die Rote Fahne*, which moreover carried two essays by Ernst Graf zu Reventlow, a co-founder of the far-right *völkisch* Freedom Party (*Deutschvölkische Freiheitspartei*, DVFP). Meetings at which speakers from both the KPD and the *völkisch* nationalist movement competed for the audience's sympathies were not uncommon at the time.⁶² The literature to date has assumed that the Left Opposition fell in line behind the 'Schlageter approach' without reservation.⁶³ To that end, Edward H. Carr invoked Radek himself, who had declared that his tactic had been executed 'arm in arm' with Ruth Fischer.⁶⁴

The crucial event in this respect was Fischer's participation in a discussion with far-right students at a meeting in Berlin on 25 July 1923.⁶⁵ During her speech, she called out to the audience:

Anyone who rails against Jewish capital, gentlemen, is already a class warrior whether he knows it or not. They are against Jewish capital and want to overcome the stock exchange dealers – rightly so. Stamp down on the Jewish capitalists, hang them from the lampposts, crush them. But gentlemen, how do you feel about the big capitalists like Stinnes and Klöckner?[66]

The text was printed in the central organ of the SPD, *Vorwärts*, a month after the event under the headline 'Ruth Fischer as Anti-Semite'. It is unclear whether the wording is exact because no record of the meeting exists. But neither Fischer nor the KPD denied the quote and we therefore have to assume that she at least condoned it. Fischer and Radek both came from Jewish families and although Radek had condemned fascism, Fischer's speech demonstrates the dubious path the new tactic had opened up. Instead of 'neutralising' the fascist movement, its ideas were seeping into the KPD. No public disavowal of Fischer's words by the Left Opposition has been found. But previously unpublished archival sources show that the KPD's new approach was the subject of considerable criticism. This was part of the ongoing conflict that Scholem and Fischer were engaged in with the *Zentrale* after they spoke out *against* a nationalist policy in the Ruhr. Other sources prove that this criticism had not let up by the summer of 1923. In two letters to Karl Radek dated 12 and 18 July of that year, Heinrich Brandler described reactions to Radek's speech, writing that: 'It turned Ruth's stomach as well as those of a whole array of leading right and left comrades'.[67] Fischer and Maslow in particular tried to sabotage the Schlageter approach by openly ridiculing it at meetings. They joked that the new policy had neutralised all of twelve fascists, but unfortunately 3000 workers had turned towards fascism. Brandler wrote that Fischer was sabotaging the campaign 'not because she has, for instance, significant factual objections but because she would exploit every foolish sentiment in order to play them against the policy of the *Z*[*entrale*] for her own interests'.[68] Given that Fischer would make her own infamous speech to the far-right students only a week later, Brandler may have been correct that Fischer had no principled objections.[69] She appeared to put aside those objections for advantage in the internal power struggle, abandoning the Left's criticisms and embracing the official 'Schlageter line'. She went even further than Radek, and her speech showed the disastrous consequences of this approach: a Communist leader suggested that the Nazis' anti-Semitism might be a basis for some kind of common anti-capitalism.

Fischer's speech, however, cannot be taken as evidence that the KPD in 1923 was an anti-Semitic party.[70] Both Radek and Fischer were from Jewish backgrounds and their agenda was to confront an emerging fascist movement. But trying to win over fascists to communism could only fail because the dialogue with fascism, as represented by the 'Schlageter line', accepted the ethnic-nationalist framing of the economic crisis. But, at the same time, other members of the Berlin KPD saw this as a disastrous error and protested against the new tactics. In Moscow, Max Hesse complained that leading far-right thinker Reventlow had been allowed to publish in *Die Rote Fahne*: 'The workers know that he is a complete swine and this man is being given many columns in our newspaper'.[71]

That the KPD had planned an 'anti-fascist day of action' for 29 July (one week after Ruth Fischer's speech), including plans for large demonstrations, is further evidence of criticism by the Berlin Opposition of the use of nationalist rhetoric.[72] However, when the Prussian Ministry of the Interior banned demonstrations, the *Zentrale* backed away from that plan – against the will of the Berlin KPD. The issue went all the way to Moscow where Radek worked energetically to prevent the 'anti-fascist day of action'. In league with Stalin, he ultimately managed to cancel the demonstration.[73]

Scholem provided another critical voice against any dialogue with the far-right movement. As a deputy of the Prussian *Landtag*, Scholem was the constant target of anti-Semitic attacks – and was aware that the radical rhetoric coming from the right had nothing in common with the goals of the KPD.[74] In his parliamentary speeches, Scholem constantly criticised the fascist movement as a continuation of the counter-revolution of 1918. In the spring of 1923, he openly turned against the nationalist fanfare and complained that Germans killed by the French military during the occupation of the Ruhr were publicly mourned, while killings of demonstrating workers by the German police were ignored.[75] For Scholem, the right-wing terror perpetrated by the likes of Schlageter complemented a police apparatus that used violence against demonstrations by unemployed workers. Unlike Radek, he was a long way from 'honouring' Schlageter.

Instead he used his position in the district leadership to call for social and anti-fascist struggles, saying that: 'An intensified struggle against the fascists and for wages must be conducted outside the Ruhr. [...] The political line in *Rote Fahne* was incorrect. It says that we should move away from the Ruhr workers in a "united front" with the Cuno government.'[76]

While Ruth Fischer was debating with far-right students in Berlin, as early as 1922 Scholem had branded the blatant anti-Semitism of the student members of fraternities and duelling societies (*Corpsstudenten*) as a 'barbaric mind-set'.[77] The very same day as Radek gave his Schlageter speech in Moscow, Scholem told the *Landtag* in Berlin that the Ruhr workforce could only effectively fight imperialism 'if it is understood that the dominance of all capitalists over production in the Ruhr must be eliminated regardless of their national flag'.[78]

These statements by the Left Opposition on the Ruhr conflict amount to a consistent critique of the nationalism in the anti-French Ruhr campaign, followed by a sudden u-turn on the part of Ruth Fischer in July 1923. The key to this volte-face may have been Maslow's cautious admiration for the 'success' of the rivalry presented by Hitler. The outward anti-capitalist appearance of the so-called National 'Socialists' raised questions about why its adherents did not feel that the KPD spoke for them. However, Maslow never expressed this publicly. After Fischer's speech to far-right students, there is no other known attempt by the Left Opposition to implement the Schlageter policy. We can, therefore, conclude that, contrary to earlier accounts by, for example, Carr and Angress, the left wing of the KPD never fully endorsed the Schlageter experiment. Scholem's numerous statements on the Ruhr question and the fascist movement in particular always took an anti-nationalist perspective.[79]

Eventually, both wings of the party agreed on a change of course in mid-1923. The Schlageter line was abandoned and – influenced by mass strikes, as Mario Kessler's chapter discusses – the KPD now advocated an uprising to be launched in October 1923. This had widespread appeal within the party. But the consequences of 'failed October' sent shockwaves through the party and precipitated a renewal of the factional infighting. This time the opposition prevailed and became the majority. At the Frankfurt Party Congress in April 1924, Ruth Fischer, Arkadi Maslow, and Werner Scholem took the party leadership.

Summary and Perspective

The current within the KPD that was called 'ultra-left' by its critics was established in Hamburg and Berlin in 1921 around a left-wing critique of the 'united front' policy as it was formulated after the failed uprising in March 1921. The 'Left Opposition' dominated the district leadership in Berlin and used its anchoring there to challenge the direction taken by the party leadership. Until mid-1922, criticism came in the context of solidarity among comrades; thereafter, it became a factional struggle. Contrary to the claims of earlier literature, the 'ultra-left' in Berlin had strong working-class support; intellectuals and proletarian radicals worked closely together in the district leadership. Both rejected 'reformism' in any form. What is less well known is that 'ultra-leftists', like Scholem and Max Hesse, also rejected the nationalist 'Schlageter approach' of 1923. However, their criticism remained within the party and, before the opening of the archives, has not previously been accounted for in the research.

The new Left Opposition distinguished itself from the syndicalist tendencies in the early stages of the KPD in 1919-1920 by its acceptance of the Comintern's '21 Conditions' and its centralist conception of the party. When the Berlin Opposition assumed the leadership in April 1924, they themselves used authoritarian measures. As head of the *Zentrale's* Organisational Division (*Orgbüro*), Scholem in particular imposed what became known as the 'Bolshevisation' of the KPD.[80] Their authoritarianism, as well as the unsuitability of their abstract radicalism during a period of global capitalist stabilisation, laid the groundwork for their overthrow in 1925 by rivals within the party. What followed was a new phase of the 'united front' policy, but also the party's Stalinisation. At that point the Left Opposition wanted to continue its old oppositional politics of 1921-1923, but that was impossible. Opposition by district leaderships was no longer tolerated under Ernst Thälmann. Werner Scholem, Ruth Fischer, Karl Korsch, and Arthur Rosenberg lost their party offices and were expelled from the KPD by 1926.

Translated by Joe Keady

Notes

1. See Ralf Hoffrogge, *A Jewish Communist in Weimar Germany. The Life of Werner Scholem (1895-1940)*, Leiden: Brill, 2017.
2. For biographical details of Fischer and Maslow, see Mario Kessler's chapter.
3. Mario Keßler, *Arthur Rosenberg – ein Historiker im Zeitalter der Katastrophen (1889-1943)*, Cologne: Böhlau, 2003.
4. 'K. Tsetkin P'ismo IKKI [letter from Clara Zetkin to the ECCI]', 23 February 1923, in Russian State Archive of Socio-Political History (RGASPI), F. 528, op. 2, d. 84.
5. Werner T. Angress, *Die Kampfzeit der KPD 1921-1923*, Düsseldorf: Droste, 1973, p288.
6. See Andreas Herbst and Hermann Weber, *Deutsche Kommunisten. Biographisches Handbuch 1918 bis 1945*, Berlin: Dietz, 2008, pp292f, 329f, 579, 671f, 791f, 1080.
7. Ralf Hoffrogge, *Working-Class Politics in the German Revolution. Richard Müller, the Revolutionary Shop Stewards and the Origins of the Council Movement*, Leiden: Brill, 2014. For biographical information, see Herbst and Weber, *Deutsche Kommunisten*. For Max Hesse and the locksmith Paul Weyer, see *ibid.*, pp369f, 1019f.
8. See Hoffrogge, *Working-Class Politics*, pp24-34; see also Dirk H. Müller, *Gewerkschaftliche Versammlungsdemokratie und Arbeiterdelegierte vor 1918*, Berlin: Colloquium, 1985, pp285-329.
9. There was also a faction from the RSS milieu that turned to Paul Levi's Communist Working Group (*Kommunistische Arbeitsgemeinschaft*, KAG) in 1921, which merged with the SPD in 1922.
10. Teacher Ernst Schwarz, who joined in 1922, should also be mentioned among the intellectuals, see Herbst and Weber, *Deutsche Kommunisten*, pp855f.
11. The first conflict of this kind arose in 1924 when Scholem wanted to unseat treasurer Arthur König due to his incompetence. Thälmann initially accused Scholem of wanting to drive workers out of the leadership. However, he eventually had to yield due to the fact that König was proven to have been behind a serious loss of party finances, see Weber, *Wandlung des deutschen Kommunismus*, p105.
12. See 'Sitzung der Bezirksleitung des KPD-Bezirks Berlin-Brandenburg-Lausitz, 2.3.1923', in Stiftung Archiv der Parteien und Massenorganisationen der DDR im Bundesarchiv (SAPMO), RY 1/I 3/1-2/16.
13. 'Letter from Werner Scholem to Gershom Scholem', 2 January 1915, in Gershom Scholem Archive, National Library of Israel, Jerusalem (GSA).
14. Herbst and Weber, *Deutsche Kommunisten*, pp925ff.
15. Angress, *Kampfzeit*, p288. For a more critical view, see Otto Langels, *Die*

ultralinke Opposition der KPD in der Weimarer Republik – zur Geschichte und Theorie der KPD-Opposition (Linke KPD), der Entschiedenen Linken, der Gruppe 'Kommunistische Politik' und des Deutschen Industrie-Verbandes in den Jahren 1924 bis 1928, Frankfurt a. M.: Peter Lang, 1984, pp20-22.
16. Ruth Fischer, *Stalin und der Deutsche Kommunismus*, Frankfurt a. M.: Verlag Frankfurter Hefte, 1950, p221.
17. Werner Scholem, 'Feinde Ringsum', in *Der Funke*, 16, 15 September 1924.
18. The first draft of this article came from Ruth Fischer and Arkadi Maslow and can be found in SAPMO, RY 5/I 6/3/128, Bl. 42. After gaining the support of the Berlin leadership, it was published as Werner Scholem, 'Skizze über die Entwicklung der Opposition in der KPD', in *Die Internationale*, 7, 2/3, 28 March 1924.
19. 'Skizze der Berliner Delegation nach Moskau, den 21. April 1923', in SAPMO, RY 1/I 3/1-2/14, Bl. 164ff.
20. *Ibid*.
21. *Ibid*.
22. Zetkin's letter to the ECCI, *op. cit*.
23. Many of the left-wing KPD officials from Berlin came from the USPD and by 1924 had been in the movement for ten years or more, see Weber, *Wandlung*, p18.
24. Angress, *Kampfzeit*, p289.
25. See Florian Wilde, 'Ernst Meyer - Vergessene Führungsfigur des deutschen Kommunismus', PhD Thesis, University of Hamburg, pp243ff; published online: http://ediss.sub.uni-hamburg.de/volltexte/2013/6009/.
26. Werner Scholem, 'Skitze über die Entstehung der linken Opposition in der KPD', in *Die Internationale* 2/3, 7, March 1924, pp.122ff.
27. See Werner Scholem, 'Der 20. April in Deutschland', in *Internationale Presse-Korrespondenz*, 52, 22 April 1922.
28. Werner Scholem, 'Entstehung der Opposition in der KPD', p125.
29. *Ibid*., p127.
30. 'Politbüro Sitzung', 11 April 1922, in SAPMO, RY 1/I 2/3/2.
31. *Ibid*.
32. *Ibid*.
33. Angress, *Kampfzeit*, p290.
34. See Ruth Fischer, *Stalin und der Deutsche Kommunismus*, pp183-186; Clara Zetkin, *Erinnerungen an Lenin*, Berlin (DDR): Dietz, 1957, p46; Angress, *Kampfzeit*, p296.
35. Scholem, *Entstehung der Opposition*, p129.
36. Angress, *Kampfzeit*, p308.
37. Scholem, *Entstehung der Opposition*, p129.
38. On the KPD in Saxony, see Norman LaPorte, *The German Communist Party in Saxony, 1924-1933: Factionalism, Fratricide and Political Failure*, Oxford: Peter Lang, 2003. On Thuringia, see Steffen Kachel, *Ein rot-*

roter Sonderweg? Sozialdemokraten und Kommunisten in Thüringen 1919 bis 1949, Cologne: Böhlau, 2011.
39. *Ibid.*, p130.
40. 'Sitzung der Bezirksleitung des KPD-Bezirks Berlin-Brandenburg-Lausitz, den 2. Februar 1923', in SAPMO, RY 1/I 3/1-2/16.
41. *Ibid.*
42. *Ibid.*
43. *Bericht über die Verhandlungen des 3. Parteitages der KPD*, p. 325f; see also Angress, *Die Kampfzeit der KPD*, p305f.
44. Werner Scholem, 'Entstehung der Opposition', p130.
45. Conan Fisher, *The Ruhr Crisis 1923–1924*, Oxford: Oxford University Press, 2003.
46. *Ibid.*
47. On KPD and nationalism see Louis Dupeux, *Nationalbolschewismus in Deutschland 1919-1933*, München: Büchergilde Gutenberg, 1985; and Otto-Ernst Schüddekopf, *Linke Leute von Rechts. Die nationalrevolutionären Minderheiten und der Kommunismus in der Weimarer Republik*. Stuttgart: Kohlhammer, 1960.
48. Scholem presented a report on this subject to the Berlin district leadership on 27 March 1923, see SAPMO, RY 1/I 3/1-2/16.
49. This meeting was held 12 March, see 'Sitzung des Berliner Zentralvorstandes vom 4. April 1923', in SAPMO, RY 1/I 3/1-2/14.
50. 'Edwin Hoernle to the ECCI', 23 April 1923, in RY 1/I 2/3/62a, Bl.132, cited in Mario Keßler, *Arthur Rosenberg - ein Historiker im Zeitalter der Katastrophen*, p90.
51. See 'Sitzung der Bezirksleitung des KPD-Bezirks Berlin-Brandenburg, 3.4.1923', in SAPMO, RY 1/I 3/1-2/16.
52. 'Sitzung des Berliner Zentralvorstandes vom 4. April 1923', in SAPMO, RY 1/I 3/1-2/14.
53. *Ibid.*
54. *Ibid.*
55. 'Berliner Zentralvorstand vom 5. April 1923', in SAPMO, RY 1/I 3/1-2/14.
56. For details see 'Sitzung der Zentrale mit den Vertretern der Berliner Bezirksleitung vom 5. April 1923', in SAPMO, RY 1/I 2/2/3.
57. 'Sitzung der KPD-Bezirksleitung Berlin-Brandenburg-Lausitz, 23.3.1923', in SAPMO, RY 1/I 3/1-2/16.
58. 'Sitzung der KPD-Bezirksleitung Berlin-Brandenburg-Lausitz, 9.3.1923', in SAPMO, RY 1/I 3/1-2/16.
59. The altered version read: 'Beat Poincaré and Cuno, on the Ruhr and the Spree'. At a meeting of the district leadership, it was reported that the entire editorial staff was unhappy with the nationalist undertones of the original text, see 'Sitzung der KPD-Bezirksleitung Berlin-Brandenburg-Lausitz, 23.1. 1923', in SAPMO, RY 1/I 3/1-2/16.

60. The speech was published in *Die Rote Fahne* on 26 June 1923; see also the reprint in Dietrich Möller, *Karl Radek in Deutschland*, Cologne: Verlag Wissenschaft und Politik 1976, pp245f. An English translation can be found online: https://www.marxists.org/archive/radek/1923/06/schlageter.htm.
61. Harald Jentsch, *Die KPD und der 'Deutsche Oktober' 1923*, Rostock: Ingo Koch Verlag, 2005, pp114-124.
62. See Angress, *Kampfzeit*, pp374ff for a more critical interpretation of these events, see also the chapter by Mario Keßler in this volume.
63. Angress wrote that, 'Because the "Schlageter approach" was a tactical matter and not doctrine, it had the support of the entire party, including the Left Opposition', see *idem*, *Kampfzeit*, p384. Conan Fisher suggests that the KPD's left wing distanced itself from the Schlageter-Line only at the beginning of 1924, see Conan Fisher, *The German Communists and the Rise of Nazism* Basingstoke: Macmillan, 1991, p68.
64. Karl Radek, *Die Lehren der Deutschen Ereignisse*, cited in E. H. Carr, *A History of Soviet Russia. The interregnum 1923-1924*, London: Macmillan, 1954, p185. Carr also regarded the 'Schlageter approach' as purely tactical.
65. See Angress, *Kampfzeit*, pp374ff.
66. 'Hängt die Judenkapitalisten. Ruth Fischer als Antisemitin', in *Vorwärts*, 22 August 1923.
67. 'Brief. KPD (*Polbüro*) an Karl Radek, Moscow (ECCI) 12 u.18 July 1923', in SAPMO, RY 1/I 2/3/ 208b, Bl.436ff, 448f.
68. Brandler also defended Radek's policy, see SAPMO, RY 1/I 2/3/208b, Bl.436ff, 448f.
69. Flechtheim proposed that, 'the Ruth Fischer-Thälmann group was attempting to push back against a wavering *Zentrale* by exaggerating the slogans behind its own policy', see *idem*, *Die KPD in der Weimarer Republik*, Bollwerk: Offenbach, 1948, p89.
70. On this point, see Olaf Kistenmacher, 'From 'Judas' to "Jewish Capital": Anti-Semitic Forms of Thought in the German Communist Party (KPD) in the Weimar Republic, 1918-1933', *Engage Journal*, 2, 2006, pp1-12.
71. For the minutes of this meeting, see SAPMO, RY 5/I 6/10/78, Bl.31.
72. Carr states that, as a manoeuvre intended to split the fascist organisations, the Schlageter approach did not rule out antifascist campaigns, see *idem*, *Interregnum*, p181.
73. *Ibid.*, p187.
74. Hoffrogge, *Werner Scholem*, pp258-271.
75. Prussian Landtag, 232nd session, 20 April 1923.
76. 'KPD-Bezirksleitung Berlin-Brandenburg-Lausitz, den 23. Mai 1923', in SAPMO, RY 1/I 3/1-2/16.
77. Prussian Landtag, 104th session, 22 February 1922.
78. Prussian Landtag, 259th session, 20 June 1923.

79. When the Left took control of the KPD in 1924, one of its first campaigns was a nationwide anti-fascist day in Halle. It was conceived of as a way to make up for the suppressed 'antifascist demonstration' in Berlin in 1923. As Arkadi Maslow stated: 'This day will have the same significance as last year's anti-fascist day with the sole difference that this time we will not pull back', see 'Protokoll der Sitzung der Sekretäre und Redakteure, 11.5.1924', in SAPMO, RY 1/I 2/2/4.
80. Hoffrogge, *Werner Scholem*, pp267-284.

Resisting Moscow? Ruth Fischer and the KPD, 1923-1926

Mario Kessler

THE COMMUNIST PARTY was one of the main political forces in the Weimar Republic. Founded in the aftermath of the First World War by leftist socialists around Rosa Luxemburg, the party became gradually more committed to the Leninist party model and, finally, to Stalinism.

A turning point on the way towards Stalinism was the policy of Bolshevisation that was adopted by the Fifth Comintern Congress in July 1924, which meant a strict centralisation of the party structure as well as suppression of internal opposition. This policy, in Geoff Eley's words:

> [D]ragooned the communist parties toward stricter bureaucratic centralism. This flattened out the earlier years of radicalisms, welding them into a single approved model of Communist organisation. Only then did the new parties retreat from broader Left arenas into their own belligerent world [...]. Respect for Bolshevik achievements and defence of the Russian Revolution now transmuted into dependency on Moscow and belief in Soviet infallibility. Depressing cycles of 'internal rectification' began, disgracing and expelling successive leaderships, so that by the later 1920s many founding Communists had gone.[1]

The history of the Bolshevisation of the KPD is inseparably bound with the name of Ruth Fischer (1895-1961). During the inter-war period she was one of the most dazzling figures of German and international communism. Immediately after the end of the First World War she co-founded the Communist Party of Austria, became famous as the chair of the KPD in the Weimar Republic, and, after 1945, was associated with the anti-communist crusade in the United States where she authored the best-selling book *Stalin and German Communism*. At the end of her life she hoped in vain that the Soviet Union under Nikita Khrushchev would move towards a more democratic variant of communism. Ruth Fischer was the sister of two other prominent Austrian-German communists: the composer Hanns Eisler (1898-1962) and the journalist Gerhart Eisler (1897-1968). The following remarks will not give a full biographical sketch, but will concentrate on the years 1923 to 1926, the years of Ruth Fischer's rise and fall within the German communist movement.

From Vienna to Berlin: Ruth Fischer and the Early Communist Movement

Ruth Fischer (born Elfriede Eisler) came from a middle-class family. She was born in Leipzig on 11 December 1895. Her parents married a few weeks after her birth and their daughter then received her father's family name of Eisler. The family soon moved to Vienna where her father held a position as lecturer in philosophy at the university. Since her father, Rudolf Eisler (1873-1926), who was of Jewish origin, refused to be baptised, he was never promoted to full professor. Elfriede's mother Maria (1876-1927), who had worked as a domestic servant until she married, was Protestant. The three children grew up in a liberal and agnostic household.[2]

After finishing high school in 1914 Elfriede Eisler studied pedagogy, economics and philosophy at the University of Vienna. Soon after the war begun in 1914, Elfriede and her brothers, who were both waiting for conscription, founded a student group that expressed a strict opposition to the war. She also belonged to a circle around the left-wing Freudian psychoanalyst Siegfried Bernfeld, with whom she probably came in contact through her brother Gerhart.[3] Another member of this circle was Paul Friedländer, a fellow-student, whom Elfriede married in 1917. In December of that same year, her son (Friedrich) Gerhard was born. The group produced and distributed anti-militarist leaflets and read the writings of radical leftist critics of war, militarism ·and imperialism, among them Lenin, Zinoviev and Rosa Luxemburg. In October 1918, Elfriede Eisler wrote a brochure on sexual policy in an anticipated communist society.⁴ At the same time she left the university without finishing her studies.

On 3 November 1918, a group of around forty people including Elfriede, her husband and brothers, founded the Communist Party of Austria. She became, as her membership card testifies, member number one.⁵ According to her later reminiscences, the Communist Party of Austria was founded on the initiative of Russian Communist Party representatives and, unlike the Communist Party of Germany, the Austrian Party owed its existence from the very beginning to the efforts and the money of Russian Communists.⁶

During the first months of 1919 armed revolts swept all over Germany. In some states, Council Republics were proclaimed and existed, most prominently in Bavaria, even if only temporarily. The failures of these revolutionary attempts were a major setback for the KPD. Following the assassination of its leaders Karl Liebknecht, Rosa Luxemburg and Leo Jogiches by the right-wing paramilitary Free Corps, Paul Levi became chair of the party. Unlike many Russian Bolsheviks who 'tended to treat every piece of news dealing with unrest in Germany as a sign of imminent social revolution', Levi led the party away from the policy of anticipating an immediate uprising.⁷ He made a serious effort to win over supporters from the Social Democratic Party and the Independent Socialists. These efforts were rewarded when a substantial section of the USPD joined the KPD in December 1920, making it a mass party.

At this time Ruth Fischer was already a rising star in German radical politics. After a failed attempt to gain exclusive leadership of the Austrian communists, she left Vienna in late August 1919.⁸ While her husband remained in Vienna, Fischer went to Berlin. Her son remained with her parents in Vienna. After her arrival in Berlin, she used the name Ruth Fischer in public. Divorced in 1922, she officially married the KPD member Gustav Golke a year later to obtain German citizenship, but the marriage remained one of convenience. Soon, she found a job at the women's office of the KPD with Paul Levi's support. A few months later, Karl Radek, the Comintern's emissary to Germany, recommended that she should work for the Western European Secretariat of the Comintern.⁹

In December 1920, Ruth Fischer was among the KPD delegates at the conference that merged with the left wing of the USPD forming the United Communist Party of Germany.¹⁰ Fischer's political activities earned her the position of chair in Berlin-Brandenburg, the party's largest district organisation (*Bezirk*). She found support from two politicians who represented the leftist opposition to Levi's more moderate course: Ernst Friesland, who became better known as Ernst Reuter, the Social Democratic mayor of post-war West Berlin, and Arkadij Maslow, who would soon become Ruth Fischer's life-long partner.[11]

Maslow (1891-1941), born in the Ukraine under the name Isaak Chemerinskij, had abandoned a promising career as a concert pianist as well as his university studies in mathematics to devote all of his time to communist politics.[12] From 1921, together with Ruth Fischer, he led the Berlin-Brandenburg district organisation of the party. The left-wing faction around Fischer and Maslow became known as the Berlin Opposition. It criticised Levi's attempts to cooperate with the SPD. Following bitter disputes within the KPD, Levi resigned from the leadership of the Communist Party in January 1921. Only two months later, under the influence of the Hungarian Comintern emissary Béla Kun, the party launched the March uprisings (or 'March Action') of 1921 in central Germany. Following the uprisings, which were soon suppressed by army and police units, Levi was expelled from the Communist Party for publicly criticising party policies.[13]

Immediately after Paul Levi's resignation, the influence of the Fischer-Maslow faction increased within the party. In November and December of 1922, Fischer participated in the Fourth World Congress of the Comintern in Moscow where she met Lenin and Trotsky. In an unofficial meeting that was arranged between the German delegation and the Soviet party leadership, she spoke, in her own words:

> vehemently and brutally against the policy of the German Central Committee, attacked the New Economic Policy irreverently and criticised the Russian Communist Party without the servile attitude of deference toward Lenin that had already become habitual with all foreign Communist leaders.[14]

Consequently, neither Fischer nor Maslow would obtain seats in the new KPD *Zentrale*, the party directorate. Control over affairs passed into the hands of Heinrich Brandler, August Thalheimer and Walter Stoecker. Brandler in particular soon realised that the vast majority of German workers refused to be dragged into revolutionary adventures without any purpose or sense. Throughout 1921-22, the moderate and the leftist tendencies were both seeking support from the Comintern headquarters in Moscow.

At that time, the Fischer-Maslow faction had Karl Radek's support. The Comintern's expert for German affairs warned the party against the 'dangers of opportunism'.[15] It was only the intervention of Lenin and of the Executive Committee of the Comintern (ECCI) that was sufficient to bring about the adaptation of a united front policy.[16]

Ruth Fischer in 1923

In January 1923, the German government claimed that it could no longer afford the reparation payments required by the Versailles Treaty. When it defaulted on some payments, French and Belgian troops occupied the Ruhr region, taking control of most mining and manufacturing companies. Strikes were called and passive resistance was encouraged. These strikes lasted eight months, further damaging the economy. The strikes meant that no goods were being produced. This infuriated the French occupiers, who began to kill and exile protestors in the region.

Since striking workers were paid benefits by the state, money was printed, further exacerbating the ongoing hyperinflation. Soon, Germans discovered that their money was worthless. This led the Comintern to conclude that a revolutionary situation had arisen in Germany, and the leftist tendency within the KPD gained ground. At the end of March 1923, Fischer and Maslow were among the organisers of a conference of trades councils of the Ruhr region in Essen (immediately after the KPD district conference at the same place) to discuss revolutionary action. Radek even went as far as proposing a united front of Communists and what he called 'revolutionary nationalists' in the struggle against Western imperialism. In an enlarged ECCI meeting held in June in Moscow, he gave a speech that became infamous as 'The Schlageter Speech'. Leo Schlageter, a young Nazi, had been sentenced to death and executed by a French military court after attempting to blow up a railway line in the occupied Ruhr region.[17]

In his speech, Radek emphasised that Schlageter, 'as a courageous soldier of the counter-revolution' deserved 'the sincere respect of us, the soldiers of the revolution'. He concluded: 'Unless patriotic circles in Germany will decide to adopt the cause of the majority of people and form a single united front against the Western capitalists and the German capitalists, Schlageter's sacrifice will have been in vain'. Radek called upon the 'hundreds of Schlageters' to participate in joint action with the Communists. The nationalist rebels should recognise that Germany 'can only be freed from the bonds of slavery with the working class, not against it'.[18] Ruth Fischer addressed similar remarks to German nationalists when she said that 'the giant who will liberate Germany is there: it is the German proletariat of which you form a part, and with which you must align yourself'.[19] According to a report in the Social Democratic press, she said to nationalist students:

> Anyone who rails against Jewish capital, gentlemen, is already a class warrior whether he knows it or not. They are against Jewish capital and want to overcome the stock exchange dealers – rightly so. Stamp down on the Jewish capitalists, hang them from the lampposts, crush them. But gentlemen, how do you feel about the big capitalists like Stinnes and Klockner?

Much later Ruth Fischer pretended that this 'episode has been cited and distorted over and over again in publications on German communism'. But she used the same form of argumentation again: 'I was obliged to answer some anti-Semitic remarks. I said that communism was for fighting Jewish capitalists only if all capitalists, Jewish and Gentile, were the object of the same attack'.[21] Here it must be noted that the notion of 'Jewish capital' confirmed the stereotype of the powerful, yet simultaneously hidden, 'alien' capital that is foreign to the German 'proletarian' nation.[22] Fischer saw on the one hand the 'rich Jews' who accumulate money and on the other hand the 'visible' German big entrepreneurs.

At the height of the Ruhr crisis Ruth Fischer called on workers to seize the factories and mines, to take political power and establish a Workers' Republic of the Ruhr. This republic would then become the base for a Workers' Army that would 'march into Central Germany, seize power in Berlin and crush once and for all the nationalist counter-revolution'.[23]

During the summer of 1923 riots and strikes against galloping inflation erupted all over Germany. Hundreds of thousands participated. There were serious differences within the KPD about how to deal with this situation. The so-called rightist group around party chair, Heinrich Brandler, stood by their view that workers' governments should be formed. Radek, who now refrained from his earlier position, supported this orientation. However, the KPD leadership's attempt to join the left-social democratic governments in the states of Saxony and Thuringia came under attack from the group around Fischer and Maslow. They saw Germany ready for revolution and criticised what they called the 'reformist passivity' of the circle around Brandler. In both states, Saxony and Thuringia, the KPD joined leftwing SPD governments on October 10 and 16 respectively.

As early as 21 August 1923, the Russian party leadership decided to prepare for a revolution in Germany and constituted a Commission for International Affairs to supervise the political radicalisation in Germany. It consisted of Zinoviev, Kamenev, Radek, Stalin, Trotsky, Chicherin, Dzerzhinsky, Pyatakov and Sokolnikov, i.e. almost all of the prominent Bolshevik leaders. Financial, logistical and even military support would be provided to arm the paramilitary units of the KPD, the Proletarian Hundreds, which had been set up over the previous months.[24] Simultaneously Gregory Zinoviev, the chair of the ECCI, helped Ruth Fischer to become a member of the KPD *Zentrale* while she was in Moscow. In October, Radek, Pyatakov and Sokolnikov were sent to Germany to assist the revolution. The date for the uprising was set for 9 November.

However, on 26 September, German chancellor Gustav Stresemann announced the end of passive resistance against the French-Belgian occupation of the Ruhr. He argued that there was no other way to get hyperinflation under control. On 13 October, the national parliament passed an 'empowerment act' that allowed the government to abolish most of the social achievements of the November Revolution, including the eight-hour working day. The SPD parliamentary faction voted in favour of this act.

With the support of the President, Friedrich Ebert, the *Reichswehr* stepped up its pressure in Saxony and Thuringia and issued a direct order banning the Proletarian Hundreds, giving them three days to give up their arms. The ultimatum was ignored. On 21 October, the army entered Saxony. The workers' protest was so massive that the SPD was obliged to resign from the Stresemann government in Berlin.

The KPD had to bring forward its plans for insurrection. It called a congress of works councils in Chemnitz, Saxony on 21 October. This congress was supposed to call a general strike and give the signal for the desired 'German October'. But because the left Social Democratic delegates disagreed, Brandler called off the uprising. 'During the Chemnitz conference I realised once we had been unable to convince the left Social Democrats to sign the resolution for a general strike that we could under no circumstances enter the decisive struggle', he wrote.[25] Brandler also saw that the Proletarian Hundreds were not well enough equipped with arms.[26] However, news of this decision did not reach Hamburg in time. Here a communist insurrection was organised and begun but it remained isolated and was quickly put down. For a few months, the KPD – together with the Nazi Party after its ill-fated Beer Hall Putsch in Munich – was outlawed, a decision that was revoked on 1 March 1924.[27]

Leader of German Communism: Rise and Fall

The end of these hopes for a 'German October' was a major setback for international communism, and the reaction of the Comintern leadership was to condemn the KPD leaders. The new turn to the left was in part a spontaneous reaction of KPD members against the so-called 'betrayal' by the rightists around Brandler. But it was also determined by a regrouping of political forces in Moscow. Zinoviev, the chair of the ECCI, refused to acknowledge for some time after the Chemnitz conference that the 'German October' was a complete failure for the KPD and not a temporary regression.[28]

As the time passed, Zinoviev's attitude began to change. The easiest way to escape the responsibility for the failed policy was to delegate it to Brandler, Thalheimer, and also to Radek. Unlike Brandler and Thalheimer, Radek was also known for his alliance with Trotsky against Zinoviev, Kamenev and Stalin. Thus, Brandler, Thalheimer, and Radek had to acknowledge sole responsibility before a special commission.[29] Zinoviev's turning against them had been prompted in part by Fischer and Maslow. At the end of 1923 both were in Moscow, where Maslow awaited an investigation concerning his past party record. They complained about Brandler's alleged incompetence in leadership. As a result Zinoviev asserted that KPD participation in the governments of Saxony and Thuringia had turned 'into a banal parliamentary coalition with the Social Democrats. The result was our political defeat'.[30]

Between 8 and 21 January 1924, the ECCI presidium and the KPD's rival factions held a conference in Moscow. Brandler and Radek defended the standpoint that the German working class had not been ready for a revolution and thus the communist retreat was necessary. Hermann Remmele represented a so-called 'centre line' which held that the KPD would have to take the road to revolution in stages.[31] This newly constituted 'Centre Group' also included Wilhelm Koenen, August Kleine, and Hugo Eberlein, and hoped to constitute the new party leadership. Ruth Fischer, speaking for the left, attacked Brandler and Radek fiercely and demanded that the leadership be changed.[32] On 19 February 1924, the KPD *Zentrale* met in Halle to elect Remmele as the party's interim chair, with Ernst Thälmann, who represented the left, as his deputy.

This centre-left coalition in the party leadership was unstable. The Centre Group had little support in either the party or in the Comintern. Its temporary influence rested on a political compromise until a new leadership could be established. The regional party organisations of Berlin-Brandenburg and the Rhineland expressed on various occasions their disgust with the idea of any cooperation with the SPD.[33] Equally important was the fact that the Left received a considerable amount of support from Zinoviev and the Comintern apparatus. As early as January 1924, Zinoviev denounced 'the leaders of German Social Democracy' as 'Fascists through and through' and concluded that only the slogan 'unity from below' – which excluded the leaders of the SPD – 'must become a living reality'.[34]

From 7 to 10 April 1924, the KPD held its Ninth Congress in Frankfurt-Main. Although the ban on the party had been repealed, the congress did not meet in the open and the protocol did not mention the names of the speakers. But it was reported that there were ninety-two congress delegates representing the Left faction and only thirty-four from the Centre Group. The Rightists had no elected representation at the congress. Only their former *Zentrale* members were allowed to participate.[35]

The congress set a tone of unbound revolutionary optimism. It stated that, despite the setbacks to the revolution and the lack of popular support for the KPD, the crisis of capitalism persisted and was even getting stronger. The conclusion was that the party would 'have to bring its members to a state of readiness for decisive struggles in the most immediate future'.[36] This would require 'a complete break with the whole ideology of the preceding period, when the incorrect applications of united front tactics filled the party with a sense of weakness'.[37]

After tumultuous debates the victory of the 'Left' was decisive: Fischer, Maslow and Werner Scholem constituted the new Political Bureau (*Politbüro*).[38] At the end of April, it was extended and renamed the Political Secretariat. Among its members were the party chairman Ernst Thälmann, one of the leaders of the defeated Hamburg uprising, and the historian Arthur Rosenberg.[39] Scholem became head of the organisational directorate. The jurist Karl Korsch became editor of *Die Internationale*, the party's theoretical journal. They were all now supporters of Fischer and Maslow. Finally, Maslow was appointed political secretary of the party – the *de facto* leader.

On 24 May 1924, Maslow was arrested and brought to court. Accused of high treason, he was sentenced to four years in prison, but because of his failing health he was released early, in May 1926. During Maslow's incarceration, the KPD *Zentrale* entrusted Ruth Fischer with the post of the political secretary of the party.[40] At this time, she was in England to participate in a congress of the Communist Party of Great Britain.[41] A few days later, after her return to Berlin, she started her work as leader of the KPD. Successively, she and her supporters took over the regional and local branches, dismissing those functionaries who had expressed their sympathy with a more moderate line and continued to seek joint actions with the SPD.[42]

This policy led towards isolation. The KPD lost its positions in the trade unions, particularly in the German Metalworkers' Union, which had been a communist stronghold. Many shop stewards left the KPD.[43] Independent observers put much of the blame for this situation on Ruth Fischer. The radical-democratic weekly *Die Weltbühne* wrote in May 1924 that, under Fischer's leadership 'radicalism has triumphed'. It argued that this kind of leadership would demand blind obedience:

> Ruth Fischer wants to command absolutely, wants to be adored [...] like the Dalai Lama. But is she the spirit capable of ruling over men? Or is she, since all good spirits seem to have deserted the KPD, the last glimmer of light that shines for the communist masses in the darkness?[44]

Throughout 1924, a process of political consolidation all over Germany followed the financial stabilisation. The parliamentary elections of 4 May were, however, still largely influenced by the recent inflation and the turmoil that resulted from it. Since the Nazi Party was still not allowed to compete, the impoverished middle-class flocked to the German Nationalists, a far-right force, while a large part of the workers who were struggling along on inadequate wages cast their ballots for the Communists. The KPD came in fourth place, polling around 3.7 million votes, or 12.6 per cent of the electorate, and sent sixty-two deputies to parliament, among them Ruth Fischer.

In her inaugural speech on 28 May, Fischer called the Reichstag 'a shadowy theatre' and its non-communist deputies 'dream-figures'.[45] A few months later she described the parliamentarians as 'puppets of heavy industry'.[46] The KPD was in staunch opposition to the bourgeois government and the Dawes Plan, which had softened the burden of Allied reparations, stabilised the economy, and brought increased foreign investments and loans to the German market. The party thus came into conflict with general public opinion. Consequently, the next elections, held in December 1924, turned out unfavourably for the KPD: the number of votes for its candidates fell to 2.7 million (8.9 per cent of the electorate), giving the party only forty-five seats. Fischer retained her seat and became a member of the Parliamentary Committee for International Affairs.[47]

It was not only the political situation in Germany but also in the Soviet Union that was of decisive importance for the KPD. In June and July 1924, the Fifth Comintern Congress took place within the context of internal Soviet power struggles. Since Trotsky had already lost decisive ground in these struggles, one of the issues for the congress was the 'fight against Trotskyism'; this meant the removal of his last supporters from every relevant political position inside the Comintern. Zinoviev and Stalin, who had recently united to defeat Trotsky, had become political rivals; both of them now pursued the aim of dominating the Comintern's 'national sections'. Lenin's principle of 'democratic centralism', which left command over party affairs in the hands of the national leaderships, was superseded by the 'Bolshevisation' of communist parties. Internal party factions no longer determined whether or not there would be promotion or expulsion of party functionaries, instead this was decided by the demands of the Soviet party leaders. The term 'Bolshevisation' was most likely coined at the session of the KPD leadership on 19 February 1924, as a letter from Zinoviev testified, in which he considered the term to be a 'wonderful expression'.[48] It became clear that the term also implied that any criticism of Soviet policy could be denounced as anti-communist. The consequence was a drastic curtailment of freedom of discussion inside every party.

The political isolation of the Soviet Union and the temporary stabilisation of capitalism in Europe, notably in Germany, strengthened the position of Soviet bureaucracy, particularly that of Stalin, who became the main proponent of the new orientation towards 'socialism in one country'. That slogan could well be seen as an ideological justification for the growing power of the state and party apparatus.[49]

It was Zinoviev who announced at the Fifth Comintern Congress that the great slogan of the coming period would be the Bolshevisation of the communist parties. The 'Theses on Tactics' adopted by the congress defined Bolshevisation as 'the transfer to our sections of everything in Bolshevism that has been and is still of international significance'. It was emphasised that every communist party 'must be a centralised party, prohibiting factions, tendencies, or groupings. It must be a monolithic party cast in a single bloc'.[50] Ruth Fischer called for a monolithic Comintern according to the Russian party model from which all dissent should be banished: 'This world congress should not allow the International to be transformed into an agglomeration of any kind of currents; it should forge ahead and embark upon the road that leads to a single Bolshevik world party'.[51] Ruth Fischer was, in Isaac Deutscher's words, a 'young, trumpet-tongued woman without any revolutionary experience or merit'.[52] She found support among the Comintern leadership and became a consultative member of the ECCI. The KPD delegation and Ruth Fischer in particular endorsed the policy of Bolshevisation and the position of the congress that declared that 'Fascism and Social Democracy are the left hand and right hand of modern capitalism'.[53]

This attitude had a fateful consequence. In March and April 1925, presidential elections were held in Germany. The refusal of the KPD to withdraw its candidate, Ernst Thälmann, from the second round of voting helped the former Field Marshal Paul von Hindenburg, the candidate of the Nationalists, to win against Wilhelm Marx, the 'bourgeois' candidate who was also supported by the SPD.[54] Thälmann gained less than two million votes, only 6.4 per cent of the electorate.

The Social Democrat Friedrich Stampfer wrote: 'When the election result became known that night there could not have been a single man among the republicans who did not feel the enemy at his throat'.[55]

This was also the opinion of the ECCI, which had moderated its tactics. It was Zinoviev who had suggested that the KPD should withdraw Thälmann and support a candidate who would at least prevent a monarchist restoration, preferably a Social Democrat.[56] While Maslow, who had just been sentenced to imprisonment, agreed, Ruth Fischer accepted this idea only very reluctantly. She ridiculed reproaches from the SPD that the Communists would effectively be helping Hindenburg by supporting Thälmann as a candidate.[57]

There were other differences emerging between the KPD leadership and the Comintern leadership, as the latter gradually moved toward a more realistic policy. Since 1924, the KPD *Zentrale* had opposed the Red International of Labour Unions' orientation to advocate negotiations with the Social Democratic International Federation of Trade Unions. Much criticism of this policy was published in *Die Internationale*; the editor-in-chief, Karl Korsch, had become a target of Zinoviev's attacks during the Fifth Comintern Congress. Korsch, once a supporter of workers' governments, now rejected co-operation between communist and non-communist representatives.[58] Zinoviev gave Korsch, who was Professor of Legal Theory at the University of Jena, the 'friendly advice' that 'he should first study Marxism and Leninism' before dealing with theoretical issues in the party's journal.[59]

Ruth Fischer realised that she had to abandon her more extreme positions. In February 1925, the *Zentrale* dismissed Korsch as editor of *Die Internationale*. A few weeks later, Werner Scholem lost his post as head of the organisational directorate. On 27 May 1925, the leadership attempted to come closer to the SPD by means of an 'Open Letter' that proposed areas of cooperation. This provoked loud objections from Rosenberg, Scholem and Iwan Katz. In a letter addressed to rank-and-file party officials, they criticised Maslow and Fischer for their statement on the 'relative stabilisation' of capitalism internationally, insisting that a new revolutionary upswing would come soon.[60]

In July 1925, the tenth party congress ratified the moderation of policy. Out of the 170 delegates, only twelve – including Rosenberg, Scholem and Katz – belonged to what was termed the 'ultra-left' tendency. In a letter addressed to the conference Zinoviev urged the party to acknowledge the 'relative stabilisation' of capitalism in

Germany. He accused Rosenberg and Scholem of trying to 'falsify' communism while Korsch's opinions disqualified him from being considered a Bolshevik.⁶¹ The insistence on Thälmann's candidacy during the second round of the presidential election had shown an 'ultra-leftist fever' that the party had to cure. Remarkably, Zinoviev did not criticise Thälmann himself.⁶² Ruth Fischer also criticised the 'ultra-leftists', if in more moderate tones.⁶³ Nonetheless, Moscow viewed Fischer's leadership with growing scepticism. The strong opposition that Dmitri Manuilsky, the ECCI emissary, had faced at the congress – he was loudly advised to 'go back to Moscow' – was seen as proof of the dwindling quality of Fischer's leadership.⁶⁴

The 'Manuilsky Affair' played a pivotal role at the meeting of the German Commission of the ECCI with the KPD leaders on 12 August. At first Fischer refused to come to Moscow, but she later changed her mind. At the meeting, she was confronted by complaints made by Bukharin and Zinoviev. Both made clear that the party needed trustworthy proletarian elements, such as Ernst Thälmann and Philipp Dengel.⁶⁵ Thälman in particular was seen as Stalin's supporter while Ruth Fischer was associated with Zinoviev. Thälmann and Dengel, unlike Fischer and the party intellectuals around her, were considered authentic representatives of a policy that should guarantee the rootedness of the KPD among the proletarian masses. An 'Open Letter' of the ECCI that was published on 1 September 1925 confirmed this agenda. It emphasised that only under a proletarian leadership would the KPD be able to practice a Leninist policy that deserved its name. The letter stated explicitly that it 'is not the left in the KPD that is bankrupt, but certain leaders of the left, and in the future the left will assert itself along different lines'.⁶⁶

Demonstrating the discipline expected from every communist, the letter was signed by all KPD delegates in Moscow. That included Ruth Fischer who, in her own words written decades later, 'was driven to sign my own political death warrant and to confess my sins in public'.⁶⁷ An extraordinary First Party Conference was held in Berlin on 31 October and 1 November 1925, which confirmed the new situation; Fischer and Maslow were expelled from the party leadership.⁶⁸

At that time, Ruth Fischer was still in Moscow. According to an unofficial order given by Stalin, she was not allowed to leave the country but had to stay in the Comintern's 'Hotel Lux'.⁶⁹ The Sixth ECCI Plenum, which Ruth Fischer was still allowed to attend, confirmed the resolutions of the previous meetings and endorsed the new leadership of the KPD. Zinoviev gave one of his last public speeches before falling from grace, and thus it was not him but rather Stalin who was elected to be the new chair of the German Commission of the ECCI, although he had only a rudimentary knowledge of the German language. The dismissed leaders, in particular Fischer and Maslow, were depicted as proponents of 'anti-communism'.[70] Ruth Fischer was able to return to Berlin only 'after a stiff fight' for her passport.[71] Shortly after her return she and Maslow, who had been released from prison, were denounced as 'renegades' and expelled from the KPD on 19 August 1926.[72]

Ruth Fischer's tragic mistake was to underestimate Stalin and the Stalinists completely. She did not realise that Stalin only needed party activists like her to remove his critics from the KPD and the Comintern. After Ruth Fischer had done this duty, she was worthless to him. Bolshevisation meant the destruction of internal party democracy; Stalinisation – the process that followed – meant the slavish subordination of the party to the short-term needs of Stalin's policies. Ruth Fischer turned out to be a suitable tool for Bolshevisation, but was totally unsuited for the tasks that were bound with Stalinisation. She and the circle around her had to be replaced by others. Thälmann's victory documented, in its essence, Stalin's dominance over the KPD after his own victory over Zinoviev in the Soviet Union. With Fischer's departure, the key positions in the party passed from intellectuals to men of proletarian origin. This had the double advantage, as Walter Laqueur pointed out: 'of making the party more attractive to the masses and its leaders easier for the Comintern to manipulate'.[73]

Notes

1. Geoff Eley, *Forging Democracy: The History of the Left in Europe, 1850-2000*, Oxford: Oxford University Press, 2002, p228.
2. For biographical introductions see Peter Lübbe (ed.), *Ruth Fischer – Arkadij Maslow: Abtrünnig wider Willen. Aus Reden und Manuskripten des Exils*, Munich: Oldenbourg, 1990, pp1-48; Sabine Hering and Kurt Schilde (eds), *Kampfname Ruth Fischer: Wandlungen einer deutschen Kommunistin*, Frankfurt-Main: dipa, 1995, pp7-75. See also two unpublished studies: Mathilde Montagnon, 'Ruth Fischer 1895-1961: Itinéraire d'une communiste oppositionnelle', Grenoble: Université Pierre Mendès-France,

Institut d'Etudes Politiques, 1998; Toralf Reinhardt, 'Zur politischen Biographie Ruth Fischers (Elfriede Friedländers) in den Jahren 1913-1941, unter besonderer Berücksichtigung ihrer frauenpolitischen Aktivitäten und Vorstellungen in den Jahren 1915-1925', Diplomarbeit, Leipzig: Pädagogische Hochschule, 1992. Most valuable are Fischer's 'Autobiographical Notes' (1944), published in *Abtrünnig wider Willen*, pp442-477. Lübbe's documentation is largely based on Fischer's papers that are deposed at Houghton Library, Harvard University, Cambridge, MA. The collection is bMS Ger 204 (henceforth: Ruth Fischer Papers). For my own wider publications, see Mario Kessler, *Ruth Fischer: Ein Leben mit und gegen Kommunisten (1895-1961)*, Cologne: Böhlau, 2013. A short version can be found as: *Communism – For and Against: The Political Itineraries of Ruth Fischer (1895-1961)*, Berlin: Trafo-Wissenschaftsverlag, 2013. See also *idem*, 'Ruth Fischer: Communist and Anti-Communist Between Europe and America, 1895-1961', in *Logos. A Journal of Modern Society and Culture*, 11, 4, 2012, http://logosjournal.com/2012/spring-summer_kessler/.
3. See Ronald Friedmann, *Ulbrichts Rundfunkmann: Eine Gerhart-Eisler-Biographie*, Berlin: Edition Ost, 2007, pp18-19.
4. See Elfriede Friedländer, *Sexualethik des Kommunismus: Eine prinzipielle Studie*, Vienna: Neue Erde, 1920.
5. Between 14 November and 24 December 1918, Fischer was briefly arrested for her communist activities, see *Abtrünnig wider Willen*, p446.
6. See Fischer, *Abtrünnig wider Willen*, p443; *idem*, 'Westentaschenrevolution in Wien', in *Heute* [Vienna], 1 April 1961, p4; see also Hans Hautmann, *Die Anfänge der linksradikalen Bewegung und der Kommunistischen Partei Deutschösterreichs 1916-1919*, Vienna: Europaverlag, 1970, pp38-39.
7. Albert S. Lindemann, *A History of European Socialism*, New Haven: Yale University Press, 1983, p213.
8. See Hautmann, *Anfänge der linksradikalen Bewegung*, p123.
9. Fischer had visited Radek at the end of 1919, while he was arrested and imprisoned in Germany. She also had good connections to Willi Münzenberg, who was responsible for communist propaganda work. See *Abtrünnig wider Willen*, pp450-451.
10. See Ruth Fischer, *Stalin and German Communism: A Study in the Origins of the State Party*, Cambridge, Mass.: Harvard University Press, 1948, pp144-146. The party soon reverted to using the name KPD.
11. Maslow's murder in Havana, Cuba, was a pivotal point in Ruth Fischer's movement from anti-Stalinism to anti-communism, a position from which she subsequently distanced herself in the 1950s. See Kessler, *Ruth Fischer*, passim.
12. On Maslow see Mario Kessler, *Sektierer, Lernender und Märtyrer: Arkadij Maslow (1891-1940)*. Pankower Vorträge 179, Berlin: Helle Panke, 2013.
13. See Sigrid Koch-Baumgarten, *Der Aufstand der Avantgarde: Die Märzaktion der KPD 1921*, Frankfurt-Main: Campus, 1986.

14. Fischer, *Abtrünnig wider Willen*, p454.
15. *Bericht über die Verhandlungen des 2. Parteitags der Kommunistischen Partei Deutschlands (Sektion der Kommunistischen Internationale), abgehalten in Jena vom 22. bis 26. August 1921*, Berlin: V.I.V.A., 1922, pp175-181.
16. See V. I. Lenin, 'A Letter to the German Communists', *idem, Collected Works*, Vol. 32, Moscow: Progress Publishers, 1970, pp512-523; *Die Tätigkeit der Exekutive und des Präsidiums des Exekutivkomitees der Kommunistischen Internationale vom 13. Juli 1921 bis 1. Februar 1922*, Petrograd and Moscow: Verlag der Kommunistischen Internationale, 1922, pp108-19. See also Ben Fowkes, *Communism in Germany Under the Weimar Republic*, London: Macmillan, 1984, pp74-79; Klaus Kinner, *Der deutsche Kommunismus: Selbstverständnis und Realität*, Vol. 1: *Die Weimarer Zeit*, Berlin: Karl Dietz, 1999, pp42-50, who characterises policy during this period as like a pendulum swinging 'between fundamental opposition and *realpolitik*'.
17. For the Schlageter affair, see Robert G. L. Waite, *Vanguard of Nazism: The Free Corps Movement in Postwar Germany 1918-1923*, New York: W. W. Norton, 1969, pp233-238; Nigel H. Jones, *Hitler's Heralds: The Story of the Freikorps, 1918-1923*, New York: Dorset Press, 1992, pp227-229.
18. *Protokoll der Konferenz der Erweiterten Exekutive der Kommunistischen Internationale (Moskau, 12.-23. Juni 1923)*, Hamburg: Carl Hoym, 1923, pp240-245.
19. Ruth Fischer, as quoted in *Die Rote Fahne*, 29 June 1923.
20. Ruth Fischer, as quoted in *Vorwärts*, 22 August 1923. The article conceded that Fischer had urged her audience to consider the activities of non-Jewish capitalists as well, but it castigated her for using demagogic language to attract anti-Semitic elements to the KPD. See also Donald L. Niewyk, *Socialist, Anti-Semite and Jew: German Social Democracy Confronts the Problem of Anti-Semitism, 1918-1933*, Baton Rouge: Louisiana State University Press, 1971, pp65-66.
21. Fischer, *Stalin and German Communism*, p283.
22. For context, see Mario Kessler, 'Die KPD und der Antisemitismus in der Weimarer Republik', in *idem, Vom bürgerlichen Zeitalter zur Globalisierung: Beiträge zur Geschichte der Arbeiterbewegung*, Berlin: Trafo Verlag, 2005, pp47-62.
23. Quoted in Pierre Broué, *The German Revolution 1917-1923*, Chicago: Haymarket Books, 2006, p702.
24. On the formation of the Proletarian Hundreds, see James M. Diehl, *Paramilitary Politics in Weimar Germany*, Bloomington and London: Indiana University Press, 1977, pp133-136.
25. Bernhard H. Bayerlein and Hermann Weber (eds), *Deutscher Oktober 1923: Ein Revolutionsplan und sein Scheitern*, Berlin: Aufbau Verlag, 2003, p359.
26. See Harald Jentsch, 'Der KP-Aufstandsversuch in Hamburg', *Junge Welt*,

23 January 2004. See also, *idem*, *Die KPD und der 'Deutsche Oktober' 1923*, Rostock: Verlag Ingo Koch, 2005.
27. See Donald W. Bryce, 'The Reich Government versus Saxony, 1923: The Decision to Intervene', *Central European History*, 10, 2, 1977, pp112-147; Hans-Joachim Krusch, *Linksregierungen im Visier: Reichsexekutive 1923*, Schkeuditz: GNN, 1998.
28. For details, see Kinner, *Der deutsche Kommunismus*, pp67-71.
29. For details see Jens Becker, Theodor Bergmann and Alexander Vatlin (eds), *Das erste Tribunal: Das Moskauer Parteiverfahren gegen Brandler, Thalheimer und Radek*, Mainz: Decaton, 1993.
30. Zinoviev's undated letter (written in November or December 1923) is quoted in Jane Degras (ed.), *The Communist International, 1919-1943: Documents*, Part II, Oxford: Oxford University Press, 1960, p65.
31. See *Die Lehren der deutschen Ereignisse: Das Präsidium des Exekutivkomitees der Kommunistischen Internationale zur deutschen Frage, Januar 1924*, Hamburg: Carl Hoym, 1924, pp38, 47.
32. *Ibid.*, pp48-57.
33. For this shift to the left on regional and local levels see Hermann Weber, *Die Wandlung des deutschen Kommunismus: Die Stalinisierung der KPD in der Weimarer Republik*, Vol. 1, Frankfurt-Main: E.V.A., 1969, pp54-62.
34. *Internationale Pressekorrespondenz*, No.22, 18 February 1924, p242.
35. *Referentenmaterial für die Berichterstattung über den 9. Parteitag der KPD* [undated], p4, cited in Weber, *Wandlung*, p65.
36. *Bericht über die Verhandlungen des IX. Parteitages der Kommunistischen Partei Deutschlands (Sektion der Kommunistischen Internationale), abgehalten in Frankfurt-Main vom 7. bis 10. April 1924*, Berlin: V.I.V.A., 1924, p370.
37. *Ibid.*, p334.
38. For the rise and fall of the Left within the KPD see, most convincingly, Marcel Bois, *Kommunisten gegen Hitler und Stalin: Die linke Opposition der KPD in der Weimarer Republik – Eine Gesamtdarstellung*, Essen: Klartext-Verlag, 2014. On Scholem see Ralf Hoffrogge, *A Jewish Communist in Weimar Germany. The Life of Werner Scholem (1895-1940)*, Leiden: Brill, 2017; Mirjam Zadoff, *Der rote Hiob: Das Leben des Werner Scholem*, Munich: Hanser, 2014.
39. Mario Kessler, *Arthur Rosenberg: Ein Historiker im Zeitalter der Katastrophen (1889-1943)*, Cologne: Böhlau, 2003.
40. See the session of the *Zentrale*, 23 May 1924, in Stiftung Archiv der Parteien und Massenorganisationen der DDR im Bundesarchiv (SAPMO), RY 1/I 2/2/16, Bl.110.
41. See her reports in: 'Einige Fragen der englischen Arbeiterbewegung', *Die Internationale*, 7, 10/11, 1924, S.356-60; 'Zum V. Weltkongress: Einige Fragen der englischen Arbeiterbewegung', *Der Funke*, 9/10, 15 June 1924.
42. See Weber, *Die Wandlung*, pp74-81.

43. See Ossip K. Flechtheim, *Die KPD in der Weimarer Republik*, Frankfurt-Main: E.V.A., 1976 [1948], pp208-210.
44. Johannes Fischart, 'Neue Politikerköpfe, IV: Ruth Fischer', in *Die Weltbühne*, 8 May 1924, S.620.
45. *Verhandlungen des Reichstages: II. Wahlperiode 1924*, 381, 1924, S.43-44.
46. *Verhandlungen des Reichstages: III. Wahlperiode 1925*, 384, 1925, S.827.
47. In this committee, Fischer's linguistic skills were undoubtedly helpful, as she was fluent in English and French.
48. Zinoviev's letter to the KPD *Zentrale*, 26 February 1924, in SAPMO, RY 16/10/5, Bl.87.
49. For the international context see, e. g., Yvonne Thron and Mario Kessler, 'Entscheidung für den Stalinismus? Die Bolschewisierung in KPD und Komintern', in Theodor Bergmann and Mario Kessler (eds), *Aufstieg und Zerfall der Komintern: Studien zur Geschichte ihrer Transformation (1919-1943)*, Mainz: Diskurs, 1992, pp85-94.
50. *Thesen und Resolutionen des V. Weltkongresses der Kommunistischen Internationale*, Hamburg: Carl Hoym, 1924, pp25-26.
51. *Protokoll: V. Kongress der Kommunistischen Internationale*, Vol. 1, Hamburg: Carl Hoym, [n.d.], p193.
52. Isaac Deutscher, *The Prophet Unarmed: Trotsky, 1921-1929*, London, New York and Toronto: Oxford University Press, 1959, p146.
53. *Thesen und Resolutionen des V. Weltkongresses der Kommunistischen Internationale*, p18.
54. In 1944, Fischer wrote that she had agreed to the demands of the ECCI to withdraw Thälmann as candidate and it was Thälmann himself who refused to withdraw. See *Abtrünnig wider Willen*, S.459.
55. Friedrich Stampfer, *Die 14 Jahre der ersten deutschen Republik*, Offenbach: Bollwerk-Verlag, 1947, p453.
56. See *Die monarchistische Gefahr und die Taktik der KPD*, Berlin: V.I.V.A., 1925, pp66-67.
57. See Ruth Fischer, 'Eberts Nachfolger heißt Hindenburg', in *Die Rote Fahne*, 28 May 1925.
58. For details see Flechtheim, *Die KPD in der Weimarer Republik*, pp205-11.
59. *Protokoll: V. Kongress der Kommunistischen Internationale*, Vol. 2, p54.
60. For these statements, see SAPMO, RY 1/I 2/3/65, Bl.5-8.
61. See *Bericht über die Verhandlungen des X. Parteitages der Kommunistischen Partei Deutschlands (Sektion der Kommunistischen Internationale), abgehalten in Berlin vom 12. bis 17. Juli 1925*, Berlin: V.I.V.A., 1925, pp167-177.
62. *Ibid.*, p176.
63. *Ibid.*, p515.
64. See Fischer's own interpretation in her *Stalin and German Communism*, pp439-42. See also, for example, Franz Borkenau, *World Communism: A History of the Communist International*, Ann Arbor: University of Michigan Press, 1962, pp60-61; Kinner, *Der deutsche Kommunismus*, pp85-86.

65. For the meeting, see SAPMO, RY 5/I 6/10/57; see also the reports in *Die Rote Fahne*, 26 September–3 October 1926; *Der neue Kurs: Reden der Genossen Bucharin und Sinowjew*, Berlin: V.I.V.A., 1925.
66. The 'Open Letter' was written on 20 August and published in *Die Rote Fahne* on 1 September 1925.
67. Fischer, *Stalin and German Communism*, p451; for her later recollections, see also *Abtrünnig wider Willen*, p460.
68. The conference proceedings were published in *Die Rote Fahne*, 3 and 4 November 1925.
69. She later recalled: 'But in fact, I was a state prisoner in the Hotel Lux, on Tverskaya Street in Moscow, under [close] supervision of the GPU, a situation which I quickly began to grasp', see *Abtrünnig wider Willen*, p460.
70. See *Protokoll der Erweiterten Exekutive der Kommunistischen Internationale, 17. Februar bis 15. März 1926*, Hamburg and Berlin: Carl Hoym, 1926, p507.
71. Fischer, *Abtrünnig wider Willen*, p461.
72. *Die Rote Fahne*, 20 August 1926.
73. Walter Laqueur, *Weimar: A Cultural History 1918-1933*, London: Phoenix Press, 2000, p51.

The Rise of Ernst Thälmann and the Hamburg Left, 1921-1923

Norman LaPorte[1]

JUST AS RUTH Fischer's leadership came to represent the Bolshevisation of the KPD,[2] Ernst Thälmann is remembered as the agent of its 'Stalinisation'. After years of endemic factional feuding, which worsened after the 'failed October' of 1923, and after an ill-fated palace coup in 1928 had tried to oust him, Stalin and Molotov intervened directly in the KPD's internal affairs to restore Thälmann as party chairman. It was at this point that Stalin announced, 'now I have the German Party in my hands'.[3] The fate of those who wanted to contest the Soviet leader's policies was sealed, and Thälmann was presented as the 'public face' and front-man of German communism, in a quasi-cult of leadership.[4] The image of Thälmann as a principal German architect of the 'party of a new type' was reinforced by the hagiographic accounts of his political life in the German Democratic Republic until the collapse of communism in 1989, in contrast to West German accounts of him being no more that Stalin's satrap.[5] Yet, this institutional, top-down way of remembering Thälmann overlooks his early location within a mass movement and ignores how domestic political developments took him from local activism to becoming the leader of the largest communist party outside Soviet Russia.

This chapter will argue that, in the early years of the KPD, Thälmann was not merely a figurehead giving 'proletarian legitimacy' to a cohort of younger, often foreign-born, middle-class intellectuals who were new to the labour movement and impatient with the older, more cautious leadership associated Heinrich Brandler and Ernst Meyer.[6] Instead, we will see below how Thälmann was an able communist politician who expressed the views of an ultra-radical minority in the Hamburg workers' movement and, disappointed with the role of social democracy, looked to Soviet Russia as an alternative to the failing Weimar Republic.

Political Socialisation

Thälmann was born into an upwardly-mobile lower middle-class family on 18 April 1886.[7] His parents, after some setbacks, ran a successful grocery and delivery business in Hamburg's docklands. Politically, his father was a member of *völkisch* political and cultural organisations and his mother was devoutly religious. However, rather than accept this life, Thälmann asserted his adult independence by leaving home, at sixteen years of age, in 1902. After some years of casual work and subsequently finding employment as a coachman in the docks he worked his passage to America as a stoker on board the freightliner *Amerika*. After spending time as a rural labourer near New York, he returned to Hamburg and the docks in 1907, resuming his political activism.

Thälmann joined the Social Democratic Party in 1903 and the transport workers' union the following year. Before the outbreak of war, he had risen to positions of local prominence; by 1914, he was the chairman of a local branch of the Hamburg SPD and headed the coachman's section of the transport workers' union in Hamburg. Between 1912 and 1922, he was a delegate to the union's national congresses and sat on the Hamburg Trades Council. As reports compiled by the political police detail,[8] he already stood on the far left of the workers' movement: he called for industrial militancy and opposed the 'reformists' in the central union and party bureaucracy who opted for compromise. He also championed street protests, aiming to give a public presence to parliamentary demands for reform of the Prussian three-class electoral franchise, which limited workers' representation.[9]

Although personally opposed to the 'imperialist war', Thälmann fought on the Western Front from January 1915 until the armistice in November 1918. The experience of 'total war' was brutalising and, in political terms, reinforced his hostility to the SPD leadership. The leadership had supported the war effort and, as the Kaiserreich fell, it acted with the officers of the old army to suppress workers' radicalism during the German Revolution.[10] As the then Hamburg-based Communist Curt Geyer observed, during 1919 and 1920 the rapid rise and radicalisation of the Independent Social Democratic Party in industrial areas was fuelled by the SPD's lack of socialist reforms, and its supporters looked to Moscow to inspire a second, socialist revolution.[11] In this milieu, Thälmann was able to represent a general political mood and to influence its development.

At the Unification Congress between the Left USPD and the KPD in December 1920, Thälmann was appointed to the *Zentralausschuss* – which represented the party's district organisations – and was elected chairman of the party in Hamburg, which had its stronghold in the city's docks. From the outset, Thälmann stood on the KPD's intransigent, ultra-radical wing and presented himself as an authentic voice of the German proletariat.

The Origins of the Hamburg Left

With some 14,000 members in 1922, Greater Hamburg – which was organised within the party district of Wasserkante – was one of the KPD's local strongholds.[12] Its radicalism was shown during the so-called 'March Action' of 1921, when Hamburg was the only major city outside of central Germany to join the uprising.[13] The outcome of what amounted to a communist putsch produced an acrimonious feud within the party. Some party leaders, most notably Heinrich Brandler and Ernst Meyer, now supported the Communist International's (Comintern) 'united front' policy, as detailed by Florian Wilde in this volume. Thälmann, however, did not. At the Third Congress of the Comintern in the summer of 1921 and at the ensuring KPD Congress in Jena, he represented the Left's continued adherence to a policy anticipating imminent revolution, opposing even tactical co-operation with the leadership of the Social Democratic Party. However, unlike in Berlin, leftists in the Wasserkante party leadership, including most notably Thälmann and Hugo Urbahns, submitted to what the Comintern termed 'international discipline' and, into the second half of 1922, set out to put the policy into practice.[14]

At this time, Thälmann presented the 'united front' as a means of strengthening the KPD for the next revolutionary 'offensive'. At various meetings of party officials and activists in early 1922, for example, he reminded those assembled that, after the disastrous impact of the ill-fated 'March Uprising', the 'united front' policy had revived the party's campaigning, increased the membership and allowed the KPD to become a strong minority in the workforce.[15] In the shipyards, Thälmann worked with Hans von Borstel, a railway worker and senior figure in the Hamburg party, to win over Social Democratic workers by pursuing a more vigorous defence of pay and conditions than their own leadership; the outcome was the KPD taking ninety-two of the shipyard's 148 works councillors in 1922.[16] Similarly, at public meetings organised to show solidarity with Soviet Russia, which also attracted Social Democrats, Thälmann moved resolutions in support of the Comintern's 'united front' policy. These meetings were drenched in an atmosphere of loyalty to the Bolsheviks, with collections for 'Aid for Soviet Russia' and the omnipresence of the symbols of the communist movement, from Soviet flags and banners and the singing of revolutionary songs to speeches by international guests from France, Italy and Britain, as well as Russian sailors passing through the harbour. Thälmann's famously theatrical speeches aimed to serve this cause fully.[17]

However, the Hamburg KPD was increasingly aware of mounting hostility to the 'united front' among party activists and officials. At one meeting, an official stated that the full-time, salaried party leadership had become divorced from rank-and-file workers, who did not want co-operation with the SPD, however tactically, and especially not in parliament.[18] Another party official opposed the Comintern's slogan 'To the Masses', stating that, 'A thousand good members who are loyal to their principles are worth 100,000 wavering comrades'.[19] Party activists even organised a protest rally in the hope of influencing the leadership before the Fourth World Congress of the Comintern met at the end of 1922.[20] Already in the spring of 1922, Thälmann had informed a meeting of the district leadership that local officials and rank-and-file members feared the 'united front' was leading to 'reformism'.[21]

The 'Monarchists Danger'

The issue making the KPD's stance towards the Weimar Republic and its self-proclaimed 'party of state', the SPD, acute was the vast upsurge in far-right 'nationalist' violence against the new political regime and the labour movement.[22] The wave of attacks hit Hamburg in May 1922. A memorial to the German Revolution was bombed, the offices of the KPD press and the Comintern publisher, Hoym, suffered arson attacks, a hand grenade exploded outside the Thälmann's family home, and other prominent local Communists received death threats.[23] In line with the 'united front' policy, Thälmann called on the SPD in the city parliament, the *Bürgerschaft*, to act against the forces of monarchism by banning their highly public commemorations of battles and regimental days and purging them from all state offices.[24] The Hamburg SPD, however, rejected the KPD 'united front' offer and refused to take legal action against these public shows of anti-republicanism.[25]

However, precisely this issue returned at the national level with the assassination of Foreign Minister, Walther Rathenau on 24 June, by the Organisation Consul – a secret organisation of former army offers. In the minds of the *völkisch* Right, Rathenau – as a politician 'fulfilling' the demands of the Versailles Treaty, an intellectual, and a Jew – was a symbolic hate figure. For the workers' movement, however, the assassination brought about a rare moment of spontaneous cooperation in many localities, including Hamburg and Berlin.[26] Under Ernst Meyer's leadership, a joint declaration was signed with the Social Democratic parties and unions, the 'Berlin Agreement', which foresaw making common cause against the enemies of the Republic.[27] However, following a letter from Zinoviev to the KPD leadership on 28 June, which insisted on maintaining 'independence of agitation', the party ended the most significant 'united front' action since the general strike against the Kapp-Lüttwitz Putsch in March 1920, which had attempted to sweep away the new democracy.[28] When the Reichstag voted for the 'Law for the Protection of the Republic' on 18 July, the KPD's parliamentary fraction now voted against it, arguing – not without some reason – that this was a weapon against communism.[29]

Crystallisation of the German Left Opposition

The outcome of the 'Rathenau campaign' ended Thälmann's attempts to implement the 'united front' policy and links between the Berlin and Hamburg Lefts were now formalised. Not only had the SPD refused to co-operate with the KPD, but the Security Police in Hamburg – which was headed by a Social Democrat – had opened fire on workers leaving a mass rally in the city's Heiligengeistfeld on

26 June. Thälmann now stated that the SPD had 'only ever left the KPD in the lurch since the November Revolution' and this meant any negotiations with the party's leadership were futile.[30] At the following meeting of the Zentralausschuss he stated that, 'the [Hamburg] party [...] could not understand why Rathenau was the best friend of the broad masses'.[31] After some initial hesitation, Urbahns also opted to join the Left Opposition, whose views he represented at the Fourth World Congress of the Comintern.[32]

At the Comintern Congress, the Bolsheviks' Germany expert, Karl Radek, supported Heinrich Brandler – who now replaced Meyer as party chairman – in advocating the continued pursuit of the 'united front' tactic, including calls for 'workers' governments' (i.e. parliamentary coalitions with left-wing Social Democrats).[33] Zinoviev, the chairman of the Executive Committee of the Communist International, however, supported the KPD's Left, conspicuously endorsing Ruth Fischer when she stated that Communists should 'not [have] ra[u]n behind the corpse of Rathenau shouting "republic, republic"'.[34] When the KPD leadership defended the 'united front' at the December meeting of the *Zentralausschuss*, Thälmann was able to point out that, '[in Moscow] the leading personalities had such different views on the united front that Brandler cannot claim the party has a united position'.[35]

The Year 1923

Between the Comintern Congress and the KPD's Reich Congress, the situation in Germany had escalated. On 11 January 1923, French and Belgian troops occupied the Ruhr after the Cuno government defaulted on reparations payments. Yet the Congress majority, under Brandler, voted down the Left's call for a debate on the political situation and the tasks of the party. This was recognised as an attempt to challenge the party majority's 'Thesis on the United Front and Workers' Governments', which reaffirmed the 'correctness' of the Comintern's 'united front' policy – or, at least, Radek's interpretation of it.[36] However, the exclusion of the Left – which dominated Berlin, Hamburg and wide sections of the now occupied industrial areas of the Ruhr and Rhineland – brought the KPD close to a party split in the course of 1923.

The core of the Left Opposition's critique was that the 'united front' policy merely awakened workers' 'democratic illusions', weakened their revolutionary élan, and pushed the party towards reformism as represented by the Social Democracy.[37] As Ruth Fischer stated, the Left did not want to negotiate with Social Democratic parliamentarians; instead, it called on Communists to push all 'current mass movements' towards revolution from below – the party 'must be active, it must act' not just make propaganda.[38] At the Party Congress in Leipzig, Thälmann had stated that negotiating with the SPD leadership during the Rathenau campaign had been a 'hindrance for the revolutionary development of the proletariat', especially the Reich leadership's readiness to sign a joint public declaration.[39]

In response to Brandler's statements, Thälmann insisted that the Left's hostility to the SPD 'does not come from intellectuals, but is born of our inner recognition of the [position of the] working class which, in the four years since the German Revolution, has registered vast distrust of the SPD as a workers' party'.[40] The party's efforts, he insisted, should focus on mobilising the workforce in the factories against the occupation of the Ruhr. On the vexed issue of 'workers' governments', Thälmann drew applause for his insistence that Communist ministers would be thrown out of any 'workers' government' at the first opportunity: 'They can only survive when [...] the workforce is already clear that they can counter the dictatorship of the bourgeoisie with their own dictatorship'.[41]

A report on the Congress sent to Edwin Hoernle, who was the party's representative to the ECCI in Moscow, emphasised that the KPD was dangerously divided along regional as well as political lines. It noted how, in its strongholds, the Left was propelled forward by a 'mood of revolutionary impatience' which was fuelled by rank-and-file hostility towards the 'betrayals' of the SPD since the German Revolution. In Saxony, Thuringia, and Halle-Merseburg, by contrast, the Brander leadership had proved able to use the 'united front' tactic in order to 'unleash strong activity' and there was the possibility of negotiating with regional SPD leaders in order to enter, or 'tolerate', 'workers' governments'.[42] Despite considerable pressure from Moscow – including leading Bolsheviks attending meetings in Berlin, such as Nikolai Bukharin in February – Brandler refused to recognise that the Left had deep roots in the membership of important districts and could not be dismissed as merely the machinations of intellectuals such as Ruth Fischer in Berlin.[43]

As the Left had been excluded from the national leadership, its leaders did not feel obliged to implement official policy locally. Throughout January and February 1923, both Thälmann and Urbahns spoke at meetings of party members and officials to promote the Left's tactics, which were endorsed at a District Party Congress in Hamburg in mid-February. The party rejected co-operation in regional parliaments with the SPD as a means of mobilising the workforce and, instead, called for a nationwide congress of works councils, which would serve as an 'alternative government' (*Nebenregierung*).[44] In the *Bürgerschaft*, the KPD attacked the SPD for supporting Chancellor Cuno's policy of 'passive resistance' and organising collections to help pay for the strikes in the Ruhr. The Communist deputy, Ernst Franke, called this a 'swindle of a national united front'.[45] On the streets too, Hamburg's SPD politicians anxiously observed an upsurge in support for the Communists. As mass unemployment hit the city, these workers turned to the KPD-led 'Committees of the Unemployed', despite the trade unions' best efforts to prevent this.[46]

In the context of a mounting crisis in the occupied areas, the Left aimed to maximise its influence.[47] Together with Ruth Fischer, Thälmann used his factional contacts with Eugen Eppstein, the political secretary of the Left-dominated Middle Rhine (*Mittelrhein*) party branch,[48] to speak at a District Party Congress in Rhineland-Westphalia North, which convened in Essen on 25 March. Although the national leadership (*Zentrale*) won the vote by a slim margin, the strength of the Left in the occupied areas had prompted the ECCI to send Radek to Essen in order to make it clear that, if there was an uprising in the Rhine and Ruhr, Moscow would disavow it.[49]

Violent unrest in the region was becoming increasingly common. The best known incident was the so-called 'Mühlheim rising' in mid-April, when price rises led to protests by relief workers (*Notstandsarbeiter*) and the unemployed which escalated into armed clashes with the authorities in which six protesters were shot dead by police.[50] After the Essen Congress, Thälmann, who had spent five days travelling around the occupied region witnessing similar events, reported that there was overwhelming support for the Left's policies among local officials in Hamborn, Essen, Dortmund and Gelsenkirchen.[51]

Already in April, the feud in the KPD and the extent of support for the policies of the Left in the occupied areas prompted party officials on the 'moderate' left to write an official letter to Zinoviev. They stressed that the Left Opposition's demand for an extraordinary party congress to discuss policy would only paralyse campaigning of any sort, while also warning that Brandler's intention to use 'organisational measures' (i.e. imposing central control over oppositional districts) would only 'tie the left workers even more to the extreme groups'.[52]

As the Comintern's efforts to bridge the growing gulf within the KPD during early 1923 ultimately came to nothing,[53] Zinoviev summoned the feuding factions to attend a conference with the ECCI in Moscow. In essence, the outcome was that, in exchange for agreeing not to take their radical agitation outside their own districts, the Left would receive four seats in the KPD's leadership. Fischer, Arkadi Maslow, Arthur König and Thälmann now sat at the top table of German communism.[54] As we will discuss below, Thälmann was then able to play a prominent role in the plans for the 'German October'.

Communism, German Nationalism and the Franco-Belgian Occupation

Before the ECCI adopted a plan for revolution, however, the KPD was forced to address the rise of the nascent fascist movement. The occupation of the Ruhr had driven a process of political radicalisation and polarisation throughout Germany. Widespread strikes, hunger riots and rocketing unemployment undermined the SPD and their bedrock of support in the trade unions, to the advantage of the KPD, which at this point almost certainly became the majority party within the workers' movement.[55]

However, the impact of the Franco-Belgian occupation produced an even greater surge on the far right. At the Fourth Congress of the Comintern, fascism as an international phenomenon was added to the agenda, following Mussolini's 'March on Rome' in October 1922, but no systematic policy was formulated.[56] In practice, there were three responses. One was to hold an 'International Antifascist Congress' in Frankfurt-am-Main in March 1923, which proved unable to win support beyond the communist movement. Another approach was to meet violence with violence, whereby workers' defence was organised by the party's recently founded paramilitary organisation, the Proletarian Hundreds, and 'anti-fascist' shows of strength were staged locally and nationally.[57] It was, however, the third approach which was by far the most controversial and amounted to extending the 'united front' to rank-and-file members of proto-fascist organisations. The means to this end was *de facto* nationalist propaganda, which had been debated in the party since the beginning of 1923 and which now culminated in Radek's 'Schlageter Speech' to the ECCI in June. It did enormous reputational damage to the KPD as an 'antifascist' party'.[58] But, as Ralf Hoffrogge discussed above, not every member of the party's Left participated in the campaign.[59] In Hamburg, Thälmann advocated the confrontational approach towards the far right on the streets and his local party organisation participated in the national 'Antifascist Day' on 29 July.[60] Despite a ban on outdoor demonstration imposed by the SPD-led Senate in the *Bürgerschaft*, several thousand Hamburg Communists attended a rally at the city's Heiligengeistfeld.[61]

The 'German October'

In late July, what amounted to a wait-and-see approach was superseded by a policy of preparing for the 'German October'.[62] On 9 August, after the ECCI had received reports detailing the depth of the revolutionary crisis in Germany, Stalin convened a meeting of the Russian Politburo. Then, on 12 September, the Cuno government fell – and with it the policy of resisting the Franco-Belgian occupation – amidst a wave of strikes in which the KPD had played a significant role.[63] The 'German October' now seemed to be a real possibility, even reviving hopes of world revolution.[64]

At the series of meetings which ensued, the Russian Politburo drew up a plan for revolution and then, in the forum provided by the ECCI, consulted the French and Czechoslovakian parties, in addition to the KPD leadership, to which Thälmann now belonged.[65] At one of the secret sessions in late September, the French delegate, Cachin, expressed anxieties about how a de facto alliance with German nationalism in a 'revolutionary war' against France would impact on his party's supporters.[66] Trotsky's reply was that, 'It is too early for sleepless nights over the Ruhr. The point is to firstly take power in Germany [...] everything else will derive from that'.[67]

The Ruhr, however, was not to be to the launch pad for the 'German October'; revolution was to be ignited using the 'united front' tactic in central Germany.[68] According to Moscow's plan, the KPD would enter 'workers' governments' in Saxony and Thuringia. These were the locations where the party had 'tolerated' left SPD administrations throughout 1923, enabling the Proletarian Hundreds – which were to fight as armed units in the anticipated civil war – to operate legally at a time when they were banned by the right SPD-led Prussian government. A general strike with left SPD support would then be declared and this would signal the armed uprising.[69]

Yet, even now, differences over tactics continued to shape the responses of the KPD leadership. During the discussions in Moscow, Thälmann expressed reservations about the revolutionary potential of Brandler's 'united front' policy. He spoke against Brandler's assessment of the influence of the left SPD and the likelihood of their supporters coming over to the side of revolution, and he questioned the value of entering regional Diets in order to procure arms. The latter was the key issue. While Brandler had stated that there were 250,000 men organised in the Proletarian Hundreds, Thälmann stressed that they were largely unarmed and, thus, militarily useless. The success of the German revolution would, therefore, depend on Soviet intervention.[70] In early October, shortly before his return to Hamburg, Thälmann concluded: 'The party is not ideologically and politically prepared for the most important matter of the revolution, the civil war'.[71]

Initially, developments proceeded without complication as the KPD entered the Saxon and Thuringian governments in mid-October.[72] Then, on 20 October, the new Reich government under Chancellor Gustav Stresemann, which included SPD Ministers, declared a state of emergency, passed political power to the military and dispatched troops into central Germany to depose these 'workers' governments'. The KPD and its Soviet advisers, who had relocated to Dresden, were left to improvise a response in a fast-moving and unanticipated situation. That evening, the leadership and its Soviet advisors resolved to use a meeting between Communist and left SPD activists, which was scheduled for the following day, ostensibly to identify the level of support for a general strike protesting the actions of the Reich government. Their actual aim was to assess the readiness of the proletariat for the German revolution. But the outcome of the so-called 'Chemnitz Conference' was negative. Speaking for the SPD, the Saxon Minister of Labour, Georg Graupe, refused to countenance an immediate general strike and, instead, proposed setting up a commission of both parties to decide on what action to take.[73] This, according to the

KPD's leading theoretician, August Thalheimer, gave the revolution a 'third-class funeral'.⁷⁴

The Hamburg Rising

Despite Thälmann's reservations in Moscow about the prospects for a successful 'German October', the only attempted uprising in 1923 took place in Hamburg.⁷⁵ It was based on an initially effective military-technical plan, especially when compared with the uncoordinated 'March Rising' of 1921, and took the city's police force by surprise – despite the KPD's public trumpeting of the coming revolution.⁷⁶ At 5am on 23 October, members of the party's *Ordnerdienst* – the militarily-trained inner core of the Proletarian Hundreds – stormed police stations in the city's suburbs, rapidly overpowering seventeen of twenty-six of them, in order to seize firearms. These units then took up position on rooftops, inside buildings and behind barricades. At the same time, Combat Groups (*Kampfgruppen*) had gone into the night with the intention of obstructing the arrival of reinforcements by blocking arterial roads and intercity railway lines, cutting telephone cables and dividing the city by occupying bridges over the river Alster. The expectation was that once the city's working-class suburbs had been taken, the insurgents would move on the city centre in concentric circles, drawing with them wider popular support.⁷⁷ After returning from Moscow in early October, Thälmann's was main role was political: he was responsibility for the agitation which aimed to bring about a mass movement.⁷⁸

Over the course of almost three days, the Hamburg KPD – with limited numbers of firearms and at most a few hundred insurgents – fought a losing battle against some 6000 well-armed members of the city's police, which drew on military reinforcements, and 800 members of the SPD's combat organisation, *Republik*.⁷⁹ By the end of the uprising, more than 100 were dead, seventeen of them police officers, and several hundred more – many of them passersby – were wounded.⁸⁰ Had the Hamburg KPD not carried out the leadership's order to 'retreat', there would have been a massacre of party activists.⁸¹

Although there had been significant support for the rising among the residents of Eimsbüttel, Barmbek, and Schiffbek – which marked the epicentre of events – it remained a putsch without wider support in the workforce, even in the giant shipyards.⁸² A dockers' strike, which began on 20 October, resolved the following day to call a general strike when workers became aware that the military had been sent into central Germany, but this was stalled by the SPD-led trade-union leadership in Hamburg. The KPD's support in the local unions and the high levels of animosity towards the actions of the SPD Ministers in the Reich government had not turned into support for revolution.[83]

Despite the more recent availability of secret communist documentation – in addition to police records and party circulars – it remains very much easier to reconstruct the specific events that took place than the internal-party dynamics that allowed them to happen.[84] The most likely interpretation is that it grew out of a confusion of central and local party responses to a series of unanticipated circumstance. Since the fall of the Cuno government in September, the KPD had been placed on a nationwide state of readiness for the German revolution.[85] In early October, a political committee was set up in Wasserkante, in which Urbahns was the political leader, (probably) Gustav Faber was responsible for organisation, and Rudolf Hommes liaised with the Military-Political Directorate (*Oberleitung*) responsible for north-western Germany. The latter was headed by Albert Schreiner and his Soviet military advisor, General Moishe Stern.[86] Urbahns then travelled to the Chemnitz Conference as the district's representative. However, in the expectation that the left SPD would adopt Brandler's call for a general strike, some twenty-five to thirty couriers were dispatched nationwide with the message that the uprising was anticipated to take place no later than Tuesday 23 October.[87] Hermann Remmele was the courier sent to Kiel – the port town which began the November Revolution five years before – in order to investigate reports that it offered the best prospects for widening the revolution. But he stopped in Hamburg for talks with the regional military and political leadership. Here, he was persuaded that Hamburg presented the better option and, laying too much emphasis on the likelihood of a resolution in support of a general strike in Saxony, stressed that the party must be ready to 'launch the attack' within 'one or two days'.[88] Remmele then travelled on to Kiel, where he received the telegram to postpone events. In Hamburg, confusion reigned: the uprising was launched in the belief that that military intervention against the 'workers' governments' in central Germany and the strike in the docks marked the moment to begin, and once launched, the uprising was not so easy to call off, especially after the party's military units had gone underground.[89]

A number of accounts attribute personal responsibility to Thälmann for this bloody fiasco, as he was the highest official present at the time the decision was taken.[90] His motivation is explained in terms of a lust for political power: expunging the competition of party rivals, above all Hugo Urbahns.[91] Yet, none of the documentation states more than his political involvement in events – and these were events clearly under the command of the party's military-technical apparatus and its Soviet advisors.[92] At a meeting of the leadership held in Berlin as the rising was still underway in Hamburg, the topic was not any breach of discipline by Thälmann and the Hamburg leadership, but rather whether some form of assistance should be given to them. The final decision, in the words of the Solomon Lozovsky, who chaired the meeting, was: 'If one does not come to the aid of Hamburg that is not a betrayal. We sacrifice a division to save an army'.[93]

Conclusion

During the KPD's 'Years of Struggle' (Angress), Thälmann had risen from being a regional to a national communist leader. This had been facilitated by his solid support within a radical workers' milieu, which was centred on the Hamburg docks, and on his political alliance with the Berlin Left around Ruth Fischer, Arkadi Maslow, Werner Scholem, and their proletarian supporters. In 1924, they came to power in the KPD leadership in a grass-roots surge of support for their policies of revolutionary intransigence and outright hostility to Social Democracy. Ironically, however, the 'failed October' had ended Moscow's residual hopes in the imminence of world revolution and Stalin announced the policy of 'socialism in one country'.[94]

Events in Germany became entwined with the power struggle in Moscow to succeed Lenin and to push aside Trotsky, which meant avoiding all blame for the 'October fiasco'. Zinoviev – who had drawn up the plan for revolution – now accused the Brandler leadership of entering into a 'banal parliamentary combination' with the SPD in Saxony and, in a private letter to the KPD leadership, chastised him for the alleged 'miscommunication' that led to the Hamburg rising.[95] But, if the Comintern was able to oust Brandler, whose support in the

KPD evaporated, it was not yet able to dominate the German communist movement and its leadership. Moscow had hoped to support the so-called 'Centre Group', which had broken with the 'old' leadership but remained avowedly 'loyal' to Comintern policy. But this failed.[96] At the party's Reich Congress in April 1924, the Left now had the support of ninety-two of the 126 delegates – leaving the 'Brandler Group' without any representation.[97]

Thälmann's ability to trade on his credentials as a revolutionary worker helped him to rise and rise in the KPD. In the course of 1924, he became deputy chairman of the party, chairman of the League of Red Front Fighters – which superseded the Proletarian Hundreds – and was the party's candidate in the presidential elections of spring 1925.[98] By the mid-1920s, he was by far Germany's best known Communist. But it was the ECCI that enabled him to become party chairman in September 1925, following a direct and highly public intervention to oust the Fischer-Maslow leadership.[99] From this time, a quasi-cult of leadership was constructed around Thälmann which resonated with the party's core supporters, who identified with the former transport worker from the Hamburg docks who looked and spoke like them.[100] Only now was his role in the 'Hamburg Rising' highlighted in a narrative that presented him as one of those in the party who were prepared to fight, even against the odds, and would ultimately win against all of the party's enemies.[101] An agent of Stalinisation in the party, as Ruth Fischer had been an agent of Bolshevisation, by the end of the decade Thälmann only had the trappings of political power – which was now instead ultimately in Stalin's hands.

Notes

1. The author would like to thank Marcus Schönewald for discussing the KPD in detail and providing some valuable documents. The funding which made this chapter possible is thanks to the British Academy grant: SG47136.
2. See the chapter in this volume by Mario Kessler.
3. Bernhard H. Bayerlein, 'Ernst Thälmann. Vom "Fall" zur Parabel des Stalinismus', in *idem* and Hermann Weber (eds), *Der Thälmann-Skandal. Geheime Korrespondenzen mit Stalin*, Berlin: Aufbau, 2003, pp58-59.
4. Rosa Levine-Meyer, *Inside German Communism: Memoirs of Party Life in the Weimar Republic*, London: Pluto, p154.

5. On the political uses of Thälmann's biography in East Germany, see Russell Lemmon, *Hitler's Rival. Ernst Thälmann in Myth and Memory*, Lexington: University of Kentucky Press, pp277-310; see also Herman Weber, 'Das schwankende Thälmann-Bild', in Peter Monteath (ed.), *Ernst Thälmann. Mensch und Mythos*, Amsterdam: Editions Rodopi, 1994, pp7-15.
6. Werner T. Angress, *Stillborn Revolution. The Communist Bid for Power in Germany 1921-23*, Princeton: Princeton University Press, 1963, pp203f, 254; see also Pierre Broué, *The German Revolution 1917-1923*, Chicago: Haymarket Books, 2005, p702 and note 13; Otto Wenzel, *1923. Die Gescheiterte Deutsche Oktoberrevolution*, Münster: Lit Verlag, 2004, p44.
7. For valuable biographical sketches, see Hermann Weber and Andreas Herbst, *Deutsche Kommunisten. Biographisches Handbuch 1918 bis 1945*, Berlin: Dietz, 2008, pp782-85; Roland Sassning, *Rückblick auf Ernst Thälmann. Der Umgang dem KPD-Führer im Widerstreit der Meinung*, Jena: Rosa-Luxemburg-Stiftung, 2006, pp22ff; Aleksandr Vatlin, 'Ernst Thälmann', in Silvio Pons and Robert Service, *Twentieth Century Communism*, Princeton: University of Princeton Press, 2012, pp792-94.
8. For reports on Thälmann's political activities before 1914, see Staatsarchiv Hamburg [henceforth: StaH], 'Politische Polizei', Bd.1-2, V 236, 3.
9. Norman LaPorte, 'Ernst Thälmann: The Making of a German Communist, 1886-1921', in *Moving the Social*, 51, 2014, p134.
10. *Ibid.*, pp130-35.
11. Curt Geyer, *Die revolutionäre Illusion: Zur Geschichte des linken Flügels der USPD*, Stuttgart: Deutsche Verlags-Anstalt, 1976, p195.
12. Angelika Voß, 'Der "Hamburger Aufstand" im Oktober 1923', in Angelika Voß, Ursula Büttner and Hermann Weber (eds), *Vom Hamburger Aufstand zur politischen Isolierung. Kommunistische Politik 1923-1933 in Hamburg und im Deutschen Reich*, Hamburg: Landeszentrale für politische Bildung, 1983, p24
13. Sigrid Koch-Baumgarten, *Aufstand der Avantgarde: Die Märzaktion der KPD 1921*, Frankfurt: Campus, 1986, pp157ff.
14. On the vexed relationship between Thälmann and Urbahns, see Marcel Bois, 'Thälmanns Gegenspieler: Hugo Urbahns in der frühen Hamburger KPD', in *Jahrbuch für Historische Kommunismusforschung*, Berlin: Aufbau, 2016, pp217-33.
15. See, for example, 'Aus der KPD, 18.5.1922', in StaH, Polizeibehörde I, 331-1, I, 898, Bl.173-74; 'Außerordentliche Mitgliederversammlung der Ortsgruppe Hamburg, 13.1.1922', in *ibid.*, Bl.24.
16. Richard A. Comfort, *Revolutionary Hamburg. Labour Politics in the Early Weimar Republic*, Stanford: Stanford University Press, 1966, p116; on Borstel, see Herbst and Weber, *Deutsche Kommunisten*, p115.
17. See, for example, 'Aus der KPD, 12.4.1922', in StaH, Polizeibehörde I, 331-1, I, 898, Bl.112-13.

18. 'Aus der KPD, 15.3.1922', in *ibid.*, Bl.72.
19. 'Lagebericht, 19.2.1922', in *ibid.*, Bl.39.
20. *Ibid.*, Bl.40.
21. 'Aus der KPD, 15.3.1922', in *ibid.*, Bl.73.
22. For an overview of these events, including assassinations of local labour leaders, see Heinrich August Winkler, *Von der revolution zur Stabilisierung. Arbeiter und Arbeiterbewegung, 1918 bis 1924*, Bonn: Dietz, 1984, pp426-28.
23. Helmut Ebeling, 'Hamburgische Kriminalgeschichte 1919-1945. Eine Stoffsammlung aus der Tagespresse. Band I (1919-1930)', Hamburg, Manuscript, 1961, in StAH, 731-1, 603, Bd. 3, p155.
24. 'Stenographische Berichte über die Sitzungen der Bürgerschaft zu Hamburg, Sitzung 27, 14.6.1922', pp667-68; see also *ibid.*, '29 Sitzung, 28.6.1922', p730.
25. On the SPD-led coalition in Hamburg, see Voß, 'Hamburger Aufstand', p24.
26. Winkler, *Von der Revolution*, p427.
27. See the chapter by Florian Wilde above.
28. Wolf-Dietrich Gutjahr, *Revolution muss sein. Karl Radek – die Biographie*, Cologne: Böhlau, 2012, pp543-44.
29. Klaus Kinner, *Der deutsche Kommunismus. Selbstverständnis und Realität*, Berlin: Dietz, 1999, p48; Ben Fowkes, *Communism in Germany under the Weimar Republic*, London: Macmillan, 1984, p82.
30. 'Bericht Nr.36, 3.7.1922', in StaH, Politische Polizei, V 236, Bd.3, Bl.238-39.
31. '5. Tagung des Zentralausschusses der KPD, 15-16.10.1922', in Stiftung Archiv der Parteien und Massenorganisationen der DDR (SAPMO), Bl.195-96.
32. *Bericht über den IV Kongress der Kommunistischen Internationale*, Hamburg, 1923, p91.
33. Gutjahr, *Radek*, p531; Marie-Louise Goldbach, *Karl Radek und die deutsch-sowjetischen Beziehungen 1918-23*, Bonn: Dietz, 1973, pp112ff.
34. John Riddell (ed. and translation), *Towards the United Front. Proceedings of the Fourth Congress of the Communist International*, 1922, Amsterdam: Brill, 2014, pp8-9.
35. '5. Tagung des Zentralausschusses der KPD, 15-16.10.1922', Bl.230-31.
36. The 'united front' section of the Comintern's theses on tactics went through more drafts than any other text, see Riddell, *Towards the United Front*, p20.
37. Angress, *Stillborn Revolution*, pp260-73.
38. Ruth Fischer, 'Der Kampf um die Kommunistische Partei', in *Die Internationale*, 3, 1 February 1923, pp.87-96.
39. *Bericht über den Verhandlungen der 8. Parteitag 1923*, Hamburg, 1923, pp289-90.

40. *Ibid.*, p375.
41. *Ibid.*
42. Heinz Möller, 'Bericht über den Leipziger Parteitag der KPD und die Lage in der deutechen Partei', [February 1923], in SAPMO, RY 5/I 6/3/425, Bl. 79-80.
43. 'Protokoll der Polbürositzung vom 22.2.1923', in SAPMO, RY 1/I 2/3/3, Bl.52.
44. 'Protokoll der BLS vom 12.1.1923', in RY 1/I 3/16/16, Bl. 9; see also, Möller, 'Bericht über den Leipziger Parteitag', *op. cit.*
45. Voβ, 'Hamburger-Aufstand', p28.
46. Comfort, *Revolutionary Hamburg*, p121.
47. Angress, *Stillborn Revolution*, pp306-8.
48. Wenzel, *1923*, pp71-72; Weber and Herbst, *Deutsche Kommunisten*, p119.
49. Winkler, *Von der Revolution*, p564; Broué, *German Revolution*, pp701-4
50. Wenzel, *1923*, p89.
51. 'Konferenz des Präsidiums des E.K. der KI mit der Delegation der KPD über die innere Lage der deutschen Partei. 4 Sitzungen, 1. 27.4.1923 (vormittags)', in SAPMO, RY 5/I 6/3/67, Bl.84-91; see also Edward H. Carr, *The Interregnum 1923-24*, London: Macmillan, 1965, p163
52. Arthur Ewert, Hans Pfeiffer, Gerhart, Hans Neumann, 'An die Exekutive der Komintern, z.H. des Genossen Sinowjew, Moskau, Berlin, den 8ten April 1923', in SAPMO, RY 5/I 6/3/125, Bl.12-15. These party leaders had broken with the Left Opposition after the Leipzig Congress, see Hermann Weber, *Wandlung des deutschen Kommunismus. Die Stalinisierung der KPD in der Weimarer Republik*, Frankfurt: Europäische Verlag, 1969, p48.
53. For the role the Comintern's emissaries Eugen Varga and Rakosi at meetings in Berlin, see 'Konferenz des Präsidiums des E.K. der KI mit der Delegation der KPD', *op. cit.*, esp. Bl.143, 175.
54. Gutjahr, *Radek*, pp566f.
55. Hermann Weber, 'Zum Verhältnis von Komintern, Sowjetstaat und KPD', in Bernhard H. Bayerlein *et al* (eds), *Deutschland, Russland, Kommintern. Neue Perspektiven auf die Geschichte der KPD und die Deusch-Russischen Beziehungen* (1918-1943), Berlin: De Gruyter, 2014, p46.
56. Riddell, *Towards the United Front*, p19.
57. On the role of the Proletarian Hundreds, see Dirk Schumann, *Political Violence in the Weimar Republic 1918-1923*, New York: Berghahn, 2001, pp115ff; James M. Diehl, *Paramilitary Politics in Weimar Germany*, Bloomington: Indiana University Press, 1978, pp116ff.
58. Gutjahr, *Radek*, pp569ff.
59. Radek made no secret of the policy serving the defence of Soviet Russia, see *idem*, *Der Kampf der Kominterns gegen Versailles und gegen die Offensive des Kapitals*, Hamburg, 1923, esp. pp28ff; See also Goldbach, *Radek*, pp199ff.

60. Eberhard Czichon and Heinz Mahron, *Thälmann. Ein Report*, Berlin: Wiljo Heinen, 2010, p150 and note 283.
61. Voβ, 'Hamburger Aufstand', p15.
62. The documentation of these key events has been published, see Bernhard H. Bayerlein *et al* (eds), *Deutsche Oktober 1923. Ein Revolutionsplan und sein Scheitern*, Berlin: Aufbau, 2003.
63. Wenzel, *1923*, pp164ff; on the efforts to coordinate Soviet foreign policy and the 'united front' tactic in Germany, see Goldbach, *Radek*, pp116ff.
64. Friedrich Firsov, 'Ein Oktober, der nicht stattfand. Die revolutionaren Pläne der RKP(B) und der Komintern', in Bayerlein *et al* (eds), *Deutscher Oktober*, p39.
65. Thälmann travelled to Moscow with Brandler in late August, see Jens Becker, *Heinrich Brandler. Eine politische Biographie*, Hamburg: VSA, 2001, p223.
66. 'Protokoll der Geheimen Moskauer Konferenz der russischen Mitglieder der Exekutiv mit der Delegation der KPD, der KP Frankreichs und der KP der Tschechoslovakia', 25 September 1923, in Bayerlein *et al* (eds), *Deutscher Oktober*, p171.
67. *Ibid.*, p166.
68. For details, see the chapter by Mario Kessler.
69. Norman LaPorte, *The German Communist Party in Saxony, 1924-1933*, Oxford: Peter Lang, 2003, pp62ff; Wenzel, *1923*, p47.
70. 'Protokoll der zweiten Sitzung der russischen Mitglieder des Exekutiv der Komintern mit den Delegationen der Kommunistischen Parteien Deutschlands, Frankreichs under der Tschechoslowakei', cited in Firsov, 'Ein Oktober', pp44-45 and note 34.
71. 'Protokoll der Sitzung der Delegation der Zentrale der KPD und der Delegation der Berliner Bezirksleitung mit den russischen Mitgliedern des Exekutivkomitees der Komintern', 2 October 1923, cited in Bayerlein *et al* (eds), *Deutscher Oktober*, p193.
72. For a valuable summary, see Harald Jentsch, '"Deutsche Oktober" 1923 und "Brandlerismus" in der KPD', in Simone Barck and Ulla Plener (eds), *Verrat. Die Arbeiterbewegung zwischen Trauma und Trauer*, Berlin: Dietz, 2009, pp67-83.
73. For a valuable report on events as reported in the SPD's central organ, *Vorwärts*, on 23 October, see Ben Fowkes (trans. and intro.), *The German Left and the Weimar Republic. A Selection of Documents*, Leiden: Brill, pp94-95.
74. August Thalheimer, *Eine Verpaβte Revolution*, Berlin: Hoym, 1931, p26.
75. The classic account remains Angress, *Stillborn Revolution*, pp444ff; see also Comfort, *Revolutionary Hamburg*, 120ff; for accounts which integrate new archival material, see Wenzel, *1923*, pp248-56; Harald Jentsch, *Die KPD und der 'Deutsche Oktober' 1923*, Rostock: Ingo Koch, 2005, pp237-44; Bernhard H. Bayerlein, 'Geschichtsmythos Hamburger Aufstand

- Thälmann und das Ende einer Ursprungslegende', in *International Newsletter of Communist Studies*, X, 17, 2004, pp45-48; for a valuable overview, see Heinrich August Winkler, *Von der Revolution*, pp653-54.
76. Voß, 'Hamburger Aufstand', p39; Weber, *Wandlung*, p50; Larry Peterson, 'A Social Analysis of KPD Supporters: The Hamburg Insurrectionaries of October 1923', *International Review of Social History* 28, 2, 1983, p206.
77. Voß, 'Hamburger Aufstand', pp10-15; from the KPD's perspective, see Valdemar Roze [Military head of the KPD's *Zentrale*], 'Bericht über den Hamburger Aufstand', 26 October 1923, in Bayerlein *et al* (eds), *Deutscher Oktober*, pp248-51; from the perspective of the Social Democratic head of the Hamburg police, see Lothar Danner, *Ordnungspolizei Hamburg. Betrachtungen zu ihrer Geschichte 1918–1933*, Hamburg: Verlag Deutsche Polizei, 1958, pp63-131; a collection of local press reports can be found in Bundesarchiv, Berlin, 1507/2913.
78. Voß, 'Hamburger Aufstand', p19; Czichon and Mahron, *Thälmann: Ein Report*, pp157-62.
79. For a discussion of the varying estimates of Communist fighters and arms, see Wenzel, *1923*, p253.
80. 'Bericht über die Unruhen vom 20-26 Oktober 1923', 6 November 1923, in StaH, Polizeibehörde I, 331/I, 903, Bl.24f.
81. 'Wilhelm Pieck to Clara Zetkin', 6 November 1923, in Bayerlein *et al* (eds), *Deutscher Oktober*, p333.
82. Hans-Ulrich Ledewig, *Arbeiterbewegung und Aufstand. Eine Untersuchung zum Verhalten der Arbeiterparteien in den Aufstandsbewegungen der frühen Weimarer Republik*, Husum: Matthiesen Verlag, 1978, pp210-11.
83. Peterson, 'KPD Supporters', p239.
84. For a discussion of the internal party documentation, see Bayerlein, 'Geschichtsmythos'; on the extent of contradictory information, see Angress, *Stillborn Revolution*, pp444ff.
85. Ledewig, *Arbeiterbewegung und Aufstand*, p207; Winker, *Von der Revolution*, pp653-54.
86. Jentsch, *Deutscher Oktober*, pp240-41.
87. Alexander Lozovsky, 'Bericht über die Lage in Deutschland', 26 October 1923, in Bayerlein *et al* (eds), *Deutscher Oktober*, pp257-59.
88. 'Pieck to Zetkin', *op. cit.*, pp332-33.
89. See Jakob Walcher, '1923', unpublished manuscript, in SAPMO, NY 4087/25, Bl.235f. This is Walcher's view, who was one of the few party leaders to remain loyal to Brandler after these events; see also 'Pieck to Zetkin', pp332-33; Roze, 'Hamburger Aufstand', p248; Lozovsky, 'Bericht über die Lage in Deutschland', p258.
90. For a discussion of the literature, see Bayerlein, 'Geschichtsmythos'.
91. Joachim Paschen, *'Wenn Hamburg Brennt, brennt die Welt'. Der Kommunistische Griff nach der Macht im Oktober 1923*, Bern: Peter Lange, 2010, esp. pp.235-37; Armin Fuhrer, *Ernst Thälmann. Soldat*

des Proletariats, Munich: Olzog, 2011, pp108ff; see also Wolfgang Zank, '"Deutscher Oktober" 1923 an der Alster: ein blutiger Reinfall – Unbekannte Briefe und Berichte zum Putschversuch der Hamburger Kommunisten', in *Die Zeit* 22 October 1923: http://www.zeit.de/1993/43/aufstand-an-der-waterkant.
92. From the police perspective, see Danner, *Ordnungspolizei*, p73.
93. Lozowsky, 'Bericht über die Lage in Deutschland', p261.
94. Kinner, *Der deutsche Kommunismus*, pp62-63.
95. Zinoviev, 'Geschlossener Brief an die Zentrale der KPD, 23.11.1923', Bl.22-26, in SAPMO, RY 5/I 6/3/116, Bl. 23
96. Weber, 'Vorwort', in Bayerlein *et al* (eds), *Deutscher Oktober*, pp28-29.
97. *Ibid.*
98. Weber and Herbst, *Deutsche Kommunisten*, p784.
99. For the text of the ECCI's 'Open Letter', see Fowkes, *Weimar Left*, pp190-94.
100. Gerd Reuter, *KPD-Politik in der Weimarer Republik. Politische Vorstellung und soziale Zusammenstellung der KPD der KPD in Hannover zur Zeit der Weimarer Republik*, Hannover: SOAK-Verlag, 1982, pp95-98.
101. Norman LaPorte and Kevin Morgan, '"Kings among their subjects"? Ernst Thälmann, Harry Pollitt and the Leadership Cult as Stalinization', in Norman LaPorte, Kevin Morgan and Matthew Worley (eds), *Bolshevism, Stalinism and the Comintern. Perspectives on Stalinization, 1917-53*, Basingstoke: Palgrave Macmillan, 2008, pp124-45.

Opposing Hitler and Stalin: Left Wing Communists after Expulsion from the KPD

Marcel Bois

JOSEPH STALIN WAS stunned. 'These people', he wrote, 'are hooligan agitators against the Comintern and the Soviet Communist Party – against our Soviet state'.[1] The leadership of the German party was also shocked. It was an 'anti-Bolshevik diatribe', 'criminal divisiveness',[2] and an 'attack on party unity'.[3]

Their outrage was in response to a statement that had been published in September 1926 by nearly 700 opposition officials in the Communist Party of Germany.[4] It said that, 'Until now, the Central Committee of the KPD has believed that the situation within the party and the Comintern could be overcome by organisational means. But the contradictions have never been so acute. The Opposition no longer has any access at all to the party press.' They called for an open discussion within the party, above all about the situation in the Soviet Union, under the slogan 'Back to Lenin and to Real, Pure Leninism'.[5]

In fact, the KPD was confronted with a serious crisis in 1926. Numerous groups had formed in rebellion against the leadership's political line and they all regarded themselves as belonging to the party's left wing. These included the tendency articulated in Karl Korsch's *Kommunistische Politik*, the all-but forgotten 'Wedding Opposition', and the group around Ruth Fischer and Hugo Urbahns.[6] Contrary to frequent assertions, these groups were by no means small sects of intellectuals. Rather, at least by the mid 1920s, they represented a not-insignificant section of the communist base. Even according to conservative estimates, more than 20,000 KPD members considered themselves part of these left opposition groups, including numerous representatives to the national and state parliaments.[7] The ratio of workers to intellectuals in these groups was comparable to that within the KPD at large.[8]

This left wing around Ruth Fischer, Werner Scholem and Arkadi Maslow held the leadership of the party from 1924. Then, in 1925, Moscow intervened to have them removed after the disastrous presidential election, when their refusal to run a joint candidate with the SPD handed victory to the monarchist Hindenburg. Along with a rejection of Stalinism, criticism of 'united front' politics remained a constant among members of the KPD's left wing. Some of these groups only changed their stance and called for extra-parliamentary cooperation with the SPD once the Nazi Party threatened to take power in the early 1930s.[9] This chapter will examine the development of the left wing of the KPD from 1925, detailing their gradual expulsion from the party, and the difficulties of finding a political strategy between left-wing radicalism and an anti-fascist 'united front'.

The Rise of Stalinism

One reason for the uproar among these opposition groups had its roots in Soviet Russia. Communists were aware that socialism could only be achieved if their 1917 revolution were to spread to other, economically advanced countries. Although a wave of strikes, demonstrations, and factory occupations washed over the European continent immediately after the First World War,[10] ultimately not a single socialist revolution succeeded anywhere. It was clear by the time of the failed communist uprising during the 'German October' of 1923 that civil war-wracked Soviet Russia would remain isolated.[11]

As the Soviet working class quickly lost political influence of any kind, the party bureaucracy became the new socially dominant stratum. Stalin, as its representative, became the leader of the state and the party. His programme proclaimed 'socialism in one country', and the subsequent programme of industrialisation was so vast that it reminded Victor Serge of 'the pages of *Capital* where Marx describes the relentless mechanism of primitive capitalist accumulation'.[12] In pursuing this policy, Stalin also annulled many of the revolution's achievements. Within a few years, he perverted Russian socialism into its opposite: workers were now exploited, dissenters were placed in labour camps, and dissident Communists were politically persecuted.

Stalin's rise in the 1920s was accompanied by a fierce factional struggle within the Communist Party of the Soviet Union (CPSU). The Stalin faction's main adversary was the 'United Opposition', which was formed in the spring of 1926 by an alliance between Lev Kamenev, Grigory Zinoviev, Leon Trotsky, and many other 'old Bolsheviks'. They criticised the party and state bureaucracy, calling for a reinforced workers' democracy and a form of industrialisation that would improve the people's social situation. They also opposed Stalin's thesis that it is possible to establish socialism in a single (economically backward) country.[13]

Stalinisation of the KPD and the Comintern

In Germany, the opposition referred to these criticisms when they published their statement in September 1926. Accordingly, it was entitled: 'Statement on the Russian Question'. At the same time, they also criticised the erosion of democracy in the KPD, a development which similarly had its origins in Moscow.

In the Soviet Union, Stalin was carrying out a policy that contradicted everything his party originally stood for; to do so, communist traditions were eliminated. This was achieved in part through the Stalin faction's increasing tendency to transform Marxism into dogma. Marx's writings were separated from their historical background and phrases were re-contextualised to explain current policy. Stalin and his supporters also removed personnel from the party, placed the old guard in camps, drove them into exile, or, later, even physically annihilated them.

At the same time, Stalin was also trying to bring the communist parties abroad into line. Sooner or later, they all underwent a transformation that historians now call Stalinisation.[14] This meant that they became increasingly dependent on Moscow, both materially and ideologically, and they ceased to be democratic organisations that engaged in debates, becoming instead bureaucratised. In the words of historians Kevin McDermott and Jeremy Agnew, even the Communist International (Comintern) changed 'from an idealistic relatively pluralist body of enthusiastic revolutionaries into a stiflingly bureaucratised mouthpiece for the Soviet state'.[15] By the end of the 1920s, the process was complete: 'advisers, emissaries, ultimately even inspectors and commissars replaced substantive debate with the demands of international solidarity'.[16] Grigory Zinoviev, the first chairman of the Comintern, was replaced in 1926 because of his opposition to Stalin. The same fate befell Nikolai Bukharin in 1929. His successors, Dmitry Manuilsky and Georgi Dimitrov, were nothing more than Stalin's 'willing executors'.[17]

The Stalinist transformation was particularly rapid within the KPD.[18] During its early phase the KPD was still a democratic party that was open to discussion. Members met regularly, the Opposition was able to stake out positions in every organisation, and controversial issues were debated in the party press. Otto Wenzel's assessment was that even in 1923 'fully free debate prevailed. Criticism of all decisions by party headquarters was allowed'.[19] It was also not the least bit unusual for the leadership to be in the minority during disputes. One prominent example was when Rosa Luxemburg was outvoted at the founding congress on the question of whether the KPD should participate in the elections to the National Assembly in January 1919.

Under the Fischer leadership from 1924, as Mario Kessler's chapter discussed, the party began a process of 'Bolshevisation', which included the creation of centralist structures. Ironically, the Left itself soon fell victim to this development and was removed from leadership in late 1926, then expelled from the KPD altogether.[20] A significant reason for this was that the leaders of the Left pursued a course that was independent of Moscow, despite their support for Bolshevisation. It was only under the leadership of Ernst Thälmann in the second half of the 1920s that the KPD began to orient itself, without significant opposition, to the Stalinised CPSU, and thus towards a strictly hierarchical organisation with military-style discipline. It was a culture that contrasted starkly with the party's early years. The formation of party factions was forbidden in 1925, debate was largely prohibited, and conflicts were not 'resolved' politically but rather organisationally – through expulsions. Thälmann's Central Committee banned critics from speaking or summarily removed them from the party. Overall, the membership and leadership underwent an enormous turnover. For example, by 1929 only two of the sixteen officials who had been top-ranking in 1923 and 1924 were still in the *Politbüro*; no fewer than eleven had been expelled.[21]

As in the Soviet Union, this bloodletting led to an ideological ossification. Political positions within the KPD became increasingly dogmatic or, in the words of historian Sigrid Koch-Baumgarten, the

Soviet Union was 'stylised as the holy land and Marx, Engels, and Lenin [...] as founders of a religion'.[22] Hermann Weber stated that Thälmann became 'as the *infallible leader* a German copy of Stalin'.[23]

Left Opposition to Stalinisation

Left Communists rebelled against this process. They fought back against bureaucraticisation and advocated a return to the 'old KPD'. Despite their heterogeneity, this resolute opposition to Stalinisation united all left-wing groups. As the 'Letter of the 700' makes clear, they also espoused a fundamental critique of the developments in the Soviet Union. On this point, they differed from, for example, the other major oppositional tendency within the KPD, namely the party's 'right wing' – around Heinrich Brandler and August Thalheimer – which in 1929 founded the Communist Party of Germany (Opposition) (KPO).[24] Although they opposed the KPD's Stalinisation, the new party refrained from criticising the Soviet Union's domestic politics under Stalin for a long time.[25]

The Left published its views in the KPD press and put its positions up for debate at party meetings for as long as it was possible to do so. But opportunities to do so became increasingly infrequent. In this respect, the 'Letter of the 700' was, in a way, the high point in the struggle for the party. Indeed, the leadership felt forced to respond to the Opposition's demand and permitted discussion of the 'Russian Question'. But, at the same time, it also intensified its fight against the Left. As Günter Wernicke wrote, 'The decisive phase of degeneration from what had once been a radical Marxist party to a Stalinised party machine had begun'.[26] Prominent representatives of the Opposition like Hugo Urbahns, Werner Scholem and Anton Grylewicz were expelled in the months that followed. The wave of repression would ultimately reach its height in March 1927 at the KPD's Eleventh Congress in Essen when in the months before, some 1300 officials were expelled, as were entire local branches.

The wave of expulsions forced the oppositional Communists to take more decisive steps. In late 1926, a national conference of the Left elected its own national leadership and passed a resolution to publish a bi-weekly newsletter. In contrast with the increasingly undemocratic party, the Opposition was 'one of the strongholds of political discussion'.[27] In March 1928, the Left finally decided to establish an independent organisation: the *Leninbund*. This was prompted by Zinoviev and Kamenev's 'capitulation' to Stalin and the ensuing collapse of the 'United Opposition' in the Soviet Union. Most of the German opposition was composed of Zinoviev supporters, but, in this instance, they did not follow his lead. Given that they regarded the Soviet Opposition's relative disorganisation as a primary reason for its failure, they instead continued to strive to unite left-wing communists.[28]

153 delegates and approximately 100 guests participated in the founding congress of the *Leninbund* during Easter 1928.[29] Most members of the new organisation came from the KPD, although the majority had already been forced to leave it. Pierre Broué thus describes the *Leninbund* as 'undoubtedly a revolutionary workers' organisation [...] a legitimate child of Spartacus, the left wing of the Independent Social Democratic Party of Germany and the United KPD'.[30] Hermann Weber pointed out that it 'included the most prominent names from all the left opposition groups'.[31] In fact, it had managed to bring together almost all well-known left-wing critics of the KPD. With Fischer, Maslow, Scholem, Urbahns, Paul Schlecht, and Fritz Schimanski, the new organisation included six former members of the Central Committee. Moreover, various representatives to the Reichstag and state parliaments also joined, including Wolfgang Bartels, Gustav Müller, Guido Heym, and Anton Grylewicz. Unfortunately, it is still very difficult to determine precisely how many members the organisation had, but was in the region of 3000 to 6000.[32]

Before the *Leninbund* was founded, its leaders explicitly stated that the organisation would not be a second communist party. However, at Hugo Urbahns's suggestion, the founding congress voted to field a candidate in the forthcoming Reichstag elections. Left Communists had previously debated this question in detail. Fischer and Maslow, for example, spoke resolutely against running an independent slate.[33] Even Trotsky, who had been following the discussion, warned from abroad that, 'Running your own candidates will mean saying that the KPD is no longer communist and down with it. It is a step that will complete the split and will make it impossible to retake the party'.[34]

The 'electoral question' broke the fragile unity of the *Leninbund*. The conflict led Scholem and Max Hesse to leave the organisation just a few weeks after it was founded. They were critical of the fact that, 'A majority guided by entirely apolitical considerations decided to run its own slate in the upcoming elections'. This decision, 'in fact means the formation of a second communist party, although it is clear that there is no possibility or justification for its existence'.[35] The Comintern's renewed 'left turn' in 1928 was also part of the controversy. Scholem and his colleagues hoped that Moscow would now orient itself to the Left's policies of 1924, which would mean rejecting the 'united front' in favour of a directly 'revolutionary' policy.[36] Shortly afterward, the German Zinoviev supporters – Fischer, Maslow, Schlecht, Bruno Mätzchen and Schimanski – also left the *Leninbund*.[37]

Consequently, the last promising attempt in the history of the Weimar Republic to unite the KPD's opposition to Stalinism in a single organisation failed. After that, the *Leninbund* fragmented in four directions: (1) some members remained under the leadership of Hugo Urbahns, but the rump organisation lost important publications, suffered from financial difficulties, and putting up candidates for the Reichstag elections proved to be a fiasco; (2) Fischer and Maslow, among others, reapplied to rejoin the KPD on the terms set out by the Comintern, but only Schimanski was readmitted; (3) other members joined the SPD, notably in the former stronghold of Suhl in Thuringia under Guido Heym, while the daily newspaper, *Volkswille*, also went to the Social Democrats; (4) contacts between the rump *Leninbund* and Trotsky, now in exile, complicated the organisation's development. Differences between Urbahns and Trotsky, over the vexed issue of whether to reform the KPD or create a new party, led to a split. In February 1930, those who supported Trotsky, like Grylewicz and Kurt Landau, were expelled and came together with part of the Wedding Opposition and the Leipzig-based Bolshevik Unity organisation to form the United Left Opposition of the KPD – the first explicit Trotskyist organisation in Germany.[38]

After this new split in 1930, 'the Leninbund, which had struggled with signs of decay since its founding, lost even more significance'.[39] In 1932, the group only had about 500 members.[40] But after a year, the newly established 'United Left Opposition' also disintegrated into two groups, each of which referred to itself as the Left Opposition of the KPD.[41] While both groups did subsequently undergo a certain 'boom', their combined membership of little more than 1000 people kept them far removed from their goal of reforming the KPD – a project that had probably been illusory from the outset. Social Democrat Walter Riest correctly stated in 1932 that, 'These splinter groups will have no influence on the fate of the KPD, to say nothing of the labour movement'.[42]

4. The KPD and Fascism

In the final years of the Weimar Republic, the remaining left-wing Communists focused their attention on fighting the growing fascist movement. Adolf Hitler's NSDAP had been transformed from being an 'irritating fringe element' of Weimar society into a mass party within a few years.[43] The National Socialists had received 2.6 per cent of the vote in 1928, but they entered the Reichstag in 1930 as the second largest faction, with 5.6 million more votes than in the previous election. Two years later they doubled their vote, reaching 37.3 per cent, and becoming the strongest party in the Reichstag. The *Sturmabteilung* – the SA, or Storm Division – their paramilitary organisation, grew to approximately half a million members.

Undoubtedly, this development would be inexplicable without reference to the 1929 world financial crisis, the impact of which was acute in Germany. The crisis bankrupted thousands of companies and impoverished a significant portion of the middle class and the country's farmers. The ranks of the unemployed grew from 1.3 million in 1929 to over 6 million in early 1933. One worker in three was jobless.

This precarious social situation for millions of people spurred on mass political radicalisation, which also benefitted the Communists. Between 1928 and 1932, their votes increased from 3.3 to 6 million and the number of KPD members grew from just under 125,000 in 1929 to 360,000 in 1932.[44] But these successes allowed the KPD leadership to overlook the fact that the National Socialists were the main beneficiaries of the crisis. After winning 2.5 per cent of the vote in the 1930 Reichstag election, the Communists, blinded by hubris, declared themselves the 'only real winner' despite the fact that the NSDAP received more votes.[45] Their error was based on a complete misunderstanding of the danger that the National Socialists presented for the entire German labour movement. Neither the Comintern nor the KPD was in any position to develop a clear definition of the phenomenon of fascism. Instead, the leaders of the KPD applied the term 'fascism' excessively. They saw fascism in power with Hindenburg's presidential cabinets from 1930 onwards.[46] They also regarded all other parliamentary parties as 'fascist': 'The fight against fascism means fighting the SPD as well as Hitler and the parties around [German Chancellor Heinrich] Brüning'.[47] Thälmann's confidant Werner Hirsch believed that it was not the Communists' job 'to look through the distorted lens of any pseudo-theory for a distinction between democracy and fascism'.[48]

The Communists' failure to comprehend the phenomenon of fascism became particularly explicit in what was known as the theory of 'social fascism'. In 1929, at the Comintern's behest, the party leadership began identifying social democracy as its 'main enemy', arguing that it discouraged workers from fighting capitalism. The KPD therefore rejected any collaboration with the SPD, even against the Nazis: 'The social fascists [SPD] know that they share no common ground with us. For us there is only a fight to the death with the party supporting building battleships, the police socialists'.[49]

In fact, there were incidents that made it easier for the KPD leadership to win over the rank and file to the 'social fascism' theory. One of the most symbolically powerful contributions to the growing split within the German labour movement was what became known as 'Bloody May', when in 1929 the Berlin police, under the direction of Social Democrat Karl Friedrich Zörgiebel, shot dozens of Communist demonstrators. But the SPD's policies appeared to support the theory in other ways as well. In the dubious hope of obstructing the National Socialists' route to power and keeping Weimar democracy alive, they pursued a 'lesser evil' policy: they supported the candidacy of archconservative Paul von Hindenburg in the 1932 presidential elections; tolerated Chancellor Heinrich Brüning's authoritarian cabinet, which imposed new taxes, reduced public services, and threatened wage and salary reductions; and sanctioned many decisions that contradicted the SPD political programme.

The KPD, however, was in no position to offer any alternative to those affected by the loss of social services. On the contrary, the fact that its rhetoric was directed primarily against the SPD not only led it to engage in bizarre alliances (in 1931 it supported a referendum initiated by the National Socialists and the German Nationalists against the Prussian state government, which was led by the Social Democrats) but also alienated the masses. Although its 'ultra-left politics brought it a certain degree of success because the desperate army of the unemployed was constantly growing and many radicalised people placed their hopes on the KPD',[50] the party addressed few people outside that circle. Contrary to the hopes of the leadership, 'many of the voters who cast their ballot for the KPD for the first time were not won over from the Social Democrats', as an analysis of the election results shows.[51] The Communists were scarcely more present in the factories. In the autumn of 1932, the ratio of wage labourers in the overall membership was still only 11 per cent.[52] The Communists' 'confusing theory of fascism' did not significantly hamper National Socialism.[53] On the contrary, it contributed to the KPD's decline: the party was banned a few months after Hitler took power. Thousands of party members soon found themselves in the Nazi regime's first concentration camps – side by side with the Social Democrats they had fought against.

Left Opposition to Fascism

Could Hitler have been prevented from taking power? In retrospect, the question seems pointless, but it was of existential importance for many of his contemporaries. At the outset of the 1930s, Germany had one of the strongest labour movements in the world. Millions of people were union members. In the last free elections, the two largest labour parties, the SPD and the KPD, jointly received more votes than the National Socialists.[54] So it seems appropriate that more than a few people placed their hopes in the ability of that movement to block Hitler's path to power. They regarded the general strike against the Kapp Putsch in March 1920, when the far right tried to seize power, as a positive example of how a dictatorship could be prevented.

The remaining left-wing Communists were among those who held this view, but they scarcely made any theoretical contribution of their own to the matter. Instead, they relied heavily on Trotsky's assessments.[55] Trotsky demonstrates remarkable foresight and an astonishing grasp of the situation in Germany – particularly given that he was in exile in Turkey.[56] Journalist Kurt Tucholsky marvelled at the time how: 'Trotsky writes magnificent things that pass through the world's press [...] Recently a Portrait of National Socialism, which is really a masterpiece. Everything – and I mean everything – is in there. Incomprehensible what one can write without living in Germany'.[57]

Contrary to the official Comintern line, Trotsky did not believe that Hitler's National Socialists were a 'creation' of reactionary finance capital.[58] He described fascism as a mass movement that recruited primarily from the petty bourgeoisie (which Trotsky understood as meaning the self-employed, higher-grade white collar workers and civil servants), but also from 'the *Lumpenproletariat* and, in a certain way, even from the proletarian masses'.[59] The crisis had hit the petty bourgeoisie particularly hard and created a sense of disillusionment in its ranks. National Socialism was so appealing to this demographic because it linked demagoguery against big capital with great hostility toward the organised labour movement.

While fascism was not invented by capital, Trotsky saw that capital was nonetheless perfectly willing to support the National Socialists at a moment of enormous social and political polarisation, such as that which prevailed in Germany. And although capital regarded bourgeois democracy as the most favourable form of domination – even with the attendant risk of proletarian revolution – fascism, with its pledge to smash the labour movement, was a palatable alternative. Trotsky compared the bourgeoisie's feeling toward fascism to the way 'a person with a toothache feels about getting their tooth extracted'.[60]

Trotsky therefore regarded the 'social fascism' theory as both incorrect and dangerous, even though he supported the Comintern's thesis that social-democratic politics had paved the way for the fascists. Nonetheless, based on the lessons learned from Italian fascism, he explained that, 'Fascism feeds on social democracy, but it must break its skull in order to achieve power'.[61] He therefore urged the SPD and the KPD, despite all fundamental differences, to work together against the increasingly powerful National Socialists. He believed that both parties were ultimately threatened by fascism in equal measure, writing that, 'Fascism is not just a system of repression, violent action, and police terror. Fascism is a particular state system based on the eradication of all elements of proletarian democracy in bourgeois society'.[62]

He believed it was necessary to pursue 'united front' politics as applied by the Comintern:

> The Communist Party must call for the defence of the material and intellectual positions that the German proletariat has won. That explicitly pertains to the fate of its political organisations, its unions, its newspapers and printing works, its homes, libraries, etc. The Communist worker must say to the Social Democratic worker, 'The politics of our parties are irreconcilable. But if the fascists come

tonight to destroy your organisation's spaces, I will come to your aid with a weapon in my hand. Do you also promise to help if my organisation is threatened?' That is the quintessence of the politics of the current period.[63]

Trotsky's pamphlets were distributed by left-wing German Communists and circulated in numbers that reached five figures.[64] The call for a 'united front' was quite obviously in keeping with a widespread mood among workers and intellectuals. Faced with the National Socialist threat, there was a great desire for unity. That is why, in advance of the July 1932 Reichstag election, 33 public figures addressed an 'urgent appeal' to the SPD and the KPD 'to finally take action to create the united workers' front'. The document was signed by, among others, Albert Einstein, Erich Kästner, Käthe Kollwitz and Heinrich Mann.[65]

SPD and KPD members flouted the ban on collaboration with one another in many localities, as several historical studies have shown in recent years. Joachim Petzold, for example, has analysed reports produced by the Ministry of the Interior during the summer of 1932 and concluded that, 'there were many Communists who wanted to unite with the Social Democrats in the struggle against fascism'. He finds 'the contrast between the party leadership and the rank and file' on this question to be striking.[66]

Thomas Kurz presents similar findings in his work on the supposedly 'hostile brothers in south-western Germany'. According to him, there were also efforts to unite the working class in Baden and Württemberg. In July 1932, for example, the chairman of the Baden SPD offered the Communists a 'party truce': 'The gravity of the moment requires that all that divides us be set aside'.[67] As Hermann Weber has shown, local KPD leaders in Tübingen and in Ebingen in the state of Württemberg made similar overtures to the SPD and the General Federation of German Trade Unions.[68] Klaus-Michael Mallmann demonstrates that there were affiliated SPD and KPD slates in municipal elections in Württemberg as early as December 1931 and in three places candidates even ran on joint lists. Workers' insistence on unity was most clearly articulated in the municipality of Unterreichenbach, Württemberg, where the local KPD branch dissolved and formed a United Workers Party together with the local SPD.[69]

German left-wing Communists likewise worked to build united front committees in the cities where they were active. They were quite successful in places where they were able to act independently of the Stalinised KPD. For example, in Bruchsal, in the state of Baden, where the 'United Left Opposition' was the only communist organisation (much to the chagrin of KPD officials), its members established an anti-fascist action committee with the participation of the local SPD and the union cartel.[70] The newspaper of the Left Opposition, *Permanente Revolution*, reported in December 1931 that:

> The action committee recently held a demonstration against cuts in wage and social welfare and against the looming threat of fascist government terror. The police estimated that roughly 1500 workers were present. This is striking evidence of the correctness of the Left Opposition's tactics given that no party has been able to mobilise such large crowds since 1923.[71]

In Oranienburg near Berlin, Trotskyists were likewise able to create a successful anti-fascist committee – not only with SPD involvement but also with the local KPD. This committee was just as successful and versatile as the action committee in Bruchsal. It organised demonstrations against the National Socialists and formed 'anti-fascist defence units'. It also established committees for the unemployed and factory workers. Moreover, it inspired workers in neighbouring localities, who also established united front committees (sometimes with active support from Oranienburg).[72]

Despite all these efforts, the rigid stance of the SPD and KPD leaderships toward one another dashed all hope of a national alliance. At the same time, the Left Opposition in the early 1930s was far too small to change the KPD's direction. It only succeeded in creating effective united front committees in those places where it was relatively large and its influence rivalled that of the two major workers' parties. This was unthinkable in a large city like Berlin, where it had fifty members to the KPD's 34,000.

The *Leninbund*, which followed a plan similar to that of the United Left Opposition in the fight against fascism, must have had the same experience. It too understood that a 'united front' of the two major workers' parties was imperative if fascism was to be averted. But, at the same time, it attempted to merge with various small left-wing groups into an 'anti-fascism defence organisation'. In March 1931, it established an 'action group against reaction and fascism', which proved to be ineffective. Even later on (now in alliance with the KPO and the Socialist Workers' Party, a left-wing split-off from the SPD), the *Leninbund* was unable to initiate anti-fascist associations that were effective nationwide.[73]

The *Leninbund* changed its strategy following the replacement of the Brüning government by the 'cabinet of barons' under Chancellor Franz von Papen in June 1932. While it had previously relied exclusively upon extra-parliamentary alliances against the rise of the National Socialists, now it was focused on the Reichstag as well. With the slogan 'For the Anti-Fascist Parliament!', left-wing Communists demanded a coalition of all anti-fascist factions. They hoped also to win over some of the non-socialist petty bourgeoisie and Christian workers to that end. In concrete terms, the *Leninbund* envisioned a resuscitation of the Weimar Coalition (made up of the SPD, Centre Party and Democratic Party) with the KPD's 'toleration'. Proposals such as these obviously failed to resonate with the relevant actors, but the leadership of the *Leninbund* did not expect that. It is certainly interesting to consider, however, that the demand for an alliance among all anti-fascist democrats was a kind of forerunner of the 'popular front politics' that the Comintern would pursue starting in the mid-1930s.[74]

Conclusion: *The Failure of the Left*

Left-wing opposition Communists fought to stop the KPD's transformation from a democratic party toward a bureaucratic instrument of Stalinist foreign policy. In the end, they failed. However, there is no single cause that explains that failure. There was instead a cluster of objective and subjective factors that ultimately contributed to their defeat. First and foremost, they had an overwhelmingly powerful adversary that had access to money and a secret service. The leaders of the Comintern recognised early on just how dangerous the left-wing opposition in the largest communist party outside the Soviet Union was – and it acted accordingly. Plans were hatched in Moscow that Thälmann's Central Committee would then execute. The 'divide and conquer' policy that the Soviet leadership recommended in the fight against the opposition was particularly successful. As sources from the KPD party archive show, the KPD leadership always exerted pressure on the ostensibly weakest link and thereby pitted various groups against one another. However, they also encountered obliging adversaries. Fear of expulsion from the party ran extremely high among some members of the opposition and as a result the mere threat was often sufficient to move one group away from another. Intense infighting within the opposition was also a factor. Situations arose again and again in which individual actors put divisive factors before unifying ones.

The fact that some members of the left-wing opposition groupings were also responsible for their party's desolate condition must not go unmentioned. Bolshevisation, meaning strict centralisation and ending internal-party democracy, ultimately began under the leadership of Fischer and Maslow in 1924 and 1925. This meant that the left within the party had created the structures that made it easier for Thälmann subsequently to push them out. But beyond that, it also explains why not all contemporary critics of Stalinisation aligned themselves with the left-wing opposition: to them, Fischer and her comrades simply appeared disingenuous.

The left wing of the KPD also made cooperation more difficult in another way. While it may still have been able to earn sympathy in the mid 1920s for its critique of events in Soviet Russia, it simultaneously repelled many Communists with radical left positions. For example, the left-wing opposition categorically refused to work with the SPD for a long time. Accordingly, in 1926 it considered the KPD-led campaign to expropriate the former imperial German monarchies, the KPD's most successful 'united front' project in the Weimar Republic, to be a mistake. The left therefore distanced itself from rank-and-file members who, while also critical of the way the party was developing, nonetheless supported the leadership's political course.

The left wing of the KPD would later abandon these positions and, under Trotsky's influence, support 'united front' politics. But by then it was too late. In its final years, the Weimar Republic became so politically polarised that it was all but impossible to build a third mass party on the left alongside the SPD and the KPD, as, for example, the *Leninbund* had attempted to do. The rising threat of fascism aligned most of the German working class with one of the two parties – despite all the mistakes they may have made. Under those circumstances, voting for a small, insignificant left-wing party – let alone joining one – looked feasible to a very small number of people.

Translated by Joe Keady

Notes

1. J.V. Stalin, 'Measures for Mitigating the Inner-Party Struggle, Speech Delivered at a Meeting of the Political Bureau of the CC, CPSU(B)', 11 October 1926, in *idem, Collected Works*, 8, Moscow: 2. Foreign Languages Publishing House, 1954, p222.
2. *Die Rote Fahne*, 17 September 1926.
3. 'Beschluss des ZK über die Erklärung zur russischen Frage der Opposition, 16.9.1926', in Stiftung Archiv der Parteien und Massenorganisationen der DDR im Bundesarchiv (SAPMO), RY 1, I 2/3/64, Bl. 500f.
4. Bundesarchiv Berlin (BArch), R 1507/1063g, Bl. 103/04, 106-39.
5. BArch, R 1507/1063g, Bl. 106, 117.
6. Marcel Bois, *Kommunisten gegen Hitler und Stalin. Die linke Opposition der KPD in der Weimarer Republik. Eine Gesamtdarstellung*, Essen: Klartext, 2014; *idem*, 'Vergessene Kommunisten. Die "Weddinger Opposition" der KPD', in *Jahrbuch für Historische Kommunismusforschung* (JHK), 2008, pp58-67; Otto Langels, *Die ultralinke Opposition der KPD in der Weimarer Republik. Zur Geschichte und Theorie der KPD-Opposition (Linke KPD), der Entschiedenen Linken, der Gruppe 'Kommunistische Politik' und des Deutschen Industrie-Verbandes in den Jahren 1924 bis 1928*, Frankfurt: Lang, 1984; Rüdiger Zimmermann, *Der Leninbund. Linke Kommunisten in der Weimarer Republik*, Düsseldorf: Droste, 1978.
7. Bois, *Kommunisten gegen Hitler und Stalin*, p449.
8. For details on the social structure of the KPD left, see Bois, *Kommunisten gegen Hitler und Stalin*, pp396-435.
9. For more on the history of 'united front' politics, see Marcel Bois, 'The Rise and Fall of United Front Politics in the Weimar Republic KPD', in *Historical Materialism* (forthcoming).
10. Marcel Bois and Reiner Tosstorff, '"Ganz Europa ist vom Geist der Revolution erfüllt". Die internationale Protestbewegung am Ende des Ersten Weltkriegs', in Ulla Plener (ed.), *Die Novemberrevolution 1918/19 in Deutschland. Für bürgerliche und sozialistische Demokratie. Allgemeine, regionale und biographische Aspekte*, Berlin: Dietz, 2009, pp41-60; Francis L. Carsten, *Revolution in Central Europe 1918-1919*, Berkeley: University of California Press, 1972; Donny Gluckstein, *The Western Soviets: Workers' Councils versus Parliament 1915-1920*, London: Bookmarks, 1985.

11. For more on the German October, see the essays by Norman LaPorte and Mario Kessler in this volume.
12. Victor Serge, *Destiny of a Revolution*, London: Jarrolds Publishers, 1937, p169.
13. Pierre Broué, 'Zur Geschichte der Linken Opposition (1923-1928)', in Helmut Dahmer *et. al.* (eds), *Leo Trotzki: Schriften, Bd. 3.1: Linke Opposition und IV. Internationale (1923-1926)*, Hamburg: Rasch und Röhrig, 1997, pp9-22.
14. See Norman LaPorte, Kevin Morgan and Matthew Worley (eds), *Bolshevism, Stalinism and the Comintern. Perspectives on Stalinization, 1917-53*, Basingstoke: Palgrave, 2008.
15. Kevin McDermott and Jeremy Agnew, *The Comintern. A History of International Communism from Lenin to Stalin*, London: Macmillan, 1996, p213f.
16. Theodor Bergmann, 'Aufstieg und Zerfall der Kommunistischen Internationale', in *idem* and Mario Keßler (eds), *Aufstieg und Zerfall der Komintern. Studien zur Geschichte ihrer Transformation (1919-1943)*, Mainz: Diskurs, 1992, p12.
17. Hermann Weber, *Die Kommunistische Internationale. Eine Dokumentation*, Hannover: J. H. W. Dietz Nachf., 1966, p21.
18. Above all others, Hermann Weber has analysed this process in detail in, *idem, Die Wandlung des deutschen Kommunismus. Die Stalinisierung der KPD in der Weimarer Republik*, Frankfurt: Europäische Verlagsanstalt, 1969. There he relies on the standard work by Ossip K. Flechtheim, *Die Kommunistische Partei Deutschlands in der Weimarer Republik*, Offenbach: Bollwerk-Verlag, 1948. The Stalinisation theory was challenged by Klaus-Michael Mallmann, *Kommunisten in der Weimarer Republik. Sozialgeschichte einer revolutionären Bewegung*, Darmstadt: Wissenschaftliche Buchgesellschaft, 1996, esp. pp54-83. For an overview of the controversy, see: Marcel Bois and Florian Wilde, 'Ein kleiner Boom. Entwicklungen und Tendenzen der KPD-Forschung seit 1989/90', in *JHK 2010*, pp309-322; Marcel Bois, 'Review article on Christian Gotthardt's "Die radikale Linke als Massenbewegung. Kommunisten in Harburg-Wilhelmsburg 1918-1933"', in *Historical Materialism*, 17, 1, 2009, pp191-200.
19. Otto Wenzel, *1923. Die gescheiterte Deutsche Oktoberrevolution*, Münster: Lit, 2003, p125.
20. Biographical works have recently been published on two figures that exemplify this process, see Mario Keßler, *Ruth Fischer. Ein Leben mit und gegen Kommunisten (1895-1965)*, Cologne, Weimar and Vienna: Böhlau, 2013. An abridged English version of the book has been published with the title: *Communism – For and Against. The Political Itinaries of Ruth Fischer (1895-1961)*, Berlin: Trafo, 2013. See also: Ralf Hoffrogge, *A Jewish Communist in Weimar Germany. The Life of Werner Scholem (1895-1940)*, Leiden:

Brill, 2017; Mirjam Zadoff, *Der rote Hiob. Das Leben des Werner Scholem*, Munich: Hanser, 2014.
21. Hermann Weber and Andreas Herbst, *Deutsche Kommunisten. Biographisches Handbuch 1918 bis 1945*, Berlin: Dietz, 2008, p21.
22. Sigrid Koch-Baumgarten, 'Einleitung', in Ossip K. Flechtheim, *Die KPD in der Weimarer Republik*, Hamburg: Junius, 1986, p39.
23. Hermann Weber, *Von Rosa Luxemburg zu Walter Ulbricht. Wandlungen des deutschen Kommunismus*, Hannover: Verlag für Literatur und Zeitgeschehen, 1961, p38.
24. K. H. Tjaden, *Struktur und Funktion der 'KPD-Opposition' (KPO). Eine organisationssoziologische Untersuchung zur 'Rechts'-Opposition im Kommunismus zur Zeit der Weimarer Republik*, Meisenheim am Glan: Hain, 1964; Theodor Bergmann, *'Gegen den Strom'. Die Geschichte der Kommunistischen-Partei-Opposition*, Hamburg: VSA, 1987.
25. See Hartmut Beseler, *Die Haltung der KPO zur Sowjetunion hinsichtlich ihrer inneren Systementwicklung, Außenpolitik und Politik im Rahmen der Kommunistischen Internationale*, PhD Thesis, Berlin, 1981.
26. Günter Wernicke, 'Die Radikallinke der KPD und die russische Opposition. Von der Fischer/Maslow-Gruppe zum Lenin-Bund', in *Beiträge zur Geschichte der Arbeiterbewegung*, 42, 3, 2000, p87.
27. Pierre Broué, 'Die deutsche Linke und die russische Opposition 1926-1928', in Annegret Schüle, *Trotzkismus in Deutschland bis 1933. 'Für die Arbeitereinheitsfront zur Abwehr des Faschismus'*, Cologne: [self-published], 1989, p17.
28. *Die Aufgaben der Linken Kommunisten. Beschlüsse der Reichskonferenz der Linken Kommunisten zur Vorbereitung der Gründung des Leninbundes*, Berlin: Verlag Fahne des Kommunismus, 1928, p25.
29. Staatsarchiv Bremen, 4,65-511; see also *Fahne des Kommunismus*, 15, 13 April 1928.
30. Broué, *Die deutsche Linke*, p22.
31. Weber, *Wandlung*, p184.
32. Bois, *Kommunisten gegen Hitler und Stalin*, p265.
33. Zimmermann, *Leninbund*, p104.
34. *Fahne des Kommunismus*, 15, 13 April 1928.
35. *Fahne des Kommunismus*, 20, 18 May 1928.
36. See Hoffrogge, *Werner Scholem*, pp335-340.
37. See the letter from Ruth Fischer, Bruno Mätzchen, A. Maslow, Fritz Schimanski, and Paul Schlecht to the Sixth World Congress of the Comintern, 23 September 1928, in SAPMO, RY 5, I 6/3/11, Bl. 1.
38. See Wolfgang Alles, *Zur Politik und Geschichte der deutschen Trotzkisten ab 1930*, Frankfurt: ISP-Verlag, 1987; Annegret Schüle, *Trotzkismus in Deutschland bis 1933. 'Für die Arbeitereinheitsfront zur Abwehr des Faschismus'*, Cologne [self-published], 1989; Maurice Stobnicer, *Le mouvement trotskyste allemand sous la république de Weimar*, PhD Thesis, Paris, 1980.

39. Alles, *Trotzkisten*, p26.
40. Zimmermann, *Leninbund*, p230.
41. For more on both groups, see Bois, *Kommunisten gegen Hitler und Stalin*, pp332-346.
42. Walter Riest, 'Die Splittergruppen der KPD', in *Neue Blätter für den Sozialismus*, 3, 1932, p209.
43. Ian Kershaw, *Hitlers Macht. Das Profil der NS-Herrschaft*, Munich: dtv, 2000, p58.
44. Mallmann, *Kommunisten*, p87.
45. Weber, *Wandlung*, p240.
46. Siegfried Bahne, '"Sozialfaschismus" in Deutschland. Zur Geschichte eines politischen Begriffs', in *International Review of Social History*, 10, 1965, p236.
47. *Die Rote Fahne*, 18 November 1931.
48. Werner Hirsch, 'Faschismus und Hitlerpartei', in *Die Internationale*, 15, 1 January 1932, p31.
49. *Die Rote Fahne*, 22 March 1931.
50. Weber, *Wandlung*, p239.
51. Conan J. Fischer, 'Gab es am Ende der Weimarer Republik einen marxistischen Wählerblock?' in *Geschichte und Gesellschaft*, 21, 1995, p78.
52. Andreas Dorpalen, 'SPD und KPD in der Endphase der Weimarer Republik', in *Vierteljahrshefte für Zeitgeschichte*, 31, 1983, p86.
53. Weber and Herbst, *Kommunisten*, p15.
54. In the November 1932 Reichstag elections, the KPD (16.9 per cent) and the SPD (20.4 per cent) won more than 37 per cent combined, whereas the NSDAP received approximately 33 per cent of the votes.
55. See Ernest Mandel, *Trotzkis Faschismustheorie*, Frankfurt: ISP-Verlag, 2nd. ed., 1977.
56. Trotsky's important writings on the rise of National Socialism can be found in the anthology Leo Trotzki, *Schriften über Deutschland*, edited by Helmut Dahmer, Frankfurt: Europäische Verlagsanstalt, 1971 (henceforth: *SüD*).
57. 'Letter from Kurt Tucholsky to Walter Hasenclever', 25 July 1933, in Kurt Tucholsky, *Gesamtausgabe, Bd. 20: Briefe 1933-1934*, edited by Antje Bonitz and Gustav Huonker, Reinbek: Rowohlt, 1996, p66.
58. See Alex Callinicos, 'Plumbing the Depths: Marxism and the Holocaust', in *The Yale Journal of Criticism*, 14, 2, 2001, pp391f.
59. Leo Trotzki, 'Was ist Faschismus? (Aus einem Brief an einen englischen Genossen)', in *SüD*, pp141-42.
60. Leo Trotzki, 'Der einzige Weg', in *SüD*, p359.
61. Leo Trotzki, 'Die österreichische Krise, die Sozialdemokratie und der Kommunismus', in *SüD*, p57.
62. Leo Trotzki, *Was nun? Schicksalsfragen des deutschen Proletariats*, Berlin: Linke Opposition der KPD, 1932, p5.

63. Leo Trotzki, 'Die Wendung der Komintern und die Lage in Deutschland', in *SüD*, pp95f.
64. Bois, *Kommunisten gegen Hitler und Stalin*, pp468-477.
65. *Der Funke. Tageszeitung für Recht, Freiheit und Kultur*, 25 June 1932.
66. Joachim Petzold, 'SPD und KPD in der Endphase der Weimarer Republik: Unüberwindbare Hindernisse oder ungenutzte Möglichkeiten?', in Heinrich August Winkler (ed.), *Die deutsche Staatskrise 1930–1933. Handlungsspielräume und Alternativen*, Munich: Oldenbourg, 1992, p94.
67. Thomas Kurz, *Feindliche Brüder im deutschen Südwesten. Sozialdemokraten und Kommunisten in Baden und Württemberg von 1928 bis 1933*, Berlin: Duncker & Humblot, 1996, p394.
68. Hermann Weber, 'Zur Politik der KPD 1929–1933', in Manfred Scharrer (ed.), *Kampflose Kapitulation. Arbeiterbewegung 1933*, Reinbek: Rowohlt, 1984, p140.
69. Mallmann, *Kommunisten*, p373.
70. *Permanente Revolution*, 1, 4, October-November 1931.
71. *Permanente Revolution*, 1, 5, December 1931.
72. Bois, *Kommunisten gegen Hitler und Stalin*, p371.
73. Zimmermann, *Leninbund*, pp211-213.
74. *Ibid.*, pp220-225.

The German Section of the International of Sailors and Harbour Workers

Constance Margain

THE GERMAN SECTION of the 'International Union of Seamen and Harbour Workers', the 'Unity Union of Seamen, Harbour Workers and Bargemen in Germany' is an unusual phenomenon because of its close links with the Red International of Labour Unions, which was a communist and Soviet organisation. It was headed initially by Johannes Koschnick, followed by Ernst Wollweber after October 1931.[1]

The statutes of the trade union were drawn up in September 1930, and this was followed by the outbreak of a series of strikes in the German ports at the beginning of the year 1931. The EVSHBD defended the interests of the German sailors, dockers, fishermen and bargemen and the interests of Soviet Russia. The links between the USSR and the EVSHBD became very clear at the time of a strike organised by the latter in Soviet ports in October 1931 with the aid of the Profintern's network of Interclubs (International Seamen's Clubs). The strike was a fiasco, but it allows us to gain a better understanding of the functioning of the trade union and its relationship with the Profintern. It is the conditions of its foundation as much as the impact of the world crisis which explain why the EVSHBD disappeared so rapidly after Hitler's seizure of power in 1933.

Strikes called to set up a new trade union

The EVSHBD was founded to fight against the Social Democratic trade unions, in particular the International Transport Workers' Federation (ITF). The Revolutionary Trade Union Opposition (*Revolutionäre Gewerkschafts-Opposition*),[2] which was the German trade union section of the Profintern, wanted to organise a dock strike in Hamburg in order to proclaim the official establishment of the EVSHBD and to recruit supporters for it. There were between 22,000 and 26,000 dockers in Hamburg, seven or eight thousand of whom were members of reformist trade unions.[3] The remainder were not particularly politicised. This made it difficult to organise the strike, which was supposed to create the conditions for the development of a revolutionary trade union movement among the dockers and sailors of Germany.

The port workers' strike committee called on 11 February 1931 for a boycott of the elections for what were called the 'free' trade unions, that is to say the Social Democratic ones. Some stokers, dockers without fixed employment and occasional labourers failed to appear for work on 11 February, but in the absence of a broader movement, work was resumed on 14 February.[4] The demands raised by the strikers were for a rise in wages, a guarantee of five days of wages a week, recruitment by number rather than name to avoid blacklisting, twelve days' holiday a year, and the provision of places where they could relax when off duty.[5]

Workers who were on permanent contracts had not joined the new trade union in this strike, because they were mainly cardholding members of the *Gesamtverband* (the Social Democratic trade union). The strike was also criticised by dockers without permanent employment (*Unständige*). This group did not want to stop work for such a long time, and they believed that the strike did not need to be so thoroughly prepared or organised.[6] This criticism, which was tinged with anarcho-syndicalism,[7] showed that the decisions taken at the Fifth Congress of the Profintern (particularly the decision to set up the EVSHBD) were at variance with the complex and shifting trade union environment among the workers of the seaboard. The strike was marked by violence. It lacked any connection with a mass basis, and was put into effect by full-time communist officials who also organised other strikes at Bremen, Stettin (Szczecin), Kiel and Nordenham.

Abortive attempts to organise strikes in the German ports in October 1931

Starting in 1928, there was an ideological turn in the USSR. The Profintern, with Solomon Lozovsky at its head, played an important role in the implementation of a new political orientation. This required, on the one hand, a struggle against Social Democracy, and, on the other, the foundation of parallel trade unions to fight against the existing trade unions. Strikes were intended to play an important part in these struggles. They were perceived henceforth as an economic approach in the service of a political objective: the world revolution. This revolution was supposed to succeed through the struggle of a class, the international proletariat, and to contribute to the protection of the USSR by preventing the 'imperialist powers' from waging a war against the new 'fatherland of the proletariat'.

Ernst Wollweber wrote an article explaining the strategy employed in this sailors' and dockers' strike.[8] The unemployed would have to be prepared, he said, so as to prevent them from becoming strike-breakers by taking the jobs refused by the strikers. Moreover, a national strike would have to be conducted simultaneously in Germany and in foreign ports. This strategy resulted in the strike movement of October 1931 organised by the EVSHBD, but also in a strike in Soviet ports upheld and organised by the ISH.

At the end of August 1931, the 'action committee' of the EVSHBD assembled to prepare the EVSHBD congress planned to take place in Hamburg between 10 and 13 September 1931. This meeting was a sign of the impending strike. The principal demand of the strike was for the authorities to reverse the reduction of dockers' wages, which was due to take place on 30 September 1931, and under which the wage would fall from 8.8 to 7 *Reichsmark* per shift. The EVSHBD sent a list of demands to the ship-owners and the harbour enterprises, with an ultimatum dated 19 September for the sailors and 23 September for the dockers. No demands were included for the bargemen.

The communist union then decided to reject the agreements made between the Social Democratic trade union and the ship-owners and port employers. There had been negotiations between the Social Democratic trade unions and the employers in the port of Hamburg on 21 and 22 September,[9] resulting in an announcement that the current wage-scales would remain valid until 15 November 1931. On 26 September, a joint appeal by the EVSHBD and the RGO vehemently denounced these agreements which, they said, did not meet the demands of the stokers and the engineers as regards the organisation of labour on the ships and the payment of overtime.[10]

This refusal to negotiate, along with the rejection of any kind of association with the Social Democrats, was the hallmark of the communist trade unionists. It also showed that the objectives of the EVSHBD were not solely of a trade union character; they were also political.

The sailors were supposed to follow the dockers in demanding improvements in labour conditions, and it was necessary to avoid destroying the common front between dockers and sailors. But the authorities reduced only the sailors' wages, and not those of the dockers,[11] which meant that a common front was therefore not possible. This first attempt by the EVSHBD proved to be completely ineffective. The strikes which broke out in different German ports had limited participation and limited results.

While attempts were being made to promote the idea of supporting the strike among the unemployed sailors and dockers, the leadership of the EVSHBD was waiting to see what kind of shape the strike would take. The national leadership of the union wanted to know what kind of atmosphere there was in the ports.[12]

On 2 October, the arbitrators agreed a 13.6 per cent reduction of wages. Two days later there was a meeting of local leaders of the communist union in the Hamburg Interclub.[13] Every local group sent delegates.[14] They came from the following towns and cities: Bremen, Bremerhaven, Nordenham, Kiel, Wismar, Rostock, Flensburg, Stettin, Emden, Harburg, and Hamburg – and numbered twenty-three representatives.

Speech after speech called on the local groups to organise strikes. Once a strike had been declared, they would be able to inform the national headquarters in Hamburg.[15] The strike movement, they said, would make it possible to create a German-Soviet fleet, and lead to the improvement of conditions of life on board ships. The strikes in Bremen, Bremerhaven, and Nordenham would be difficult to organise, however, because there was less work in those ports.[16] Nevertheless, the meeting voted in favour of a strike.[17]

But on the prescribed day, 5 October, there was no strike movement in the port of Hamburg. The police arrested the militants who distributed the tracts, and agitators were prevented from entering the port. When the strike committee met on that day, the EVSHBD complained of a lack of support from the German Communist Party. The strike had in fact ended without having begun, but the EVSHBD wanted to wait for the decision of Profintern and its European secretariat. On 6 October, fighting broke out among the sailors in front of the employment offices; the Communists wanted to prevent anyone from being hired. But the crews of the ships did not follow their lead, and on 6 October the strike was broken off. According to a Social Democratic newspaper, this abrupt decision had been taken by the KPD because there were four Soviet ships in the port.[18] They could now be unloaded by communist dockers.

A second strike movement took place in November 1931 in the port of Hamburg. The Association of Port Enterprises had announced the wage reduction from 8.8 to 7 *Reichsmark*. Finally, the ship-owners decided that the wage per shift would be 8.30 *Reichsmark*. Faced with this decision, many dockers were ready to go on strike, but the *Gesamtverband* declared its opposition to the idea. It described the strike the EVSHBD was planning as 'unofficial'.[19]

The communists made very thorough preparations for this dock strike. The police later discovered a plan of the port, including the names of the streets. The militants were subdivided into groups so as to occupy the whole area, in order to ensure the success of the strike and thwart the activities of strike-breakers. The location of each police station was indicated on the plan.[20] The aim was to control the streets and keep under observation the movement of transport, the deployment of the police and the spots where dockers were being hired. But all this surveillance did not prevent the police from making arrests.

The strike made some progress in Stettin and Hamburg. At Bremerhaven, the strike call was only partially successful. In Hamburg, the police wounded one person and arrested three.[21] The police intervened each time a strike picket-line was put in place. This resulted in the arrest of sixty militants in Hamburg, who were sent before the courts. The police protected people who wanted to work.[22]

The strike front crumbled away little by little. By 5 November, the situation was critical. The EVSHBD met on 7 November in Hamburg to decide whether the strike should be continued. Twenty-three delegates were present.[23] The dockers called on the sailors for support. At Bremen, all the sailors were against the strike, and lacked any commitment to the communist union. The militants accordingly decided that the two parts of the maritime profession should separate. The strike ended.

Permanently-employed workers had not participated in this strike,[24] and the employment offices continued to function. Dockers who participated in the strike had their labour cards withdrawn. Indeed, the labour cards had a stamp which indicated the number of hours worked. If there was no stamp, the docker in question had been on strike.[25]

The strike of November 1931 was one of the last social struggles in the port of Hamburg during the years of the Weimar Republic. In January 1932, the EVSHBD attempted to mount an offensive by the dockers in various German ports (Danzig, Kiel, Stettin, Bremerhaven, Hamburg, and other ports of North Germany and the Baltic coast) in reaction to Chancellor Brüning's decree of 8 December 1931 which reduced the salaries and wages of state employees and workers.[26] However, the union failed in its objective, and the movement it started remained limited. Owing to the catastrophic economic situation, there was a mood of resignation among the dockers and the sailors. They knew that it was risky to strike, particularly after their experience of the October 1931 strike in the ports of the Soviet Union.

The strike organised by the EVSHBD and the ISH in the USSR in October 1931

A strike by German sailors in the Soviet ports began officially on 7 October. It lasted until 22 October in Poti, and until 17 October in Leningrad. In the Soviet ports the Interclubs were the organisational centres for the strike.[27] At Leningrad, Odessa, Batumi and Poti, the sailors' refuges provided food for the strikers and organised strike meetings. They also sent ISH agitators onto the German ships to encourage the crews to go on strike. It was their activities that made it possible for the strike to last, because organising a strike at sea required a central headquarters on shore.

A telegram sent from Hamburg on the evening of 6 October 1931 was read out in the Leningrad Interclub.[28] This telegram announced that a strike had been launched in Hamburg and other German ports, with the support of certain foreign crews. At that point in time, however, no strike had in fact broken out in Hamburg.

The demands formulated by the ISH in Hamburg concerned the struggle against capitalism, the refusal to accept wage reductions and the lengthening of working hours, as well as a demand for paid leave. More precisely, one leaflet demanded the following: more watches on the ships, hence more men, two or three weeks of paid leave each year, and, above all, fraternal international action to prevent any reduction in wages.[29]

Strengthened by the news of this movement, 240 out of the 300 sailors present at the Leningrad meeting, the majority of them German, came out in support of the strike.[30] The strike itself did not have any economic objectives. It was primarily political: it was aimed at promoting military intervention in Germany to establish a Soviet government there.

By the morning of 7 October 1931, the decision of the strikers was known in the port of Leningrad. There, the crews of thirty-two ships stopped work.[31] By 12 October 1931, according to the Soviet newspaper *Pravda*, thirty-six ships were on strike.[32] The newspaper reported that it had received a message from the strike leadership in Germany, stating that ninety-two boats were on strike there, and that fifty-seven of them were barricaded against penetration from outside. That brought the total number of ships held to 149. This information was in fact false. But the newspaper was not only the principal source of information for the Interclub, and thus for the strikers, but also for Profintern officials. As a result of receiving this false information, the Profintern encouraged the sailors to continue their action.

The Interclub of Leningrad played an important part in giving logistical support to the strikers.[33] It distributed food coupons, for example,[34] and it offered the sailors transport passes to enable them to move around the city. The sailors only returned to their ships to sleep. Membership of the EVSHBD was a matter of course from the moment someone became a striker, granting them access to the facilities of the Interclub. Without it, the strike would not have been able to last for such a long time.

The strike finally ended on 16 October without gaining any concessions from the ship-owners. By 19 October, according to the German government, the maritime traffic of the German ships in the port of Leningrad had returned to normal.

The strike in the other Soviet ports

A German sailor, Emil Winkels, was the animating force behind the strike of twenty-eight sailors on the ship *Godfried Bueren* at the port of Odessa.[35] He was the shop steward of this ship, and an EVSHBD member. He was chosen at a meeting of the Odessa Interclub to lead the strike on all the German ships in the Black Sea. The Odessa Interclub, which nurtured the strikers, giving them money and cigarettes,[36] served as a link between the strike committee and the EVSHBD.

The steamer *Godfried Bueren* came out on strike on 7 October. Another ship, the *Amantea*, left Novorossiisk on 13 October, arriving at Odessa on 15 October. The next morning, the crew of the *Amantea* discovered that the whole port of Odessa was on strike. The strike committee led by Winkels was blockading the entrance to the ship's stokehold. The crew of the *Amantea* thereupon also went on strike.[37] Even so, the ship succeeded in leaving the port on 18 October, under a hail of stones thrown by the strikers.[38]

On the occasion of the strike on the *Amantea*, Emil Winkels and five other sailors physically attacked the German consul in Odessa, Paul Roth,[39] who had boarded the ship and thrown the notice-board marked '*STREIK*' ('STRIKE') into the sea. According to his own report, he suffered scratches and bruises, and his clothing was torn. An hour later, the harbour-master and two other political representatives managed to remove him from the ship. He called for the arrest of the sailors who had attacked him, armed protection for the ship and its rapid departure from the port. The Russian authorities apologised for the attack and promised that one of the sailors who had attacked him, Jan Janssen, would be arrested. Nothing was done.[40]

In the port of Batumi, the strike broke out with some delay, on 17 October (the militants had not yet learned that the strike had ended in Leningrad), with the assistance of the local Interclub. On 16 October, fifty sailors went on strike, on three steamers: the *Biskaya*, the *Schindler*, and the *Afrika*.[41] This was principally the work of young seamen (cabin-boys and stokers), whose demands, which were relayed by the Interclub, were essentially concerned with the need to cancel the reduction in wages ordered by the German government.

The Soviet authorities refused to allow the ships to leave because there was not a complete crew and the strikers were demanding their wages. The ships finally left the port a few days later: the *Biskaya* and the *Schindler* on 20 October, the *Afrika* the next day.

At Poti, similarly, the strike broke out on 17 October. It affected two ships, the *Angora* and the *Thessalia*. There, too, the port's Interclub played a major role. Its director, who according to the German authorities was a German-speaking Hungarian, invited the crews into the Interclub and harangued them. After his speech, the whole crew of the

Angora went on strike. On the *Thessalia*, just two men went on strike, then four more followed them. The captain of the *Thessalia* had forbidden his men from going to the Interclub. According to the German consulate, this was the reason why the strike did not take hold completely on this ship. The strike ended on 21 October in the *Thessalia*, and on 22 October in the *Angora*.[42]

The Hamburg Interclub initiated and organised this strike. But the organisers of the strike in Hamburg were not prosecuted when it ended, because there was a lack of proof of their role.[43] The sailors who went on strike on the spot in the USSR were arrested and brought before a court on their return to Germany. But sixty-eight sailors decided to remain in the USSR.

The specific methods adopted during the Leningrad strike

In order to organise the strikes, the EVSHBD and the militants in the Interclubs of Odessa, Leningrad, Batumi, Poti, and Novorossiisk falsified, or at least amplified, a movement which was actually much smaller than they claimed. Perhaps they had also been misled by Russian communist newspapers, which gave the impression of a much broader movement than the reality justified.

The strike was also being conducted by violent means. The Leningrad Interclub organised *Rollkommandos*, or mobile columns, groups of men who went from ship to ship to call for a strike from 7 October onwards. These mobile detachments used violence and threats to impose their views, not just on the officers, but on recalcitrant sailors as well. In the opinion of the German police, fear was the reason the strike lasted for ten days.[44] The strikers steamed around in a tug, and forced the sailors to get on board as a way of going on strike. Once they were on the tug, the militants added their names to the list of strikers. These tugs moved around under the flag of the Soviet police.

According to the police, the cudgels used by the strikers to compel other sailors to participate in the strike or to join the *Rollkommandos* were stored in the Interclub. It is impossible to know how many sailors went on strike because of the threat of force, but it is known that one officer was wounded. At Leningrad, twenty German sailors wanted to board the steamer *Pinnau* on 8 October, but the First Officer and the First Engineer refused them access. There is no record of any wounded sailors. This suggests that if the cudgels did exist, as the police report claimed, they were not used much, even if the presence of these weapons contributed to instil a climate of fear among the sailors. The Interclub and the militants of the EVSHBD organised and participated in these missions of intimidation.

However, the threat of force was not the sole reason why the strike continued for so long. Despite the German Consul's proposal that they return to work on 10 October, the sailors refused, replying that only their trade union, the EVSHBD, could end the strike.[45] This refusal does not in itself invalidate the thesis that force played a role in prolonging the strike. The sailors could have been forced to refuse the Consul's offer under the threat of physical reprisals.

However, the testimony of two sailors interrogated by the German police does provide some clarification. On 22 October, the German Embassy made a list of those who had volunteered to work during the strike, or at least those who had kept away from the action. It questioned some of the sailors. Two stokers stated that they had been forced to go on strike between 9 and 17 October. Their trade union, which was of a Social Democratic orientation, considered the strike to be unofficial, indeed, worse than that, a piece of 'stupidity'.

The two men had taken the opportunity to make excursions to the Winter Palace, the city's House of Culture, the district around Leningrad, a collective farm and the town of Vyborg. The food had been very good. The *Rollkommandos* who came on board the ship boasted about the merits of the USSR and stated that the sailors did not need to fear punishment because they could remain in the country, where there was no shortage of work. The tugs that made it possible for the *Rollkommandos* to move from ship to ship belonged to the Soviet authorities. According to one of the sailors, the Soviet authorities did not view this strike unfavourably and probably supported it.[46]

This testimony by two striking stokers partly confirms the reports by the German police and diplomatic authorities. Although they may have felt that they had been obliged to go on strike, this 'obligation' at least allowed them to profit from Russia's culinary arts and cultural treasures!

Diplomacy and Politics

Several agencies were involved in the course of this strike in the USSR: the port authorities, the GPU (the Soviet State Political Police), the harbour police, the Profintern, the Interclubs and the diplomatic representatives of various countries. If the strike lasted a long time in some ports (approximately ten days) this was because it was supported, or at least tolerated, by the Soviet authorities.

Contrary to received ideas, the Soviet authorities were far from having a uniform opinion about these events and they did not all pursue the same objectives. There were several issues involved here: the diplomats wanted to avoid a diplomatic incident with Germany, the port authorities wanted to continue loading and unloading Soviet ships, the police wanted to avoid disorder, and the Profintern wanted to mobilise militant forces for the success of the strike. This multiplicity of distinct objectives gives us some inkling of the complex character of these events.

On 7 October 1931, the German consulate in Leningrad sent a telegram informing the German embassy in Moscow, and therefore the German government, that a strike was imminent.[47] According to the Consul, the Soviet authorities seemed astonished that a strike had been triggered. It created a difficult situation for the port authorities, because they feared that they would fall behind in the loading and unloading of the ships, and some of the merchandise was perishable. But the strike committee responded to the demand of the Soviet authorities by authorising the loading and unloading of Russian vessels.

The Consul demanded the assistance of the GPU to protect the ships, the officers and those who wished to work. He also wanted that organisation to prohibit all unauthorised persons from boarding the ships, and to enforce the prohibition. Right from the start of the strike, the GPU promised to put these measures in place.[48] Even so, thirty-two steamers went on strike in Leningrad and the political police force made no move to intervene, even when violent acts were perpetrated before its officers' eyes.

On 9 October, the German Consul in Leningrad met a representative of the People's Commissariat of Foreign Affairs to discuss the protection of the ships.[49] This official, whose name we do not know, stated that the strike was legal and the strike leadership had been recognised. There was therefore no reason to protect the ships, or to prohibit the *Rollkommandos*. The Soviet authorities considered that the protection demanded by the German diplomatic authorities constituted an interference in German internal affairs, with the aim of protecting the interests of the ship-owners.[50] The Soviets recognised the strike leadership and invariably replied to the German diplomats that the ships could leave port provided that they had a full crew on board.

According to the German Embassy in the USSR, the Soviet Commissariat of Foreign Affairs did not approve of this strike.[51] For this reason, it tried to exert pressure on the Soviet communist party and the trade unions to put an end to the conflict.[52] On 11 October, on the occasion of a fresh discussion between the German Ambassador Herbert von Dirksen and the representative of the Commissariat of Foreign Affairs,[53] the latter told him semi-officially that he had not been able to find a compromise with the party and the trade unions to stop the strike. Officially, however, he said that the strike movement was not only authorised but legitimate. He added that paragraph three of article twenty-five was only applicable to the personal protection of the Consul. This paragraph did in fact specify that the Consul had to be protected by the Soviet authorities. He apologised for the aggressive acts committed by German sailors against Consul Roth,[54] but he added that these sailors were not Soviet citizens but German communists. Total confusion!

On 13 October, the German consul in Leningrad declared that he lacked the competence to continue the negotiations, and he called on the Ambassador to intervene politically by approaching Chancellor Brüning's government in Germany.[55] The Ambassador stated on 14 October that the Soviets seemed incapable of putting a stop to the movement, while admitting that the affair was serious. At the People's Commissariat of Foreign Affairs, officials began to fear that the whole matter would reflect back on them.

On 15 October, a member of the consulate staff, a number of ship's captains and a representative of the Soviet Commissariat of Foreign Affairs had a meeting with the strike committee. According to the Consul's representative, only one of the three people on the strike committee was a striking crew member. The other two were professional militants. While the captains accused the Soviets of supporting the strike, the strike committee stated that it needed to account for its actions only to the EVSHBD in Germany. They were warned by the consular representative that the movement was illegal, the ringleaders would certainly be arrested, and there would be serious consequences for Russo-German relations.

The same day, the German Ministry of Foreign Affairs addressed a note to the regional transport ministers of the German ports affected by the strike movement (whether because the ships in question belonged to a local company, or because the transport of the goods needed to be carried out by the ports in question) informing them that the German Ambassador in Moscow had received positive signs from the Soviet government concerning an imminent end to the strike.

The Profintern had been against the idea of a strike by German ships in Soviet ports, but the organisation could not avoid giving support to a movement it had not anticipated. It did demand, however, that in future the ISH should inform the Profintern before starting movements like this, and that the strike should be organised by the EVSHBD and not by the ISH.[56] Lastly, the slogan of such a strike should not be 'abolish the Brüning decrees' but 'fight against the reduction in wages and the Brüning decrees'. The Profintern was trying to recover the original initiative, in the face of a movement which had outrun those original objectives. The strike, it said, should have been extended to all the German ports and should only have been launched in the capitalist countries.[57] In Moscow, the German Ambassador informed the German Ministry of Foreign Affairs that the funds needed to finance the strike had come from the Russian sailors' union, the Profintern, the Soviet Communist Party and the Soviet port authorities.

This strike ran counter to the line adopted by the Comintern and the Soviet Communist Party, which was to oppose strikes on Soviet ships in foreign ports and on foreign ships in Soviet ports. In practice, however, the divergences within the communist apparatus did not affect relations between the Soviet communist party and the Profintern, but rather relations between the Commissariat of Foreign Affairs and the government of the Weimar Republic, as represented by its Ambassador. On 16 October, under the pressure of the KPD, the Hamburg headquarters of the EVSHBD declared the strike at an end. The Soviet government had intervened to secure this result, in response to a demand by the German government.[58] The strike ended in Leningrad and Odessa on 17 October. Maritime activity began again, the German ships were unloaded, and they left the ports. The tugs sent by the ship-owners and the German government returned to Holtenau because there was no longer any use for them. The Commissariat of Foreign Affairs in Moscow had been opposed to the strike from the outset and it regarded the cessation of the strike as a strengthening of its own position.[59]

This strike placed the Russian authorities at the heart of the paradox of a state which regarded itself as proletarian: they had to weigh the organisation of a strike with revolutionary objectives in their country, against the respect due to the diplomatic relations forged with Weimar Germany on the other. The agitators in Hamburg and the Interclubs drew support from the existence of the USSR to justify the demands they made of the German government, but the crisis brought to light the contradictory character of the diplomatic relations in which the Soviet state had become entwined in order to ensure its legitimacy.

Before Hitler Comes to Power: New Strike Appeals

The national conference of the EVSHBD took place on 27 December 1931 in Hamburg. It was proposed at the conference that there should be a total strike in the port on 2 January 1932.[60] This decision was in response to a decree issued by Chancellor Brüning on 8 December 1931 imposing a reduction in wages for state employees and workers. No strike took place, however.

In February 1932, the EVSHBD demanded an increase in payment per shift to 11 *Reichsmark* (the payment was then 8.8 *Reichsmark*), a guarantee of a minimum of five days' salary, hiring by number not by name, and paid holidays for all dockers.[61]

In September 1932, a new wave of discontent affected the sailors of Germany.[62] A decree issued by the new German Chancellor, Franz von Papen, indicated that sailors' wages were to be reduced by 23 per cent, while the crews were not up to full strength and the hours of work had become longer. On 15 September 1932, being faced with this new threat, the leadership of the EVSHBD got together to discuss its response.[63] No immediate action came out of the meeting. For one thing, the imprisonment of the sailors who had taken part in the strikes of October 1931 in the USSR had dampened the group's spirits. There had also been an increase in police repression directed against communist activities, while street battles with the Nazis were becoming more frequent, leading to an atmosphere of tension, and sometimes a climate of terror, which affected every political demonstration.

The EVSHBD organised another strike by the bargemen in the autumn of 1932, and there was a strike in France in the December of that year. On 15 December 1932, the EVSHBD issued an appeal for the formation of a united fighting front of all organisations.[64]

Conclusion

The total membership of the EVSHBD at its height in Germany was slightly under 10,500. The majority of its adherents were unemployed seamen. The union only had a short history, because on 5 March 1933, all trade union activities were prohibited throughout Germany. The end of the Weimar Republic brought with it the end of the organisation, although there were numerous militants who were involved in resistance after 1933.

The EVSHBD liked to describe itself as a trade-union organisation.[65] In actual fact, it was predominantly a communist organisation. Defence of the Bolshevik revolution took precedence over the needs of the working masses, and as a result the workers' combative energy was frittered away. The only debates that took place inside the EVSHBD were over whether to strike and, then, the best moment to do so.

The decision to establish the EVSHBD should be placed in the context both of the world economic crisis and a political crisis, or at least a major change, at the summit of Soviet power. Stalin then dominated the USSR. The history of the EVSHBD was characterised throughout by an intricate relationship between two elements: the Bolshevisation of the communist parties and the rise of unemployment.

Translated by Ben Fowkes

Notes

1. The EVSHBD was a section of the International of Seamen and Harbour-Workers, the international communist trade secretariat founded on 3 October 1930 in Hamburg.
2. See among other works on the RGO: Werner Müller, *Lohnkampf, Massenstreik, Sowjetmacht. Ziele und Grenzen der Revolutionäre Gewerkschafts-Opposition (RGO) in Deutschland 1928 bis 1933*, Cologne: Bund-Verlag, 1988.
3. Russian State Archive of Socio-Political History (RGASPI), 534/5/221, 68.
4. *Die Rote Fahne*, 15 February 1931, p10.
5. See the documentation in Stiftung Archiv der Parteien und

Massenorganisationen der DDR im Bundesarchiv (SAPMO), RY/1/1 2/8/70.
6. Klaus Weinhauer, *Arbeitsvermittlung, Arbeitsalltag, Arbeitskampf. Sozialgeschichte der Hamburger Hafenarbeiter 1914-1933*, Schöningh: Paderborn, 1994, p319 note 67.
7. *Ibid.*, p318, note 68.
8. Ernst Wollweber, 'Seeleute und Hafenarbeiter rüsten zum Streik', *Internationale Gewerkschafts-Pressekorrespondenz*, 72, September 1931, p5.
9. Bundesarchiv, Berlin (BArch) R 1501/20/106, Bl.43.
10. *Ibid.*, Bl.38.
11. 'Polizei-Direktion, Bremen, den 28 September 1931', in *ibid.*, Bl.32.
12. *Ibid.*, Bl.54.
13. RGASPI, 534/5/223, Bl.54.
14. BArch, R 58/2026.
15. 'Polizei-Direktion, Bremen, 5 October 1931 an die Reichsministerium des Innern', in *ibid.*, R 1501/20/106, Bl.63.
16. *Ibid.*
17. *Ibid.*
18. *Deutsche Allgemeine Zeitung*, 7 October 1931.
19. Ludwig Eiber, *Arbeiter und Arbeiterbewegung in der Hansestadt Hamburg in den Jahren 1929 bis 1939. Werftarbeiter, Hafenarbeiter und Seeleute: Konformität, Opposition, Widerstand*, Bern: Peter Lang, 2000, p188.
20. BArch, R 1501/20 106, Bl.274.
21. *Ibid.*, Bl.208.
22. *Op. cit.*, Bl.264.
23. 'Polizei-Direktion Bremen an dem Reichsministerium des Innern, 9.11.1931', in *ibid.*, Bl.231.
24. Klaus Weinhauer, *Arbeitsvermittlung*, p324 note 97.
25. *Ibid.*, pp321ff, 359. According to this research, between 360 and 400 cards were withdrawn.
26. BArch, R 1501/20 471, Bl.404.
27. *Ibid.*, Bl.508.
28. *Ibid.*, R 1501/20, 471, Bl.106.
29. Geheim Staatsarchiv Preussischer Kulturbesitz (GStAPK), 1 – HA Rep. 120 C XVII, 3 92:1, Bl.223.
30. BArch, R 1501/20 471, Bl.509.
31. *Ibid.*, R 1501/20 106, Bl.205, 143.
32. *Ibid.*, R 1501/20 471, Bl.539.
33. *Ibid.*
34. GStaPK, I-HA Rep. 120 C XVII 3, 92:1, Bl.294.
35. BArch, R 1501/20 471, Bl.500.
36. BArch, R 1501/20 106, Bl.330.
37. GStAPK, I-HA Rep. 120 C XVII 3, 92:1, Bl.277.

38. *Ibid.*, Bl.216.
39. GSta PK, 1-HA Rep. 120 C XVII, 92:1, Bl.227.
40. BArch, R 1501/20 471, Bl.547.
41. GStAPK, 1-HA Rep. 120 C XVII 3, 92:1, Bl.337.
42. *Ibid.*, Bl.307.
43. BArch, R 1501/20 106, Bl.304.
44. SAPMO, NY 4321/60.
45. BArch, R 1501/20 106, Bl.304.
46. GStAPK, I-HA Rep. 120 C XVII 3, 92:1, Bl.332.
47. *Ibid.* Bl.203.
48. BArch, R 1501/20 471, Bl.491.
49. 'Leiter der Westlichen Abteilung II des Aussenkommissariats', in *ibid.*, Bl.520.
50. GStAPK, I-HA Rep. 120 C XVII 3, 92:1, Bl.258.
51. *Ibid.*, p212.
52. BArch, R 1501/20 471, Bl.520.
53. Gerald Mund, *Ostasien im Spiegel der deutschen Diplomatie. Die privatdienstliche Korrespondenz des Diplomaten Herbert v. Dirksen von 1933 bis 1938*, Munich: Franz Steiner, 2006.
54. GStAPK, I-HA Rep. 120 C XVII 3, 92:1, Bl.260-262.
55. *Ibid.*, Bl.294.
56. RGASPI, 534/3/627, 210.
57. GStAPK, I.HA Rep. 120 C XVII 3, 92:1, Bl.363; RGASPI, 534/5/222.
58. BArch, R 1501/20 106, Bl.140.
59. *Ibid.*, R 1501/20 224, Bl.100.
60. BArch, R 1501/20 471, Bl.418-424; RGASPI, 534/7/191, 167.
61. SAPMO, SgY2/VDF/VIII/33, Bl.12.
62. BArch, R 1501/20 471, Bl.626.
63. SAPMO, SgY2/VDF/VIII/31.
64. *Ibid.*, Bl.20.
65. BArch, R3003/8J/137433, Bl.15.

The 'Red Unions' and their Resistance to National Socialism: The Unity Union of the Berlin Metal Workers, 1930-1935

Stefan Heinz

RECENT DEBATES ABOUT the history of the German Communist Party have not looked closely enough at its trade union politics to enable a conclusive assessment in this field of activity. This is particularly true of the period from late 1930, when KPD supporters attempted to establish 'red unions' within the Revolutionary Trade Union Opposition. This practice began with the formation of the 'Unity Union of Berlin Metalworkers'. The Unity Union's politics were derived from a very radical conception of what a union should be, which, in the long term, proved to be incommensurate with the directives of the KPD leadership. A few years ago, a monograph and an anthology were published that analysed the reasons why the Unity Union was established, its objectives, and its relationship to the KPD.[1] These texts did include descriptions of RGO activities in the struggle against the Nazi regime, but they paid it only minimal attention despite the fact that it was among the most significant union-based resistance. This chapter will address the history of the Unity Union and the features that distinguish it from other union organisations, for example its appeal to female workers.

RGO Politics and the Establishment of the Unity Union

One important aspect of the KPD's history is its relationship to the unions organised within the General Confederation of German Trade Unions.[2] During the 'ultra-left turn' of 1927-28, the KPD attempted to exacerbate tensions between the union leadership, which was allied to the Social Democratic Party, and its rank-and-file members. This development should be viewed in connection with the Comintern change in strategy. But it was also the result of political and social developments in Germany as well as the practices of the ADGB.[3] The KPD leadership had been making clear for years that it wanted to systematically 'conquer' the unions. Yet the KPD realised that it could not undertake successful 'factional work' unless communism enjoyed greater popularity among rank-and-file party members.[4] This laid the groundwork for the KPD's turn toward 'ultra-left politics'.

Following the Comintern's lead, the KPD leadership also identified 1928 as the point at which capitalism was entering its 'Third Period' and thus beginning its inexorable slide into crisis. The Communists assumed that the class struggle would intensify and the workers would be increasingly radicalised.[5] They declared the SPD to be the 'main enemy',[6] arguing that a 'united front' would only be possible 'from below' – that is to say, with rank-and-file SPD members incorporated into the Communists' actions. In this context, the task of the RGO was to carry out factional work within the unions to support the anticipated leftward shift in their membership. This is why the RGO tried to establish its own strike leaderships, which attempted to conduct 'independent' economic struggles (i.e. against the will of the ADGB leadership) and to lead strikes as political conflicts. This policy aimed to enable the formation of the RGO within the ADGB but, in fact, it had the opposite effect: ADGB officials expelled communist activists. Those expulsions increased anti-union sentiment among RGO members, who thought it was pointless or misguided to operate within the ADGB. The KPD leadership, however, did not believe that any of its supporters should leave the unions voluntarily – a demand that was ignored by more than a few Communists. From 1929, there were attempts to organise independent 'red unions' within individual industries in KPD strongholds, notably Berlin, the Ruhr, and Hamburg. These differences of opinion over organisational issues and autonomy were expressed at the RGO's first national conference in late 1929.[7] But, at this point, the official aim was to expand the RGO into a body which operated as a consolidated block within the ADGB and the creation of 'rival unions' was officially rejected.

In the meantime, supporters of forming 'red unions' felt sufficiently encouraged by political developments to push ahead with the RGO's transition into an organisation independent of the SPD-led unions. They created associations for expelled union members and previously unorganised workers, particularly in Berlin. In the process, RGO supporters intensified their antagonistic stance toward Social Democracy. Given the worldwide economic crisis that broke out in 1929 and the onset of Chancellor Heinrich Brüning's rule by deflationary emergency decrees, which the SPD Reichstag fraction 'tolerated', social-democratic officials within the ADGB were fighting an increasingly defensive battle against wage cuts.[8] Having been weakened by a declining membership and constantly rising unemployment, the ADGB adopted a stance of avoiding strikes during the crisis. That defensive approach was in keeping with their officials' legalistic conception of the state and their commitment to the SPD – a position that, despite protests, was shared by most union members. In this way, as the crisis set in, the ADGB had failed to raise workers' readiness to strike and failed to reduce the risk of strike-breaking. The RGO, by contrast, wrongly believed that growing impoverishment would raise workers' readiness to strike, and understood the crisis as capitalism's death throes, even though there were fewer and fewer strikes during the final years of the Weimar Republic.

The second national conference of the RGO in November 1930 passed a resolution to transform the RGO into a 'fighting organisation'.[9] Franz Dahlem, the national leader of the RGO, analysed the situation in which workers and the unemployed found themselves. In particular, he addressed the Berlin metal industry where, despite a strike by some 130,000 metalworkers, a significant wage reduction could not be averted.[10] On 4 November 1930, a few days before Dahlem spoke, the Unity Union was founded in the Berlin district of Wedding. Its purpose was to continue the metalworkers' strike against the will of the German Metalworkers Union (*Deutscher Metallarbeiter-Verband*, DMV). It was unsuccessful. However, some of Berlin's metal workers were radicalised by the strike and expressed their dissatisfaction with the DMV, especially that it had not exhausted all avenues in resisting the wage cuts, which affected female workers more than their male counterparts.[11] Nonetheless, the RGO ignored the fact that the strike had shown workers' general reluctance to fight rather than expressing a revolutionary awakening. This attitude was also seen in the founding of other 'red unions' where communist influence was relatively strong locally, notably for coal miners and building workers in early 1931. In contrast, in the opinion of the RGO leadership, the hurried establishment of very small 'red unions' meant skipping necessary stages of struggle.[12] The central committee of the KPD shared this view. The party leadership had called for 'red unions' to be created only under specific circumstance – namely when the working masses rebelled against the ADGB and when, in the course of a major strike, union members either left the union or were expelled.[13]

The RGO leadership foresaw an organisational structure modelled on industrial unions, with groups of factory workers and the unemployed at local, district and national level. Within the framework of a complicated dual strategy, the factory groups, which were affiliated to an 'industry group', were tasked with continuing 'fractional work' within the SPD-led unions.[14] At the same time, 'red unions' were to exist as part of their respective industrial groups with their own sections within the factories. Thus, the 'red unions' were formally separate at the lower levels while, at the higher level, they were accountable to the RGO authorities.[15] But the constantly changing rules concerning the relationship between the RGO authorities and the 'red unions' were seldom thoroughly implemented. Difficulties soon arose, particularly where tasks were to be divided between industrial RGO groups and 'red unions' (as in the case of the Unity Union and the RGO in Berlin). This often led to personal rivalries and turf wars at various levels.[16]

Unity Union Politics and Practices

In the weeks after the Unity Union was founded in November 1930, the 'red union' made numerous attempts to convince DMV members to defect to them. Alongside the senior leadership of the Unity Union, the city-district leader also had important functions. Together with forty representatives from large factories, they formed an 'enlarged executive' which, combined with the senior leadership, made up the overall Unity Union leadership. The proportion of non-party workers on the 'enlarged executive' is thought to have been very high, although its precise composition is not known.

In response to an ADGB official's jibe that the Unity Union was insignificant, Paul Peschke, its chairman, announced in November 1930 that the 'red union' had 11,473 members with some half of them previously unorganised workers. The Unity Union's subsequent claim to organise up to 18,000 members was inflated: internal police reports from early

1931 show approximately 4000 workers and 4000 unemployed members, with combined figures later rising to a total of 10-11,000. Those numbers declined from the end of 1931 and it was only in late 1932 that the membership again grew to over 10,000. The number of factory sections in 1931 was between 300 and 350; in late 1932 there were 260.[17] By contrast, the number of unemployed sections in the Unity Union increased from twenty in early 1931 to seventy-four in late 1932.

As a communist organisation, the Unity Union was committed to class struggle with the objective of 'eliminating capitalist wage slavery and replacing it with working-class rule and the construction of a socialist society'.[18] Low membership dues, an organisational structure based on the workplace rather than place of residence and pledges towards workers disciplined by the DMV and strikers should have made the Unity Union attractive and facilitated opposition to the ADGB. But the Unity Union's success was limited. Its members were concentrated in only a few departments in large factories and in about twenty smaller factories that primarily employed lathe operators, moulders, machinists and fitters. The Unity Union was able to organise more than half the employees in some of those shops, but it was unable to initiate large-scale strikes or, moreover, to lead strikes as political struggles. The KPD soon abandoned its intention to expand the 'red metalworkers union' into a 'national metalworkers union of Germany'.

By late 1931, independent unions had become more controversial in the KPD leadership and parts of the RGO. The KPD began to scale back its newfound engagement with the metal workers' Unity Union and the other 'red unions' which had been set up earlier that year.[19] The KPD again prioritised the RGO's call to intensify 'offensive factional work' within the ADGB. But the party's criticism made little difference to how the Unity Unions acted. Once the Unity Union had enticed workers away from the DMV, these workers then found it all the more difficult to be reintegrated into the DMV and many were not readmitted. Particularly as the Unity Union had had a degree of independence, many members resisted the new political orientation: some left in frustration while others advocated pragmatic union politics that could hardly be called revolutionary. Given that the Unity Union's strike policy was so risky that workers were constantly in danger of being sacked, its influence remained limited. Nonetheless, it did do well in some works council elections in 1931. Overall, however, its day-to-day activities created many difficulties, which led the KPD leadership to view the Unity Union as a problem. As an organisation hostile to the state, it was not officially recognised as a negotiating partner in industrial relations, nor was it recognised by the labour courts. Unemployment and its radical approach to strikes (without a well-endowed strike fund) help to explain why the Unity Union had only a very limited base of support.

RGO and Unity Union Policies Regarding Women

The RGO and the KPD both worked to enable women's active participation in industrial conflict, and initiated campaigns to improve working conditions for women. The proportion of women workers in the metal industry had been increasing since 1925, and that growth accelerated during the Great Depression. This was partly due to the fact that women were paid far less than their male colleagues and employers wanted cheap labour for automated procedures. When the Unity Union was founded in 1930, women's wages in the Berlin metal industry were 30 per cent lower than men's. At that time, 35,874 female workers were employed in Berlin's metal factories.[20] Overall, this amounted to 25 per cent of Berlin's metalworkers, while in some departments in the larger factories it rose to 40 per cent. Because the companies used women for jobs that did not require extensive training, women's work only occasionally qualified as skilled labour. A large number of women performed work that required no training period; many others had 'semi-skilled' jobs as lathe operators in tool shops or in the electrical industry. In addition to wage discrimination, there was also inadequate sanitary provision.

The proportion of women in the DMV was higher than the national average of 6.7 per cent in 1930 and 5.7 per cent in 1932.[21] However, the rate at which women were organised in the Berlin DMV decreased astonishingly quickly after 1924, despite the fact that the proportion of women in the workforce was constantly increasing. The DMV leadership used women's unwillingness to join the union to explain wage disparities and employers' minimal awareness of women's interests. Apart from the DMV leadership's own reservations about treating women on an equal basis, the union's basis among skilled-workers was also a factor. Most skilled male workers felt that female labour was a threat to their own livelihood. As the DMV took the view that men should be responsible for earning money and women for the family and household, the union's newspaper called on married women to leave working in paid employment to their husbands.[22] Notably, too, many DMV members feared female employment would put downward pressure on their wages. This stance did not go unchallenged, but the DMV nonetheless never passed any resolutions that might have promoted gender equality. In 1931, some DMV reports showed a greater awareness of the problems women faced, but it was still thought that they should leave the workforce when the economy picked up again.

The RGO and the Unity Union tried to take up these issues in cities like Berlin, where female union membership was relatively high and they were particularly affected by wage cuts. Obviously, there were regional differences within the DMV in terms of women's needs. In Berlin, female workers were, for example, alienated by the failure of the union's efforts to account for them in collective bargaining.[23] Yet, in Nuremberg, the RGO gained little interest in a locality with strong female support for the DMV. Here many women stood for election to works councils and took on roles as officials, which explains the DMV's greater attraction to female workers in southern Germany.

There is a clear link between poor representation of women's interests and strong approval for the policies of the RGO and Unity Union, as was evident in Berlin. RGO publications not only emphasised that gainful employment for women was necessary for economic reasons; it also promoted their social liberation. From the RGO's perspective, the DMV's stance was akin to those of a small-minded petty bourgeois (*Spießer*) who would banish women to the kitchen.[24] By contrast, the principles of the Unity Union aimed to end gender discrimination as part of the struggle against capitalism, so demands that conflicted with men's interests were presented as anti-capitalist. For this reason, Silvia Kontos' thesis that there was no specific RGO policy towards women cannot be upheld.[25] Indeed, draft policy resolutions called for minimum wages that would be applied to women as well as men,[26] and demands were made to ban nightshifts and to end exhausting piecework. Strike committees' programmes addressed these workplace grievances; they also called for the creation of washrooms and cloakrooms, protective clothing, breaks for washing, and ventilation.[27] The Unity Union led numerous strikes to implement demands like these,[28] and fielded female candidates in works council elections.[29]

In Berlin's metal industry, we can safely assume that a higher than average number of women sympathised with the Unity Union, beyond what its actual membership suggests. Other 'red unions', such as in mining and construction, rarely addressed female workers' interests, which is attributable to so few women working within their remit. During this period, some 15 per cent of the KPD's membership comprised women, of whom approximately 75 per cent were unemployed. The RGO tried to organise housewives into groups, but very few complied. There were also men in the unity unions who resisted the idea of gender equality. At unity union conferences, women were drastically underrepresented, even in proportion to their membership. Although women were more strongly represented in leadership positions in the metal workers' Unity Union than in the DMV, they were minimally represented in the highest level.[30] Many members remained unaware of how patriarchal structures related to their own organisation in terms of both their function in the economy and the existence of restrictive gender roles. But the fact that the Unity Union demanded equal pay for women and espoused politicising struggles with the explicit aim of gender equality was sufficient to give many female workers the sense the Unity Union was responding to their needs. This explains why the Communists in the Berlin metal industry attracted more women than any other 'red union' throughout the country; the proportion of female members reached between 30 and 43 per cent.[31] This figure is clearly exceptional: there is probably no other example of a German metalworkers' union with such a high proportion of women.

The Unity Union's Opposition to National Socialism

Although the Unity Union had begun to address concerns about a possible ban of trade unions from early 1931,[32] it was nonetheless caught off guard by repressive acts following Hitler's appointment as Chancellor on 30 January 1933. Once the Nazis took power, however, union officials called for resistance.[33] After the Reichstag fire of 28 February, the Berlin Stormtroopers and Gestapo occupied the Unity Union's offices.[34] Some documents were safeguarded, but the Nazis nonetheless found material with sensitive information which was used to arrest officials.[35] Despite these difficulties, the RGO district committees were able to meet, and representatives from the unity unions were able to participate. Greater independence for all of the RGO's member organisations was discussed, with the aim of facilitating activity during a period in which such actions were illegal.[36] The 'red union' also resolved to make contact with former members in the hope that small groups could be set up.

Although arrests meant that the resistance groups lost members, some 100 individuals remained active. There was also an attempt to organise a courier service between the RGO leadership and the factories.[37] Fritz Rettmann, Paul Gericke, Rudolf Lentzsch and August Bolte assumed leadership of the metal workers' Unity Union; Walter Kautz, Oskar Walz, and Wilhelm Bielefeld were also important officeholders.[38] From mid May 1933, contacts with former members were used to obtain information about working conditions, the mood in the factories, and opportunities for distributing literature. In the ensuing months, the Unity Union was able to grow into a relatively large resistance organisation. It focused on revolutionary propaganda, distributing leaflets and newspapers, collecting dues and evaluating reports about the mood among the workers in the factories.

By August 1933, with a membership now reaching several hundred, a decision was made to rebuild the organisation to enable systematic activity.[39] This attempt, however, suffered from arrests owing to a lack of due care in actions, but also the lack of 'safe houses' and printing facilities.[40] Nevertheless, from mid 1933, Rudolf Lentzsch and Walter Kautz, who worked with rank-and-file members, were able to further develop the Unity Union.[41] They assumed that Hitler would soon fall, and a revolution would wipe out fascism. The group of conspirators divided the Berlin metropolitan area into eighteen union districts.[42] The new leadership consisted of Lentzsch and four instructors (Walter Kautz, Wilhelm Bielefeld, August Bolte, and Oskar Walz), each of whom was responsible for several districts. The outlawed labour organisation consisted of the executive and district leaders, and their wider contacts.[43] There was also a 'parallel organisation' that collected dues and coordinated the distribution of fliers, but the 'courier apparat' did most of the work as too few members were willing to take on those tasks. However, the organisation did at least manage to reconsolidate itself throughout the metropolitan area.

Information that was secretly distributed in autumn 1933 provides some insight into the organisation's goals:

> We must accelerate the process of the decomposition of the fascist front by debating with Nazi supporters in the factories and at the

dole offices in order to make it clear to them that Adolf Hitler will not lead the workers to socialism but only to barbarism. Socialism can only be achieved when the working class establishes the dictatorship of the proletariat.[44]

Actions at that time consisted of short demonstrations, leaflet distribution, and painting slogans on house and factory walls.[45] Despite its illegal status, the Unity Union had a constituency in some of Berlin's specialised foundries and metalwork factories where it had been relatively strong before 1933.[46]

The Gestapo soon managed to seriously weaken the 'red union'; having incorporated 800 to 1000 workers, the Unity Union was forcibly disbanded in December 1933 and approximately fifty people were arrested.[47] The Gestapo's investigations led it to conclude that, while the Unity Union had not mobilised the masses of workers, it had nonetheless created the most dangerous union organisation in Berlin.[48] The Unity Union leadership, instructors, individual district leaders and couriers were interrogated in the Gestapo prison (*Hausgefängnis*) and then sent to Berlin's Columbia-Haus concentration camp.[49] Then, after a stay in the Oranienburg concentration camp, they were held in the detention centre in Berlin's Moabit district. The prosecutor's office charged thirty-three officials with conspiracy to commit high treason in two trials,[50] and, in June 1934, the Berlin court of appeals condemned almost all of the defendants to sentences of up to three years in prison.[51]

Although this period of repression came close to ending the Unity Union's illegal activities in December 1933, the union proved able to reconstitute itself – albeit on a more modest scale than before. In the spring of 1934, together with some members of the RGO leadership – which had returned from exile in Prague – members set about rebuilding.[52] In this 'reorganisation' key roles were played by Ewald Degen, Max Gohl, and Ernst Altenkirch, but what made activity possible after the Gestapo's repression was the decision that local groups would work without the direct input of the leadership. According to their own account, the Unity Union organised 400 members in thirty factory-based and seventeen unemployed-members' groups.[53] In the interim, contact with the KPD was broken off. This was not only out of caution. Trust in the KPD had waned because its officials were interested only insofar as the Unity Union intended to use loyal operatives for party work. The RGO leadership stated that: 'Although the connection between [the RGO] and the party leadership was critically important, it became less intense at the lower levels and was often a point of conflict [...] Even in Berlin, where the party did in fact have some power, we noted that it had underestimated the RGO's work'.[54]

From the summer of 1934, the KPD leadership felt compelled to implement a fundamental policy change. It now declared that its central task was to establish contact with Social Democratic groups in order to create the basis for joint action.[55] The creation of 'unity' with the SPD-led unions was now given as the reason for another reorganisation. After the Unity Union rejected this policy, the KPD leadership denounced its stance as left-wing 'sectarianism'. Nevertheless, its members continued to distance themselves from Social Democrats. Because the Unity Union did not disband itself, conflict with the KPD's instructors intensified in the second half of 1934. Moreover, the Unity Union insisted on continuing to be a radical leftist union; it did not want to yield to the party and its members did not bow to the KPD leadership's recommendation to illegally reconstitute the ADGB and the DMV within the Nazis' 'German Labour Front' (*Deutsche Arbeitsfront*, DAF).[56] They rejected further contact with Social Democrats, including refusing to work to recruit for their trade unions. The Berlin KPD described the consequences of these tensions in terms of party cells and RGO groups in the factories working 'without connection to each other, in complete isolation and, consequently, often against each other'.[57] The Unity Union worked on the assumption that it could forge a 'class-based union' in opposition to the DAF; this stance was made public in the pages of the illegal publication, *Der rote Metallarbeiter*. But, by late 1934, the Unity Union could no longer withstand the pressure from the party leadership and the KPD dissolved it through 'organisational measures'. Party leaders labelled Unity Union activists 'wreckers', and declared a 'relentless battle' against them.[58]

At the same time, the RGO leadership – in agreement with the KPD, Comintern and Red International of Labour Unions – announced that the entire RGO had dissolved itself.[59] In its final act, the RGO leadership proclaimed that the most pressing need of the moment was to create a broad-based mass organisation. They stated that it should incorporate their 'former Social Democrat and Christian union colleagues, members of the RGO and red unions, along with discontented members of the National Socialist Factory Cell

Organisation and *Sturmabteilung* members in order to enable action against the common enemy: capitalism and its fascist gangs'.[60] Despite the fact that the Unity Union officially ceased to exist in 1935, individual groups nonetheless continued to operate, issuing leaflets under the rubric 'Red Union'.[61] Among those who remained active, it took some time to acknowledge that they had suffered a defeat. What remained of the proscribed Unity Union became the point of departure for resistance by other significant underground factory organisations in Berlin – which were now independent of the KPD.[62]

Conclusion: The Unity Union within a heterogeneous communist movement

This case study of the Berlin metal industry at the end of the Weimar Republic shows that trade union policy can only be explained if we assume the leadership's policy corresponded with developments in the rank and file.[63] Opposition to the ADGB among grassroots Communists gained currency when more radical 'faction work' was pushed by the party in 1927-28. That opposition to the SPD-dominated unions from below affected the RGO's transition to a policy of organisational independence from the ADGB and the establishment of independent communist unions, or so-called Unity Unions. KPD representatives in the Comintern and the RILU had a role in all of the important decisions taken on union issues, and these developments reflected longer-term developments in communist union policy. A particularly radical view of union politics, which had been developed over the longer term by some Berlin Communists in the metal-working factories, correlated with then current modes of radicalisation. Over time, that process gained considerable momentum. Elements of syndicalist politics, which had a long local tradition in Berlin, were also evident in Unity Union policy. These included radical aspirations with an essentially social revolutionary character, demands for autonomy in decision-making and a critique of excessive union financial support.

There is evidence that these specific forms of consciousness carried over into a strategy of 'isolation' (*Abgrenzung*) from Social Democracy. This was nourished not only by a disposition to see social democracy as 'social fascism'; it also drew on local syndicalist traditions. Perspectives like these influenced the formation of 'red unions'. Throughout Germany, these autonomous trade unions only existed at the regional level in certain union branches where the rank and file had been open to this form of autonomous organisation, and where syndicalism had made a relatively strong impact by 1918-19 at the latest.[64] The actions of the Unity Union show how little its members could be mobilised to serve the policy of the KPD leadership, the Comintern and the RILU, or at least that they could not be pressed into action when they were not convinced that the actions being called for were necessary. In this case, the 'Stalinisation' model is ill-suited to explaining developments, as it obscures more than it clarifies,[65] applying only to the surface level of the KPD and its ancillary operations – to their resolutions and propaganda. The actions of Communists were not necessarily an expression of party authority. Despite orders from above, autonomous rank-and-file actions were strengthened as the leadership's directives were ambiguously worded and left room for interpretation. From mid 1931, when the KPD leadership no longer permitted the foundation of 'red unions' on account of their lack of success, resistance to party resolutions increased. The Berlin metal workers' Unity Union at times developed such intensively independent momentum that interventions by the KPD leadership were unsuccessful. This was an expression of the Unity Union's call for independence and, from this time onwards, there were always tensions between the Unity Union and the KPD.[66]

In 1932, the KPD again had greater leeway in formulating RGO policy. However, fundamental policy change was not possible, partly due to the actions of rank-and-file Communists in strongholds like Berlin, the Ruhr and Hamburg. Because of these actions, the KPD and RGO leadership's attempts to impose a schematised or prescribed radicalism could not be successful.[67] The movement was not unified; many Unity Union members were so radical that their aims went far beyond those of the KPD. For a time, the party and the RGO were able to overcome their differences, at least to a certain extent, but from 1933 onwards, the KPD leadership made it clear that, under National Socialism, safeguarding the party was a much higher priority than maintaining the 'red unions'. The Unity Union fought the Nazi regime within the framework of the policy of outright hostility to Social Democracy, and in that respect, it was far more radical than the KPD. By mid 1934 at the latest, the Unity Union and the KPD were openly antagonistic to one another.[68] However, the outlawed 'red union' could not continue for long by itself and ultimately folded.

Due to its deviation from official policy and its 'sectarian' leftist stance, the Unity Union was hardly mentioned into the GDR's historiography, which focused predominantly on the KPD, and the Unity Union was also unknown in the former West Germany. The fact that research on resistance movements (despite its problematic orientation) now views the underground Unity Union as a significant locus of labour union resistance to the Nazi regime is an achievement. For the general public, however, the Unity Union remains largely unknown.

Translated by Joe Keady

Notes

1. Stefan Heinz, *Moskaus Söldner? Der 'Einheitsverband der Metallarbeiter Berlins': Entwicklung und Scheitern einer kommunistischen Gewerkschaft*, Hamburg: VSA, 2010; Stefan Heinz and Siegfried Mielke (eds), *Funktionäre des Einheitsverbandes der Metallarbeiter Berlins im NS-Staat. Widerstand und Verfolgung*, Berlin: Metropol, 2012.
2. ADGB unions were known as Free Trade Unions. The term 'free' refers to the claim that they represented workers' interests independently of the state and employers. However, for clarity, we have tended to avoid this term. For a discussion of related issues, see Michael Schneider, *Kleine Geschichte der Gewerkschaften. Ihre Entwicklung in Deutschland von den Anfangen bis heute*, Bonn: Dietz, 2000.
3. For extensive coverage, see Heinz, *Moskaus Söldner?*; Werner Müller, *Lohnkampf, Massenstreik, Sowjetmacht. Ziele und Grenzen der 'Revolutionären Gewerkschafts-Opposition' (RGO) in Deutschland 1928 bis 1933*, Cologne: Bund, 1988; Eva C. Schöck, *Arbeitslosigkeit und Rationalisierung. Die Lage der Arbeiter und die kommunistische Gewerkschaftspolitik 1920-1928*, Frankfurt a. M.: Campus, 1977; Lore Heer-Kleinert, Die Gewerkschaftspolitik der KPD in der Weimarer Republik, Frankfurt a. M.: Campus, 1983; Klaus-Michael Mallmann, *Kommunisten in der Weimarer Republik. Sozialgeschichte einer revolutionären Bewegung*, Darmstadt: WBG, 1996; Reiner Tosstorff, *Profintern. Die Rote Gewerkschaftsinternationale 1920-1937*, Paderborn: Schöningh, 2004.
4. Ulrich Eumann, *Eigenwillige Kohorten der Revolution. Zur regionalen Sozialgeschichte des Kommunismus in der Weimarer Republik*, Bern: Peter Lang, 2007, pp299-301.
5. Bert Hoppe, 'Stalin und die KPD in der Weimarer Republik', in Jürgen

Zarusky (ed.), *Stalin und die Deutschen. Neue Beiträge der Forschung*, Munich: Oldenbourg, 2006, pp31ff.
6. For details, see Hermann Weber, *Hauptfeind Sozialdemokratie. Strategie und Taktik der KPD 1929-1933*, Dusseldorf: Droste, 1982; Bernd Faulenbach, 'Zur Rolle von Totalitarismus- und Sozialfaschismus-'Theorien' im Verhältnis von Sozialdemokraten und Kommunisten in den zwanziger und frühen dreißiger Jahren', in Mike Schmeitzner (ed.), *Totalitarismuskritik von links. Deutsche Diskurse im 20. Jahrhundert*, Göttingen: Vandenhoeck & Ruprecht, 2007, pp119-131.
7. 'Protokoll des I. Reichskongress der revolutionären Gewerkschafts-Opposition Deutschlands', 30 November/1 December 1929, Manuscript, Berlin 1930; Berlin police surveillance report in Landesarchiv Berlin (LAB), A Pr. Br. Rep. 030, no. 21797, 4 January 1930, Bl.1ff.
8. For details, see Eberhard Heupel, *Reformismus und Krise. Zur Theorie und Praxis von SPD, ADGB und AfA-Bund in der Weltwirtschaftskrise 1929-1932/33*, Frankfurt a. M.: Campus, 1981; Klaus Schönhoven, 'Von der Kooperation zur Konfrontation. Gewerkschaften, Arbeitgeber und Staat in der Weimarer Republik', in Hans-Jochen Vogel and Michael Ruck (eds), *Arbeiterbewegung und soziale Demokratie in Deutschland. Ausgewählte Beiträge*, Bonn: Dietz, 2002, pp257-275; see also, Petra Weber, *Gescheiterte Sozialpartnerschaft – Gefährdete Republik? Industrielle Beziehungen, Arbeitskämpfe und der Sozialstaat. Deutschland und Frankreich im Vergleich (1918-1933/39)*, Munich: Oldenbourg, 2010.
9. For documentation concerning these events, see 'Stiftung Archiv der Parteien und Massenorganisationen der DDR' im Bundesarchiv Berlin (SAPMO), RY 1/I 4/6/2.
10. For details of relations between the Unity Union and the Profintern, KPD and RGO, see 'Bericht von den beiden Sitzungen der Reichsfraktionsleitung Metall am 6. und 21. Januar 1930', SAPMO, RY 1/I 2/708/78, Bl.47.
11. For details, see Heinz, *Moskaus Söldner?*, pp123-148.
12. For the discussion surrounding this, see SAPMO, RY 1/I 4/6/2, 16.
13. 'Anweisungen und Resolution des Politbüros im ZK der KPD', 15 November 1930, Bundesarchiv Berlin (BArch), R 1501/20461, Bl.234ff; further, 'Die Lehren des Berliner Metallarbeiterstreiks. Resolution des Politbüros des ZK der KPD', in Staatsarchiv Bremen (StAB), 4, 65-1207, Bl.9.
14. See the Gestapo surveillance report in SAPMO, RY 1/I 4/6/37, 15 June 1933, Bl.18.
15. 'Rundschreiben des RGO-Reichskomitees. Anlage zu den Anweisungen des KPD-Sekretariats an die Bezirksleitungen', 15 November 1930, in BArch, R 1501/20461, Bl.244.
16. 'Rundschreiben des Sekretariats des RGO-Reichskomitees, 6/33', 24 January 1933, in SAPMO, RY 1/I 4/6/13, Bl.399ff.
17. For further details on membership figures, see Heinz, *Moskaus Söldner?*, pp486-506.

18. *Die Rote Fahne*, 25 December 1930.
19. Heinz, *Moskaus Söldner?*, pp207-235, 277-285.
20. *Jahresbericht für das Geschäftsjahr 1930 der DMV-Verwaltungsstelle Berlin*, Berlin: 1931, p221.
21. In 1929, of the Berlin DMV's 82,067 members, there were 7944 (9.7 per cent) women; of 78,035 members in 1930, 6861 (8.8 per cent) were women and in 1932 there were 3515 women out of 57,971 members (6.1 per cent). See *Jahresbericht für das Geschäftsjahr 1929 der DMV-Verwaltungsstelle Berlin*, Berlin: 1930, p241; *Jahresbericht für das Geschäftsjahr 1931 der DMV-Verwaltungsstelle Berlin*, Berlin: 1932, p261; Brigitte Kassel, *Frauen in einer Männerwelt. Frauenerwerbstätigkeit in der Metallindustrie und ihre Interessenvertretung durch den Deutschen Metallarbeiter-Verband (1891-1933)*, Cologne: Bund, 1997, pp202, 678.
22. *Metallarbeiter-Zeitung*, 19 April 1930.
23. Kassel, *Frauen in einer Männerwelt*, p636.
24. 'Verbandstag des D.M.V. und Reichstagswahl. Referentenmaterial der RGO', [mid 1930], SAPMO, RY 1/I 4/6/31, Bl.19.
25. Silvia Kontos, *Die Partei kämpft wie ein Mann. Frauenpolitik der KPD in der Weimarer Republik*, Frankfurt a. M.: Stroemfeld/Roter Stern, 1979, p81.
26. *Die Rote Fahne*, 24 May 1930.
27. *Die Rote Fahne*, 5 September 1930.
28. 'RGO-Arbeitsplan zur Arbeit unter den Arbeiterinnen für die Zeit von Mai bis August 1932', May 1932, in SAPMO, RY 1/I 4/6/27, Bl.88ff.; for criticism of strike action for 'women's demands', see DMV-Berlin (ed.), *Die Kommunisten und die Gewerkschaften*, Berlin: 1932.
29. 'Rundschreiben an alle Bezirks-Arbeiterinnen-Kommissionen', 30 March 1931, in SAPMO, RY 1/I 4/6/27, Bl.51ff.
30. At most, 15 per cent of the participants in the delegate conference were women. Female officials in the Unity Union's 'narrow executive' only occupied positions that addressed women's issues, although the proportion of women was considerably higher among lower functionaries, see 'Bericht über die Lage im EVMB', 11 April 1931, SAPMO, RY 1/I 2/708/77, Bl.255; 'Resolution der EVMB-Sektion des Siemens-Konzerns zur außerordentlichen Generalversammlung', 16 January 1933, BArch, R 58/3302, Bl.38.
31. Heinz, *Moskaus Söldner?*, p499.
32. Berlin police surveillance report, Geheim Staatsarchiv Preußischer Kulturbesitz (GStaPK), I. HA Rep. 219, no. 162, 25 August 1931, Bl.15.
33. Berlin police surveillance report in BArch, R 58/3302, 1 February 1933, Bl.144.
34. Approximately 1700 arrests were made, primarily of Communists, see Martin Schuster, 'Die SA in der nationalsozialistischen "Machtergreifung" in Berlin und Brandenburg 1926-1934', PhD Thesis, Berlin, 2005, p230.

35. Gestapo surveillance report in SAPMO, RY 1/I 4/6/37, 15 June 1933, Bl.9ff; *idem*, BArch, R 58/3294a, 27 June 1933, Bl.63ff.
36. Gestapo surveillance report in BArch, R 58/3302, 30 June 1933, Bl. 179.
37. Berlin police surveillance report in BArch, R 58/3290, 9 March 1933, Bl. 238 ff.
38. For more on the lives of Unity Union officials, see Heinz and Mielke (eds), *Funktionäre des Einheitsverbandes*.
39. There were between 250 and 700 members, see 'Anklageschrift A gegen Rudolf Lentzsch und andere', 28 March 1934, in BArch, NJ 4301, Bl.7, 10.
40. 'Bericht der RGO Berlin-Brandenburg-Grenzmark vom 19.9.1933 bis 1.1.1934', in SAPMO, RY 1/I 4/6/14, Bl. 247.
41. 'Schlussbericht der Gestapo im EVMV-Strafverfahren', 13 January 1934, in BArch, R 58/3329, Bl.1ff.
42. 'Anklageschrift B gegen Willi Schulz und andere', 28 March 1934, in BArch, NJ 15018, Bl.5.
43. Heinz, *Moskaus Söldner?*, pp312-326; Hans-Rainer Sandvoß, *Die 'andere' Reichshauptstadt. Widerstand aus der Arbeiterbewegung in Berlin von 1933 bis 1945*, Berlin: Lukas Verlag, 2007, pp367-368.
44. 'EVMB-Informationsmaterial', September 1933, in 'Urteil des Kammergerichts Berlin in der Strafsache gegen Willi Schulz und andere', 26 June 1934, in BArch, NJ 15018, Bl.5.
45. 'Bericht des EVMB über durchgeführte Besprechungen zur Herstellung der Aktionseinheit', [August/September 1934], in SAPMO, RY 1/I 4/6/16, Bl. 408ff.
46. 'Betriebsbericht für die Berliner KPD', [early 1934], in SAPMO, RY 1/I 3/1-2/108, Bl.140.
47. Gestapo reports in BArch, R 58/3302, Bl.10ff.
48. Gestapo surveillance report in BArch, R 58/3293, 19 December 1933, Bl.100.
49. Information derived from the 'detention log' of the Gestapo prison in Berlin, in BArch, R 58/742 Bl.1ff; Kurt Schilde and Johannes Tuchel, *Columbia-Haus. Berliner Konzentrationslager 1933-1936*, Berlin: Edition Hentrich, 1990, pp144-201.
50. 'Anklageschrift A gegen Rudolf Lentzsch und andere', 28 March 1934, in BArch, NJ 4301; 'Anklageschrift B gegen Willi Schulz und andere', 28 March 1934, in BArch, NJ 15018.
51. Heinz, *Moskaus Söldner?*, pp324-326.
52. Gestapo surveillance report in BArch, R 58/3290, 7 February 1934, Bl.242.
53. 'Bericht über den Stand der RGO-Berlin', [May 1934], in SAPMO, RY 1/I 4/6/14, Bl.258; EVMB organisational report, [mid 1934], in SAPMO, RY 1/I 3/1-2/108, Bl.142.
54. See the minutes of the RGO national committee meeting of 24-5 August 1934, in SAPMO, RY 1/I 4/6/5, Bl.534.

55. Siegfried Mielke and Matthias Frese (eds), *Quellen zur deutschen Gewerkschaftsbewegung im 20. Jahrhundert, Bd. 5: Die Gewerkschaften im Widerstand und in der Emigration 1933-1945*, Cologne: Bund-Verlag, 1999, p41.
56. For details of this policy, see Matthias Frese, *Betriebspolitik im 'Dritten Reich'. Deutsche Arbeitsfront, Unternehmer und Staatsbürokratie in der westdeutschen Großindustrie 1933-1939*, Paderborn: Schöningh, 1991; Rüdiger Hachtmann, *Das Wirtschaftsimperium der Deutschen Arbeitsfront 1933-1945*, Göttingen: Wallstein, 2012.
57. 'Für bolschewistische Klarheit in der Gewerkschaftsfrage', [December 1934], in SAPMO, RY 1/I 3/1-2/109, Bl.381.
58. Heinz, *Moskaus Söldner?*, pp326-363, 466-483.
59. 'Meldung der Geheimen Staatspolizei über die Liquidierung der RGO', [December 1934], in GStAPK, I. HA Rep. 90 P, Bd. 2, Bl.195.
60. *Unabhängige Gewerkschafts-Zeitung*, 3, 1934.
61. Gestapo memorandum in BArch, R 58/3300, 3.4.1935, Bl.45; Gestapo surveillance reports in *ibid.*, 5 January 1935, Bl.21, 27.
62. Heinz, *Moskaus Söldner?*, pp472-474.
63. *Ibid., passim*; see also Bert Hoppe, *In Stalins Gefolgschaft. Moskau und die KPD 1928-1933*, Munich: Oldenbourg, 2007; Eumann, *Eigenwillige Kohorten*.
64. For further details, see Heinz, *Moskaus Söldner?*, pp474-483.
65. Cf. Hermann Weber, 'Die Stalinisierung der KPD. Alte und neue Einschätzungen', in *Jahrbuch für Historische Kommunismusforschung*, 2007, pp221-244. For an influential critique of Weber's 'Stalinisation thesis', see Mallmann, *Kommunisten in der Weimarer Republik*, pp1-17.
66. Heinz, *Moskaus Söldner?*, pp178-285, 326-363, 466-483.
67. For a discussion of these issues, see Mallmann, *Kommunisten in der Weimarer Republik*, pp304-394; Heinz, *Moskaus Söldner?*, pp364-483.
68. *Ibid.*, pp326-363, 470-483.

The KPD and Farmers: Approaches to a Neglected Research Problem

Sebastian Zehetmair

IN BOTH ITS programmatic self-conception and its social structure, the Weimar-era German Communist Party was a class party rooted primarily in the industrial proletariat. However, its political goal of overthrowing the existing social order required the party to clarify its relationships with the various non-proletarian groups in German society. The Weimar Republic included a wide spectrum of middle-class groupings that could not be strictly classified as either working-class or bourgeois yet whose various political perspectives were significant for the Communists' political prospects. Peasants, who constituted about one quarter of the German population at the time, were the largest of these non-proletarian groups.

The KPD's policies toward farmers have scarcely factored into discussions of the Party's history.[1] And given that the issue of peasant policy has received little attention in the existing research literature, the prevailing view has held that the KPD was indifferent to or even dismissive of peasants' interests.[2] But even a cursory look at party congress and journalistic records show that this perception is problematic: the KPD repeatedly debated the agrarian question in detail at its congresses and in its press starting in 1920, and was the first party in the Weimar Republic to specifically adopt an agrarian programme. The party published a series of newspapers specifically for farmers and agricultural workers, and for many years had a separate department within its leadership, the Rural Department (*Abteilung Land*), that was responsible for agitation among farmers and farm labourers. These efforts, however, were vastly disproportionate to their results. Despite everything, only an infinitesimally small number of peasants turned to the KPD. According to an internal survey conducted by the *Zentrale*, only 0.15 per cent of the members were peasants in 1927 (in absolute figures that means approximately 200 people among some 140,000 Party members), and only 2.2 per cent were agricultural workers as opposed to 68.1 per cent industrial workers and at least 9.5 per cent journeymen.[3] Peasants therefore made up a significantly smaller portion of the KPD's membership than was the case in several other communist parties in Western Europe, such as in Italy and France.[4]

To understand the reasons for this imbalance between effort and outcome, we need to consider two fields of historical research that have traditionally been investigated and discussed relatively independently of one another: the agrarian history of the Weimar Republic and labour movement history. The programmatic bases of communist agrarian policy are relatively easy to deduce from the party's congress debates, press, and the two official agrarian programmes of 1920 and 1931. More recently, the opening of the archives has also allowed historians to reconstruct the KPD's organisational practices in rural areas.

Agrarian history has produced many promising approaches to research in the past three decades. These include analyses of traditions in peasant and Junker political organising and analyses of rural social movements;[5] inquiries into the dynamics of economic and social development in the relationship between urban and rural spaces and the resulting shifts in workers' and peasants' social interests and lines of political conflict;[6] as well as the issue of the distinct mental and cultural preconditions for the process of developing political consciousness and for peasants' and workers' political practices.[7] The most pressing task in investigating rural communist agitation consists of utilising the knowledge that has been acquired in recent years about the Weimar Republic's agrarian history to analyse rural communist agitation.

Given the current state of the research, what follows can only point towards a project that still essentially remains to be done. This essay will address only three aspects of this subject. Firstly, it will address the agrarian programme of 1920; then it will address the ways in which uneven development in the agricultural and urban-industrial economies affected relations between industrial workers and peasants, paying close attention to the political economy of urban-rural relations during the inflationary period of 1919-1923; and, finally, it will engage with the problem of distinct organisational traditions in rural and urban politics and their implications for rural communist agitation.

The Agrarian Programme of 1920 and the Onset of the Agrarian Debate in the KPD

The *Zentrale* published an initial draft of an agrarian programme in the summer of 1919, just a few months after the party was founded.[8] However, the programme would not be systematically discussed until the unification congress of the KPD and the left wing of the Independent Socialists in the autumn of 1920. The question of land ownership had been at the heart of the agrarian debate among socialists prior to 1914 and it was once again central to the first agrarian debate in the KPD.[9] The Communist International's (Comintern) 'Twenty-One Conditions' for entry called for the establishment of an alliance between industrial workers and poor agricultural workers. That requirement was derived from the experience of the Russian Revolution in October 1917, in which the Bolsheviks won support for their policies from portions of the rural populace.[10]

The core of Bolshevik agrarian policy in October 1917 focused on the redistribution of large estates among the peasants. Rosa Luxemburg was critical of this as early as 1918. It was a move that had created a political base for the Bolsheviks among the peasants, but she believed that it would lead to long-term problems for Soviet power because Bolshevik agrarian reform had strengthened the land-owning farmers, who would put up strong resistance to future agricultural socialisation efforts.[11]

When the 1920 party congress discussed the unified party's agrarian programme, the question of whether Bolshevik agrarian policy could serve as a model for a German party had not yet been resolved. August Thalheimer, author of the KPD's agrarian programme and long-time political companion of Rosa Luxemburg, defended the Bolshevik land reform at this party congress. He argued that there had been no alternative – it was a step that made a political alliance between the relatively small number of Russian workers and the far larger population of poor farmers possible in the first place. According to Thalheimer, economic conditions in Germany demanded a different route to an agrarian policy. Germany had a broad stratum of small- and mid-scale farmers who had not been as badly pauperised as Russia's peasants. That populace had occasionally offered active support for counterrevolutionary movements in Germany and would, at least, need to be politically 'neutralised', which is to say liberated from fealty to the large estate owners and wealthier farmers. To that end, he believed that distributing the existing large estates to the small- and mid-scale farmers would make political sense under certain circumstances (for example, if that ownership were leased in parcels and cultivated on a small scale) even though such actions might mean a step backward from the *economic* standpoint of socialisation. Thalheimer was convinced that only cooperatively run large-scale operations could serve as a basis for agricultural socialisation.[12]

The most important question in the agrarian debate at the congress concerned the party's attitude toward land ownership by small-scale farmers, and whether it would be better to directly socialise the existing larger estates or to redistribute them among the farmers. There were groups that agreed with Rosa Luxemburg's critique of Bolshevik-style agrarian reform and pushed for complete expropriation of rural property, or opposed the redistribution of large estates, but they were a distinct minority.[13] With respect to socialisation, the agrarian programme that the congress passed differentiated between forms of agricultural operation based on the size and type of cultivation. Large estates that were cultivated by peasants as fragmented, leased parcels were to be expropriated without compensation and reassigned to the former tenants, who would then be able to decide for themselves how cultivation should proceed. Estates that were already being cultivated on a large scale were to be taken over and managed by newly formed estate councils made up of farmworkers, estate artisans, and administrators.[14] The small- and mid-scale farmers' land ownership, on the other hand, was explicitly guaranteed. The programme thereby facilitated socialising individual estates while simultaneously accounting for small farmers' need to augment their own property.

The programme emphasised the principle of self-management by agricultural producers in lieu of state regulation or nationalisation of agriculture. The leaders of the KPD were aware that the war economy had left the farmers with a distinct aversion to any form of command economy. According to a 1921 manual for rural communist agitation, no state mandate could ever lead to the consolidation of small-scale agricultural operations with larger production entities. That could only happen voluntarily, although the party did pledge economic support for farmers in the event of cooperative consolidation.[15]

Beyond that, however, the programme did not at first provide a particularly concrete answer to the question of the political means by which small- and mid-scale farmers could be won over to form an alliance with urban workers. The text includes a series of individual demands on behalf of and promises to small-scale farmers, but most of those demands were essentially to be fulfilled after the workers had seized political power, which could not have had much practical meaning for farmers as long as the bourgeoisie still had the upper hand in the struggle for control of industry and the state apparatus. The KPD's agrarian programme was still significantly lacking in transitional demands which were tied to the needs of small-scale farmers in any form that would have made it practically possible to build the intended alliance.

The party would only develop such transitional demands in the years that followed. The 1931 'Farmers' Aid Programme' (*Bauernhilfsprogramm*) comprised a total of twelve individual demands, which ranged from tax and customs policy to socio-political demands and measures to reduce the burden of leases for tenant farmers.[16] By way of comparison with the agrarian programme of 1920, the Farmers' Aid Programme was not only geared more specifically toward meeting farmers' short-term political needs in general but also, more positively, toward protecting the property of mid-sized farmers in particular. This is worth noting as this programme was published during a period in which the Soviet state leadership began to implement forced collectivisations. While the Farmers' Aid Programme painted a rosy picture of forced collectivisation in the Soviet Union, it also promised to safeguard German farmers' property.

The Political Economy of Urban-Rural Relations

Although the commercial dynamics of Weimar industry and agriculture were extremely closely linked to one another, urban and rural economic development did not occur in parallel. At various times during the Republic's tenure, this unevenness created various problems that led to changing political possibilities and degrees of manoeuvrability for communist agrarian policy. Between 1919 and 1923, inflation made KPD agitation among farmers far more difficult.

On one hand, it made food drastically more expensive in the cities and on the other it created relatively stable economic development in the rural parts of the country.[17] The coexistence of hunger in the cities, and relative prosperity in the villages exacerbated urban-rural tensions that had been latent since the war.[18] These tensions became evident in the debates around the idea of a command economy, which set the terms for the discussion of agrarian policy in the early 1920s.[19] A command economy had been introduced during the war and instituted price controls for agricultural products as well as production requirements for farmers that were intended to help stem the rising cost of food. Elements of the command economy would remain in force until 1923 despite the farmers' bitter political opposition. The KPD found itself faced with a permanent dilemma. Its supporters among the urban workforce needed affordable food, while a command economy would have made any alliance with the farmers impossible. The stereotype of the 'profligate farmer' enriching himself through high food prices at the workers' expense was widespread among urban workers in the early 1920s, and that resentment radiated beyond the ranks of the KPD.[20]

Until 1923, the KPD's stance toward a command economy was contradictory. Its agrarian programme of 1920 advocated suspending it while at the same time rejecting a return to 'free' agriculture, which is to say farming not regulated by production requirements and price controls. Instead, the party proposed the direct exchange of goods between city and country, which would be mediated through cooperatives and farmers' associations, thus eliminating middle men in order to reduce prices.[21] But because the most important condition for this exchange of goods – workers' control of industrial production in the cities – could never be realised, this concept never became attractive to farmers or workers.

At the height of hyperinflation in 1923, the KPD, in diametric opposition to its own programmatic creed, called for a command economy for farmers again, in order to safeguard the food supply for the cities.[22] The primary distinction between the steps that the party began to promote and the existing command economy was that deliveries and prices were not to be under the control of state or municipal institutions, but rather managed by bodies within the labour movement itself. Additionally, the KPD that same year threatened draconian repercussions against farmers who inflated prices or refused to feed the cities. At regional and municipal level, the KPD also voted for Social Democratic legislative proposals that would have continued a diluted form of governmental controls over the wheat market.[23]

In 1922 and 1923, the conflict between farmers and workers was not limited to parliamentary debates about a command economy. In the provinces, a number of clashes flared up between workers and villagers due to a new form of what was termed 'proletarian self-help': direct appropriation of food by organised groups of workers in the villages. Workers who could no longer afford the price of potatoes or other vegetables stole food from the fields – and in doing so frequently clashed with farmers who were protecting their land.[24] In some rural areas, these massive conflicts intermittently brought public order to the brink of collapse and intensified the alienation between farmers and workers, particularly during the summer of 1923. The party leadership rejected such crimes against property for political reasons, but it nonetheless had to take the mood and the needs of its proletarian base into consideration. At the height of hyperinflation, workers often simply had no other choice but to steal from the fields to secure food and it was not uncommon for party leaders to be implicated in these confrontations themselves.[25]

Tensions between workers and farmers eased as the urban food situation improved following the stabilisation of the currency in the autumn of 1923. The command economy was lifted. For agriculture, unlike urban industry, the currency stabilisation meant the start of a new crisis that came on slowly at first but escalated substantially at the end of the 1920s. Poverty was widespread in the rural areas during the last few years of the Republic and it also affected middle-class farmers. What had been a widespread stereotype of the 'profligate farmer' who enriched himself at the workers' expense became implausible.

In an attempt to arouse farmers' interest in the fate of urban workers,[26] the KPD then focused its rural agitation on urban consumers' drop in mass purchasing power due to increasing unemployment and declining wages. But whenever party members discussed wage issues in the villages, they inevitably touched on the question of wages for farmhands, milkmaids and agricultural workers in general. Farmers' responses to this new form of rural communist agitation have yet to be researched in detail.

The Political Public Sphere in the Villages and the Role of the Farmers' Associations

Wolfram Pyta contends that the failure of communist rural agitation was primarily due to the KPD's poor understanding of the particular mechanisms through which villagers formed political opinions.[27] This argument should be incorporated into considerations of the KPD's relations with farmers. Urban workers at that time had a more or less firmly established milieu that was structured and organised by workers' parties, union organisations and other proletarian cultural, sports and leisure associations. These organisations defined the political space in which the KPD acted, and the Party's strategy was always primarily directed toward gaining political hegemony within that space. Village agitation, however, required an entirely different approach because the local political-public sphere in the villages was structured differently from the public sphere in the cities. Rural areas often had no tradition of organised workers' parties, no unions and no independent proletarian associations.

The provinces were dominated by conservative agrarian associations that had been organising in the villages since the late nineteenth century.[28] These associations' politics were estate-based, which is to say that they emphasised the common interests of small- and large-scale farmers in opposition to urban consumer groups. The largest of these agrarian associations, the League of Farmers (*Bund der Landwirte*) – which had merged with the German Rural League (*Deutscher Landbund*) in 1921 to form the National Rural League (*Reichslandbund*) – as well as the Christian Farmers' Association (*Christliche Bauernverein*) were mass organisations with rank-and-file memberships numbering into the hundreds of thousands of farmers.[29] Unlike the left-wing proletarian parties, they had access to a tightly woven organisational network in the provinces.

The farmers' associations were Janus-faced. On one hand, they were organisations for political lobbying which influenced parliamentary processes, but on the other, they were also organisations for economic self-help (with affiliated taxation consultancies and access to credit and trading associations), whose services were indispensible for many farmers' everyday business. These associations had a leading position in the political public sphere in the provinces – they were more firmly rooted in farmers' everyday lives than the political parties themselves.

The associations' leaders were very close to the right-wing bourgeois parties, above all the German National People's Party in the north and the Centre Party and the Bavarian People's Party (*Bayerische Volkspartei*, BVP) in the Catholic south. But these associations also organised huge numbers of poor farmers and occasionally tens of thousands of farmhands, whom the KPD wanted to win over politically.[30]

The rural organisational power of the farmers' associations, their dominant position in the political public sphere and their socially and politically integrative function that transcended the agricultural population's various classes created serious problems for the KPD. The party rejected the associations' estate-based ideology and their links to conservative parties, yet it also wanted to win over at least the smallholders. It occasionally attempted to create independent farmers' associations alongside these established organisations, though at the same time it also wanted to build a political opposition among smallholders within the existing associations. The KPD made its first attempt at autonomously organising independent farmworkers' associations in 1919-1920 with the formation of the 'Communist Farm Workers' and Smallholders' Association' (*Kommunistischen Landarbeiter- und Kleinbauernverbandes*), but this ceased to play any role in the party's rural agitation after a few months.[31] In the mid-1920s, communist Reichstag deputy Ernst Putz founded the 'League of Working Farmers' (*Bund der Schaffenden Landwirte*), which later merged with several other smaller tenant farmers' associations to form the 'Association of Producing Farmers, Tenants, and Planters' (*Arbeitsgemeinschaft der Schaffenden Landwirte, Pächter und Siedler*).[32] The organisation was highly political in nature and received the KPD's support. Yet it also had a political dynamic of its own that the party leadership could not completely control. The question of the sense – or lack thereof – of a separate farmers' party alongside the KPD first arose within the League of Working Farmers in 1924. The party leaders remained indecisive for years, and that indecision was reflected in a general uncertainty in its tactics with regard to small-scale farmers.[33]

The party leadership hoped that an independent farmers' party would be able to weaken both the influence of the established farmers' associations and the link between smallholders and the conservative parties. However, it also quickly became clear that the members of the smallholders' associations by no means shared a universal tendency toward the political left. As economic interest organisations, these associations were far more heterogeneous than the Social Democratic-led unions. Despite the political differences between the SPD and the KPD, these unions shared common, overarching ideological horizon that crossed party lines, due to both parties' relationship with class struggle and socialism. The political alliances that the KPD entered into in the smallholders' associations in contrast were far more brittle. In the end, the results of the party's attempt to build its own smallholder organisations were disheartening. Even at their height, these communist-influenced organisations only comprised a few thousand members – a fraction of the membership of the National Rural League or the Christian Farmers' Association.[34]

Along with building its own smallholder organisations, early on, the KPD began agitating within the large agricultural associations themselves.[35] The party congress in Essen in 1927 passed a resolution stating that members should also build organised political opposition to the dominance of large agricultural interests among small- and mid-scale farmers within existing associations.[36] The practical outcome of this resolution is unclear. It was changed only two months after the Essen congress, when it was decided that the party should attempt to split the agricultural associations whenever the opportunity arose, rather than working within them.[37] Whether this change was primarily connected to the failure of the previous line or a response to a new dynamic within the agricultural associations themselves is yet to be investigated.

The KPD's rural tactics took a new turn in the late 1920s. The political cohesion of the existing agricultural associations, especially the National Rural League in northern Germany, declined noticeably over the course of the agrarian crisis. Large portions of the rural population underwent a remarkable political radicalisation that rearranged the rural political landscape (primarily in Mecklenburg and Schleswig-Holstein, although to a lesser extent in other regions as well). The most significant organisational expression of the farmers' radicalisation process was the peasants' movement, a new kind of social movement that began with a series of large protest actions by farmers in 1928 and soon transitioned into various forms of civil disobedience directed at state institutions and, ultimately, in a few cases, into terrorist activities.[38]

Starting in the late 1920s, the KPD attempted to link its own demonstrations in the core regions of the peasants' movement with the farmers' radicalisation process. But the radicalism of the peasants' movement could not easily be integrated into the KPD's familiar system of coordinating political action. In both its rhetoric and its practice, the peasants' movement took up established self-help traditions of village life, and in that respect, it was an expression of a particularly rural form of political radicalism. It invoked archaic images of pre-modern peasant class solidarity. Its politics revealed a clear sense of alienation from the state among broad swathes of the peasant populace, and showed a break with the politics of the established agricultural associations, which primarily focused on lobbying and saw themselves as thoroughly statist. But the peasants' movement was also a continuation of traditional peasant class politics in that its ideas were based on the shared interests of the peasantry, and consequently united large landowners and small-scale farmers within a single movement. In ideological terms, large portions of the peasants' movement, with its antiparliamentarian and *völkisch* ideology, were far removed from the labour movement; many of its adherents would later transition into the National Socialist camp. To date, the KPD's relationship with the peasants' movement has only been subjected to rudimentary research, and assessments of the communists' peasant policy are highly contradictory.[39] Yet this is a critical matter for any understanding of the KPD's rural organisational ideas during the latter stages of the Weimar Republic.

When considering Communist agrarian policy, the reality of the KPD's political experience cannot be analysed solely on the basis of party sources. Further research must also take account of the social conditions that impacted on the practical implementation of communist agrarian policy. It therefore seems reasonable to take the changing relationship between the world of urban workers and that of the farmers as a point of departure. In terms of its agrarian policy, the KPD was responding to precisely this fundamental political and social fault line within Weimar society. Approaching the party's history from this angle could open up new perspectives on some of the reasons for the failure of organised communism in the Weimar Republic.

Translated by Joe Keady

Notes

1. This is certainly the case for the standard texts in the KPD historiography. For an exception, see Wolfram Pyta, *Dorfgemeinschaft und Parteipolitik 1918-1933. Die Verschränkung von Milieu und Parteien in den protestantischen Landgebieten Deutschlands in der Weimarer Republik*, Düsseldorf: Droste, 1996, pp279-282; Martin Schumacher, *Land und Politik. Eine Untersuchung über politische Parteien und agrarische Interessen 1914-1923*, Düsseldorf: Droste, 1978, pp370-386.
2. Eric D. Weitz, *Popular Communism. Political Strategies and Social Histories in the Formation of the German, French and Italian Communist Parties 1919-1948*, New York: Ithaca, 1992.
3. Klaus-Michael Mallmann, *Kommunisten in der Weimarer Republik. Sozialgeschichte einer revolutionären Bewegung*, Darmstadt: Wissenschaftliche Buchgesellschaft 1996, p96.
4. Weitz, *Popular Communism, passim*. They probably also made up a significantly smaller proportion than in the more agrarian countries in South-Eastern Europe. Figures for countries like Yugoslavia, Bulgaria, and Romania provide good points of comparison in this regard because they were the focus of the Comintern's rural agitation in Europe in the 1920s. See George D. Jackson, *Comintern and Peasant in East Europe (1919-1930)*, New York: Columbia University Press, 1966.
5. Among others, see Schumacher, *Land und Politik*; Richard Evans and W. R. Lee (eds), *The German Peasantry: Conflict and Community in Rural Society from the Eighteenth to the Twentieth Centuries*, London: Croom Helm, 1986; Robert Moeller (ed.), *Peasants and Lords in Modern Germany: Recent Studies in Agricultural History*, Boston: Allen & Unwin, 1986; Stephanie Merkenich, *Grüne Front gegen Weimar. Reichs-Landbund und agrarischer Lobbyismus 1918-1933*, Düsseldorf: Droste, 1998; Robert G. Moeller, *German Peasants and Agrarian Politics 1914-1924: The Rhineland and Westphalia*, Chapel Hill: University of North Carolina Press, 1986; Jens Flemming, *Landwirtschaftliche Interessen und Demokratie. Ländliche Gesellschaft, Agrarverbände und Staat 1890-1925*, Bonn: Dietz, 1978; Jonathan Osmond, *Rural Protest in the Weimar Republic: The Free Peasantry in the Rhineland and Bavaria*, Basingstoke: Palgrave, 1993; Klaus Megerle, 'Protest und Aufruhr der Landwirtschaft im der Weimarer Republik (1924-1933). Formen und Typen der politischen Agrarbewegung im regionalen Vergleich', in Jürgen Bergmann (ed.), *Regionen im historischen Vergleich. Studien zu Deutschland im 19. und 20. Jahrhundert*, Opladen: Verlag für Sozialwissenschaft, 1989, pp200-287.
6. Research on the period of hyperinflation between 1919-1923, which will be discussed in greater detail in the section on the political economy of the urban-rural relationship below, is particularly instructive in this regard.

7. See in particular Pyta, *Dorfgemeinschaft und Parteipolitik*; Onno-Hans Poppinga, *Politisches Verhalten und Bewusstsein deutscher Bauern und Arbeiter-Bauern, unter besonderer Berücksichtigung revolutionärer und gegenrevolutionärer Bewegungen und Ansätze*, Hohenheim: EVA, 1973. Other valuable studies include: Josef Mooser, *Arbeiterleben in Deutschland 1900-1970, Klassenlagen, Kultur und Politik*, Frankfurt/Main: Fischer, 1984; Klaus Tenfelde, *Proletarische Provinz. Radikalisierung und Widerstand in Penzberg/Oberbayern 1900-1945*, Munich: Oldenbourg, 1982; Martin Müller-Aenis, *Sozialdemokratie und Rätebewegung in der Provinz. Schwaben und Mittelfranken in der Revolution 1918-1919*, Munich: Oldenbourg, 1986.
8. *Das Agrarprogramm der KPD* [undated: 1919].
9. For details, see Hans-Georg Lehmann, *Die Agrarfrage in der Theorie und Praxis der deutschen und internationalen Sozialdemokratie. Vom Marxismus zum Revisionismus und Bolschewismus*, Tübingen: Mohr, 1970.
10. See point 5 of the 'Twenty-One Conditions', which are available in English at: https://www.marxists.org/archive/lenin/works/1920/jul/x01.htm.
11. Rosa Luxemburg, 'Die russische Revolution', in *Rosa Luxemburg und die Freiheit der Andersdenkenden*, Berlin: Dietz, 1990, pp130-131.
12. *Bericht über die Verhandlungen des Vereinigungsparteitages der USPD (Linke) und der KPD (Spartakusbund)*, Berlin: 1921, p74. See also Emil Unfried, 'Die Landarbeiter- und Kleinbauernbewegung und die Aufgaben der KPD', *Die Internationale*, 15, 1 March 1922, pp340-341.
13. This tendency is apparent in, for example, the speeches of Iwan Katz, see the *Verhandlungen des Vereinigungsparteitages*, pp85-89.
14. The final version of the 1920 agrarian programme can be found in *ibid.*, pp237-242.
15. Emil Unfried, *Die Agrarfrage. Leitfaden zum Kursus 1921*, Hamburg: Carl Hoym, 1921, pp19-20.
16. *Kampf um die Scholle. Das Bauernhilfsprogramm der KPD*, Hamburg: Carl Hoym, 1931.
17. For these relations during the inflationary period, see Robert G. Moeller, 'Winners as Losers in the German Inflation: Peasant Protest over the Controlled Economy' in Gerald D. Feldman *et al* (eds), *Die deutsche Inflation: eine Zwischenbilanz*, Berlin: De Gruyter, 1982, pp255-289; Jonathan Osmond, 'German Peasant Farmers in War and inflation, 1914-1924: Stability or Stagnation?' in Feldman *et al* (eds), *Die deutsche Inflation*; Schumacher, *Land und Politik*, pp271-294; Pyta, *Dorfgemeinschaft und Parteipolitik*, pp163-183.
18. Klaus Tenfelde, 'Stadt und Land in Krisenzeiten. München und das Münchener Umland zwischen Revolution und Inflation 1918 bis 1923' in Wolfgang Hardtwig and Klaus Tenfelde (eds), *Soziale Räume in der Urbanisierung. Studien zur Geschichte Münchens im Vergleich 1850 bis 1933*, Munich: Oldenbourg, 1990, pp37-57.

19. Schumacher, *Land und Politik*, pp130-188.
20. See in particular, *Verhandlungen des Vereinigungsparteitages*, esp. pp85-87, where, among other things, it is said that, 'The farmer today is a usurer to the point of oblivion; there is no limit to his greed'.
21. *Ibid.*, pp95-96; Unfried, *Die Agrarfrage*, pp23-27.
22. See the KPD pamphlet, *Wie sichert die Arbeiter- und Bauernregierung die Volksernährung*, Berlin: 1923. Other pamphlets held large estate owners and 'usurers' responsible for the food crisis, see Heinrich Rau, *Was wollen die Kommunisten?*, in Heinrich Rau (ed.), *Für die Arbeiter- und Bauernmacht. Reden und Aufsätze 1922-1961*, Berlin [DDR]: 1984, pp26-36.
23. Wilhelm Koenen, 'Der Kampf um die Getreideumlage in Deutschland', *Internationale Pressekorrespondenz*, 113, 24 June 1922, pp770-771. The KPD subsequently pointed out that it had unsuccessfully tried to exempt small farmers from these requirements and was only prevented from doing so by the SPD. But this did not change the KPD's identification with the hated wheat allocations in the minds of the farmers. See the KPD publication *Bauernfrage und Landarbeiterfrage. Referentenmaterial für die Reichstagswahl 1924*, Berlin: 1924.
24. On the conflicts between workers and farmers over the food supply, see, for example, Schumann Dirk, *Politische Gewalt in der Weimarer Republik 1918-1933. Kampf um die Straße und Furcht vor dem Bürgerkrieg*, Essen: Klartext, 2001, pp64-69, pp152-157, 192-202; Klaus Tenfelde, *Proletarische Provinz*.
25. See *Bericht über die Verhandlungen des Vereinigungsparteitages*, pp72-105.
26. *Bauernhilfsprogramm der KPD*, pp17-18.
27. Wolfgang Pyta, *Dorfgemeinschaft und Parteipolitik*, esp. pp279-281.
28. On the history of the largest agrarian associations generally, see Merkenich, *Grüne Front*; Flemming, *Landwirtschaftliche Interessen*; Schumacher, *Land und Politik*.
29. The research literature on this includes only estimates as to the growth of membership in the farmers' associations. An analysis of the most important German farmers' associations from the perspective of the Comintern with estimates of their membership figures can be found in Eugen Varga (ed.), *Materialien über den Stand der Bauernbewegung in den wichtigsten Ländern*, Hamburg: Carl Hoym, 1925.
30. Varga estimated that the National Rural League and its affiliated farmhand organisations alone organised between 150,000-200,000 farmworkers in the mid 1920s – numbers that roughly equate with membership figures for the independent German Agricultural Labour Union, see *ibid.*, pp68-71.
31. The organisation is named in the first draft of the KPD's agrarian policy programme, but ceases to be mentioned in later publications, see *Agrarprogramm der Kommunistischen Partei Deutschlands*, p7; see also Poppinga, *Politisches* Verhalten, pp143-144.

32. An outline of these organisations was produced by the KPD leader Edwin Hoernle, see *idem*, 'Die Arbeitsgemeinschaft der schaffenden Landwirte Deutschlands und die Bewegung der Kleinbauern, Pächter und Siedler, nachgedruckt' in *Edwin Hoernle. Ein Leben für die Bauernbefreiung. Das Wirken Edwin Hoernles als Agrarpolitiker und eine Auswahl seiner agrarpolitischen Schriften*, Berlin: Dietz, 1965, pp288-301.
33. Edwin Hoernle, 'Zur Frage der Bauernpartei in Deutschland' in *ibid.*, pp302-313; see also Varga, *Materialien*, pp77-79; 'Bericht der Abteilung Land' in the *Bericht des Zentral-Komitees der KPD an den XI. Parteitag*, Berlin: 1927, pp99-104, here the question of forming an autonomous farmers' party is characterised as an important tactical problem for rural party agitation.
34. On the organisational strength of the smallholders' associations affiliated with the KPD, see Varga, *op. cit.*, pp75-78, which mentions approximately 10,000 members of these organisations. Poppinga estimates that there were some 2000 members of the communist 'National Peasants' League' (*Reichsbauernbund*) in 1927 and regards the figure of 10,000 that was occasionally cited by the party and in the subsequent DDR literature to be excessive, see *idem, Politisches Verhalten*, pp143-144.
35. The report by the Rural Department to the Leipzig Party congress in 1923 discusses systematic agitation at meetings of the Rural League, see *Verhandlungen des III. (8.) Parteitages der Kommunistischen Partei Deutschlands*, Berlin: 1923, p80.
36. See *Thesen und Resolutionen des XI. Parteitages der Kommunistischen Partei Deutschlands*, Essen, Berlin: 1927, pp83ff.
37. Heinrich Rau, 'Bauernbewegung und unsere Taktik' [15 January 1928], in *idem* (ed.), *Reden und Aufsätze 1922-1961*, pp62-67.
38. On the history of the peasants' movement, see Gerhard Stoltenberg, *Politische Strömungen im schleswig-holsteinischen Landvolk 1918-1933. Ein Beitrag zur politischen Meinungsbildung in der Weimarer Republik*, Düsseldorf: Droste, 1962; Rudolf Heberle, *Landbevölkerung und Nationalsozialismus: Eine soziologische Untersuchung der politischen Willensbildung in Schleswig-Holstein 1918 bis 1932*, Stuttgart: De Gruyter, 1963; Bergmann and Megerle, *Protest und Aufruhr*, which places locates the northern German peasants' movement within the national context.
39. Cf. Poppinga, *Politisches Bewusstsein*; Christof Ostheimer, *Vom Agrarprogramm zum Bauernhilfsprogramm. Ein Beitrag zur Entwicklung agrarpolitischer Parteiprogramme in der Weimarer Republik*, Diploma Dissertation, University of Hohenheim, 1976.

Communism and the Cultural Avant-Garde in Weimar Germany

Ben Fowkes

THIS CHAPTER INVESTIGATES the cultural avant-garde in Weimar Germany, which has not previously been examined in isolation. Partial examinations of it can be found embedded in more general studies of Weimar culture,[1] and intensive studies have been made of various individual aspects of the subject, such as Expressionism, Dadaism, and the proletarian literature movement. I intend here to build on these very useful contributions, to form a picture of communist policy in Germany towards avant-garde experiments, a policy which passed through five distinct stages. The first stage was an alliance with the avant-garde between 1918 and 1919; the second stage was a break with the avant-garde and a reversion to cultural conservatism between 1920 and 1924; the third stage was an attempt to create a new, proletarian culture combined with a partial return to the avant-garde alliance, between 1925 and 1928; the fourth, after 1928, was a renewed rejection of the avant-garde cultural producers and the development of a 'proletarian-revolutionary literature and art' which closely followed the Soviet example; and the final stage, after 1932, was the move towards 'socialist realism'.[2] But before considering the first four of these stages we need to examine the background, and in particular to depict the cultural situation the German communists inherited in 1918.

The German communist movement in its early years preserved to some extent the inheritance of the pre-1914 socialist movement. This applies particularly to cultural policy, and so requires consideration of the relationship between the socialist movement and the producers of culture before the catastrophic break marked by the First World War, a relationship which naturally depended on the attitudes of both groups. The views of cultural producers in Wilhelmine Germany can be analysed via the replacement of Naturalism by Aestheticism in the 1890s.[3] Aestheticists favoured the idea of 'art for art's sake', and the producers of literature, art and music therefore steered clear of assigning any political or social relevance to their activities. This was a crucial moment in the institutionalisation of art, and the later rebellion of the 'historical avant-garde' was a response to it (to use Peter Bürger's pioneering insight, as reformulated by Richard Murphy).[4] The period of Aestheticist dominance was then followed by a change of atmosphere, which can be dated from the 1900s. A new, modernising movement emerged, which has generally been called 'Expressionism'. Expressionism aimed at 'a radical demarcation from Wilhelminism on all levels of cultural practice'.[5] In other words, it explicitly identified existing German culture with a political regime – that of Wilhelm II – and utterly rejected it. The Expressionists who founded the journal *Die Aktion* in 1911 opposed the materialism and respectability of official Wilhelmine culture, and called for poets to associate with the marginal groups in society: prostitutes, thieves, the unemployed. The poet should 'break out of his social isolation' said the Expressionists, and 'lead the battle for the victory of the spirit [*Geist*]'.[6]

Did that mean that the pre-1914 avant-garde saw itself as engaged in a kind of revolution? It has been suggested that the avant-garde was 'politics, or even revolution, in the form of literature' and that 'most avant-garde authors in Germany understood revolution in leftist terms'.[7] This goes a little too far. It is true that some of the artists and writers of the German avant-garde were not opposed to collaborating with political revolutionaries; indeed they often thought of themselves as more revolutionary than the revolutionary politicians. But this was not the *general* attitude of the pre-1914 European avant-garde. The Russian avant-gardists of the early twentieth century, for instance, were not revolutionaries in a political sense, although like the German Expressionists they were usually hostile to the existing regime. The revolution they wanted was 'the acquisition of a new vision',[8] rather than political upheaval. Their aim, in Katerina Clark's striking phrase, was 'revolution as revelation'.[9] The difference between the German and the Russian avant-garde was that in Russia, unlike in Germany, a successful Bolshevik revolution took place, and so the artists and writers of the avant-garde were confronted with new tasks. They realised 'that the zero point had been reached [...] and they had a singular opportunity to translate their aesthetic intuitions into reality'.[10] Or, as Camilla Gray has put it: 'to the artists, the October Revolution was the signal for the extermination of the hated old order and the introduction of a new one'.[11] The artists of Russia did not make the October Revolution; they responded to it. It gave them the opportunity to display their artistic talents in the service of the revolution.[12]

Political activists' attitudes are also relevant to this interaction between politics and culture. People on the radical left, whether anarchist, socialist, or communist, might be expected to be in favour of all the forms of cultural innovation mentioned above, if they were aware of them. As David Cottington has recently written, 'the idea of the avant-garde [...] has become almost inseparable from that of political activism; indeed, from [...] revolutionary politics'.[13] But he adds this qualification: 'the assumption of a necessary relation between the cultural avant-garde and left politics is misleading'.[14] Moreover, the communists had serious reservations about the avant-garde's form of cultural innovation (though they were very aware of the merits of other cultural innovations, namely new methods of communication such as film and photography).[15]

Communist cultural conservatism was inherited from the pre-war SPD. The SPD displayed no evident reaction to what happened around 1910 in all branches of cultural activity, when, to use Adorno's striking expression, 'revolutionary artistic movements ventured out onto the ocean of the previously unimagined'.[16] There were no socialist debates about Expressionism in the 1910s, in contrast to the fierce battles in the 1890s over Naturalism.[17] The Social Democrats found literary Naturalism shocking, but Expressionism in literature and abstraction in painting, on the other hand, were simply incomprehensible. Neither Mehring nor any other leading Social Democratic critic paid any attention to the Expressionists or the Futurists; this is why Mehring was able to claim that the contemporary scene in Germany was an artistic desert. The writer Herwarth Walden complained with some bitterness that 'the spokesmen for the masses are against the Futurists. I expected nothing else. They want people to be ordinary, the same as each other and straightforward.'[18] The intellectual gap between the avant-garde and the German public increased considerably during the decade before 1914, and this also applied to the socialist movement, even the left of it. Modern poetry, said Rosa Luxemburg, 'produces in me an impression of vacancy';

because its view of the world 'has neither grandeur nor nobility', its 'formal artistic beauty becomes a grimace'.[19]

The First World War did not bring the avant-garde and the socialist movement any closer together at first, but it was of vital significance in the long run in bringing cultural producers out of the ivory tower they had largely inhabited before 1914. As the theatre director Erwin Piscator wrote later: 'My calendar begins on 4 August 1914'.[20] The Expressionist poet Johannes Becher expressed the same view, with characteristic pathos: 'The war was the thunderclap which roused the enslaved earth to spring free of its chains'.[21] Indeed, the carnage of the war compelled artists and writers to take up a political position. They did not necessarily side with the anti-war left, who were a tiny minority in 1914, in Germany as elsewhere.[22] In the years before the war broke out, some Expressionists – the predominant field of the avant-garde – had actually hoped for the outcome of war, seeing it as one way of breaking through what they perceived as the stagnation of German society. The poet Georg Heym wrote in 1910: 'If only someone would start a war. It could even be an unjust one'. It should be added, though, that Heym also expressed a longing for revolution: 'Why doesn't something extraordinary happen? Why doesn't someone murder the Kaiser or the Tsar? Why does no-one make a revolution?'[23] When the war did break out, Germany's young Expressionist poets flocked to join the military.[24] Many of them were killed in the first few months of the conflict. But one domestic counterpart of military activity was the patriotic poetry produced by those authors who remained at home. Practitioners of the visual arts similarly welcomed the war; Käthe Kollwitz, whose art had long expressed her passionate sympathy with the sufferings of Germany's poor, initially viewed the war as a healthy development: 'I had the feeling: all right, now the pressure has gone, now we can live again. I also felt a sense of renewal. As if nothing of the old values still remained intact', she wrote in her diary, adding: 'I experienced the possibility of voluntary sacrifice'.[25] These remarks, at the outset of a war which produced millions of deaths, are now difficult to comprehend, but they were characteristic of the general mood in Germany (and elsewhere) at the time, from which few were able to escape.

A year later, however, hostilities were continuing their violent course without reaching a decisive conclusion, and so, after 1915, there was increasing artistic resistance to the war, both in literature and the visual arts. Soon the only Expressionist writer who continued to support the war in public was Alfred Döblin.²⁶ Käthe Kollwitz completely changed her position after her son's death at the Front.²⁷ Franz Pfemfert's journal *Die Aktion* had opposed the war from the start, but he was now joined by others and René Schickele's journal *Die Weissen Blätter* started its criticism in 1915, having moved to Switzerland.²⁸ Kurt Hiller was surprisingly able to publish the first issue of his anti-war yearbook *Das Ziel* in Germany in 1916, which looked forward to a future in which 'war would no longer be permitted'.²⁹ It was prohibited immediately after publication. The artist Franz Marc, who volunteered in 1914, had decided by July 1915 that the war had 'lasted too long and become meaningless' and that 'the sacrifices it exacts are senseless'.³⁰ The poet Ludwig Rubiner went into exile in Switzerland and agitated against the war in the Munich journal *Zeit-Echo,* which he edited. He welcomed the Russian revolution of February 1917 and 'called on intellectuals to devote themselves to mankind [...] and expound the ideas of brotherhood and peace'.³¹ In burning words, Rubiner expressed the regret and sense of guilt of many German Expressionists at the false turning they had taken three years previously:

> We were the leaders. We towered over the rest. We sent out waves that moved the masses. That was our sin! Now the world is being made anew. We no longer have the right to exist. We no longer lead humanity to freedom, humanity is freeing itself over our dead bodies.³²

The Expressionists, in their turn, would soon be challenged by two other movements, which found the Expressionist stress on the need for inner spiritual renewal to be too vague and too far removed from concrete reality: their rivals demanded more down to earth, practical action.

These newly emerging cultural movements were Proletkult (which began in Russia) and Dada (which began in Switzerland). The ideas put forward by the Proletkult ('Proletarian Culture') movement spread from Russia to Germany after the October revolution of 1917, although they did not really surface in public in the latter country until 1919. This movement, founded by Aleksandr Bogdanov, was inspired by Marxist ideas. Bogdanov maintained that since all art and literature always reflects the ideas of the dominant social class, the proletariat must have its own class art to 'organise its own forces in social labour, struggle and construction'. This art would 'reflect the world from the point of view of the workers' collective'.[33] Proletkult in its original form did not last very long in Soviet Russia, but its ideas found expression in the All-Russian Association of Proletarian Writers (VAPP),[34] which was founded in October 1920, with the programme of 'creating the proletariat's own class culture as a mighty instrument for influencing the perceptions of the masses'.[35] By 1928, proletarian writers had achieved almost complete (though not permanent) dominance over the Soviet literary scene.

The tone of the Dada revolt, on the other hand, was more anarchist than Marxist, although its rejection of existing culture, and the society that underpinned it, was as uncompromising as that of the Proletkult. It began in neutral Switzerland in 1916, and was essentially a reaction by a number of exiled avant-garde artists (including three Germans, Hugo Ball, Hans Richter and Richard Huelsenbeck) to the brutality and mechanised slaughter of the war. It did not draw explicit political conclusions at first. In Hermann Korte's words, 'as a literary avant-garde, it expressed the crisis of art at the very moment of its crisis'.[36] The poet, abstract artist and sculptor Hans Arp, who joined Ball in Zürich in 1916, has provided a graphic description of Dada's activities at this time:

> Revolted by the butchery of the First World War, we in Zürich devoted ourselves to the fine arts. While the guns rumbled in the distance, we recited, painted, made collages and wrote songs with all our might. We were seeking an art based on fundamentals, to cure the madness of the age.[37]

A branch of the movement emerged in Berlin towards the end of the war,[38] and it was much more directly political than Zürich's Dada. The first German Dada manifesto, issued in Berlin on 12 April 1918, voiced its authors' disappointment over the tendency of the Expressionist movement to float around in the realms of the spirit:

> The highest art will be that which in its conscious content presents the thousand-fold problems of the day. Have the expressionists fulfilled our expectations of an art which should be an expression of

our most vital concerns? No! No! No! Under the pretext of turning inward, the expressionists in literature and painting are already looking forward to an honourable mention in the histories of literature and art and aspiring to the most respectable civic distinction.[39]

Instead of Expressionism, the Dadaists offered 'a new art' symbolising 'the most primitive relation to the reality of the environment', an art in which 'life appears as a simultaneous muddle of noises, colours and spiritual rhythms'.[40] This manifesto was immediately confiscated by the German police, and as a result it did not become known to the general public until 1919.[41] These artistic rebels intended to revolutionise the whole cultural sphere, and when the November 1918 revolution came along they hoped to broaden and deepen it through their cultural activities.

The Communist Party of Germany, which was founded a month later, at first had no definite policy towards the rebellion of the avant-garde cultural producers, though it shared their general attitude of rejecting existing German society and the German past. Most of the German avant-gardists of this time regarded themselves as communists, although they were highly unorthodox in their views, with a tendency towards anarchism. There was therefore a basis for an implicit alliance with the KPD. This did not last very long, however, as the party soon reverted to cultural conservatism. This partly reflects the influence of Gertrud Alexander, the literary editor of *Die Rote Fahne* throughout the period between 1919 and 1924. Alexander poured scorn on the endeavours of the Dadaists, and she took up the defence of 'bourgeois' culture against the onslaught mounted against it by George Grosz and John Heartfield (seconded by a fair number of other veterans of the November period) in the so-called *Kunstlump* ('art scoundrel') controversy of 1920. Grosz and Heartfield responded to the news that a painting by Rubens had been damaged by a stray bullet during the fight against the Kapp putsch of March 1920, and that the Expressionist artist Oscar Kokoschka had issued a plea to the combatants to avoid damaging the cultural treasures of the past, by describing Kokoschka as a *Kunstlump,* and proclaiming that the whole of the existing artistic inheritance was worthless and reactionary. Such monuments of culture as Rubens' paintings, they said, were part of the 'whole insolent art and culture swindle of our times'. High culture was not just bourgeois; it was 'one of the instruments of oppression used by the ruling class'.[42]

The cultural inheritance of the past, wrote Alexander, though it was decried as 'bourgeois', was a universal human achievement and should not be blotted out or ignored but rather transferred from the former ruling classes to the proletariat. This view, which triumphed in the party for the next few years, was actually in line with the traditions of the pre-war SPD. It appears somewhat paradoxical that the 'Alexander line' in culture coincided with a time when socialist revolution was on the agenda in Germany. The explanation is fairly simple, however: the efforts of the party were concentrated on the political sphere, and it was not thought (by orthodox Communists) that the attempt to change culture could make any serious contribution to the revolution. The situation was different in Soviet Russia, where the political revolution had already taken place, and a cultural revolution seemed to Communists to be its natural accompaniment. In Germany, the general attitude of the KPD until 1924 was that a cultural revolution would merely be a substitute for political action, a diversion and a useless waste of energy.

This changed after 1924. Revolution in Europe had ceased to be a realistic prospect, and no amount of overheated rhetoric from Zinoviev could hide this fact. Planning for the long term was now on the agenda, and communist cultural policy therefore entered a third stage. For the first time, the KPD set itself the objective of a direct transformation of culture. Where previously the KPD had seen culture as a benefit created by the servants of the old ruling classes for their enjoyment, which only needed to be spread more widely among the mass of the people, now it began the attempt to create a new, proletarian culture. This change of direction was intimately connected with the party's move towards factory cell organisation and the concomitant rise of the worker-correspondent movement (itself derived from Soviet experience). Worker-correspondents were factory workers who were members of the party, and they sent in reports on conditions in the factories to the party's local newspapers, or to the central organ, *Die Rote Fahne*. They were now expected to move on to the next stage, and become the creators of an independent proletarian culture. However, this did not settle the question of what to do with the existing culture.

In practice, the Communists now began to take up a less hostile attitude towards current avant-garde culture. The return of the 'united front' policy was underlined by the letter of 1925 from the Executive

Committee of the Communist International condemning the ultra left, which was welcomed by potential cultural allies of the KPD who had been spurned by the party until then. They began to bask in 'the sunshine of the ECCI's letter', to quote the Expressionist writer Kurt Hiller, who was one of the beneficiaries of the new line.[43] This third stage of communist cultural policy is thus marked by a dual process: the development of a separate proletarian culture through the worker-correspondent movement, and an uneasy alliance between communists, such as the poet Johannes Becher and the artist George Grosz, and leading cultural producers who were often of a social-democratic, liberal or indeed completely non-political orientation. The high-point of this cultural alliance was the successful joint KPD-SPD campaign against the 1926 attempt by the Right to impose censorship in Germany by passing a law against 'Trashy and Filthy Writings'.

The alliance did not last long. 1928 marked the beginning of a fourth stage of Communist cultural policy. It coincided (not by accident) with the KPD's move towards a leftist 'Third Period' policy, in line with the new approach of the Communist International (Comintern). Political cooperation with non-communists now came to an abrupt halt. This was paralleled by the ending of cultural cooperation, as the communists began to engage in ferocious polemics against leading former literary allies like Döblin. There was also sharp criticism of artists such as Grosz, who decided to leave the KPD at this time.

More positively, there now began an attempt to create, not just a proletarian culture, but a 'proletarian-revolutionary culture', and the KPD set up a series of unified proletarian cultural organisations. The visual arts were covered by the Association of German Revolutionary Visual Artists (ARBKD), which was established in March 1928,[44] and the League of Proletarian-Revolutionary Writers (BPRS) took care of the literary sphere. The latter was founded as part of an international communist writers' organisation, the International Association of Revolutionary Writers, which was strongly influenced by its Soviet counterpart, the Russian Association of Proletarian Writers (RAPP). The BPRS and its journal *Die Linkskurve* initially saw their main task as to give support to those literary works that emerged out of the worker-correspondent movement: 'proletarian literature'. In other words it ruled out cooperation with 'bourgeois' (in other words non-communist) writers, despite offers of alliance from progressive intellectuals like Toller and Ossietzky, who were increasingly concerned with the mounting danger of Nazism. Such people, said the BPRS, were dangerous 'because they had left liberal illusions about the class character of the Weimar Republic'. Literature should see the world from the standpoint of the revolutionary proletariat, and only writers of proletarian origin could do this.[45] Perhaps surprisingly, the organisation did not receive as much support for this rigid view as it would have liked from the KPD. In 1929, in its annual report, the BPRS complained that KPD leaders despised proletarian literature and paid much more attention to bourgeois writers, 'irrespective of whether their work contributed to the development of a new, proletarian literature or not'.[46] It was important to correct this, because 'deviations on literary matters are closely associated with deviations from the political line'.[47] The low opinion held by leading KPD officials of the efforts of proletarian authors was also shown (allegedly) 'by their demand that they give readings from Marx, Engels and Lenin at public literary gatherings rather than from their own works'.[48]

The party's Central Committee did not share the BPRS's view that 'left bourgeois' writers should be ignored. It was more interested in the *political attitudes* the writers took up. If they publicly supported the party they could be welcomed. Conversely, writers of genuine proletarian origin could not guarantee that their works would be published if they were not deemed to be of good literary quality. In March 1930, a member of the Central Committee criticised an article in *Die Linkskurve* for 'bowing down before worker-correspondents and factory newspapers'.[49] This intrusion by the party into the affairs of the BPRS resulted in the removal of the leftist Andor Gábor from the editorial board of *Die Linkskurve*. There followed a series of articles in the journal on Marxist aesthetics by Karl August Wittfogel, who proposed that the bourgeois heritage should not be rejected in its entirety but critically evaluated.[50] Later in the year Ernst Schneller, another member of the KPD leadership, criticised inadequacies in the BPRS's work,[51] and the line against left tendencies in the BPRS was confirmed at an international conference held in the Ukrainian city of Kharkiv in November 1930.[52]

But the Kharkiv meeting did not bring an end to disputes on cultural questions within the party. For instance, *Die Rote Fahne* consistently supported Erwin Piscator's theatrical experiments against attacks by critics in *Die Linkskurve*. Meanwhile, 'Leftists' such as Karl Biro-

Rosinger and Aladár Komját, as well as worker-correspondents from Essen and Berlin, and the literary critic Lu Märten, were fighting things out with Becher, Wittfogel and Biha. In the May 1931 issue of *Die Linkskurve*, Märten replied to Wittfogel's earlier criticism of her 1924 book in which she had endeavoured to make a historical-materialist investigation of what she called 'the essence and the changes in artistic forms'.[53] Here, she had developed the idea that artistic forms emerged from the dialectic of practical necessities, i.e. economic purposes, under the given technical conditions, and then later on they took on the character of fetishes, after their purpose had ceased to operate. Wittfogel attacked this approach as 'undialectical formalist barbarism'.[54] Märten replied that Wittfogel's thinking was 'organicist' because he had said that new forms 'grow out of' new materials, and that he was wrong to contrapose Hegel to Kant in this instance because they both proceeded from the 'absolute existence of art', positing art as an immanent and eternal human capacity. For a Marxist, she said, the aesthetic of both of these writers could only be of historical interest. Forms of art were of historical origin and could only be handed down to a limited extent. The proletariat would find adequate expression for its purposes not in existing artistic forms but in entirely new forms which did not necessarily need to be regarded as art. Film was an example of such a form.[55] Wittfogel issued a rejoinder the next month. He accused her of taking both a 'Trotskyist' position (by denying the possibility of a proletarian literature) and an 'ultra-left' position (by denying the 'continuity of cultural development').[56] These accusations contradicted each other, and in fact there was no real justification for the claim that Märten had denied the possibility of a proletarian literature. The accusation of 'Trotskyism' was a technique sometimes used by communist literary polemicists at this time, whether justified or not.

According to the draft programme of the BPRS, writers should raise their sights to creating the 'great proletarian work of art' which would 'grasp the daily life of the proletariat in its interaction with the lives of the other classes in such a deep and all-round manner as to reveal the great driving forces of social development'.[57] In other words, to out-Tolstoy Tolstoy. Rather a tall order! This was a sign that a new phase of literary policy was about to begin. There was a growing mood of dissatisfaction in Moscow in the summer of 1931 with what had been achieved so far.[58] RAPP was repeatedly called upon to carry out a frank self-criticism. Averbakh, the head of that organisation, responded by giving the signal for an attack on the proletarian writers, which was printed in *Die Linkskurve* in November 1931:

> The continuing backwardness of proletarian literature demonstrates the inadequate level of Bolshevik culture among the majority of writers. This is the reason for the weakness of their work. Inadequacy of form is only the expression of inadequacy of content.[59]

Now the famous George Lukács entered the picture. Having moved from Moscow to Berlin in the summer of 1931 he announced his arrival by making a fierce critique of two novels by the proletarian author Willi Bredel. 'These works are dry and artistically uninteresting. They present the world not as it is in reality but as it ought to be in the view of the author'. 'Bredel's work fails to portray real human beings', he added. 'Its linguistic level is that of press reportage'. Bredel's work was characterised, he said, not only by 'a lack of technique' but by 'a failure to apply dialectics in the literary field'. Moreover, its deficiencies were 'less individual failings than the general failings of the whole literary movement' (namely proletarian-revolutionary literature).[60]

Lukács also criticised Ernst Ottwalt, contrasting him with Tolstoy, to the former's disadvantage, of course. Tolstoy gives us 'stinking bug-ridden prison cells [...] and the real sufferings of real people', while Ottwalt offers only 'informed *discussions between lawyers* about criminal justice and a fleeting visit to the penitentiary by a judge'.[61] Ottwalt replied in *Die Linkskurve* by saying that Lukács was unable to point to a single example 'of a text which he sees as fulfilling his requirements for a proletarian-revolutionary work of literature. Since he does not do this it may be assumed that he is unaware of any work of this kind'. Moreover, he added, 'the fighting working-class comrade seeks support from his writer comrades' and where party brochures fail 'he reaches for proletarian-revolutionary literature'.[62] Lukács's rejoinder, backed up by extensive quotations from Marxist texts, was that Ottwalt's views were 'diametrically opposed to those of Marx, Engels and Lenin', because those great Marxists 'repeatedly referred to art as something to be enjoyed'.[63] As Ottwalt had predicted, Lukács was unable to point to any proletarian-revolutionary literature he approved of in this rejoinder.

Bertolt Brecht came into the firing-line as well. The editorial board of *Die Linkskurve* had never been particularly favourable to him, and it had ignored all the didactic plays he wrote between 1929 and 1932. They did not fit in at all with the above-mentioned programme of creating 'the great proletarian work of art'. Now *Die Linkskurve* went over to attacking Brecht openly for 'abandoning realism', to use Lukács's phrase. According to Lukács, Brecht was wrong to oppose 'eternal realities' to 'changeable and changing human beings' and to reject old-fashioned dramatic, Aristotelian theatre in favour of epic theatre. 'This contraposition', he said, 'is mechanical, and falsifies the real meaning of Marx's thesis on Feuerbach', which distinguishes between 'interpreting' and 'changing' the world. He argued that Brecht's views were 'a superficial vulgarisation of Marxist theory' devoid of any element of dialectical materialism. They amounted to a crude call for a 'radical break with all old art'.[64]

The former leftist Andor Gábor, who had now changed sides, made an attack on two plays in which he detected Brecht's influence. The authors had produced a 'montage' instead of a 'portrayal', and a 'report' instead of 'action'. 'Epic theatre' of this type was a theatre of 'consciousness and not of being', and it therefore represented 'an idealist standpoint', he claimed.[65] The proletarian writers tried to counterattack by denouncing intellectual know-alls who had no right to criticise; only the masses had this right, they said. But they were in a weak position. The BPRS programme drafted by Komját and Biro had already been rejected, and Brecht's attempt to join the BPRS was rebuffed by Becher and Lukács.[66] Around this time, the KPD Central Committee joined the anti-proletarian cultural chorus by issuing a resolution against the narrowness of the BPRS's approach. It had made a mistake in 'glorifying the working-class writer' at the expense of the 'need to learn and to raise the ideological level'. It had failed to gain the support of proletarian writers who were still outside it, according to the Committee, and it had failed to struggle against the 'danger from the right'.[67]

These attacks coincided with a decisive change in Soviet cultural policy, which transformed the situation of communist cultural producers everywhere. In April 1932, the Soviet party decided to dissolve the Russian Association of Proletarian Writers and the musicians' association, and then two months later, the corresponding association for artists was also abolished.[68] These decisions were aimed in part against 'leftism' in the arts, since the main reason given for dissolving RAPP was that it had had a negative attitude towards 'many groups of writers and artists who sympathise with socialist construction', the 'fellow-travellers'.⁶⁹ Thus, in Germany, the position of the radical left was weakened still further, and Lukács's view became paramount, in favour of retaining the traditional literary inheritance, and on this basis forming an alliance with left bourgeois writers.

This fourth and final phase in the history of the BPRS is marked, says Helga Gallas, by 'the rejection of new literary techniques and the return to an emphasis on the classical literary tradition'.⁷⁰ Lukács wrote five articles in *Die Linkskurve* in the next six months, attacking 'leftist' views of literature. He struck a few obligatory blows at 'Trotskyism' on the way, although in truth his opposition to the 'proletarian culture' approach and his respect for the literary inheritance was much closer to Trotsky's views expressed in *Literature and Revolution* than to those of the RAPP theorists. His criticisms ridiculed the theatrical experiments of Piscator and Brecht, and advanced the idea of *Parteilichkeit* (Party-mindedness), in contrast to *Tendenz* (tendency, or political commitment).⁷¹ This distinction was somewhat obscure. *Tendenz* meant simply commitment, which in the given circumstances could not be other than a commitment to the communist party, and the *Parteilichkeit* with which Lukács proposed to replace it, also meant commitment to the communist party (or as he put it, quoting Marx, 'partisanship for the class that is the bearer of historical progress, the proletariat, and specifically for [...] the communists').⁷² But this was exactly what the communist advocates of *Tendenz* also demanded. The fact that Lukács had just arrived from Moscow may be significant, as the slogan of 'party-mindedness' had been raised there a few months earlier by a RAPP writer: 'Party-mindedness [...] functions as the main driving-force, the essence, of our artistic method'.⁷³ The Fifth RAPP Plenum in December 1931 had accordingly adopted a resolution calling for 'greater efforts to ensure party-mindedness [*Partiinost*'] in the whole system of work of RAPP',⁷⁴ which might have influenced Lukács's thinking.

He went on to claim even more than this. His 'new' concept, he said, had rendered the old dispute between *Tendenz* and 'pure art' irrelevant. It was clear from his definition of Tolstoy's work as exemplary, that he entirely rejected the experiments with form carried out by the supporters of proletarian literature. As Helga Gallas has put it, 'it was characteristic of Lukács' critique that he [...] completely rejected methods of construction such as montage, documentation and epic forms of narration'.[75] He 'used the categories of dialectics to reaffirm what classical bourgeois aesthetics regarded as the function of art: to establish a harmonious unity, to create another world, as the highest form of manifestation of humanity'.[76] It was therefore not surprising that in the November/December 1932 double issue of *Die Linkskurve*, he moved on to include Brecht in his criticisms. In the Soviet Union, meanwhile, the aesthetic doctrine of Socialist Realism was being promulgated, at the first plenum of the newly-founded committee of Soviet writers, held from 29 November to 3 December 1932. Lukács's ideas fitted in very well with this new doctrine.

Shortly afterwards, however, the German situation was completely transformed by political events. The connection between communism and cultural innovation, which had persisted, if tenuously, throughout the whole Weimar period, was now brought to a sudden end by external developments. Hitler's assumption of power in January 1933 meant the end of open communist literary activity. All the communist writers, musicians, critics and artists were forced into exile, imprisoned, murdered or silenced. Discussions of Marxist aesthetics continued, particularly in Moscow, but these were now divorced from current German reality. A small BPRS group survived in Berlin for a couple of years after 1933, conducting illegal work, but eventually, in 1935, the turn to the Popular Front meant the dissolution of the BPRS and the final abandonment of the project to create a proletarian culture.[77]

Developments in the Soviet Union, the country to which many of the leading participants in the cultural debates of the Weimar period now fled, pointed in the same direction. 'Socialist Realism', which was officially adopted in 1934, had cast its shadow before it, with the earlier suppression of all separate cultural organisations and the unification of cultural producers into a number of single, overarching and centralised bodies. It was a culturally conservative doctrine, as the word 'realism' indicates, and from 1934 onwards, its adoption was practically compulsory for communists. There were one or two exceptions: surrealism in art was tolerated by Communists both in France and in Czechoslovakia in the late 1930s. But the general rule everywhere else was to stick to realism. Abstract art was naturally out of the question, as was literary or musical experimentation. The artistic activities and discussions of the left in the 1920s now fell into an oblivion from which they were not rescued until their disinterment in the completely different political and cultural context of the 1960s.

Notes

1. For example in John Willett, *The New Sobriety*, London: Thames and Hudson, 1978.
2. The development of 'socialist realism', which took place in exile, mainly in the Soviet Union, is outside our consideration here.
3. This was the general trend. Developments were naturally more complex in reality.
4. Richard Murphy, *Theorizing the Avant-Garde: Modernism, Expressionism, and the Problem of Postmodernity*, Cambridge: Cambridge University Press, 1999, p11.
5. Wilhelm Korte, 'Expressionismus und Jugendbewegung', *Internationales Archiv für Sozialgeschichte der deutschen Literatur*, 13, 1988, p93.
6. Ludwig Rubiner, 'Der Dichter greift in die Politik', *Die Aktion*, 2, 1912, p647.
7. Ingo R. Stoehr, *German Literature of the Twentieth Century. From Aestheticism to Postmodernism*, Rochester, NY: Camden House, 2001, pp54, 56.
8. Katerina Clark, *Petersburg: Crucible of Cultural Revolution*, Cambridge, Mass.: Harvard University Press, 1995, p30.
9. *Ibid.*, p29 (the title of chapter one of her book).
10. Boris Groys, *The Total Art of Stalinism: Avant-Garde, Aesthetic Dictatorship, and Beyond*, Princeton, New Jersey: Princeton University Press, 1992, p20.
11. Camilla Gray, *The Russian Experiment in Art, 1863-1922*, 2nd edn, London: Thames and Hudson, 1986, p219.
12. It was easy, and tempting, to identify aesthetics with politics in the post-1917 Soviet context. Whether the members of the artistic and literary avant-garde went as far as, in the words of Boris Groys, to 'call insistently upon the state to repress their [aesthetic] opponents', is questionable, though they certainly applied political terms of abuse to them. See Groys, *Art of Stalinism*, p23.
13. David Cottington, *The Avant-Garde. A Very Short Introduction*, Oxford: Oxford University Press, 2013, p98.
14. *Ibid.*, p100.
15. See chapters 4, 10 and 15 of Bruce Murray, *Film and the German Left in the Weimar Republic*, Austin: University of Texas Press, 1990. This is an illuminating and thorough treatment of the relationship between the German communists and film, which brings out the changing political context.
16. Theodor Adorno, *Ästhetische Theorie (Gesammelte Schriften*, vol.7), Frankfurt: Suhrkamp, 1970, p1.
17. I have excluded the debate over Naturalism for reasons of limited space.
18. Herwarth Walden, 'Abwehr I', *Der Sturm*, 3, 108, May 1912, p25.

19. 'Letter of 24 November 1917 to Sophie Liebknecht', in Rosa Luxemburg, *Herzlichst Ihre Rosa. Ausgewählte Briefe*, Berlin: Dietz Verlag, 1990, p403.
20. Erwin Piscator, *The Political Theatre*, tr. by Hugh Rorrison, London: Eyre Methuen, 1980, p7.
21. Johannes R. Becher, 'Unsere Front', in *Die Linkskurve*, 1, 1, August 1929, p1.
22. See Frank Trommler, *Sozialistische Literatur in Deutschland. Ein historischer Überblick*, Stuttgart: Kröner, 1976, p372.
23. Georg Heym, *Dichtungen und Schriften. Gesamtausgabe*, vol.3, ed. by K. L. Schneider, Hamburg: H. Ellermann, 1968, p169.
24. Max Beckmann, Otto Dix, Oskar Kokoschka, Rudolf Leonhard, Alfred Lichtenstein, Franz Marc, and Ernst Toller volunteered for military service in 1914.
25. *Käthe Kollwitz. Die Tagebücher*, ed. by Jutte Bohnke-Kollwitz, Berlin: Siedler, 1989, p151.
26. Thomas Anz and Michael Stark, eds, *Expressionismus: Manifeste und Dokumente zur deutschen Literatur, 1910-1920*, Stuttgart: Metzler, 1982, p295.
27. Käthe Kollwitz, *Tagebuchblätter und Briefe*, ed. by Hans Kollwitz, Berlin: Gebrüder Mann, 1948, p65.
28. Eva Kolinsky, *Engagierter Expressionismus: Politik und Literatur zwischen Weltkrieg und Weimarer Republik*, Stuttgart: Metzler, 1970, p45.The third major expressionist journal of the time, Herwarth Walden's *Der Sturm*, remained resolutely apolitical throughout the war.
29. Seth Taylor, *Left-Wing Nietzscheans. The Politics of German Expressionism 1910-1920*, Berlin: Walter de Gruyter, 1990, p72.
30. Franz Marc, *Briefe, Aufzeichnungen und Aphorismen*, Berlin: Paul Cassirer, 1920, pp46-7.
31. Theda Shapiro, *Painters and Politics. The European Avant-Garde and Society 1900-1925*, New York: Elsevier, 1976, pp162-3.
32. As quoted in Klaus Petersen, *Ludwig Rubiner. Eine Einführung mit Textauswahl und Bibliographie*, Bonn: Bouvier Verlag Herbert Grundmann, 1980, p60.
33. Aleksandr A. Bogdanov, Aleksandr A. 'Kritika proletarskogo iskusstva', in A.A. Bogdanov, *Voprosy Sotsializma. Raboty raznykh let*, Moscow: Izdatel'stvo politicheskoi Literatury, 1990 [1918], pp421-2.
34. There was a key difference: Proletkult in its heyday sought to act completely independently of, and almost in rivalry with, the Bolshevik party, while VAPP aimed to use the support of the party to impose its views on Soviet literature.
35. 'Ideologicheskaia i khudozhestvennaia platforma Oktiabria', quoted in Nikolai L. Brodsky and N.P.Sidorov, eds, *Literaturnye Manifesty ot simvolizma do 'Oktiabria'*, *Sbornik Materialov*, 2nd edn, Moscow: Agraf, 2001, p183. This was the platform adopted at the First Congress of the

VAPP in October 1920. For a succinct examination, still worth reading, of the complexities of the Soviet cultural situation, see Edward J. Brown, *The Proletarian Episode in Russian Literature, 1928-1932*, New York: Columbia University Press, 1953, pp7-15.
36. Hermann Korte 'Spätexpressionismus und Dadaismus', in *Literatur der Weimarer Republik 1918-1933*, ed. by Bernhard Weyergraf, Munich: Hanser, 1995, p115.
37. Hans Arp, *Unsern täglichen Traum ... Erinnerungen, Dichtungen und Betrachtungen aus den Jahren 1914-1954*, Zürich: Verlag der Arche, 1955, p51.
38. The main participants in the Berlin Dada movement were Huelsenbeck, Hannah Höch and her partner Raoul Hausmann, George Grosz, John Heartfield, Werner Herzfelde, and Johannes Baader.
39. Richard Huelsenbeck, 'First German Dada Manifesto', in Charles Harrison and Paul Wood, eds, *Art in Theory 1900-2000. An Anthology of Changing Ideas*, 2nd edn, Oxford: Blackwell, 2003, p257.
40. *Ibid.*
41. Dietmar Elger and Ute Grosenick, eds, *Dadaism*, Cologne: Taschen, 2009, p16.
42. Walter Fähnders, 'Literatur zwischen Linksradikalismus, Anarchismus und Avantgarde', in *Literatur der Weimarer Republik 1918-1933*, ed. by Bernhard Weyergraf, Munich: Carl Hanser Verlag, 1995, p161.
43. Frank Trommler, *Sozialistische Literatur in Deutschland. Ein historischer Überblick*, Stuttgart: Kröner, 1976, p585.
44. See Jürgen Kramer, 'Die Assoziation Revolutionärer Bildender Künstler Deutschlands (ARBKD)', in *Wem gehört die Welt: Kunst und Gesellschaft in der Weimarer Republik*, ed. by the Neue Gesellschaft für Bildende Kunst, Berlin: Die Gesellschaft, 1977, pp174-204. The ARBKD's manifesto and statutes are printed on pp315-7 of the same publication.
45. *Die Linkskurve*, 1, 5, December 1929, p24.
46. See 'Bericht über die Tätigkeit des Bundes proletarisch-revolutionären Schriftsteller im Jahre 1929', in *Zur Tradition der sozialistischen Literatur in Deutschland: eine Auswahl von Dokumenten*, vol. 1 1926-1935, ed. by Deutsche Akademie der Künste, Berlin: Aufbau-Verlag, 1979, p191.
47. *Ibid.*
48. Helga Gallas, *Marxistische Literaturtheorie*, Neuwied: Luchterhand, 1971, p17, quoting the 1929 report of the BPRS mentioned in the previous note.
49. N. Kraus, 'Gegen den Ökonomismus in der Literaturfrage', *Die Linkskurve*, 2, 3, March 1930, pp11-12.
50. Karl August Wittfogel, 'Zur Frage der marxistischen Ästhetik', *LK*, 2, 5, May 1930, pp6-7 and 6, June 1930, pp8-11; 'Weiteres zur Frage einer marxistischen Ästhetik', *LK*, 2, 7, July 1930, pp20-24, and 8, August 1930, pp15-17; 'Nochmals zur Frage einer marxistischen Ästhetik', *LK*, 2, 9, September 1930, pp 22-6; and 'Noch einmal zur Frage einer marxis-

tischen Ästhetik', *LK*, 2, 10, October 1930, pp20-23, and 11, November 1930, pp8-12.
51. Ernst Schneller, 'Offensive für das proletarische Buch', *Die Linkskurve*, 2, 12, December 1930, p3.
52. Gallas, *Marxistische Literaturtheorie*, p55.
53. Lu Märten, *Wesen und Veränderung der Formen und Künste. Resultate historisch-materialistischer Untersuchungen*, Weimar: Werden und Wirken, 1949 [1924].
54. Wittfogel 'Nochmals zur Frage einer Marxistischen Ästhetik', *Die Linkskurve*, 2, 9, September 1930, p23.
55. Lu Märten, 'Zur Frage einer Marxistischen Ästhetik', *Die Linkskurve*, 3, 5, May 1931, p15.
56. Wittfogel, 'Antwort an die Genossin Lu Märten', *Die Linkskurve*, 3, 6, June 1931, p23.
57. 'Entwurf zu einem Programm des BPRS', in *Zur Tradition der sozialistischen Literatur in Deutschland. Eine Auswahl von Dokumenten*, vol. 1 1926-1935, 1979, pp434-5.
58. Brown, *Proletarian Episode*, p191.
59. Averbakh, 'Zur Programmdiskussion', *Die Linkskurve*, 3, 11, November 1931, pp22-23.
60. Lukács, 'Willi Bredels Romane', in *Die Linkskurve*, 3. 11, November 1931, p26.
61. Lukács, 'Reportage oder Gestaltung? Kritische Bemerkungen anläßlich des Romans von Ottwalt (Teil II)', in *Die Linkskurve*, 4, 8, August 1932, p27.
62. Ernst Ottwalt, 'Tatsachenroman und Formexperiment. Eine Entgegnung an Georg Lukács', in *Die Linkskurve* 4, 10, October 1932, p24.
63. Lukács, 'Aus der Not eine Tugend', in *Die Linkskurve* 4, 11/12, November-December 1932, p17.
64. Lukács, 'Aus der Not eine Tugend', in *Die Linkskurve*, 4, 11/12, November-December 1932, p18.
65. Gábor, 'Zwei Bühnenereignisse', in *Die Linkskurve*, 4, 11/12, November-December 1932, p29.
66. Gallas, *Marxistische Literaturtheorie*, p225, note 64.
67. 'Resolution des Sekretariats des ZK der KPD zur Arbeit des BPRS' [undated], in *Zur Tradition der sozialistischen Literatur in Deutschland. Eine Auswahl von Dokumenten*, vol. 1 1926-1935, 1979, p441.
68. 'O perestroike literaturno-khudozhestvennykh organizatsii' [On restructuring literary and arts organisations], in *Pravda*, 24 April 1932; Brandon Taylor, *Art and Literature under the Bolsheviks. Volume 2: Authority and Revolution 1924-1932*, London: Pluto Press, 1992, p186.
69. See the resolution itself, as quoted in *Die Rote Fahne. Kritik, Theorie, Feuilleton 1918-1933*, ed. by Manfred Brauneck, Munich: Wilhelm Fink Verlag, 1973, p462.

70. Gallas, *Marxistische Literaturtheorie*, pp64-65
71. Lukács, 'Tendenz oder Parteilichkeit?', in *Die Linkskurve*, 4, 6, June 1932, pp13-21.
72. Georg Lukács, *Essays on Realism*, tr. David Fernbach, London: Lawrence and Wishart, 1980, p42.
73. G. Korabel'nikov, 'Za partiinost' literatury', *Na literaturnom postu*, 6, 1931, p16.
74. Karl Eimermacher, *Die Sowjetische Literaturpoliltik 1917-1932. Von der Vielfalt zur Bolschewisierung der Literatur. Analyse und Dokumentation*, Bochum: Universitätsverlag Dr. N. Brockmeyer, 1994, p137, note 183.
75. Gallas, *Marxistische Literaturtheorie*, p129.
76. *Ibid.*, p165.
77. Walter Fähnders, *Proletarisch-revolutionäre Literatur der Weimarer Republik*, Stuttgart: Metzler, 1977, p86.

Willi Münzenberg: A Propagandist Reaching Beyond the Party and Class

Fredrik Petersson

I am ready, with all my strength, to contribute to this campaign [...] in order to carry it out on as broad a basis as possible, to support it in this way.

Willi Münzenberg to West European Bureau in Berlin, 18 May 1928[1]

The socialist movement had been familiar with the term and concept of 'propaganda' for a long time [...] The word propaganda belongs to the most used terms in the socialist lexicon [...] According to socialist terminology it means something great, something valuable, scientific. Here propaganda is the term for the lesson of theory, of the scientific rational of socialism.[2]

Willi Münzenberg, Paris 1937

THE LIFE AND persona of Willi Münzenberg (1889-1940) has aroused both interest and conflict in scholarly debate over the years. A charismatic character in the international communist movement between the wars, Münzenberg was a German Communist and General Secretary of the international mass organisation International Workers' Relief. However, his mysterious death and the discovery of his body in a forest outside of the small French town St Marcellin in October 1940 continues to cast a shadow over his life. The British author and literary critic Michael Scammel did much to summarise the debate in his article 'The Mystery of Willi Münzenberg' in the *New York Review of Books* when he articulately re-assessed the erroneous and sensationalist biographies of Münzenberg by Stephen Koch and Sean McMeekin.[3] Yet it is the ongoing perception of Münzenberg as a 'mystery' that needs to be further addressed.

To avoid turning Münzenberg into a modern myth in the history of twentieth-century communism, we need to address the different layers of Münzenberg's life. This chapter will continue building on the representation of Münzenberg as the 'organisation man', as argued by Jorgen Schleimann in 1965, a depiction composed with extraordinary insight, which concluded that 'in death, as in life, Willi Münzenberg's name was a legend'.[4] This point of departure is detailed further by one of Münzenberg's colleagues, the author Arthur Koestler. After escaping from Germany following Hitler's 'seizure of power' on 30 January 1933, Koestler crossed paths with Münzenberg in Paris and contributed to his publishing empire up until the outbreak of the Second World War in 1939. Babette Gross, Münzenberg's partner and close ally in developing his media empire in Berlin and Paris, asked Koestler to author the foreword in her seminal political biography of Münzenberg. According to Koestler, Münzenberg was 'a political realist' who was devoted to three central principles: the struggles against war, exploitation and colonialism. Koestler concluded that Münzenberg's close relations with the Comintern and its hierarchical structures determined his life: not as politician or theoretician, but rather as a propagandist and activist.[5]

It is from this perspective that we should analyse Münzenberg's role as a propagandist and how he assumed a central role in developing numerous campaigns, committees, associations and organisations during the tumultuous years of the Weimar Republic. Yet, it is crucial to make a distinction between an initiator and a leader of propaganda campaigns. Münzenberg initiated and developed radical left-wing solidarity campaigns for the communist movement; but once they had been set in motion, the idea was for them to act independently of him while other actors arose from the background to assume control of either the campaigns or the organisations in public. This notably included the apparatuses of the German Communist Party and the Comintern. However, this does not diminish Münzenberg's role and position as one of the leading propagandists for the communist cause between the wars in Europe and beyond. Although Münzenberg was dependent on the consent of the KPD and the Comintern, documents in archives in Moscow, Berlin, Amsterdam, and London have disclosed how he was also at some level an independent entrepreneur in the way he established propaganda campaigns.[6] Despite of his intimate ties to the Bolsheviks and the international communist movement, he succeeded in reaching beyond party and class in numerous cases between the wars. Indeed, Babette Gross later concluded that Münzenberg was without a doubt one of the best-recognised 'actors on the political stage' in this period.[7] Even if we consider Gross's claims to be somewhat exaggerated, how do we assess an individual who continues to arouse vociferous political and academic debate?

One way of doing so is to focus attention on Münzenberg as a propagandist and organiser, and to consider how the interaction between the IAH's Berlin headquarters and the Comintern headquarters in Moscow functioned and determined the outcome of Münzenberg's propaganda operations. This approach allows a further understanding of Münzenberg as the 'organisation man', and demonstrates his part in developing the techniques and modes of propaganda that enhanced the public representation of European left-wing radicalism in an era characterised by hopes, uncertainty and political unrest. These political methods are taken for granted nowadays, but at that time they were new.

This chapter discusses Münzenberg's role as a propagandist in campaigns against oppression. It focuses on his different roles in the preparations for and convening of the First Congress Against Colonialism and Imperialism in Brussels from 10-14 February 1927, which established the international sympathising organisation, the League Against Imperialism and for National Independence (LAI); the plans for an international Anti-Fascist Congress, which culminated in Berlin on 9-10 March 1929; and, finally, the part Münzenberg and the LAI had in placing the anti-war issue on the political agenda in the Weimar Republic, generating mass mobilisation, and resulting in a successful political demonstration at the Amsterdam Anti-War Congress in 27-29 August 1932. A closer reading of archives and documents identifies Münzenberg's crucial role, and shows a second aspect of his propaganda enterprises: the centrality propaganda had in displaying the need for the labour and communist movement to act in the defence of the Soviet Union – an omnipresent slogan intertwined in the campaigns against oppression.[8] In the conceptualisation of these political projects, we see how Münzenberg reached beyond party and class and amassed support through struggle against colonialism, imperialism, fascism, and the threat of war. Münzenberg lived in a milieu profoundly influenced by the political context of the Weimar Republic, and this shaped his development as a propagandist. It also provides insights into why these campaigns attracted attention in circles outside of the German and international communist movements. For Münzenberg, propaganda was a means to achieve political goals, and in 1937, he outlined his Marxist-Leninist understanding of propaganda in *Propaganda als Waffe* (Propaganda as a Weapon). In its narrowest sense, the book was a polemic against Hitler, Goebbels, and the Nazi regime. But in it he also detailed how agitation and propaganda had to work hand-in-hand in order to mobilise the masses, forging a strong and coherent movement capable of realising the ultimate goal of revolution.[9]

From the beginning of his political career, Münzenberg's involvement in resistance movements against oppression was prolific. During the First World War, he met Lenin in Zürich and became involved with the far-left, anti-war Zimmerwald movement in 1915.[10] But what we are concerned with here begins in the mid 1920s, and ends with Münzenberg's successful appearance at the Amsterdam congress in 1932. After this, he was forced to move to Paris – where the setting and language was alien to him.[11] Münzenberg's conception of anti-colonialism, anti-imperialism, anti-fascism and the anti-war issue were, as we shall see, interconnected; they shared and benefitted from each other in the public spaces his propaganda reached and shaped. Regardless of how these campaigns were initiated in the 1920s, Münzenberg masterminded them, and, in some cases, the congresses that grew out of them introduced grandiose and ambitious political expectations to those who attended. The political demonstrations deriving from his campaigns shared similar organisational qualities, as well as expressing contemporary anxieties, given shape by populist strategies. Münzenberg retained control from the onset of the organisational process. The process also relied on the inclusion of prominent intellectuals, such as the French author Henri Barbusse, who was a left-wing radical and communist, and fronted all of the campaigns and congresses mentioned above. Barbusse, author of the war novel *Le Feu*, was one of the founders of the radical left-wing organisation *Clarté* in Paris after the ending of the First World War and was a close friend and collaborator of Münzenberg. His role was to aid the campaigns by securing moral support from Western intellectuals, especially those who practised radicalism at a 'distance', beyond and outside of communist circles.[12] According to Schleimann, however, Münzenberg realised that intellectuals should have no role in advancing political goals; their role was merely to fulfil 'public utility' and propaganda. Margarete Buber-Neumann, Babette Gross's sister and married to the German communist Heinz Neumann, put it more bluntly: Münzenberg respected the intellectuals, but had 'little respect for their work'.[13]

Some leading authorities in the apparatuses of the Comintern and the KPD received Münzenberg's activity with hesitancy and suspicion. For example, before the Brussels Congress began on 10 February 1927, Münzenberg also hoped to organise an international congress against fascism in connection with the demonstration against colonialism and imperialism and, with this intent, he approached the Comintern headquarters in January 1927. In response, the Secretariat of the Executive Committee of the Communist International told him to abandon any such idea, because the anti-fascist campaign was a 'campaign of the Comintern and its parties'.[14] Thus, if Münzenberg acted as an agent of ideas which were shaped by his understandings of class and solidarity, ultimately, the realisation of those ideas depended on the consent of the ECCI's decision-makers.

But Münzenberg's relationship with the KPD was different. Although he was a KPD Reichstag deputy from 1924 until 1933, he actually held the party at arm's length – not least to avoid the factional disputes discussed by Marcel Bois and Mario Kessler elsewhere in this volume. Instead, he cultivated informal, personal contact with influential figures, such as Leo Flieg and Heinz Neumann.[15] This method of working allowed Münzenberg to avoid the restrictions that would have otherwise been imposed on him and enabled his rise to prominence as an independent actor: the dichotomy between being a party soldier and working independently was a precondition for his success, which continued until his death in 1940. Münzenberg's position was secured by his masterful orchestration of political propaganda campaigns, using his media empire of newspapers, journals and films, and the launching of numerous committees, associations, organisations and initiatives, which were all loosely connected to the organisational hub of the IAH. This earned him a reputation among his antagonists (mainly the Social Democratic Party of Germany) as the 'red Hugenberg', a sardonic reference to Alfred Hugenberg, the German industrialist and conservative politician who owned a vast multimedia company during the Weimar republic.[16]

Münzenberg's role as a propagandist from the mid 1920s, including reaching beyond the party's core support, took place during the Bolshevisation and then Stalinisation of the Comintern and its 'national sections' – above all the KPD.[17] In the period from 1926 until 1933, the Comintern changed its tactics from the relative moderation and flexibility of the 'united front' policy to the infamous intransigence of the 'class against class' doctrine, which was introduced at the Sixth World Congress of the Comintern in 1928 and endorsed at the Tenth ECCI Plenum in Moscow July 1929.[18] The belief that communists should not work with Social Democrats went counter to how Münzenberg worked as a propagandist. But, typically of the enigmatic Münzenberg, it is difficult to pin down his stance towards Stalinisation in terms of how it impacted on his party work. It is, however, likely that he was able to act more flexibly because of his longstanding association with the Bolshevik 'old guard', from Lenin to Nikolai Bukharin and the Finnish Communist and Comintern secretary Otto W. Kuusinen. In 1927, he contacted Kuusinen and made a pointed reference to his work developing the communist movement's auxiliary organisations – which organised sympathisers as well as party members in *one* movement – declaring that it was 'a very personal question' for him.[19]

Ultimately, then, Münzenberg – as propagandist and 'organisation man' – developed and promoted ideas that united movements of people, beliefs and practices in a manner cutting across real and imagined borders. As discussed below, he developed a modus operandi based on his instinct as well as his experience as a party organiser who understood that anti-colonialism and anti-imperialism, anti-fascism and the anti-war issue had the potential to reach beyond party and class. In effect, he proved to be a visionary that, in some way, transcended the confines of narrowly communist party politics.

Willi Münzenberg: Propagandist against Colonialism, Fascism and War, 1926-1932

In January 1927, Münzenberg conceptualised a large number of ideas for new campaigns. He was involved in the preparations for the international anti-colonial congress which was to convene in Brussels

– a project that was jointly organised by the IAH and the forerunner of the League Against Imperialism: the League Against Colonial Oppression. He also participated in drawing up guidelines for new ventures, for example, for the founding of the Friends of the Soviet Union to promote the tenth anniversary celebrations of the October Revolution – attracting interest and involvement beyond the party – which would take place in Moscow in November 1927. He had also suggested that the ECCI strengthen support for anti-fascism by organising an international congress against Italian fascism. Alongside all of this, Münzenberg's activities as a propagandist were focused on Berlin. In January 1927, at the *Festsaal des Herrenhaus* – a ballroom in the capital – Münzenberg staged an event in which anti-colonialist and anti-fascist sentiments were expressed in speeches by Italian trade unionist Guido Migliolo, Afro-American William Pickens from the National Association for the Advancement of Coloured Peoples, and Chinese Ch'ao-Ting Chi, who visited Berlin as the representative of the Association for Spreading of Sun-Yat-Senism in America.[20]

All of these actions and events, however, also needed the Comintern's input. For example, in a session of the Political Secretariat in Moscow and during the preparations for the October Revolution's tenth anniversary celebrations, Münzenberg was told that he must 'connect the campaign' concerning colonialism and fascism with the continued 'risk of war' against the Soviet Union, according to a comment made by Mauno Heimo ('Lindberg'), a Finnish Communist who was Münzenberg's contact at Comintern headquarters.[21] Evidently, it was believed that the anti-fascist campaign should and could be intertwined with the defence of the Soviet Union and the perceived threat of war.

In February 1927, the First International Congress Against Colonialism and Imperialism took place in Brussels. It aimed to report 'on the oppression by the imperialist powers in the colonies' and to build up 'a great international organisation' capable of uniting and coordinating the 'fight of the oppressed nations'. There were 174 delegates representing 134 organisations, associations or political parties from thirty-four countries. It was seen as an 'anti-colonial pilgrimage' to celebrate the foundation of the League Against Imperialism.[22] The Brussels congress was, however, only one of several public propaganda efforts. A second event, of a similar political magnitude, took place in Berlin on 9 March 1929, as Henri Barbusse, the leader of the

International Anti-Fascist Committee (IAFC), opened the International Anti-Fascist Congress. The event aimed at mobilising 'every anti-fascist force' and would lead to the creation of a strong movement capable of enhancing the 'struggle against fascism and the danger of war', the IAFC stated after the congress. In attendance were 531 delegates, who represented communist, social-democratic, trade union, anarchist, and non-party interests.[23]

In 1932, a third event took place: the Amsterdam Anti-War Congress, which convened from 27-29 August and was attended by 2165 delegates from twenty-seven countries. To some extent, the Amsterdam congress witnessed the culmination of Münzenberg's skills as a political entrepreneurial force and established his status as 'the organisation man' of Communism in the Weimar Republic. The congress grew out of the German context – and Münzenberg's integration within the communist milieu there – and was held in a year that witnessed frequent major elections and the sidelining of parliamentary government by a presidential dictatorship.[24] Staging the event in Amsterdam offered a wider platform for communist propaganda and was seen by Münzenberg as a way of challenging the established order; the political content and propaganda connected to all of the congress themes mentioned above – anti-imperialism, anti-fascism and the anti-war issue – were continuously tested through Münzenberg's networks at political rallies in Berlin and all over the Weimar republic.[25]

The three congresses against colonialism, fascism and war between 1927 and 1932, represented crucial turning points in Münzenberg's career as a propagandist. However, these ideas and events were not isolated from each other and should be interpreted as a progressive development in the overall aim of bringing together perspectives that seemed disparate but that shared themes, aims and objectives.

The anti-colonial project had been initiated by the IAH after 1924, in response to demands made by the KPD and the Comintern that it should broaden its activities. In 1925, the IAH's proletarian solidarity campaigns Hands off China and the Committee against the Cruelties in Syria had made Münzenberg aware of the potential for putting the colonial question on the agenda.[26] In order to capitalise on anti-colonialism, which had generated extensive attention in Western Europe, Münzenberg contacted Grigori Zinoviev, the Comintern's chairman at this time, about the prospect of organising an 'all-encompassing congress against imperialist colonial politics [to be held] in Brussels or Copenhagen'.²⁷ The intention was to use the political impetus gained from the work of the Committee against the Cruelties in Syria and the Hands off China campaign. In January 1926, Münzenberg proposed the Action Committee against the Colonial Politics of the Imperialists to the Eastern Secretariat in Moscow; this would be a broad organisation capable of coordinating organisational issues and political matters linked directly with anti-colonialism. The idea was to hold an inaugural congress at the *Rathauskeller* in Berlin on 10 February 1926. Münzenberg himself kept a low profile and, on 5 February, invitations to attend were sent out to those who were considered suitable delegates from anti-colonial and radical left-wing associations in Berlin. According to the invitation, the conference aimed to discuss measures to raise awareness about the atrocities in the colonies across the 'entire civilised world' and to consider how to undertake 'preparations for an international congress against colonial atrocities and oppression'.²⁸ The *Rathauskeller* conference was attended by forty-three delegates and lasted for two-and-a-half hours, ending with the solemn declaration that the IAH should organise the international congress. Rather than form an action committee, the delegates sanctioned Münzenberg and the IAH to establish the League Against Colonial Oppression (LACO) in Berlin, which would function as the centre for a 'permanent campaign' against colonialism on an international level.²⁹

Invitations to attend the congress against colonialism and imperialism were circulated by the Berlin-based LACO. But, at the same time, Münzenberg negotiated with the Comintern on how to realise their wider objective. The Indian nationalist revolutionary and Communist, Manabendra Nath Roy, was Münzenberg's contact in Moscow. On 29 May 1926, Roy informed Münzenberg that the work to prepare the congress had to be 'done very cautiously' in order to not disrupt the general objective of the enterprise: 'to act as a neutral intermediary between the Communist International and nationalist movements in the colonies'.³⁰ Münzenberg's role was to perform organisational duties, including a mass demonstration against colonialism and imperialism. Despite tensions between Münzenberg and the Comintern – including his threat to turn the congress into 'a genuine' IAH event – the Brussels Congress convened on 10 February 1927.³¹ Before the event, Heimo reminded Münzenberg that the primary aim was to 'set up an International Committee of the League

Against Imperialist Oppression' in order to 'draw all political and industrial working class organisations, bourgeois radical, pacifist and cultural bodies [...] into the League'.[32] For Münzenberg, the aims were in perfecting anti-colonial and anti-imperialist propaganda and, in this way, finding new recruits for communism.

After the congress had successfully taken place, Münzenberg wrote to the Comintern to ask: 'what will happen now?'[33] The congress's successes were manifest. It had been supported by leading anti-colonialists such as the Indian nationalist Jawaharlal Nehru, the Indonesian Mohammad Hatta, Henri Barbusse, Albert Einstein, and, from the USA, Roger Baldwin, the leader of the American Civil Liberties Union. Yet, for Münzenberg, the issue appeared to be all about refining his skills as a propagandist in 1927.[34]

In the first months of 1928, Münzenberg began discussing with the ECCI means to realise his idea for an international anti-fascist congress. His contact in Berlin was the Ukrainian communist and high-ranking Comintern Secretary, Dmitry Manuilsky ('Numa'), who, at this time, had travelled to Berlin to coordinate the setting up of the Comintern's West European Bureau (WEB) there.[35] On 3 May 1928, Manuilsky informed Heimo in Moscow about decisions on how to develop the anti-fascist campaign. He stated that the WEB had issued a circular demanding that all communist parties give their full attention and support to the anti-fascist question.[36] The second step was getting Münzenberg to formulate a coherent plan to bring about the international congress.

It did not take Münzenberg long to respond to this request. On 18 May, he sent the WEB a detailed plan of action, which was then sent on to Heimo in Moscow. The document details how he anticipated developing his methods and strategies in the pursuit of effective propaganda and it explains the role of the IAH in this. In unleashing 'mass agitation in the [European] countries', Münzenberg's benchmark was the Brussels Congress.[37] But he also wanted to connect this anti-fascist congress with his longer-term involvement with the cause, which dated back to 1923 when he had assumed a leading position in setting up the International League of Antifascism (*Antifaschistische Weltliga*), with its inaugural meeting in Berlin on 10 December 1923.[38] In 1928, Münzenberg aimed to bring together new anti-fascist mobilisation with the memory of events in 1923, with particular emphasis on protesting against fascist rule in Italy and the thwarting of the German communist movement's failed attempt at seizing power in October 1923. In 1928, Münzenberg wanted to further the campaign by highlighting the murder of the Italian reformist Socialist, Giacomo Matteotti, whose death in June 1924 was suspected of being on the personal orders of Benito Mussolini. Münzenberg declared in 1928 that the stated aim of the congress was to 'win over' and 'consolidate' the support of 'pacifist and anti-fascist circles' in France, England, the US and Germany, and stated that it would work under the official leadership of a French committee represented by the French authors Henri Barbusse and Romain Rolland. According to the action plan, Münzenberg was explicit about two particular points: firstly, the anti-fascist campaign should follow a 'distinctly political programme' with wide appeal; and, secondly, once the latter was decided upon, the administrative and organisational work would follow.[39] Thus, approval from the Comintern in Moscow was necessary for Münzenberg, before proceedings could begin, first in Berlin, and then on an international level.

All of this took place during the period when international communism was about to break with the 'united front', as the Sixth World Congress of the Communist International met in the summer of 1928 to announce the sectarian policies of the so-called 'Third Period'. Yet, this did not deter Münzenberg from pursuing his ambition of bringing about a mass demonstration, which would include those from beyond communism's ranks. Several months before the event convened in Berlin on 9-10 March 1929, he produced an 'urgent' and 'confidential' report explaining that preparations were in their final stages and that the focus would be placed on 'the struggle against international fascism'. Italian fascism, however, would be used to symbolise the evils of this ideology in power. In the report, he stressed that Barbusse's International Anti-Fascist Committee had a broad-based character and that the KPD should stand only in the background to prevent the risk of damaging this wider appeal.[40] According to the Bulletin of the Organising Committee, which was published by the IAFC on 4 February 1929, several organisations and 'personalities' had answered the 'call against fascism'. In addition to publishing the names of its supporters, it carried reports on Austrian fascism and the prohibition of anti-fascist demonstrations across Europe. The agenda of the conference would emphasise: 'fascist terror and the persecution of national minorities'; the situation of 'workers, peasants and intellectuals' in fascist countries; and the interrelated theme of 'fascism, imperialism and the threat of war'.[41]

The congress followed Münzenberg's plan and covered all of the themes he regarded to be invaluable as propaganda. However, a secret report sent from the WEB to the ECCI on 12 March showed that the anti-fascist movement was caught up in the political maelstrom of Stalinisation and the Comintern's 'left turn', which attacked all non-Communists as 'enemies'. The report alleged 'poor preparations' – though without laying the blame openly on Münzenberg – and refuted the claim by the Italian Communist, Guilio Aquila, that the project and the congress had achieved its objective in full; instead, the report stated that the congress had merely created an 'international anti-fascist committee'.[42]

Here too we can identify some separation between Münzenberg's organisational role and his political commitments. To have adopted more rigidly the Comintern's 'Class Against Class' policy would have questioned the role of his mass and sympathising organisations. Yet, moving ahead in time, the impressive congress in Berlin in October 1931 to mark the tenth anniversary of the IAH,[43] brought Münzenberg no solace, as the communist milieu in Weimar Germany continued to radicalise in response to the advancing National Socialist movement, while, at the same time the German authorities stepped into action against communist networks. Indeed, on 21 December 1931, the LAI's headquarters in Berlin were raided, ransacked by the Berlin police force and closed indefinitely – finally re-opening at a new location in the city in April 1932.

These events took place when the LAI was preparing to mark its fifth anniversary in February 1932; instead, it was forced underground throughout Germany on account of what the Reich Commissioner for Public Order categorised as its subversive nature and communist connections. However, Münzenberg used this crisis as an opportunity. He publicised the now banned organisation's anniversary, and linked this to his campaigns against imperialism and the threat of war. The new international campaign was to be based around the implications and consequences of the crisis in Manchuria following the Japanese invasion of 1931.[44] Initially, the campaign was rooted in Germany – and subsequently France, where Barbusse was the key figure – with a mass rally in Berlin's Sportpalast on 3 March 1932, which gave prominence to the anti-war campaign. In this way, Münzenberg developed further the themes of fascism, imperialism and war, which had been first expounded at the Anti-Fascist Congress of 1929.

Münzenberg now sent a proposal to the Comintern's Political Commission to establish a 'fighting congress against war'. According to his proposal, it should take place on the anniversary of the murder of Archduke Franz Ferdinand in Sarajevo on 28 July 1914 in Geneva, close to the headquarters of the League of Nations. The objective was to give maximum impact to the event's slogan of a 'Red Anti-Militarist Week Against War'. Similar to the congresses in Brussels and Berlin, he aimed to unite every proletarian mass and sympathising organisation; these would stand side-by-side with prominent authors, academics and artists. Leading roles were to be played by Barbusse and Romain Rolland, with a preparatory committee consisting of Maxim Gorki, Albert Einstein, Heinrich Mann, Upton Sinclair, Bernard Shaw, Clara Zetkin and Ernst Thälmann. In August, however, Swiss authorities refused to approve the congress and forced the organisers to shift location to Amsterdam.[45] This change did not limit the interest stirred up by the Committee for the Preparation for the Geneva Anti-War Congress, who made public statements by Einstein and H.G. Wells showing their support for the anti-war cause and congress. And, on 5 June, Barbusse declared that the congress would expose the 'increasing chauvinism' and the 'militarist wave' that currently was spreading itself across the world.[46]

Münzenberg and the WEB entertained high hopes for the congress.[47] However, at this point, Barbusse was forced to address the criticisms of leading European socialists towards the event, charismatic figures who were hostile to the communist movement's use of war in their propaganda. The Austrian-born Friedrich Adler, who headed the Labour and Socialist International, and had a long-standing opposition to Münzenberg's involvement in campaigns of 'proletarian solidarity', played a key role in this counter-campaign. Adler called for a strong rebuttal of the way Münzenberg presented the issue of war historically, and how he linked together the issues of imperialism, fascism and the war threat. Seeking advice and support in his rebuking of Münzenberg's methods, on 8 July, Adler contacted the Belgian socialist Emile Vandervelde, who, in 1926-27 had been acting Foreign Minister, and had given permission for the First International Congress Against Colonialism and Imperialism in Brussels. Adler stressed that the anti-war congress was part of

Münzenberg's usual ploy of organising congresses, using as examples the two LAI congresses in Brussels 1927 and Frankfurt in 1929 and the Anti-Fascist Congress in Berlin in 1929.[48] Adler was not content, however, with writing letters; he also acted publicly, publishing an article making these criticisms of the coming Anti-War Congress explicitly evident in the newspaper of the Socialists in Vienna, *Arbeiter-Zeitung*.[49] Barbusse appeared to have been disturbed by Adler's behaviour, contacting Münzenberg on 14 July, stating that something should be done about his 'hypocritical attitude'. On the following day, Barbusse wrote to Adler to ask him to reconsider his harsh criticisms of Münzenberg and the congress.[50]

Nevertheless, the preparations for the conference continued on several organisational levels and at different locations in Paris, Berlin and Moscow after it became clear that the event would convene in Amsterdam. It opened on 27 August, and it confirmed Münzenberg's role as 'the organisation man', regardless of the involvement of the Comintern's control organ, the WEB, in Berlin and Amsterdam. In fact, the congress manifested Münzenberg's ability to organise a massive anti-war demonstration. As had been planned, the event found support across the political and cultural spectrum of left-wing radicalism in Europe and beyond. For Münzenberg himself, the events taking place in Amsterdam must have seemed a sharp contrast to events facing the KPD in Weimar Germany. For example, the congress bulletin reported how Münzenberg entered the rostrum while the 'Internationale' was being sung. It must have been a moment of euphoria for him, showing his ability to direct propaganda so powerfully in public spaces.[51]

Willi Münzenberg: Propagandist and Visionary

It is difficult – perhaps even impossible – to summarise the extent of Münzenberg's role as a propagandist. That has not been the aim here; rather, it has been to elucidate some of the complexities around his pioneering role in advancing methods of propaganda in public spaces in the Weimar Republic, across Europe, and beyond, between the wars. He was a forerunner of what have today become accepted methods in political and social campaigning, such as including singing and an array of cultural events in political rallies, and having appearances by artists and intellectuals who support political parties or causes. In this sense, Münzenberg was not only a propagandist and 'organisation man', the great impresario of the communist movement, but also a visionary. And, as a visionary, he also realised that his role was coming to an end as Stalinisation spiralled out of control in the 'Great Terror' in 1937-38. Although it is beyond the chronological scope of this volume, it is also worth noting Münzenberg's reaction to the signing of the Nazi-Soviet Pact on 23 August 1939. One month later, and after the outbreak of war between Germany and Poland on 1 September, in his publication *Die Zukunft* – which called for a socialist and communist alternative to Stalinism – Münzenberg stated: 'The traitor, Stalin, is you!'[52]

Münzenberg was shaped by the horrors of the First World War and by political modernity, including Leninism, as well as by the possibilities and, ultimately, the limitations offered by the Weimar Republic. He was an individual who shaped – and witnessed the advantages of using – various strategies to support campaigns against oppression. But he was never an ideologue: he was the product of a pacifist and socialist background, and the First World War had an impact on this political framework, as did the establishment of the Communist International in 1919. Unlike the biographical treatments of Münzenberg by McMeekin and Koch, which present him as a ruthless man who served only his own agenda, this chapter emphasises his complexity, and even more, the various spatial contexts and networks that flowed through or ran parallel with his life as 'the organisation man' and a political activist in the Weimar Republic. This is not a nostalgic reconstruction of a lost history nor an effort to expunge his life and work, as was done in the German Democratic Republic after 1945.[53] Quoting Münzenberg at the Brussels Congress in 1927 sums up his view of himself as a pioneering political propagandist: 'We are neither visionaries nor utopian dreamers; we know very well the limits of our strength and possibilities'.[54]

Notes

1. From Münzenberg's campaign plan, in the Russian State Archive for Social and Political History (RGASPI, Moscow) 542/1/29, 20-22.
2. Willi Münzenberg, *Propaganda als Waffe*, Paris: Carrefour, 1937, pp174-5
3. Michael Scammel, 'The Mystery of Willi Münzenberg', in *New York Review of Books*, 3, 11, 2005; Stephen Koch, *Double Lives. Stalin, Willi*

Münzenberg and the Seduction of the Intellectuals, London: Harper Collins, 1995; Sean McMeekin, *The Red Millionaire. A Political Biography of Willi Münzenberg, Moscow's Secret Propaganda Tsar in the West*, New Haven: Yale University Press, 2003; Babette Gross, *Willi Münzenberg. Eine politische Biographie*, Stuttgart: Deutsche Verlagsanstalt, 1967. Gross, who was Münzenberg's partner, remains to this day the authoritative source on his life and career in the German and international communist movement. Since the archival revolution in Russia and Germany in the 1990s, several studies have addressed Münzenberg's enterprises and involvement in developing propaganda. See: Tania Schlie and Simone Roche (eds), *Willi Münzenberg (1889-1940). Ein deutscher Kommunist im Spannungsfeld zwischen Stalinismus und Antifaschismus*, Frankfurt am Main: Peter Lang, 1995 for a good companion to Gross's narrative in comparison to Koch's and McMeekin's sensationalist accounts. For Münzenberg and the IAH, see Kasper Braskén, 'The Revival of International Solidarity. The Internationale Arbeiterhilfe. Willi Münzenberg and the Comintern in Weimar Germany, 1921-1933', PhD Thesis, Åbo Akademi University, 2014.
4. Jorgen Schleimann, 'The Organisation Man. The Life and Work of Willi Münzenberg', in *Survey: A Journal of Soviet and East European Studies*, 55, 1965, pp64-91. In the West, following the Cold War division of the world, see: Arthur Koestler's *The Invisible Writing*, London: Vintage, [1954] 2005; Gustav Regler's *Das Ohr des Malchus* Köln: Kiepenheuer & Witsch, 1958. These texts introduced readers to the enigmatic life of Münzenberg. Koestler and Regler had both worked with Münzenberg in Paris. Koestler acted as editor of Münzenberg's publishing project *Die Zukunft* in 1939.
5. Arthur Koestler, 'Vorwort', in Gross, *Münzenberg*, pp9-11.
6. The question of Münzenberg's central role in establishing political campaigns against various forms of social oppression is highlighted in my dissertation on the sympathising organisation the 'League against Imperialism and for National Independence' (LAI, 1927-37), see Fredrik Petersson, '"We Are Neither Visionaries Nor Utopian Dreamers". Willi Münzenberg, the League against Imperialism, and the Comintern, 1925-1933', PhD Thesis, Åbo Akademi University, 2013. (Published in 2013 as *Willi Münzenberg, the League against Imperialism, and the Comintern, Vol. I-II*, Lewiston: Queenston Press, 2013.)
7. Gross, *Münzenberg*, p14.
8. For a typical case on how the slogan 'in defence of the Soviet Union' was implemented in practice, see, for example the document 'For Immediate Action! All-America Anti-Imperialist League [LAI USA Section]', New York, 15 June 1929, in RGASPI 542/1/35, 10ob. The topic is addressed further in Petersson, *Willi Münzenberg*; see also Ludmila Stern's discussion on the implementation of this agenda, idem, *Western Intellectuals*

and the Soviet Union, 1920-40. From Red Square to the Left Bank, Oxon: Routledge, 2007.
9. Til Schulz (ed.), *Willi Münzenberg. Propaganda als Waffe. Ausgewählte Schriften 1919-1940*, Frankfurt am Main: März Verlag, 1972, p175.
10. Alexander Vatlin, *Die Komintern. Gründung, Programmatik, Akteure*, Berlin: Dietz Verlag, 2009, pp11-38; Gross, *Münzenberg*, pp125-39.
11. Koestler, *Invisible Writing*, p255. Documents in the Comintern Archive (part of the RGASPI in Moscow) show how secretaries translated documents into German for Münzenberg to read, for example, from English to German.
12. This kind of practice among Western intellectuals and their flirtation with communism is further discussed in, for example, Michael David-Fox, 'The Fellow Travellers Revisited: The "Cultured West" through Soviet Eyes', in *The Journal of Modern History*, 75, 2003, pp300-335.
13. Schleimann, 'The Organisation Man', p69.
14. 'Letter from ECCI Secretariat, Moscow, to Münzenberg, Berlin', 7 February 1927, in RGASPI 495/3/5, 102-04.
15. Martin Schumacher (ed.), *M.d.R. Die Reichstagsabgeordneten der Weimarer Republik in der Zeit des Nationalsozialismus. Politische Verfolgung, Emigration und Ausbürgerung 1933-1945*, Düsseldorf: Droste Verlag, 1991, p918; Koestler, *Invisible Writing*, p9.
16. McMeekin, *Red Millionaire*, pp210-12.
17. See, for example, Brigitte Studer, 'Stalinization: Balance Sheet of a Complex Notion', in *Bolshevism, Stalinism and the Comintern*, Basingstoke: Palgrave Macmillan, 2008, pp45-65.
18. The files containing the protocols of the Tenth ECCI Plenum in Moscow disclose how the decision-makers at Comintern headquarters favoured a harsher attitude towards Social Democracy, emphasising the belief that the communist movement had the inherent strength to act independently, without any support from other political parties or groups, see *fond* and *opis* RGASPI, 495/168.
19. 'Letter from Münzenberg, Berlin, to Kuusinen, Moscow', 24 January 1927, in RGASPI 538/2/40, 37-41.
20. 'Betr. Antifaschistische Kampagne, Münzenberg, Berlin, to Sekretariat des EKKI, Moscow', 25.1.1927, in RGASPI 495/3/5, 95; Secret report from unknown informant, in Auswärtige Amt, Abt. III a1, Berlin, Wilhelmsstr.74, 14.1-1927, in Stiftung Archiv der Parteien und Massenorganisationen der DDR im Bundesarchiv, Berlin (SAPMO BA-ZPA) R1001/6751, 30-31.
21. M. Heimo, Politsekretariat, 'Kampagne zum 10.Jahrestag, Moscow', 6.2.1927', in RGASPI 495/3/5, 47.
22. Petersson, *Willi Münzenberg*, pp112, 136. The original sources that summarise the intent and aim of the Brussels Congress are as follows: Louis Gibarti, 'Warum Kolonial-Kongress', in *Der koloniale Freiheitskampf.*

Mitteilungsblatt der Liga gegen koloniale Unterdrückung, 3, Berlin, 5 July 1926; Instructions ECCI Secretariat, Moscow, to Willi Münzenberg, Berlin, 2 July 1926, in RGASPI 542/1/3, 15-17; and Transcript of Willi Münzenberg's speech, Brussels, 13 Feburary 1927, in RGASPI 542/1/69, 37-49.

23. 'Internationaler Antifaschisten-Kongress. Bulletin des Initiativ-Komitees, Sekretariat Berlin, No.1', 30 January 1929, in RGASPI 543/1/4, 33; 'Informationsabteilung des EKKI, Bericht Nr.812, Moskau', 25 April 1929, in RGASPI 495/33/203, 107; 'Einige statistische Daten über den Kongress, Berlin', March 1929, in RGASPI 543/1/5, 108; 'The IAFC Appeals for a Struggle Against Fascism and against the Danger of War, IAFC, Paris-Berlin', [undated: 1929], in RGASPI 543/1/4, 132.
24. Eric D. Weitz, *Weimar Germany. Promise & Tragedy*, Princeton: Princeton University Press, 2007, pp122-3.
25. A typical example of this was how the LAI and the IAH organised an 'international demonstration against war' at the Sportpalast in Berlin on 3 March 1932. The event included fiery speeches from Münzenberg, the French communist leader Marcel Cachin, pacifist and member of the Communist Party of Great Britain Isabel Brown, the Japanese activist Nakanome Otsuka, the communist Chuang Tang from China, and KPD representative Albert Kuntz, see Petersson, *Willi Münzenberg*, p464, and 'Internationalen Kundgebung gegen den Krieg', 3 March 1932, in RGASPI 543/1/17, 320ob.
26. Petersson, *Willi Münzenberg*, pp61-90.
27. 'Letter from Münzenberg, Berlin, to Zinoviev, Moscow', 18 August 1925, in RGASPI 538/2/27, 108-09.
28. Petersson, *Willi Münzenberg*, p84; 'Einladung, Sekretariat G/E, Berlin', 5 February 1926, in RGASPI 542/1/4, 1.
29. 'Protokoll der im Berliner Rathauskeller, Berlin', 10 February 1926, in RGASPI 542/1/4, 2-4.
30. 'Confidential. Letter from ECCI Secretariat, Moscow, to Münzenberg, Berlin', 29 May 1926, in RGASPI 542/1/3, 10-11.
31. 'Letter from Willi Münzenberg', Berlin, to M. N. Roy, Moscow, 24 June 1926, in RGASPI 542/1/3, 13-14.
32. 'Letter from Heimo, Moscow, to Münzenberg, Berlin', 26 January 1927, in RGASPI 538/2/40, 55-58.
33. 'Letter from Münzenberg, Berlin, to ECCI Secretariat, Moscow', 21 February 1927, in RGASPI 542/1/7, 120-23.
34. For a full account of the Brussels Congress, see Petersson, *Willi Münzenberg*, pp135-48.
35. The West European Bureau (WEB) was established on the direct instructions of the ECCI for the sole reason of having a 'foreign bureau of the ECCI' in Western Europe, to exist as a 'contact between the ECCI and the West European sections [i.e. communist parties]'. This

was a process set in motion on 13 April 1927 by the ECCI Political Secretariat, but it was not until the beginning of 1928 that the WEB could begin its operations, using Berlin (the 'Comintern village') as its base. See '(Vertraulich). Entwurf eines Beschlusses des EKKI über die Errichtung eines Westeuropäischen Büros, Moskau', [1928], in RGASPI 499/1/33, 132.

36. 'Report from 'Numa [Manuilski], Berlin, to Lindberg [Heimo]', Moscow', 3 May 1928, in RGASPI 499/1/7, 134-35.
37. '[Plan of action] Münzenberg, Berlin, to WEB', Berlin, 18 May 1928, RGASPI 542/1/29, 20-22.
38. 'Protokoll der 1. Internationalen Sitzung der Antifaschistischen Weltliga, Berlin', 10 December 1923, in RGASPI 542/1/1, 15-17. The meeting coincided with the aftermath of the KPD's disastrous attempt to seize power in Germany in October 1923.
39. '[Plan of action] Münzenberg, Berlin, to WEB', Berlin, 18 May 1928, RGASPI 542/1/29, 20-22.
40. For Münzenberg's report, see 19 December 1928, RGASPI 543/1/5, 53. In 1929, Münzenberg was also heavily involved in the preparations for the LAI's Second International Congress Against Colonialism and Imperialism, which took place in Frankfurt am Main, 21-27 July 1929.
41. IAFC, 'Bulletin des Initiativ-Komitees, Berlin', 30 January 1929, in RGASPI 543/1/4, 33; IAFC, 'Bulletin des Initiativ-Komitees, Berlin', 4 February 1929, in RGASPI 543/1/4, 36.
42. 'Der Internationale Antifaschistenkongress, Berlin, to Moscow', 12 March 1929, in RGASPI 543/1/5, 99-102.
43. Willi Münzenberg, *Solidarität. Zehn Jahre Internationale Arbeiterhilfe, 1921-1931*, Berlin: Neuer Deutscher Verlag, 1931.
44. Petersson, *Willi Münzenberg*, pp451-65.
45. 'Bulletin über die Ärztearbeit des vorbereitenden Komitees zum Antikriegskongress', August 1932, in RGASPI 543/1/17, 209-11.
46. 'Circular. Committee for the Preparations of the Geneva Anti-War Congress, Berlin', 5 June 1932, in RGASPI 543/1/17, 73-79.
47. Petersson, *Willi Münzenberg*, p472.
48. 'Letter from Friedrich Adler, Zürich, to Emile Vandervelde', Brussels, 8 July 1932, in RGASPI 543/1/17, 146-149.
49. A copy of the article, marked 'confidential' can be found in RGASPI 543/1/17, 142-144.
50. The correspondence and other related material can be found in RGASPI 543/1/17, 169.
51. See 'Bulletin Nr.6', 27-28 August 1932, in RGASPI 543/1/18, 127.
52. For the article, 'Der russische Dolchstoss', see Bernhard H. Bayerlein, *'Der Verräter, Stalin, bist Du!' Vom Ende der linken Solidarität, Komintern und kommunistischen Parteien im zweiten Weltkriege, 1939-1941*, Berlin: Aufbau-Verlag, 2008, pp159, 164.

53. On these treatments of Münzenberg, see See K. Haferkorn, 'Münzenberg, Wilhelm', in *Geschichte der deutschen Arbeiterbewegung. Biographisches Lexikon*, Berlin [Ost]: Dietz Verlag, 1970, pp340-42; and the response by Hermann Weber, 'Das verschwundene Lexikon', in *Die Zeit*, 15 October 1970.
54. Transcript of W. Münzenberg's speech at the Brussels Congress delivered on 13 February 1927, in RGASPI 542/1/69, 37-69.

The Entangled Catastrophe: Hitler's 1933 'Seizure of Power' and the Power Triangle – New Evidence on the Historic Failure of the KPD, the Comintern, and the Soviet Union

Bernhard H. Bayerlein[1]

A CATASTROPHE OF GLOBAL proportions, Hitler's peaceful accession to power on 30 January 1933 was an epochal shift in politics, society and culture, and a particular tragedy for the German labour movement and social movements around the world. After the failed revolutions in Germany in 1923, Bulgaria, China, and other countries in the 1920s, this meant meant the calamitous defeat of the Communist Party of Germany. For the Comintern, it represented the beginning of the end as any sort of 'cultural international'. This chapter will first look at the scale and background of that defeat in three sections followed by a chronology of the year 1933, detailing the entanglement of the Russian Communist Party, the Comintern and the KPD, and offering a new interpretation to explain the conditions that made such a collapse possible.

'The two largest German labour parties, the Social Democratic Party of Germany and the KPD, sowed the seeds of their own demise with their individual failures and omissions as well as their processes for rationalising them'. Werner Thormann, a left-wing member of the Catholic Centre Party and future editor of Willi Münzenberg's journal *Zukunft*, wrote these words without a trace of schadenfreude, in a secret memorandum to the French government. Thormann argued that the effortless defeat of the world's largest and best organised labour movement was due to 'the bureaucracy of the anti-fascist parties and organisations' and the fact that, 'contrary to the desires of the masses, the organisational dictatorship that they wielded [...] prevented unity of action and consequently became the final, decisive cause of their defeat'.² Trotsky, now expelled from the RKP, offered prophetic criticism that was even more emphatic. He compared the events of 30 January 1933 with the actions of the SPD on the 4 August 1914, when it had supported a civil peace (*Burgfrieden*) and voted for the Kaiser's war loans. This led to the disastrous turn toward Stalinism, which made this historical defeat possible. This, he believed, definitively brought an end to the revolutionary path that the KPD and the Comintern had been on and necessitated the formation of a new communist party and a new international.³

The blame laid by one party on the other and vice versa had a lasting effect on the historiography, which served to obscure the parties' common responsibility for this global catastrophe.⁴ After 1945, the conservative thesis that the labour movement had been incapable of presenting an alternative in 1933 became the mainstream view. The Second World War victory against Hitler overshadowed the question of who was responsible for his accession to power and effectively rehabilitated Stalinism, while the division of the continent and the 'nightmare world of the Cold War' ensured that alternative democratic socialist prospects were no longer realistic options.⁵

This essay will present a new argument based on a wide range of new sources, which extend beyond the official level of high politics. The argument is based on the interconnected histories of three distinct yet complementary levels of action in the triangle of forces in which the KPD, the Comintern and the Soviet Union operated. It draws on research for the three-volume edited documentary collection *Deutschland, Russland, Komintern* (cited hereinafter as *DRK*), which was the first project to systematically explore these modes of action.⁶ Because Soviet policy was always multipolar and the lines between foreign and domestic policy were unclear, we can only establish a well-founded explanatory model by cross-reading the documentation covering all of these interconnected layers.

It is in this way that traditional interpretations, both of Stalin's tactical cleverness and his anti-fascist objectives, can be challenged and qualified. In some publications, Stalin continues to be wrongly portrayed as a global revolutionary and anti-fascist politician.⁷ Yet Stalinism and the RKP in fact contributed to the defeat of anti-fascist social movements and, indeed, to the traumatic catastrophes of the twentieth century. As Teddy J. Uldricks has pointed out, 'Stalin's reputation as clear-sighted statesman and brilliant tactician is undermined by the new sources, which show him all too often misunderstanding other leaders, misperceiving the international situation, launching mistaken policies, and missing promising opportunities'.[8]

The dual nature of the Comintern: Between internationalism and Russian nationalism, 1918-1929

In the mid-1920s, the Comintern gave up its independence in favour of supporting 'socialism in one country' and became a mouthpiece for the greater Russian state. In pursuit of the chimera of this 'socialism in one country', and in the interest of Russo-centrism and Stalinism, the global function of communist parties was increasingly reduced to building influence within both national governmental apparatuses and national liberation movements in the colonial periphery and semi-periphery.[9] The alleged imminence of war was used by the newly established Stalinist Empire to instill in the 'national parties' a sense of looming danger threatening Soviet Russia. Eliminating opposition within these parties was therefore only superficially a matter of party leadership and policy; in reality, it was not connected to the theory and practice of international revolution but rather to the position of the Soviet Union internationally.[10]

In its early days, the Soviet Union had contested the hegemonic concept of the nation. But the 'nationalisation process' that communist parties would later undergo at Stalin's behest caused the Comintern to become de-internationalised and deprived it of its relative independence as a global actor. The policies of the Comintern and the RKP that had been directed toward global proletarian liberation were revised, ostensibly in the interest of supporting the Soviet Union, but in fact for the benefit of Stalin's autocracy; and international networks and communication systems were realigned to the same ends. Globally oriented social, anti-fascist and anti-colonial movements were made ideologically compatible with the current 'general line' and utilised as part of the communist parties' 'Stalinisation'.[11] The final period in this process took place in the second half of the 1930s as a result of the 'Great Terror' in the Soviet Union. Stalin then used the Comintern to undermine and even suppress 'emancipatory alternatives' at the global level.[12] In fact, not a single revolutionary uprising succeeded anywhere in the world under the aegis of pre-1945 Stalinism.

The retreat from the original Bolshevik project in the capitalist west, however, corresponded to that of the 'Baku perspective' in the east.[13] The League against Imperialism and for National Independence, which had been founded in 1926 at Willi Münzenberg's initiative, was incrementally liquidated. The mood of anti-colonial awakening that had been widespread in the 1920s – a time when Lenin, not Wilson, was regarded as the personification of global leadership and thinking about anti-colonialism and national self-determination – was not revitalised.[14] The existing 'cultural' International, as seen in the anticipatory ambitions of the new anti-colonial, anti-racist organisations, vanished from the agenda. The Comintern's 'solar system' (Otto Kuusinen) of internationally-active mass organisations, like the International Workers' Relief, deteriorated along with the Comintern's transnational structures of communication and affiliation, which had been its nervous system. At the same time, Stalinism had the capacity to charm intellectuals and to use propaganda and worldwide cultural diplomacy to project the charisma, and appeal, of the October Revolution. In doing so, it moved swathes of world opinion, using seeming 'anti-fascism' to support the 'fatherland of the working people'.

The 'German-Russian complex' from Lenin to Stalin: The Soviet Union, the Comintern and the KPD in the world system

Researchers have not yet fully accepted that the policies pursued by Stalin and the Soviet Union towards Hitler's government were, all in all, far more conciliatory than has been assumed.[15] Nonetheless, there is a growing body of empirical evidence demonstrating exactly that; it shows that throughout the 1930s, Stalin had his sights set on a longer-term agreement with Nazi Germany – despite Hitler's clearly evident plans to eradicate Marxism, destroy the Soviet Union, and liquidate the Comintern. Soviet foreign policy, bilateral relations and the role of the RKP need to be reassessed in this sense, particularly with respect to Soviet-German relations.

Despite the radicalisation of Comintern policy, the German-Russian axis, which had been established at the start of the Weimar Republic on the basis of both countries' opposition to the Treaty of Versailles, continued to serve as a political tool under Stalin, principally for safeguarding Russia's industrial modernisation.[16] Rather than condemning the Nazi terror against German Communists and Hitler in general, policy was to continue to regard Trotskyism and social democracy as the main enemies until 1934. The documentary edition *Deutschland, Russland, Komintern* brings to light the shameful silence of the Soviet Politburo after Hitler's rise to power and, particularly, their benign non-interference toward the bloody suppression of tens of thousands of Communists and other opponents of the Hitler regime.

The highest-ranking Russian diplomats and their German counterparts were by no means silent: there was a spirit of mutual understanding between them and, to this end, there were explicit confirmations that the violent crushing of the KPD was perfectly compatible with good neighbourly relations. Litvinov considered it 'natural' that Communists in Germany were treated 'in the same way Russia treats subversives'.[17] Economic relations with Germany were initially also left intact. Even while millions of Russians, Ukrainians, and members of other ethnic groups were dying in the famines of the early 1930s, Stalin continued sending grain shipments to Germany.

The 'German-Russian complex', and its sense of privileged mutual relations, remained in effect for Stalin's regime as well as for Nazi and part of conservative Germany. The difference was, however, that the anti-Versailles strategy was no longer a part of a revolutionary concept.[18] Germany was no longer considered to be the epicentre of world revolution which, it was once hoped, would surpass even the October Revolution.[19] Despite its radical narrative, the Comintern did not classify the situation in 1930s Germany as revolutionary or even pre-revolutionary. It proclaimed China, India, and, later on, Latin America to be the new battlegrounds, although these were confined within the framework of collaboration with nationalist bourgeois movements. Contrary to Münzenberg's genuine anti-fascism, the defeat in Germany in 1933 soon it made clear that German communism and anti-fascism would never fulfil any function in the global system other than an auxiliary role for the Soviet leadership.[20]

The Comintern and the KPD during the 'Third Period', 1929-1933

After the Comintern proclaimed the 'Third Period' (1929) of capitalist crisis, looming war against the Soviet Union and the radicalisation of struggles and ideologies, the main enemy was held to be not Nazism but social democracy, which was declared to be 'social fascist'. In these years, party programmes for 'National and Social Liberation' and the so-called *Volksrevolution* – associated with Ernst Thälmann, who was presented as the party's alternative to Hitler – alternated with ostensibly revolutionary propaganda within the framework of 'class-against-class' politics.[21] What these policies had in common was defending the Soviet Union by any available means. The Comintern's assumption, that it was impossible to 'defeat fascism without first defeating social democracy' and defeating all other left-wing, non-communist movements, created a global schism within the labour movement, from the parties to the trade unions and to the cultural associations. At the same time, the Nazis were becoming the most powerful political force in Germany. Yet the KPD and the SPD were not only mistaken in their political assessments and mutual hostility, they also missed the critical moment for resistance – from activists on the shop floor to the party leadership, and, thus, they were defeated in 1933. The KPD had entirely disbelieved that the Nazi Party could take power and failed to give sufficient attention to it as a mass movement able to mobilise large numbers of people. And the party therefore failed to develop a strategic anti-fascist line before or even after Hitler took power.

Stalin's dominance meant that the Comintern could not change the German party's leadership or policy. However, it did attempt to moderate policy in some areas (for example, working against the entirely arbitrary use of the term 'fascism' for everything and everyone) and tried to rein in some of the KPD's worst excesses. But party leaders like Heinz Neumann, Hermann Remmele, and Willi Münzenberg, who had pushed for a more consistent anti-fascist engagement, a revolutionary orientation and – only after the catastrophe – a 'united front' policy, were sidelined. Münzenberg, the Comintern's most talented anti-fascist propagandist, was given little leeway in the KPD. In July 1933, he wrote to Stalin stating that, 'If there hadn't been so many obstructions, if I could have had as much freedom as the Nazi propagandists had, I would have given them a run for their money every day'.[22] Neumann and Remmele were killed in the Soviet Union. Münzenberg died in June 1940 under circumstances that remain unclear.[23]

Germany, Russia, the KPD, the RKP and the Comintern: The triangle of forces and their global failure

During the first two years after the Nazis took power, there was no mass propaganda against Hitler's Germany in the Soviet Union; the media did not inform the populace about the actual nature of the regime or the real situation in Germany. As noted above, the Soviet Union did not ever protest against what was certainly the twentieth century's most serious attack on the international labour movement. The Soviet Union only intervened when, for example, Soviet citizens were involved, or when journalists were refused entry to the Reichstag fire trial in Leipzig. But there was a strongly held mutual agreement between the Soviet Union and Germany that these conflicts should not be exacerbated.[24] Not only did Soviet communism fail to anticipate Hitler's 'seizure of power', but the KPD warned against an 'opportunistic overestimation of Hitler's fascism' (Thälmann).[25] When the Nazis' stormtroopers marched outside the KPD's headquarters, the party even saw it as a sign that class power was shifting in favour of proletarian revolution.[26]

The first few weeks following the Nazis' 'seizure of power' saw paralysis in the KPD. Rather than approaching the majority of German workers to forge genuine unity of action with the Social Democrats and the politically unaffiliated, the KPD opted to proclaim a 'mass strike', which remained an empty gesture. Karl Volk, one of the spokesmen for the secret opposition group within the party, the 'Conciliators', would later say that, 'the Central Committee could have prevented or at least seriously weakened the Nazi-form of fascist dictatorship if it had opted for an appropriate policy of unleashing mass struggle'.[27] The KPD demonstration against the Brown Shirts at Bülowplatz (now Rosa-Luxemburg-Platz) on 22 January and the SPD's 'Iron Front' rally in the Lustgarten in central Berlin on 7 February 1933, with a combined total of more than a half million participants, indicate that there was still the power to mobilise working people and offer resistance. Yet the Comintern was unable to organise any widespread anti-fascist mobilisation. Instead, it initially pursued what amounted to a generalised anti-war campaign, limited to the 'fight for peace'. The view that the peace campaign was embedded in a larger revolutionary strategy has become indefensible today.[28] Indeed, new documents attest to the fact that Comintern leaders had no overarching strategy.

The KPD was in a state of shock in January and February 1933. Both the party and the Comintern had lost their connection to reality, and they succumbed to incredulousness and internal chaos. The leadership failed to recognise this historical turning point because the Comintern expected that the Nazi regime would come to an end very quickly. It is telling that it was not the Comintern but the Labour and Socialist International (LSI) that proposed a united front on 19 February 1933, but the subsequent approach by Moscow included conditions that could not realistically be met.[29] During the decisive six weeks between Hitler taking power and the Reichstag fire on the night of 27-28 February 1933, there was apparently no direct communication at all between the KPD leadership and the Comintern in Moscow.[30]

It is difficult to understand that, despite the fact that Hitler had come to power with the avowed goal of destroying the Soviet Union and liquidating the international communist movement – KPD intelligence had informed Moscow of this strategic plan – Moscow did not take any defensive measures in advance.[31] For its part, the Comintern continued in its refusal to adopt a defensive strategy with the wider labour movement against Hitler. On 22 February 1933, five days before the Reichstag fire, the editor-in-chief and the foreign politics editor of the SPD newspaper *Vorwärts*, Friedrich Stampfer and Victor Schiff, going against their own party leadership, raised the possibility of creating an anti-fascist united front made up of both parties. They went to see Boris Vinogradov, the Secretary at the Soviet Embassy in Berlin, to ask whether there was a last chance for joint action against the Nazis. However, Vinogradov (an officer of the Soviet secret police) answered that the persecution of German Communists would be regarded as a German domestic matter, arguing furthermore that Hitler's accession to power would accelerate the demise of German capitalism. At the end of the meeting, he asked the obviously shaken Social Democrats not to publish any reports in *Vorwärts* that might imply the destruction of the KPD would motivate the Soviet side to break off German-Soviet relations.[32]

Thälmann's last speech at what became known as the 'illegal Central Committee meeting' in a tavern in Ziegenhals to the southeast of Berlin on 25 February 1933 was recast in the East German politics of memory as evidence of the continuity of anti-fascist resistance and it thus achieved quasi-mythical status. The record of the speech, which was probably amended after the fact, aimed to present a consistent anti-Nazi line under Thälmann. In reality, Thälmann himself almost desperately asked Moscow what he should do and in what direction he should lead the party. A series of messages smuggled out of prison after Thälmann's arrest show that the main focus of the conference was preparation for the Reichstag elections, which had been called for 5 March 1933, and had nothing to do with actively toppling Hitler.[33]

On 28 February, at an extraordinary session of the Presidium of the Executive Committee of the Communist International (ECCI) on the 'United Front in Germany', Dmitri Manuilsky, the most important Comintern secretary, stated that despite the disastrous consequences of the Reichstag fire,[34] the situation was better than it had been in a long time – indeed, he suggested that the fire was a sign of a 'revolutionary revival'. The only way to defeat fascism, he believed, was to build a 'united communist front with the working class'; he added that 'mines should be laid within social democracy' in order to destroy it once and for all.[35] These policies, and the fact that Stalin saw Thälmann as being more useful to communist propaganda by being in Hitler's jails rather than by being released to the Soviet Union, saw him spend a decade behind bars before being executed in 1944. Abandoning Thälmann was symbolic of Stalin's wider abandonment and betrayal of German communism.

Despite all this, the Reichstag elections of 5 March 1933, which were far from free and fair, showed that the KPD was still able to garner 4.8 million votes and the SPD 7.2 million. The Nazis, however, won 17.2 million votes, thereby confirming the failure of both the KPD's anti-SPD campaign, and the election-oriented, legalistic turn at Ziegenhals.

After the Reichstag elections: too little, too late

Only in mid-March did the Comintern and the KPD begin to take a more serious approach to the situation in Germany. The Comintern's initial reports, along with completely unrealistic assessments of the Nazi terror, showed the bitter mood among KPD members, even an outright hostility towards the party's leadership – many of whom had now been imprisoned. The ECCI failed to accept responsibility for the catastrophe and was unable to understand what was called the widespread passivity of the German masses. Ossip Pyatnitsky, head of the Comintern's department for international connections, at an ECCI-session exclaimed: 'Had the German Party carried out even half [of the resolutions it had adopted with the Comintern], the situation never would have come to this!' He saw the party's adjustment to illegality as its most important task and urged it to engage in 'smaller struggles'.[36] Yet the failures of the ECCI and the KPD – in addition to Thälmann's arrest – were corroborated by the arrest of Georgi Dimitrov as head of the Berlin-based Western European Bureau of the Comintern in early March 1933. Berlin's period as the Comintern capital in the West had come to an end.[37]

It took Moscow three months to send the KPD its first policy instructions. In a highly bureaucratic process, drafts were sent to Stalin, Molotov and Kaganovich for review on 20 March; these were then sent to the Presidium of the ECCI and only finally ratified on 4 April by a resolution of the Soviet Politburo.[38] In fact, the Soviet leadership believed that the masses would now see concrete evidence that the Communists had been right to reject 'democratic illusions' all along. The Nazi terror, the logic went, would ultimately have a positive effect because it would accelerate the arrival of the proletarian revolution. But the ECCI resolution – influenced by a report by the leading German Communist Fritz Heckert on the reasons for the defeat, what actions to take and Stalin's reflections on the situation – in April 1933, for the first time described the German executive as a 'government of fascist counter-revolution' committed to 'fighting against the workers'.[39] However, Heckert also continued to think that 'Hitler's government cannot last long' and believed that the fall of his dictatorship would be accelerated through a combination of strikes, speeches in parliament, mass rallies and the subversion of Nazi organisations from within. While proletarian revolution was still perceived as inevitable, the Communists, as the only party of the working class, were 'to be on target for an armed uprising', as Pyatnitsky argued in April 1933, but were not permitted to proclaim it yet.[40]

Meanwhile, the Comintern continued not only to act against the 'left', but also against the 'right' communist oppositions and intermediate socialist groups.[41] On 9 April 1933, the ECCI's Political Commission resolved to expel Felix Wolf (alias Werner Rakow), Erich Wollenberg and others for 'anti-party activities'. What this in fact meant was that these people had criticised the Communists' role in the defeat of the German labour movement and argued against their refusal to bring about joint resistance with the SPD against Hitler.

Even in April 1933, the Comintern still did not engage in mass anti-fascist propaganda. Instead, it continued to focus its efforts on opposing the SPD and the generalised threat of war, without identifying Hitler as the primary enemy. This line characterised Soviet as well as Comintern and KPD politics. While the Soviet media attacked the SPD as 'social fascists' and condemned Trotsky (with anti-Semitic overtones) as the 'eternal' enemy, Hitler's regime was spared any systematic critical propaganda.[42] While the Comintern continued to downplay Hitler's accession to power, the Soviet Politburo adhered to a posture that was by no means hostile to the Hitler government. Even Nikolai Krestinsky, a Soviet expert on Germany and Deputy Commissar for Foreign Relations, dismissed Hitler's desire for 'Living Space' (*Lebensraum*) in the East and plans for racial annihilation as empty campaign promises. Yet the KPD's secret military apparatus had informed Stalin that Hitler had unveiled such plans in a speech to military top brass on 3 February 1933.[43]

An admission of failure by a member of the KPD's Politburo: the Remmele Memorandum

It has been overlooked that the KPD leadership had indeed been subjected to a great deal of criticism from within the party for its obvious incompetence and its cautious, election-oriented posture. Steps had been taken to stamp out this dissent, yet it reappeared and even extended into the KPD's leadership itself. On 12 April 1933, Hermann Remmele, a veteran Communist, who belonged to the KPD triumvirate, accused the KPD's politburo of being collectively responsible for 'the German proletariat's worst defeat since 1914'. Remmele stated that they had 'drastically underestimated the gravity of the situation of the German as well as the international proletariat … in the wake of the victory of German fascism'; 'biased by legalistic cretinism', he continued, they had also deliberately avoided analysing the German fascist dictatorship because 'such an analysis would have revealed the falsity of certain historical assumptions held by the party leadership'.[44] In speaking out, Remmele had been urged by his close political ally, Heinz Neumann, to take on in the KPD leadership 'the role of Karl Liebknecht', who had opposed the SPD's support for the German war effort in 1914.⁴⁵ The historic defeat suffered by German communism motivated Remmele to take his protest to the Comintern, stating that: 'The Thälmann gang wants to use the 4.7 million [KPD votes in the Reichstag election] to save itself'. Implicitly distancing himself from Stalinism, Remmele pointed out that those German leaders who had supported Thälmann were now 'violently suppressing criticism of party policy'. They had failed to foresee and, thus, to prepare for a ban on the party, and the 'public's passive acceptance of the bloody mass terror' had undermined any ability to pursue a 'forceful defence'.⁴⁶

It is noteworthy that Remmele explicitly excluded the party's rank and file from criticism. The crisis was not the fault of members 'who did not follow our recommendations':

> It is us, the leadership, without exception, who are to blame. [The defeat is] because we were fooled into reckless swaggering instead of building a fighting army. In doing so, we did not safeguard the crucial positions from which we could have struck and shown that Germany is not Italy.⁴⁷

The Comintern responded by condemning Remmele for sectarianism. Four months later, on 27 October 1933, already in the Soviet Union, he was forced to resign his seat on the ECCI Presidium and was expelled from the KPD leadership. He was shot dead on 21 January 1938.⁴⁸

Even in September 1933, with the start of the Reichstag fire trial against Georgi Dimitrov and the other Communist defendants – which drew international attention thanks to Willi Münzenberg – the Comintern did not change its stance. Pyatnitsky, the organisation's *éminence grise*, clung to his assessment that National Socialism would prove to be a positive force in the process of the labour movement's purification. Solomon Lozovsky, the head of the Red International of Labour Unions, advanced a similar argument. He stated that the Nazis' dissolution of the General Federation of German Trade Unions had to be regarded as a service rendered on behalf of the communists, since it guaranteed that the Social Democrat-led unions had been smashed.⁴⁹ However, Vilgelm Knorin, the Latvian Secretary of the ECCI and head of the Central European Secretariat, spoke against this 'optimism' at the same meeting. He pointed out the consequences of Nazi repression of the KPD, and argued that, if the party's errors were not rectified, there would be no elder comrades left at all in two or three months.[50] Knorin was to become one of the first victims of the Stalinist terror within the Comintern apparatus, and was shot in 1938.

The slaughter of KPD members in the German Reich versus the goodwill policy of the Soviet Union

While the Comintern were continuing to argue that they were facing mere temporary setbacks in early 1933,[51] thousands of KPD members were becoming victims of the Nazi terror. Indeed, as these German Communists were arrested and imprisoned, Stalin continued to maintain and develop German-Soviet relations. After the Reichstag ratified a protocol extending the 1926 Berlin Treaty between Germany and the Soviet Union, on 5 May 1933 Moscow followed suit. Positive economic relations also continued unhindered. On 28 April 1933, Hitler, in a conversation with Soviet ambassador Lev Khinchuk, stated that, 'both our states must acknowledge the existence of the other for a long period as inescapable fact and act accordingly'. Hitler went on to concede that 'despite the different worldviews that they espouse' the Russo-German alliance had 'an enduring nature' based on their 'common interests'.[52] The attitude of the Soviet Politburo confirms that what amounted to a policy of goodwill was pursued toward the Nazi government. At no time during 1933 or 1934 did the highest political body of the Soviet Union pass any measures explicitly directed against the Nazi regime.[53]

Given the massive repression, the theory of the coming 'revolutionary revival', and the fact that the KPD did not begin to develop structures for work under conditions of illegality until the summer of 1932, there was initially no basis for organised KPD resistance. At first it was enough to escape the Gestapo's clutches: seventeen of the twenty-two district leaderships of the regional party organisations were arrested in early July 1933 alone. The Nazi repression of the KPD reached terrifying proportions, ultimately claiming 20,000 lives, while 150,000 people were arrested, and many of them were sent to concentration camps over the course of the Third Reich.[54]

Willi Münzenberg and the anti-fascist campaign

After the Reichstag fire trial came to an end in December 1933, the Comintern used propaganda to reframe the acquittal of Georgi Dimitrov and his co-defendants as a great victory over the Nazis. The 'Freedom for Dimitrov and Thälmann' campaign, which had been organised by Münzenberg and his helpers from Paris and London, and which had influenced the collective memory of events, was used to give the Comintern anti-fascist credibility. But Münzenberg had taken most of the initiative in presenting anti-fascist propaganda to a mass audience, and acted despite the stance of the KPD and the Soviet leadership's only lukewarm support. Nevertheless, the outcome of the trial was a blow to Hermann Göring, whose intention had been to organise a major show trial against the KPD, the Comintern and the international communist movement.

The initiatives undertaken by Münzenberg and his colleagues Otto Katz (alias André Simone) and Louis Gibarti, and the role of numerous intellectuals and writers, such as Romain Rolland and Henri Barbusse, were in some ways approved by the Stalinist leadership, with Karl Radek acting as mediator. Yet it is not possible to entirely disprove that these initiatives were used as a Stalinist smoke screen to obscure continued goodwill between Soviet Russia and Nazi Germany – including with regard to the role played by the Soviet secret police.[55]

Nevertheless, by the summer of 1933, Münzenberg was calling (initially in vain) for systematic counter-propaganda against Hitler's Germany.[56] His internal report from this time states, in summary, that neither the Comintern nor the KPD had provided any support 'with respect to mass [anti-fascist] propaganda or the means and methods for its execution'. Among other things, he cited a letter that writer Bernhard von Brentano had written to Bertolt Brecht on 18 July 1933 as evidence of both the 'monstrous acrimony' of the struggle for an anti-fascist policy and the reasons why 'this work must be done over the official party's objections and resistance'.[57] In the letter, Brentano had informed Brecht that he rejected the ECCI's already mentioned 'Heckert Resolution', which recast the labour movement's defeat as a victory. He had described the 'waste of human life' as 'horrifying' and argued that it should be no surprise that 'people are again leaving us in droves'. He had even claimed that regional KPD branches were cooperating with the Nazis' stormtroopers and denouncing Trotskyists and members of the non-communist left to the police: 'I didn't want to believe it. So now in Frankfurt [...] I'm told that denunciation has cost the lives of four competent workers (who were admittedly Trotskyists)'. Brentano finally turned to Münzenberg to ask, 'Can you do something?'[58]

Stalin's duplicity continued as Münzenberg and others tried to change communist responses towards Hitler. For example, Avel Enukidze, one of the highest ranking officials of the Soviet state and a personal friend of Stalin's, saw a positive side to the ending of all remaining vestiges of democracy in Germany. On 16 August 1933, he commented that the German administration's 'internal forcible co-ordination' (*Gleichschaltung*) would probably now give Germany the same 'free hand in foreign policy that the Soviet government had been enjoying for several years'.[59] Stalin's own overtures are still largely unknown: further archival access is required to shed more light on this matter.

The foreign-policy editor for *Vorwärts*, Victor Schiff, who we noted above had tried to convince Moscow to defend German communists, wrote the following prescient words: 'We have deluded ourselves and we must recognise that Stalin's government has shown less solidarity with the men who have fought and suffered for it in Germany than, for example, the American Jews have for their persecuted brethren'.[60] It should not be forgotten that, in April 1933, the Comintern refused to endorse the call for an international boycott of Hitler's Germany, despite its support from international union organisations, Social Democratic and Socialist organisations and the World Jewish Congress. Leading Comintern voices conceded that it was 'distasteful to us to support the interest of the German fascists' but 'the CP itself is not calling for a boycott at this time'.[61] The KPD, for its part, saw anti-Semitism as at most a marginal concern, even a contrived Nazi distraction from the class struggle. The Nazis, it believed, had acted against petty bourgeois Jews, seeking to prove that they were a workers' party. It was stated that Hitler had already taken the 'Jewish question' as far as it could go and, although anti-Semitism had temporarily helped the regime, Jewish businesses were obviously doing as well as ever and anti-Jewish methods were no longer having any effect.[62]

Communist officials continued to be reprimanded by their own leadership for trying too hard to pursue an anti-fascist policy. Such was the fate of Alfred Kurella, the Secretary of the World Committee against Fascism and War, who was subsequently Dimitrov's secretary.

Documents from his personal file in the Comintern archive show that, in April 1933, the leadership of the Comintern voted against mass anti-fascist agitation. The ECCI rebuked Kurella for having permitted Henri Barbusse, in his role as chairman of this committee, to invite Social Democrats to an international conference in order to find ways to take joint action in support of the German workers.[63] Cynical Soviet thinking persisted, despite increased pressure from rank-and-file Communists, such as in the French Communist Party and also German Communists active within the World Committee. Indeed, anti-fascism remained marginalised and the focus remained on a less direct form of anti-war propaganda, as Kurella's file details.[64] The shift only came with the subsequent adoption of the Popular Front Policy at the Seventh (and final) World Congress of the Comintern in 1935. But this was after the ruin of the KPD, a party of 300,000 members in 1933, which had arguably been destroyed in Germany by Hitler and ECCI policies – while Dimitrov's acquittal at the Reichstag Fire Trial and rise to become the head of the Comintern covered over these facts.

Concluding Comments

The depicted entangled catastrophe of the defeat without a fight in 1933 marked the destruction of German communism, and paved the way for what became the greatest trauma of the twentieth century, the Second World War with all its consequences. Insights into the power triangle of the KPD, the Comintern and the Soviet Union not only show how their practices were intertwined, but also demonstrate the extent of the German-Russian complex and the communist leadership's betrayal of its cause. These have hitherto been underestimated in communist studies.

The doctrine of 'socialism in one country' and the rise of Stalin and Stalinism meant that the German revolution was no longer needed for the survival of the Soviet state. All that was left of the original ideas of the communist project was a form of abstract solidarity, but only until this too no longer served Soviet interests. This, however, only comes as a surprise to those who accepted mainstream historiography and took it for granted. Research shows that the historic catastrophe grew out of the power triangle of inter-communist relations and – unlike the failure of the SPD and the trade unions – coalesced around the emergence of a new political system in the Soviet Union. These Soviet policies, both those officially pursued and those agreed and implemented in secret, found their nadir in 1939, when the pact with Nazi Germany was concluded, which, in effect, meant the outbreak of the Second World War. In 1941, Nazi Germany attacked the Soviet Union, as Hitler had long said that it would. These developments cannot be reduced only to the political defeats of the KPD in Germany – from the 'German Revolutions' of 1918 and 1923 to the Nazi 'seizure of power' in 1933; nor can they be reduced to structural or socio-historical factors, or patterns of perception. The explanation lies in the strategic choices made by the Soviet Union.

Newly available documentation raises significant questions about the Soviet Union's anti-fascist orientation throughout the interwar period, and especially after Stalin's rise to unrestricted power. In fact, Stalinist 'anti-fascism' before 1941 can be seen as pure pretence or, as the Italian oppositional Communist and intellectual, Pietro Tresso, termed it – a 'pretext'. From the outside, Stalin may have appeared to be a staunch opponent of Hitler. But the Stalinist Soviet Union did not operate according to a fascism/anti-fascism dichotomy but one of friend/foe. For the clique of Soviet leaders, which comprised only a few men gathered around the General Secretary, collective security, a 'democratic constitution', the popular front, even anti-war policies, were only a useful cover for what best suited their interests. The German Communists and other Communist parties were sacrificed to these machinations, as were millions of workers who were ultimately abandoned to fascist barbarism and the subsequent world war. The demise of the inter-war KPD, which lost all political relevance in 1933, can be interpreted as a form of 'betrayal to their proper cause' (Walter Benjamin).[65] The long twentieth century was an era of 'betrayed revolutions' and this is how it was depicted at the time by critical intellectuals like Benjamin and Kurt Tucholsky, and far-sighted politicians like Leon Trotsky and Willi Münzenberg. The latter, who was by far the most important international anti-fascist propagandist, finally has made history with his apposite statement in 1940: "The traitor, Stalin, is you!"[66]

What the 'archival revolution' makes clear is the need for more research of this sort, spanning the full documentary record, and especially uncovering the histories of the Communist parties.[67]

Translated by Joe Keady

Notes

1. The author would like to thank Gleb Albert, Jan Foitzik, Gerd Koenen, and Norman LaPorte for the collegial support.
2. German National Library, Frankfurt am Main, Deutsches Exilarchiv, NL 114 (Werner Thormann), EB 97/145, 101.0029, Bl. 6.
3. Leon Trotsky, 'To Build Communist Parties and an International Anew' (July 1933), https://www.marxists.org/archive/trotsky/germany/1933/330715.htm.
4. However it is no longer necessary to confront the myths of the earlier official party histories, which have now largely been settled.
5. Helmut Dahmer, 'Trotzki, Biermann und Moneta', in *Sozialistische Zeitung*, 10, 2010, http://www.sozonline.de/2010/10/trotzki-biermann-und-moneta/.
6. Bernhard H. Bayerlein *et al* (eds), *Deutschland, Russland, Komintern. Vol. I, Überblicke, Analysen, Diskussionen. Neue Perspektiven auf die Geschichte der KPD und die Deutsch-Russischen Beziehungen (1918-1943); Vol. II, Dokumente. Nach der Archivrevolution. Neuerschlossene Quellen zu der Geschichte der KPD und den deutsch-russischen Beziehungen*, Berlin-Boston: De Gruyter, 2014/2015 [henceforth: *DRK*]. The three volumes of a total 2317 pages are freely available online in open access: http://www.degruyter.com/view/product/186108 and http://www.degruyter.com/view/product/212875.
7. See Andreas Hilger (ed.), *Die Sowjetunion und die Dritte Welt. UdSSR, Staatsozialismus und Antikolonialismus im Kalten Krieg 1945-1991*, Munich: Oldenbourg, 2009.
8. Teddy J. Uldricks, 'Icebreaker Redux: The Debate on Stalin's Role in World War II Continues', in *Kritika*, 3, 11, 2010, p660.
9. Gleb Albert, 'From "World Soviet" to "Fatherland of All Proletarians": Anticipated World Society and Global Thinking in Early Soviet Russia', in *InterDisciplines* 3, 1, 2012, pp85-119.
10. Jan Foitzik, 'Der proletarische Internationalismus des sozialistischen Weltsystems. Die Mythologisierung des sowjetischen Führungsanspruchs', in *Vorgänge. Zeitschrift für Bürgerrechte und Gesellschaftspolitik* 46, 1, 2007, pp109ff.
11. Norman LaPorte, Kevin Morgan, Matthew Worley (eds), *Bolshevism, Stalinism and the Comintern. Perspectives on Stalinization, 1917-53*, Basingstoke: Palgrave Macmillan, 2008.
12. Armin Stickler, *Nichtregierungsorganisationen, soziale Bewegungen und Global Governance. Eine kritische Bestandsaufnahme*, Bielefeld: Transcript, 2005.
13. John Riddell (ed.), *To See the Dawn: Baku 1920. First Congress of the Peoples of the East*, New York: Pathfinder, 1993.
14. Erez Mancla, *The Wilsonian Moment: Self-Determination and the

International Origins of Anticolonial Nationalism, Oxford: University Press, 2007, pp7ff.
15. Bernhard H. Bayerlein, 'Abschied von einem Mythos. Die UdSSR, die Komintern und der Antifaschismus', in *Osteuropa*, 59, 2009, pp125-148.
16. See, Oleg W. Chlewnjuk, *Stalin, Eine Biographie*, Munich: Siedler, 2015.
17. Bianca Pietrow, *Stalinismus, Sicherheit, Offensive. Das 'Dritte Reich' in der Konzeption der Sowjetischen Aussenpolitik 1933-1941*, Melsungen: Bernecker, 1983, p190.
18. See, for example, Gerd Koenen, *Der Russland-Komplex. Die Deutschen und der Osten. 1900-1945*, Munich: Beck, 2005.
19. For the earlier commitment to the German revolution under Lenin, see Bayerlein *et al* (eds), *DRK II*, Doc. 4.
20. Siegfried Grundmann, *Der Geheimapparat der KPD im Visier der Gestapo. Das BB-Ressort. Funktionäre, Beamte, Spitzel und Spione*, Berlin: Dietz, 2008.
21. For a critique of Thälmann, see Hermann Weber and Bernhard H. Bayerlein, *Der Thälmann-Skandal. Geheime Korrespondenzen mit Stalin*, Berlin: Aufbau-Verlag, 2003.
22. Bayerlein *et al* (eds), *DRK II*, Doc. 330.
23. Kurt Kersten, 'Das Ende Willi Münzenbergs. Ein Opfer Stalins und Ulbrichts', in *Deutsche Rundschau*, 83, 5, 1957, pp496-499. New insights will be published in the volume announced by the First International Willi Münzenberg Kongress in Berlin at the website of the International Willi Münzenberg Forum www.muenzenbergforum.de.
24. See, for example, Gennadij Bordjugov, 'Die Machtergreifung Hitlers: Dominanten aussenpolitischer Entscheidungen des Stalin-Regimes 1933-1934', in Ludmilla Thomas *et al* (eds), *Zwischen Tradition und Revolution. Determinanten und Strukturen sowjetischer Außenpolitik 1917-1941*, Stuttgart: Franz Steiner, 2000, p377.
25. Bayerlein *et al* (eds), *DRK II*, p852, n24.
26. Bayerlein *et al* (eds), *DRK II*, Doc. 321.
27. *Ibid.*, Doc. 303.
28. See Wim Pelt, 'Vrede door Revolutie. De CPN tijdens het Molotov-Ribbentrop Pact 1939-1941', PhD Thesis, University of Amsterdam, 1990.
29. Bayerlein *et al* (eds), *DRK II*, Docs 307, 310, 311, 314.
30. *Ibid.*, Doc. 348.
31. According to Russian historian Lew Besymenski, this would have frustrated ongoing attempts at rapprochement. See Lew Besymenski, *Stalin und Hitler: Das Pokerspiel der Diktatoren*, Berlin: Aufbau, 2002, p78.
32. Bayerlein *et al* (eds), *DRK II*, Doc. 307.
33. *Ibid.*, Docs 308, 309.
34. On this key event, see Benjamin Carter Hett, *Burning the Reichstag. An Investigation into the Third Reich's Enduring Mystery*, Oxford: Oxford University Press, 2014.

35. Bayerlein *et al* (eds), *DRK II*, Doc. 310.
36. *Ibid.*, Doc. 314.
37. Marrietta Stankova, *Georgi Dimitrov: A Biography*, London: I.B. Tauris, 2010, pp91ff.
38. Bayerlein *et al* (eds), *DRK II*, Doc. 316.
39. *Ibid.*, Doc. 317.
40. *Ibid.*, Doc. 319.
41. See recently: Marcel Bois: *Kommunisten gegen Hitler und Stalin. Die linke Opposition der KPD in der Weimarer Republik. Eine Gesamtdarstellung*, Essen: Klartext, 2014.
42. Siegfried Bahne, *Die KPD und das Ende von Weimar. Das Scheitern einer Politik*, Frankfurt am Main: Campus, 1976, pp58ff, 68ff.
43. Bert Hoppe, *In Stalins Gefolgschaft. Moskau und die KPD 1928-1933*, München: Oldenbourg, 2007, p317.
44. Bayerlein *et al* (eds), *DRK II*, Doc. 321.
45. *Ibid.*, Doc. 312.
46. *Ibid.*
47. *Ibid.*, Doc. 320.
48. Hermann Weber and Andreas Herbst, *Deutsche Kommunisten. Biographisches Handbuch 1918 bis 1945*, Berlin: Dietz, 2008, p605.
49. *Ibid.*, Doc. 328.
50. *Ibid.*, Doc. 335.
51. 'Resolution des Präsidiums des EKKI zum Bericht des Gen. Heckert über die Lage in Deutschland', 1 April 1933, in Russian State Archive of Socio-Political History, Moscow (RGASPI), 495/2/203, 10-12.
52. This report on the meeting with Hitler has recently been published in Sergej Slutsch and Carola Tischler (eds), *Deutschland und die Sowjetunion 1933-1941. Dokumente aus russischen und deutechen Archiven*, Munich: Oldenburg, 2014, pp345-347. This edition of new diplomatic documents corroborates the conciliatory and cooperative attitude towards Hitler.
53. Bernhard H. Bayerlein, 'Deutscher Kommunismus und globaler Stalinismus – Komintern, KPD und die Sowjetunion 1929-1943', in *idem et al* (eds), *DRK I*, p297.
54. Andreas Herbst, *Kommunistischer Widerstand*: http://www.ddr-biografien.de/00000095890f9bc01/0000009589137ed36.html
55. For details, see Stephen Koch, *Double Lives. Stalin, Willi Münzenberg and the Seduction of the Intellectuals*, London: Harper Collins, 1995, pp335ff, 349. See also Walter G. Krivitsky, *I Was Stalin's Agent*, Bristol: Hamilton, 1939. Krivitsky was the original source of this interpretation.
56. For a report from Münzenberg in July 1933, see Bayerlein *et al* (eds), *DRK II*, Doc. 330. In 1937, Münzenberg summarised his concept of anti-fascist counter-propaganda, see Willi Münzenberg, *Propaganda als Waffe. Ausgewählte Schriften 1919-1940*, Til Schulz (ed.), Frankfurt am Main: März, 1972.

57. Bayerlein *et al* (eds), *DRK II*, Doc. 330.
58. Gerhard Müller, '"Warum schreiben Sie eigentlich nicht?" Bernhard von Brentano in seiner Korrespondenz mit Bertolt Brecht (1933-1940)', in *Exil*, 9, 2, 1989, pp42-53.
59. Bayerlein *et al* (eds), *DRK II*, Doc. 332.
60. *Ibid.*, Doc. 307.
61. *Ibid.*, Doc. 333.
62. *Ibid.*, Doc. 335.
63. 'Personalakte Alfred Kurella', in RGASPI, 495/205/6339, 373-376.
64. *Ibid.*
65. Walter Benjamin, 'Thesis on the Philosophy of History', in *Illuminations*, ed. Hannah Arendt, New York: Schocken, 1968, p250.
66. Willi Münzenberg: 'Der russische Dolchstoß', in *Die Zukunft*, Paris, 22 September 1939. See: Bernhard H. Bayerlein, *'"Der Verräter, Stalin, bist Du!": Vom Ende der linken Solidarität. Komintern und kommunistische Parteien im Zweiten Weltkrieg 1939-1941*, Berlin: Aufbau, 2008, p148.
67. See Reiner Tosstorff's review of Bayerlein *et al* (eds), *DRK* in *H-Soz-Kult*, 21 October 2015, at: http://www.hsozkult.de/publicationreview/id/rezbuecher-22480.

Notes on Contributors

Bernhard Bayerlein has a doctorate and a higher doctorate and is a linguist and translator of French, Spanish and Portuguese – including his role in publishing the important Dimitrov Diaries in German. He is senior researcher at the Institute of Social Movements, Ruhr-University of Bochum. He specialises in global communist studies in comparative perspective, political science and he is a leading light in the digitisation of the Comintern Archive (the INCOMKA project with the European Council). He has published widely, including his most recent major scholarly and editorial role in *Deutschland-Russland-Komintern 1918-1943*, 3 vols (2014/15), *German October* (2003), *Moscou-Paris-Berlin* (2003), *The Thälmann-Scandal* (2003), and *'The Traitor, Stalin is You'* (2008). He is co-editor of the *Jahrbuch für historische Kommunismusforschung* and founding editor of the *International Newsletter of Communist Studies*. At present, he continues to be a strong presence in the International Willi-Münzenberg Forum.

Marcel Bois has a doctorate in communist history and is currently an associate researcher at the Research Centre for Contemporary History in Hamburg. His research focuses on the history of the KPD in the Weimar Republic. He has published widely on this subject and is author of *Communists against Stalin and Hitler* (*Kommunisten gegen Hitler und Stalin. Die linke Opposition der KPD in der Weimarer Republik. Eine Gesamtdarstellung*, 2014). Currently, he is working on a biographical study of the Austrian communist and architect Margarete Schütte-Lihotzky (1897-2000).

Gerhard Engel was formerly a professor at the Humboldt University, Berlin. His research is on the history of the German workers' movement, and his main publications include: as co-editor, *Groß-Berliner Arbeiter- und Soldatenräte in der Revolution 1918/19* (1993 and subsequent reissues); *Rote in Feldgrau. Kriegs- und Feldpostbriefe junger linkssozialdemokratischer Soldaten des Ersten Weltkrieges*

(2008); *Johann Knief – ein unvollendetes Leben* (2011); and *Dr Rudolf Franz 1882-1956. Zwischen allen Stühlen – ein Leben in der Arbeiterbewegung* (2013).

Ben Fowkes taught at the Universities of Sheffield and North London for many years, but is now retired. He has written extensively on German and communist history, including, in 1984, the first book ever published in English specifically on the history of communism under Weimar entitled *Communism in Germany under the Weimar Republic* (there have been many more since). He has translated a number of texts from German, mainly works by Karl Marx, including *Capital Volume 1* (1976) and *Marx's Economic Manuscript of 1864-1865* (2015).

Stefan Heinz has a doctorate in political science and is presently a researcher, lecturing at the Centre for Labour Relations at the Otto-Suhr Institute of Political Science, which is part of the Free University, Berlin. His research covers trade unions and their resistance to national socialism (1933-1945) and industrial relations. Among his recent publications are: Siegfried Mielke and Stefan Heinz (eds), *Emigrierte Metallgewerkschafter im Kampf gegen das NS-Regime* (2014); idem. (eds), *Gewerkschafter in den Konzentrationslagern Oranienburg und Sachsenhausen. Biographisches Handbuch* (2013); idem. (eds), *Funktionäre des Einheitsverbandes der Metallarbeiter Berlins im NS-Staat. Widerstand und Verfolgung* (2012).

Ralf Hoffrogge is a post-doctoral Research Fellow at the Institute for Social Movements at the University of the Ruhr in Bochum. He has published widely on German labour history and the history of German communism. Among his most recent publications are: *Working-Class Politics in the German Revolution: Richard Müller, the Revolutionary Shop Stewards and the Origins of the Council Movement* (2014) and *A Jewish Communist in Weimar Germany – The Life of Werner Scholem (1895-1940)* (2017).

Mario Kessler is a Professor at the Centre for Contemporary History, Potsdam and Associate Professor at the University of Potsdam. His most recent books include: *Alfred Meusel: Soziologe und Historiker zwischen Bürgertum und Marxismus, 1896-1960* (2016); *Revolution* *und Konterrevolution: Studien über Gewalt und Humanität aus dem Jahrhundert der Katastrophen* (2016); and *Grenzgänger des Kommunismus* (2015).

Norman LaPorte is Reader in History at the University of South Wales. His research interests are (mainly) the German Communist Party (KPD) during the Weimar Republic, and relations between Britain and the GDR. He is author of *The German Communist Party in Saxony: Factionalism, Fratricide and Political Failure* (2003) and (with Stefan Berger) *Friendly Enemies: Britain and the GDR, 1949-1989* (2010). He was contributing guest editor of a special issue of *Moving the Social* (2014) entitled 'Lives of the Left'.

Ottokar Luban studied history, psychology, education, and political science at the Free University in Berlin (West). From 1960, he was a teacher in Berlin (West) and is now retired. Since 1993, he has published widely on labour movement history, including on Rosa Luxemburg's concept of grassroots democracy (*Rosa Luxemburgs Demokratiekonzept*, 2008). From 1999 until the present he has served as honorary secretary of the International Rosa Luxemburg Society.

Constance Margain is a post-doctoral researcher. Her research focuses is on the international history of communism, and her doctoral thesis, which addresses the role of the International Union of Seamen and Harbour Workers, will soon be published in French by Libertalia Edition. Her recent publications in English include 'The International Union of Seaman and Harbour Workers 1930-37', in *Twentieth Century Communism*, 8, 2015. At present, she is writing a short biography of the German Communist Kurt Rittwagen.

Fredrik Petersson now holds the post of Associate Professor in Colonial and Post-Colonial Global History at Åbo Akademi University. His doctoral thesis – *'We Are Neither Visionaries Nor Utopian Dreamers'. Willi Münzenberg, the League against Imperialism, and the Comintern, 1925-1933* – was published in 2013. His research interests include twentieth century anti-colonialism and anti-imperialism. Petersson is completing the monograph *The Elephant and the Porcelain Shop. Transnational Anti-Colonialism and the League against Imperialism, 1927-1937* and is also working on a biography of Willi Münzenberg.

His publications include articles on twentieth century anti-colonialism, anti-imperialism, and international communism.

Florian Wilde is a post-doctoral Research Fellow at the Rosa Luxemburg Foundation's Institute for Social Analysis in Berlin, where he works on the history and politics of European trade unions. His most recent publications include: *Ernst Meyer (1887-1930). Vergessene Führungsfigur des deutschen Komunismus. Eine politische Biographie* (2013); '"Freedom of Discussion inside the Party is Absolutely Necessary": KPD Chairperson Ernst Meyer 1921/22', *Historical Materialism*, 22, 2014, pp104-28; and, with Alexander Gallas and Jörg Nowak (eds), *Politische Streiks im Europa der Krise* (2012).

Sebastian Zehetmair is a Labour historian based in Berlin. He is currently researching the history of the KPD in Bavaria in the early 1920s. His research topics also include the history of the Bavarian Council Republic of 1919, the problems of industrial democracy and the rise of fascism in Germany.

Index

1914-18 world war 1, 3, 4, 5, 14, 15, 16, 28, 130, 210, 223-4
anti-war activity 32-3, 45, 46, 47-8, 66, 89, 110, 224, 225, 243, 270-1
  see also SDP/and, 1914-18 war
1939-45 world war 254, 276

ADGB see General Confederation of German Trade Unions
Adler, Friedrich 252-3
Adorno, Theodor 222
Alexander, Gertrud 226, 227
All-Russian Association of Proletarian Writers (VAPP) 225
Altenkirch, Ernst, 196
Amsterdam Anti-War Congress, 1932 242, 247, 252-3
Anspach, Erich 48
Anti-fascism 97, 101-2, 108(n), 137, 151, 162-3, 243, 244, 245, 246, 247, 249, 250, 251, 260; see also fascism, KPD attitude towards
Anti-Fascist Congress, 1929, 242, 247, 249, 250-1, 253
Anti-imperialism 1, 15, 26-7, 34, 96, 113, 243, 244, 245, 247, 248, 249, 252;
  see also Congress Against Imperialism and Fascism; League Against Imperialism and for National Independence (LAI); League Against Colonial Oppression (LACO)

Anti-semitism 8, 88, 89, 95, 101, 102, 270, 274
  Ruth Fischer controversy 88, 100-1, 102, 114
Aquila, Guilio 251
Arbeiterpolitik 29, 33, 34, 35
Arp, Hans 225
Association of German Revolutionary Visual Artists (ARBKD) 228
Association of Producing Farmers, Tenants, and Planters 213
Averbakh, Leopold 230-1

Balabanoff, Angelica 55
Baldwin, Roger 15, 249
Ball, Hugo 225
Barbusse, Henri 15, 243, 246-7, 249, 250, 251, 252, 253, 273, 275
Bartels, Wolfgang 155
Barth, Emil 49
Bavarian People's Party (BVP) 213
Becher, Johannes 223, 228, 230, 232
Becker, Karl 39
Benjamin, Walter 16, 276
Bielefeld, Wilhelm, 195
Biha, Otto (Bihalji-Merin) 230
Biro-Rosinger, Karl 230, 232
Bogdanov, Aleksandr 224-5
Bolshevik Revolution, see Russian Revolution
Bolsheviks x, xi, 1, 3, 32, 35, 36, 38, 54, 55-6, 93, 115, 132, 134,

135, 151, 152, 207, 208, 242, 245, 263
Bolshevisation 4, 8-9, 40, 41, 103, 109, 111, 119-20, 123, 129, 143, 153, 164, 184, 245
Von Borstel, Hans 132,
Brandler, Heinrich 9, 10, 11, 66, 67, 81, 93, 95, 97, 100, 112-3, 115, 116-7, 129, 131, 134-5, 137, 139, 141, 142-3, 154
Brecht, Bertolt 231-2, 233, 234, 273
Bredel, Willi 231
Bremer Bürgerzeitung (BBZ) 26, 27, 30, 31, 32, 33, 34
Von Brentano, Bernhard 273-4
Broué, Pierre 3, 155
Brüning, Heinrich 13, 158, 163, 175, 181, 182
Buber-Neumann, Margarete 244
Building Workers Union 80
Bukharin, Nikolai 122, 135, 153, 245

Cachin, Marcel 138
Carr, E.H. 99, 102
Centre Party (Catholic Centre Party) 213, 260
Chi, Ch'ao-Ting 246
Chicherin, Georgy 115
Christian Farmers' Association 212, 214
Comintern (Communist International) 1, 2, 4, 5, 13, 18, 61, 87, 90, 93, 119, 120, 133, 134, 153-4, 156, 157, 159, 160, 245, 246, 247, 251, 260, 261, 262-3, 268, 269-70, 271, 273, 275
  Second World Congress, 1920 66
  Third World Congress, 1921 67, 78, 131
  Fourth World Congress, 1922 66, 72, 76, 79, 81, 93, 112, 132, 134, 137
  Fifth World Congress, 1924 8, 109, 119-20, 121
  Sixth World Congress, 1928 245, 250
  and Class against Class 17, 87, 245, 251, 265
  Executive Committee (ECCI) 99, 117, 120, 121, 122, 123, 136, 137, 138, 143, 228, 244, 245, 246, 249, 251, 275
  and KPD 6, 8, 9, 10, 12, 18, 40, 81, 90, 93, 111, 112, 113, 116, 117, 120, 121, 122, 123, 131, 134, 137, 142-3, 150, 151, 152-3, 158, 163, 182, 188, 197, 198, 199, 203, 213, 228, 241, 263-76
  and Willi Münzenberg 14, 15, 241, 242, 244, 245, 246, 247, 248, 249, 251, 252, 253, 263, 265, 273-4
  and Popular Front 163, 275, 276
  and Twenty-One Conditions x, 4, 87, 90, 103, 172, 207
  and United Front 8, 67, 79, 113, 131, 132, 134, 156, 160, 188, 245, 250, 267, 268
  See also Stalin; Stalinisation; Stalinism
Communist Farm Workers' and Smallholders' Association 213
Communist Party of Austria 109, 111
Communist Party of Great Britain 118
Communist Party of Germany (KPD)
  Founding convention, 1918 x, 5, 39, 53-4, 55, 56, 153
  Heidelburg Congress, 1919 x, 5
  1920 Congress 207-8

1921 (Jena) Congress x, 66, 68, 78, 131,
1923 (Leipzig) Congress 80, 81, 92, 94, 95, 96, 134, 135
1924 (Frankfurt) Congress 102, 117-8, 143
1925 Congress xi, 121-2
1927 (Essen) Congress xi, 154, 214
and the arts 16-17, 220-239
agrarian policy 13-14, 205-219
and Berlin uprising, 1919 56-61
Centre group 26, 31, 81, 117, 143
Class against class 15, 17, 87-108, 265
Control Committees 79, 95
Left Opposition 7, 8, 27, 87, 133-4, 136, 150, 154-5, 156, 159, 162
and Popular Front 16, 17, 234
and Proletarian Hundreds 79, 115, 116, 137, 139, 140, 143
and trade unions 11-13, 14, 40, 54, 80, 91, 118, 137, 172, 173, 187-90, 191, 194, 197, 198, 199, 271; *see also* Red International of Labour Unions; Revolutionary Shop Stewards; Revolutionary Trade Union Opposition; Unity Union of Berlin Metalworkers; Unity Union of Seamen, Harbour Workers and Bargemen
and United Front 7, 9, 10, 11, 12, 16, 17, 18, 66-86, 87, 90, 91, 92, 93, 94, 95, 102, 103, 113, 114, 118, 131-2, 133, 134-5, 136, 138, 139, 151, 156, 161, 162, 164, 188, 227, 265, 267, 268
and SPD 6, 7, 8, 11, 17, 18, 36, 37, 66, 69, 70, 90, 91, 92, 95, 112, 115, 117, 118, 120, 121, 132-4, 135, 136, 138-41, 142, 151, 158-9, 160, 161-2, 164, 188, 214, 228, 265, 266, 268, 270; *see also* Communist Party of Germany/Berlin uprising (above); united front; social fascism
See also Comintern/relationship with KPD; fascism/KPD attitude towards; 'German October'; March action, 1921
Communist Party of Germany (Opposition) (KPO) 41, 154
Communist Party of Russia (RKP) 2, 112, 260, 261, 262, 263
Communist Party of the Soviet Union 150, 152, 153, 182
Communist Working Group (KAG) 91
Congress against Colonialism and Imperialism, 1927 242, 245-6, 247-8, 249, 252, 254
Councils movement 4, 5, 37, 38, 48, 49-50, 51, 52, 54, 55, 59, 60, 77, 111, 208
National Conference of Councils, Berlin, 1918 39, 52, 55, 61
Cuno, Wilhelm 98, 102, 134, 136, 138, 141,

Dada 220, 224, 225, 226
German Dada Manifesto 225-6
Dahlem, Franz 189
Däumig, Ernst 48, 52, 58
Dawes Plan 119
Degen, Ewald, 196
Democratic Party 163
Dimitrov, Georgi 153, 269, 271, 273, 274, 275
Döblin, Alfred 224, 228
Duncker, Hermann 46, 55
Duncker, Käte 55
Dzerzhinsky, Felix 115

EVMB *see* Unity Union of Berlin Metalworkers
EVSHBD *see* Unity Union of Seamen, Harbour Workers and Bargemen
Eberlein, Hugo 46, 56, 67, 117
Ebert, Friedrich 49, 52, 56, 57, 58, 59, 61, 70, 115
Eichhorn, Emil 52, 56
Eildermann, Wilhelm 34,
Einstein, Albert 15, 161, 249, 252
Enukidze, Avel 274
Eppstein, Eugen 136

Faber, Gustav 141
Fascism 94, 159-60, 161, 162-3, 164, 261
   KPD attitude towards 8, 94, 97, 99, 100, 101-2, 109(n)137-8, 151, 157-9, 160, 162, 163, 195-6, 264, 265, 266, 267-8, 269, 270-1, 274-5
   Willi Münzenberg anti-fascism 243, 244, 246, 247, 249, 250, 258, 265, 273-4, 276
   see also United Front; Class against Class, 'social fascism'
Farmers' Aid Programme 209
Fischer, Ruth (born Elfriede Eisler) 8-9, 11, 81, 87, 88, 89, 90, 92, 93, 95, 96, 97, 98, 99-101, 102, 103, 109-128, 129, 134, 135, 136, 137, 142, 143, 150, 151, 153, 155, 156, 164
Flieg, Leo 244
Franke, Ernst 136
Free Workers' Union of Germany (FAUD) 40
Friedländer, Paul 110
Friesland, Ernst (Ernst Reuter) 112
Frölich, Paul 29, 31, 32, 35, 41, 67
Fuchs, Eduard 55, 56

Gábor, Andor 229, 232
General Confederation of German Trade Unions (ADGB) 11, 70, 73, 79, 80, 188, 189, 190, 191, 197, 198
German Democratic Republic (GDR) 2, 129, 200, 254
German Freedom Party (DVFP) 99
German Labour Front (DAF), 197
German Metalworkers Union (DMV) 12, 80, 89, 118, 189, 190, 191, 192-3, 194, 197
German National People's Party (DNVP) 75, 213
'German October', 1923 6, 8, 11, 102, 129, 138-40, 151, 250
   Hamburg rising 140-2
German Railway Workers' Union (DEV) 70, 80
German Revolution, 1918-19 3, 4, 5, 8, 11, 35, 36, 37, 45, 46, 48, 49, 50, 51, 58, 115, 130, 132, 134, 135, 141
   Berlin uprising January, 1919 5, 56-61
German Rural League (*Deutscher Landbund*) 212
Gericke, Paul, 195
Geschke, Ottomar 89
Gesamtverband 171, 174
Geschke, Ottomar 89
Gibarti, Louis 273
Goebbels, Joseph 243,
Gohl, Max, 196
Golke, Gustav 111
Göring, Hermann 273
Gorter, Hermann 87
Graupe, Georg 139
Gross, Babette 241, 242, 244
Grosz, George 226, 228
Grylewicz, Anton 89, 154, 155, 156

Haase, Hugo 59
Hatta, Mohammad 249
Heartfield, John 15, 226
Heckert, Fritz 269, 273
Heimo, Mauno ('Lindberg') 246, 248, 249
Henke, Alfred 27, 28, 29, 30, 31, 33
Hesse, Max 89, 101, 103, 155
Heym, Georg 223
Heym, Guido 155, 156
Hilferding, Rudolf 52
Hiller, Kurt 224, 228
von Hindenburg, Paul 120, 121, 151, 157, 158
Hirsch, Werner 158
Hitler, Adolf 17, 98, 102, 159, 234, 241, 243, 260, 261, 263, 264, 265
   attitude of Comintern/Soviet Union/KPD towards 18, 102, 157-9, 194, 243, 263-5, 266, 267, 268, 269, 270, 272, 273-6
   'seizure of power', 1933 xii, 170, 194-5, 234, 241, 261, 266-7, 268, 270
Hoernle, Edwin 135,
Hommes, Rudolf 141
Hugenberg, Alfred 244
Huelsenbeck, Richard 225

Independent Social Democratic Party (USPD) 3, 4, 34, 35, 36, 40, 47, 54, 55, 56, 60, 61, 70, 72, 73, 74, 131, 155, 49
   SPD/USPD government, 1918 49, 50, 52, 56
   USPD left x, 4, 5, 48, 49, 52, 53, 54, 58, 111, 131
   and Spartacus Group 35, 36, 37, 39, 40, 45, 52, 53, 54, 55
Interclubs (International Seamen's Clubs) 13, 170, 173, 175, 176, 177-8, 179, 180, 183
International Anti-Fascist Committee (IAFC) 247, 250-1
International Communists of Germany (IKD) 5, 25-44, 54
International Group 46
International Federation of Trade Unions (IFTU) 121
International League of Antifascism 249
International Socialist Party of Germany (ISPD) 32, 33, 34, 35-6
International Transport Workers' Federation (ITF) 170
International Union of Seamen and Harbour Workers (ISH) 12, 13, 1
International Workers' Relief (IAH) 15, 240, 242, 244, 246, 247, 248, 249, 251, 263

Jacob, Mathilde 48
Joffe, Adolph 55
Jogiches, Leo 45, 46, 47, 48, 49, 50, 55, 56, 58, 59, 111

Kaganovich, Lazar 269
Kamenev, Lev 115, 116, 152, 155
Kapp Putsch 73, 133, 159, 226
Katz, Iwan 10, 90, 121
Katz, Otto (alias André Simone) 273
Kautsky, Karl 3, 26-7
Kautz, Walter, 195
Khinchuk, Lev 272
Kleine, August 117
Klöckner, Florian 100, 114
Knief, Johann 5, 26, 27-8, 29-31, 33-4, 35, 36, 37, 38, 39, 41, 55
Knorin, Vilgelm 271, 272
Koch, Stephen 240, 254

Koenen, Wilhelm 53, 73, 117
Koestler, Arthur 241, 255(n)
Kokoschka, Oscar 226
Kollwitz, Käthe 161, 223, 224
Komját, Aladár 230, 232
König, Arthur 137, 104(n)
Korsch, Karl 8, 10. 103, 118, 121, 122, 150
Korte, Hermann 225
Koschnick, Johannes 170
Krestinsky, Nikolay 270
Kun, Béla 112
Kunstlump controversy 226
Kurella, Alfred 274, 275
Kuusinen, Otto 245, 263

Labour and Socialist International (LSI) 252, 267
Landau, Kurt 156
Laufenberg, Heinrich 29
Law for the Protection of the Republic 75, 133
League Against Colonial Oppression (LACO) 246, 248
League Against Imperialism and for National Independence (LAI) 242, 246, 251, 253
League of Farmers 212
League of Working Farmers 213
League of Proletarian-Revolutionary Writers (BPRS) 228, 229, 230, 232, 233, 234
League of Red Front Fighters (RFB) 6, 17, 143
Ledebour, Georg 48, 52, 57, 58, 59
Lenin, Vladimir 3, 15, 32, 34, 40, 55, 56, 90, 110, 112, 113, 119, 142, 154, 229, 231, 243, 245, 263
Leninism x, 4, 5, 7, 8, 87, 90, 109, 121, 122, 150, 254
Leninbund 11, 155-6, 162, 163, 164

Lentzsch, Rudolf, 195
Leonhard, Susanne 48
Levi, Paul 40, 58, 90, 91, 111, 112
Liebknecht, Karl 3, 5, 8, 29, 30, 31, 32, 33, 45, 46, 47, 48, 49, 51, 53, 54, 56, 57, 58, 59, 60, 61, 111, 270
Litvinov, Maxim 264
Lozovsky, Solomon 18, 142, 171, 271
Lukács, George 231-4
Luxemburg, Rosa 3, 5, 8, 9, 29, 31, 45, 46, 47, 48, 50, 51-2, 53, 54, 55-7, 58-9, 60, 61, 66, 109, 110, 111, 153, 207, 208, 222

McMeekin, Sean 240, 254,
Mann, Heinrich 161, 252
Manuilsky, Dmitry ('Numa') 18, 122, 153, 249, 268
Marc, Franz 224
March action, 1921 7, 11, 67, 76, 79, 81, 90, 91, 93, 112, 131
Marchlewski, Julian (Karski) 46
Märten, Lu 230
Maslow, Arkadij (b. Isaak Chemerinskij) 11, 81, 87, 88, 89, 98, 100, 102, 108(n)
Matteotti, Giacomo 250
Mätzchen, Bruno 156
Marx, Karl 1, 14, 36, 151, 232, 229, 233
Marxism, Marxism-Leninism 1, 4, 25, 27, 30, 121, 152, 154, 224, 225, 229, 230, 231, 232, 234, 243, 263
Marx, Wilhelm 120
Mehring, Franz 31, 46, 2
Meyer, Ernst 66-86, 93-4, 129, 131, 133, 134
Meyer-Leviné, Rosa 66
Migliolo, Guido 246

Molotov, Vyacheslav 129, 269
Müller, Gustav 57, 155
Münzenberg, Willi 14-16, 17, 19,
    240-59, 260, 263, 264, 265,
    271, 273-4, 276
Mussolini, Benito 137, 250

National Rural League 212, 214
National Socialist German Workers'
    Party (NSDAP)/Nazis 98, 157,
    158, 159, 160, 161, 162, 163,
    194, 197, 199, 215, 229, 243,
    251, 254, 264, 265, 266, 267,
    268, 269, 271, 272, 271, 272,
    273, 274; see also Hitler, Adolph
Nehru, Jawaharlal 15, 249
Neumann, Heinz 244, 265, 270

October Revolution (Russia) see
    Russian Revolution
November Revolution (Germany) see
    German revolution, 1918-19
Von Ossietzky, Carl 229
Ottwalt, Ernst 231

Pannekoek, Anton 5, 26, 27, 87
Von Papen, Franz 163, 183
Peschke, Paul, 190
Pfeiffer, Hans 89
Pfemfert, Franz 224
Pickens, William 246
Pieck, Wilhelm 46, 56, 57, 58, 59
Piscator, Erwin 223, 229, 233
Poincaré, Raymond 98
Popular Front see Comintern/Popular
    Front; Communist Party of
    Germany/Popular Front
Profintern see Red International of
    Labour Unions
Proletarian Hundreds see
    Communist Party of Germany/
    Proletarian Hundreds

Proletkult 224, 225, 236(n)
Putz, Ernst 213
Pyatakov, Georgy 115
Pyatnitsky, Ossip 269, 271

RGO see Revolutionary Trade
    Union Opposition
RSS see Revolutionary Shop
    Stewards
Radek, Karl 5, 6, 8, 27, 32, 34, 38,
    54, 55, 57, 93, 98, 99, 100, 101,
    102, 111, 113, 114, 115, 116,
    117, 134, 136, 138, 273
Rathenau, Walter 7, 72-3, 74, 76,
    78, 79, 92, 133, 134, 135
Red International of Labour Unions
    (RILU, Profintern) 11, 13, 18,
    121, 170, 171, 173, 176, 180,
    182, 197, 198, 199, 271
Reichstag fire, 1933, 194, 266, 267,
    268, 271, 273, 275
Remmele, Hermann 117, 141, 265,
    270-1
Rettmann, Fritz, 195
Reuter, Ernst (Friesland) 112
zu Reventlow, Ernst Graf, 99, 101
Revolutionary Shop Stewards (RSS)
    5, 33, 48, 49, 54, 56, 57, 59,
    60, 89
Revolutionary Trade Union
    Opposition (RGO) 12, 170,
    172, 187-90, 191, 192-3, 194,
    195, 196, 197-8, 199
Richter, Hans 225
Riest, Walter 156
Rolland, Romain 250, 252, 273
Rosenberg, Arthur 12, 88, 89, 95,
    103, 118, 121, 122
Rosenfeld, Kurt 52
Roy, Manabendra Nath 248
Rubiner, Ludwig 224
Rühle, Otto 30

Russian Association of Proletarian Writers (RAPP) 228, 230, 232, 233
Ruhr crisis 94, 96-102, 113, 114, 115, 134, 135, 136, 137, 138
Russian Revolution 1, 3, 10, 14, 19, 36, 55, 109, 207, 199, 221, 222, 246, 263, 264

SPD *see* Social Democratic Party of Germany
Von Salomon, Bruno 14,
Scammel, Michael 240
Scheidemann, Philip 49, 56, 58, 59, 61
Schickele, René 224
Schiff, Victor 267, 274
Schimanski, Fritz 155, 156
Schlageter, Leo 98, 99, 101, 113-4
Schlageter approach 8, 98-102, 103, 113-4, 138
Schlecht, Paul 89, 155, 156
Schleimann, Jorgen 241, 244
Schneller, Ernst 229
Scholem, Werner 98, 100, 101-2, 103, 118, 121-2, 142, 151, 154, 155-6
Scholze, Paul 57
Schreiner, Albert 141
Schulz, Karl 48
Serge, Victor 151
Severing, Carl 17
Social Democratic Party of Germany (SPD), 3, 4, 5, 6, 7, 11, 18, 26, 27, 29, 32, 25, 40, 52, 60, 61, 69, 70, 72, 74, 79, 80, 91, 111, 115, 130, 131, 137, 138, 141, 156, 188, 189, 222, 227, 244, 260, 266, 268, 275
SPD/USPD government November-December, 1918 49, 50, 51, 52, 56
SPD government, 1918-19 5, 56, 57, 58, 59, 60, 61, 68; *see also* 'German October'
and, 1914-18 war 3, 8, 28-32, 33, 34, 35, 36, 45, 46, 130
opposition to SPD war policy 3, 28, 29, 30, 34, 36, 46, 47, 130
vote for war credits 4 August, 1914, 28, 33, 34, 45, 46, 223, 261
Social Democratic Working Group (SAG) 33, 34, 35
and trade unions 7, 18, 71, 75, 79, 92, 133, 137, 141, 170, 171, 172, 179, 188, 189, 197, 198, 214, 271
See also Communist Party of Germany/and SPD
Social Democratic Organisation of Bremen (SDVB) 26-36
'social fascism' 117, 120, 158, 160, 198, 264-5, 270
Socialist Workers Party (SAPD) 41, 163
Sokolnikov, Grigori 115
Soviet Union, Soviet state *see* USSR
Spartacus Group 3, 4-5, 19, 25, 31-2, 33-4, 35, 37, 38, 39, 40, 45-65, 66, 89, 155
and USPD 35, 36, 37, 39, 40, 45, 52, 53, 54, 55
Stalin, Joseph 10, 18, 87, 101, 110, 115, 116, 119, 120, 122, 123, 129, 138, 142, 143, 150, 151, 152, 153, 155, 184, 254, 261-2, 263, 264, 265, 268, 269, 270, 272, 274, 275, 276
Stalinisation xi, 4, 9-10, 17, 18, 40, 103, 123, 129, 143, 152-4, 162, 164, 199, 245, 251, 254, 261, 262
Stalinism/Stalinists 9, 10, 11, 15, 16,

61, 90, 109, 123, 151-2, 153, 156, 163, 254, 261, 262, 263, 271, 272, 273, 275, 276
Stampfer, Friedrich 121, 267
Stern, Moishe 141
Stinnes, Hugo 70, 83(n), 100, 114
Stoecker, Walter 112
Stresemann, Gustav 115, 139
Strikes 5, 7, 12, 13, 25, 32, 59, 72-3, 74, 75, 114, 115, 116, 133, 138, 139, 140, 141, 159, 183, 184, 188, 189, 190, 191, 192, 193, 269
  Bremen shipyard workers' strike, 1916 32
  General strike, 1918 57-8
  Mass strikes 26, 27-8, 47-8, 57, 102, 266
  Ruhr strikes, 1923 94, 96, 97, 113, 136, 137
  Railway workers strike, 1922 7, 69-72, 78, 80
  Sailors and harbour workers' strikes, 1931 13, 170-83
  Shipyard workers strike, 1913 28

Thalheimer, August 50, 67, 112, 116, 140, 154, 207-8
Thälmann, Ernst 9, 10, 11, 81, 90, 103, 117, 118, 120, 121, 122, 123, 129-149, 153, 154, 158, 163, 164, 252, 265, 266, 267-8, 269, 271, 273
Tolstoy, Leo 230, 231, 233
Trade unions xi, 2, 5, 6, 7, 8, 9, 26, 28, 35, 66, 69, 73, 80, 136, 170-1, 184, 194, 198, 199, 275
  See also Communist Party of Germany/trade unions; General Confederation of German Trade Unions; strikes; SPD/ trade unions

Treaty of Versailles 68, 98, 113, 133, 263, 264
Tresso, Pietro 276
Trotsky, Leon 11, 93, 112, 115, 116, 119, 138, 142, 152, 155, 156, 159-61, 164, 233, 261, 270, 276
Trotskyism/Trotskyists 119, 156, 162, 230, 233, 264, 273, 274
Tucholsky, Kurt 159, 276

Union of Manual and Intellectual Workers 11
United Communist Party (VKPD) 6, 67, 112
United Front *see* Comintern/United Front; Communist Party of Germany/United Front
United Left Opposition of the KPD 156, 162
United Workers Party, Unterreichenbach 161
Unity Union of Berlin Metalworkers (EVMB) 12, 187-204
Unity Union of Seamen, Harbour Workers and Bargemen (EVSHBD), 12-13, 170-86
Urbahns, Hugo 11, 90, 93, 131, 134, 136, 141, 142, 150, 154, 155, 156
USPD *see* Independent Social Democratic Party
USSR 10, 110, 119, 120, 123, 150, 152, 154, 155, 170, 171, 172, 209, 234, 242, 246
  Policy on Germany 261, 263-76
  See also strikes/Sailors and harbour workers' strikes, 1931

Vandervelde, Emile 252
Vinogradov, Boris 267
Volk, Karl 266

Walcher, Jacob 53, 148(n)
Walden, Herwarth 222
Walz, Oskar, 195
Winkels, Emil 176, 177
Wirth, Joseph 69, 70, 71, 72
Wischeropp, Oskar 89
Wittfogel, Karl August 229, 230
Wolf, Felix (alias Werner Rakow) 269
Wolffheim, Fritz 29
Wollenberg, Erich 269
Wollweber, Ernst 170, 172
Works councils 79, 85(n), 95, 132, 136, 191, 193
  National Works Council Congress, 1922 79

Congress of Works Councils, Chemnitz, 1923, 116, 136, 139, 141

Zetkin, Clara 45, 46, 51, 53, 61, 88, 91, 252
Zietz, Luise 52
Zimmerwald movement/left 32, 36, 40, 66, 243
Zinoviev, Gregory 72, 81, 93, 110, 115, 116, 117, 119, 120, 121-2, 123, 133, 134, 136, 137, 142, 152, 153, 155, 156, 227, 247
Zörgiebel, Karl Friedrich 17, 158